Border Crimes

Sydney Institute of Criminology Series 29

Series Editors: Professor Chris Cunneen, University of New South Wales
Professor Mark Findlay, University of Sydney
Associate Professor Gail Mason, University of Sydney
Professor Julie Stubbs, University of Sydney
Professor Pat O'Malley, University of Sydney

Titles in the Series

Lines in The Sand Noble, G (ed) (2009)
Criminal Discovery Moisidis, C (2008)
Conflict of Interest in Policing Davids, C (2008)
Recapturing Freedom Goulding, D (2007)
Imprisoning Resistance Carlton, B (2007)
Interrogating Images Dixon, D (2007)
Reshaping Juvenile Justice Chan, J (ed) (2005)
Refugees and State Crime Pickering, S (2005)
Aboriginal childhood separations and guardianship law Buti, A (2004)
Global Issues, Women and Justice Pickering, S & Lambert, C (eds) (2004)
Bin Laden in the Suburbs Poynting, S; Noble, G; Tabar, P & Collins, J (2004)
A History of Criminal Law in New South Wales Woods, G (2002)
Regulating Racism McNamara, L (2002)
When Police Unionise Finnane, M (2002)
Indigenous Human Rights Garkawe, S; Kelly, L & Fisher, W (eds) (2001)
Developing Cultural Criminology Banks, C (ed) (2000)
Defining Madness Shea, P (1999)
A Culture of Corruption Dixon, D (ed) (1999)
Reform in Policing Bolen, J (1997)
Anatomy of a French Murder Case McKillop, B (1997)
Gender, 'Race' and International Relations Cunneen, C & Stubbs, J (1997)
Fault in Homicide Yeo, S (1997)
Women, Male Violence and the Law Stubbs, J (ed) (1994)
The Prison and the Home Aungles, A (1994)
Cricket and the Law Fraser, D (1993)
Psychiatry in Court Shea, P (1996)
Doing Less Time Penal reform in crisis Chan, J (1992)
Aboriginal Perspectives on Criminal Justice Cunneen, C (1992)

Border Crimes
Australia's war on illicit migrants

Michael Grewcock

Sydney 2009
The Institute of Criminology Series 29

Published by
Institute of Criminology Press
Sydney Institute of Criminology
University of Sydney Law School
Sydney NSW 2006
www.criminology.law.usyd.edu.au

Distributed by
The Federation Press
PO Box 45 Annandale 2038
www.federationpress.com.au

National Library of Australia Cataloguing-in-Publication entry

Author: Grewcock, Michael.
Title: Border crimes : Australia's war on illicit migrants / Michael Grewcock.
ISBN: 9780975196793 (pbk)
Notes: Includes index.
Bibliography.
Subject: Illegal aliens--Government policy--Australia.
Illegal aliens--Crimes against--Australia.
Refugees--Government policy--Australia.
Political crimes and offences--Australia.
Dewey Number: 323.6310994

©2009 The Institute of Criminology

This publication is copyright. Other than for purposes of and subject to the conditions prescribed under the Copyright Act, no part of it may in any form or by any means (electronic, microcopying, photocopying, recording or otherwise) be reproduced, stored in a retrieval or transmitted without prior written permission. Enquiries should be addressed to the publisher.

Cover design by Judith Love
Typeset by The Institute of Criminology
Printed by University Publishing Service

Table of Contents

Acknowledgements	ii
Introduction 'I was like a camera, I remember everything'	1
Chapter 1 Border policing, criminology and state crime	12
Chapter 2 Forced migration, refugees and the state	39
Chapter 3 From white Australia to multiculturalism: exclusion, hegemony and unauthorised migrants	75
Chapter 4 State of denial: the creation of the illegitimate refugee	119
Chapter 5 Declaring war in the Pacific	152
Chapter 6 A system of abuse: the Australian gulag	196
Chapter 7 State crime and the ideologies of exclusion	242
Epilogue: A new beginning?	278
References	287
Index	333

Acknowledgements

I want to acknowledge and thank the many people who provided information, ideas and encouragement during the years it took to write this book. In particular, thanks are due to David Brown, Penny Green, Phil Griffiths, Phil Marfleet and Ian Rintoul. I would also like to thank the Faculty of Law at the University of New South Wales for its financial assistance. Special thanks are due to Audrey and Kyle, whose tolerance of this project extended to them becoming truly global citizens.

Michael Grewcock teaches criminal law and criminology at the University of New South Wales, Sydney, Australia.

Introduction

'I was like a camera, I remember everything'

On 18 March 2006, 52 year-old Amal Basry died from breast cancer in Melbourne. Her death prompted six obituaries in the Melbourne *Age* and tributes from federal senators Andrew Bartlett, Claire Moore and Kerry Nettle, but was not headline news. A courageous and dignified woman, who had never made claim to the public memory, had quietly passed away. However, Amal Basry had a story that deserved to be told.[1] She had survived and born witness to some of the most highly publicised events in recent Australian political history; she had given a human face to a group of people who had been condemned by the Australian state as 'queue jumpers' and possible terrorists; and she had endured levels of insecurity, displacement and loss sharply at odds with the life experiences of those whose decisions decided her fate.

Amal Basry and her family came from Iraq. Amal's journey had begun in 1997 when she and her family fled to northern Iraq following extensive threats and harassment by the Iraqi regime. One brother and her brother-in-law had been executed in 1991; her husband and two of his brothers had been jailed and tortured in 1995; and the police had placed her entire family under surveillance. In 1999, the family escaped to Iran from where her husband Abbas Akram, believing Australia to be 'a potential haven' (Zable, 2003), had flown to Malaysia. There he made contact with some of the illicit migration networks operating in the region, eventually managing to secure unauthorised boat passage to Australia's northwest coast. On arrival in January 2000, he was detained and transferred to the Woomera detention centre in South Australia, while his claim for refugee status was processed. After eight months he was granted a three year temporary protection visa and settled in Melbourne.

Border Crimes

The terms of Abbas Akram's visa meant that he had no automatic entitlement to family reunion and could not leave Australia in order to visit his family. Faced with years of separation and threats of deportation back to Iraq, Amal decided to try and follow her husband's path. Leaving her elder son behind, she flew with her younger son Rami to Malaysia. From there, the pair travelled to Jakarta, where they bought passage to Australia on a boat organised by a people smuggler named Abu Quassey. The boat, later codenamed 'the SIEV X',[2] left Indonesia on 18 October 2001 carrying 421 asylum seekers, mainly from Iraq, Afghanistan and Iran. The 19 metre fishing vessel was ostensibly bound for Christmas Island off Australia's north-west coast. Had it reached its destination, its passengers would probably have been taken by the Australian navy to Nauru, to be detained under the terms of the Australian government's 'Pacific Solution'.

However, the overcrowded and unseaworthy boat started taking on water almost immediately and had little hope of completing the journey safely. Before the day had ended, 24 Mandaeans, a minority religious group persecuted in Iraq and Iran, had persuaded the crew to let them off near a small group islands. For those left on board, the conditions got worse. By the second day, the weather had deteriorated and the ship was rocked by a heavy swell. By early afternoon the engine and the pump had ceased to function. At approximately 3pm, the SIEV X sank in the Indian Ocean. 353 people – 146 children, 142 women and 65 men – drowned, while the survivors, including Amal and Rami, spent nearly 24 hours in the water before being rescued by an Indonesian fishing boat. The Australian authorities were not about to welcome the survivors. Amal and Rami were returned to Jakarta, where they had to wait for over seven months before Amal was granted a temporary protection visa and allowed to reunite with her husband. After a further three year wait, Amal and Rami were finally given permanent protection visas in 2005.

The SIEV X tragedy and Amal Basry's story provide a confronting metaphor for Australia's border policing policies, which remain framed by the punitive logic of 2001. The SIEV X sank during a federal election contest dominated by the incumbent

Introduction

Howard government's claims that Australia faced serious threats from terrorism and people smuggling. In this context, public debate about the individual lives and experiences of those seeking entry and protection was not to be encouraged. The logic of 'border protection' precluded any meaningful concessions to the humanity of people like Amal and Rami. However, for SIEV X survivors like Amal Basry, being able to speak of their experiences was an important part of trying to reconstruct their lives. On the first anniversary of the sinking, she told a memorial gathering in Melbourne:

> I would like to welcome you all. It means a lot to me. It gives me hope....because this time last year I was fighting for my life, fighting like many others who were with me last year. When our boat sank we felt we were going to die...I can never forget the unbelievable pictures in front of my eyes. Some people...in the water, some swallowing the water and choking and choking. I will never forget the bodies lying on the sea. And the moment that pushed me into...the water....and...I saw my son fighting for his life as well...finding a piece of wood, my son started to scream 'Mum, Mum, we will choke, we will die. God please save us.' At this point I was anxious to get where my son was but I saw a dead woman's body beside me. And with my heart burning I feeling very scared and try to hold the hand of the dead body to support myself to swim to my son's side. Thank God I could arrive near my son. We kissed each other. [sobbing] Then he said 'Give me a kiss mum, we are going to die'...where some other people were still fighting for their lives. The screaming still rings in my ears. And one man screams 'All my family drown' and my friend who was holding onto a piece of wood had all her children's dead bodies floating around her. Next morning we were still waiting for death the Indonesian fishermen help us and save us. And now I am living in Australia and all my dreams come true... (transcript in Hutton 2006a).

When recalling these awful experiences, Amal Basry did not seek pity. Instead, she wanted to ensure the story of the SIEV X was properly understood. 'I was like a camera', she told Michael Gordon (2002) of the Melbourne *Age*, 'I remember everything'. She also sought a sense of legitimacy for herself and other forced migrants that was otherwise being denied. Writer Arnold Zable (2003) noted:

> More than one year later, the memory of the tragedy remains a raw wound. But before she recounts the story, Amal insists on telling me why she was so desperate to make the journey. 'I want people to know why I stayed on the boat even when I saw it was very dangerous', she says.
>
> 'I want people to know who I am. Why I escaped from Iraq. Why I risked my life. Why I wanted to come to Australia. Maybe then they will understand.'

Unlike comparable human disasters, such as plane crashes or train derailments, there was little official enthusiasm[3] for memorialising the loss of the SIEV X or paying homage to those who perished. The Australian Federal Police (AFP) resisted repeated calls to release their list of those who died, while the Howard government's myopic focus on deterring people smuggling dominated its responses to the tragedy. Only five survivors of the SIEV X were permitted to live in Australia. The remainder were resettled elsewhere; a policy designed to dispel ideas that Australia was a safe haven for refugees not seeking entry through 'proper channels' and proof, according to the Howard government, of the 'success' of the Pacific Solution.

The use of terms like 'solution' in relation to population control has a grotesque pedigree. While not comparable to the Holocaust, the Australian government's appropriation of the term nevertheless symbolised state actions that were intended to be resolute, uncompromising and in their own way, final. After 2001, this 'solution' evolved to the point where all asylum seekers attempting unauthorised entry into Australia were detained offshore while their claims for protection were processed. Those whose claims were unsuccessful risked being forcibly removed to dangerous and insecure environments, while those who were successful faced being resettled in states other than Australia. Moreover, the Australian government's response provided an attractive if not entirely practical model for other governments seeking to police unauthorised migration and deter asylum seekers. When members

Introduction

of the Australian Special Air Services seized control of the *Tampa* in 2001 and the navy was mobilised to forcibly remove refugees from their ramshackle boats to detention centres in Papua New Guinea and Nauru, there was little concern for human rights abuses shown by the major Western states.

At the time, I was working as a solicitor in London, where the Blair government made little attempt to disguise its sympathy for the Howard government's actions. This was consistent with the attitudes of governments across Europe, where there was growing official hostility to refugees, who in the aftermath of the Cold War, were being redefined as 'economic migrants' and physically targeted by elements of the far-right. During the early 1990s, I had represented some of these migrants, mainly Somalis and Kurds, whose claims for refugee status often failed to meet the strict legal criteria required, but whose need for protection was obvious. Most of them were eventually allowed to stay in Britain;[4] Somalia was in a state of crisis and had no functioning ports or government infrastructure that could facilitate return, while the governments of Iraq and Turkey were unremittingly and indisputably hostile to their Kurdish minorities, especially those associated with campaigns for national rights. This did not prevent Home Office officials, often very young and with minimal knowledge of the countries concerned, showing obvious disdain for asylum seekers during formulaic interviews and exercising in an arbitrary and inconsistent way their discretionary powers to detain; or local politicians from across the spectrum combining with the British media to whip up racist scare campaigns about 'floods' of asylum seekers. However, to that point in time, blanket interdiction or removal was not on the agendas the mainstream political parties, although it was a central demand of neo-fascist organisations such as the British National Party.

Thus, by 2001, political elites internationally were receptive to the Howard government's decision to turn round all boats attempting unauthorised entry into Australia. The unilateral nature of Howard's stance mirrored the decision of the Hawke Labor government ten years earlier to introduce a unique system of mandatory detention of all 'unauthorised non-citizens'. This had led to the establishment of a network of mainly desert based detention camps, the remote locations and isolation from Australia's civil institutions of which presaged the abandonment of refugees on Nauru. Mandatory detention failed in its stated aim of deterring refugees but the camps quickly became centres of organised abuse, where even young children were drawn into systemic patterns of violence and self-harm.

As the extent of the impact of detention became more widely documented and debated, public disquiet over the detention policy within Australia began to grow, although it retained bi-partisan support from the Coalition and Labor parties. While this bi-partisanship was maintained during the events of 2001 and allowed the government's 'border protection' policies to become firmly entrenched, there was visible and sustained extra-parliamentary opposition to the government's actions, which succeeded in forcing some partial retreats. These were consolidated in December 2007, when the newly elected Rudd Labor government announced it would close the detention centre on Nauru and instead use the detention facilities on Christmas Island. In July 2008, the government further announced that while it would maintain mandatory detention, those deemed not to represent a risk to the community would be released after initial health and security checks. However, many of the key elements of the former Pacific Solution remain in place with a renewed cycle of boat arrivals during 2009 resulting in burgeoning offshore detention centres, naval interception, elaborate regional policing operations and shrill denunciations of people smugglers.

By contrast, this book offers a criminological perspective on the Australian state's responses to unauthorised migrants. It counterposes the exclusionary and abusive measures implemented by the state to the rights and aspirations of people like Amal Basry and contrasts the alleged deviance of unauthorised migrants with the organised and deviant human rights abuses perpetrated by the Australian state. The book's main argument is that through the systematic alienation, criminalisation and abuse of unauthorised migrants, the Australian state has engaged in state crime. While this can be measured to some degree by breaches of international

Introduction

humanitarian law, the acts in question are criminal according to broader sociological understandings of state crime as organised human rights abuses (Green and Ward 2004: 2). Such a critique inevitably confronts both official explanations for the Australian state's actions and many of the accepted wisdoms about border policing, such as the inviolable nature of sovereignty and the necessity of the state to control migration. Nevertheless, in identifying the state as a source of criminality, rather than protection, my aim is to engage with the ongoing debates over migration policy as well as develop criminological notions of state crime.

Chapter one outlines the most significant dimensions of a state crime paradigm. In particular, it develops the above definition of state crime by emphasising the centrality of the state's use of force to conceptions of state deviance. The chapter examines the mechanisms by which state's right to exercise its monopoly of force is legitimised and how these can be challenged from within civil society, or from below. The contradictory nature of human rights discourse is pivotal in this process. The chapter outlines the recent origins of human rights discourse and points to the fundamental contradictions and disjunctures between those rights which Western states such as Australia are prepared to formally embrace and the more dynamic and radical conceptions of rights that inform many of the contemporary challenges to state power. The enduring tensions between different notions of rights are further examined in relation to the formal rights of refugees, which have always been narrowly construed by Western states, and implemented according to criteria often far removed from the immediate survival and protection needs of those seeking some recognition of them.

Chapter two addresses these fundamental contradictions by arguing that refugees ought to be reconceptualised as part of the more complex phenomenon of the forced migrant. The chapter examines the global context of forced and illicit migration; and considers the various social, economic and political factors underpinning unauthorised human movement. This approach is taken in order to emphasise the lack of meaningful choice many unauthorised migrants have in their decisions to move. In this context, their deviance is largely manufactured by Western states seeking to exclude them, rather than by any criminality or serious risk that they might represent. The chapter argues that the construction of Western exclusion zones, in which the Australian government has played a central role, has been crucial to legitimising punitive border control measures that range from the corralling of refugees in camps near their zones of flight through to full scale 'wars' against people smuggling and trafficking. These exclusion zones provide the infrastructure for state deviance through the measures of force and deterrence they impose and are legitimised by the state through sustained attempts to portray unauthorised migrants as alien outsiders. The chapter concludes by highlighting the increasing tension at a global level between aspirations and pressures to migrate and the increasingly restrictive nature of border controls. This provides the immediate context for understanding the development of state crime.

One of the book's central arguments is that while definitions of state crime are most easily applied to measures such as the mandatory detention policy and the Pacific Solution, the ideological justifications for such policies have a deeply rooted and complex lineage. Chapter three therefore begins the task of examining the development of Australia's migration control regime and the ideologies of exclusion historically used to justify it. The chapter's starting point is the hegemonic role of the White Australia policy in the formation of the Australian state. From federation, the Australian state had specific powers to regulate 'aliens', and was instrumental in the development of particular notions of Australian identity. The transition from the White Australia policy to a formally instituted multiculturalism reflected how conceptions of that identity have changed. However, the official policies of multiculturalism were always more contested and the consensus around them more fragile than was the case with the White Australia policy. Therefore, while the Australian state's responses to Indo-Chinese refugees in the late 1970s and early 1980s symbolised a break from the tenets of White Australia, aspects of the old policy, combined with the Australian state's desire to resettle refugees on its own rather than the refugees' terms, could be used to justify the exclusion of unauthorised migrants. The ways in which the state

Introduction

alienated certain types of migrant might have changed, but the fundamental dynamic of alienation remained the same.

Chapter four extends this analysis by discussing how prevailing notions of the illegitimate refugee in Australia developed in response to two phases of illicit boat arrivals between 1989 and 1992, and 1994 and 1998. This was the period during which mandatory detention was introduced and clear institutional distinctions established between the official, acceptable refugee and the unauthorised 'queue jumper' refugee. Although introduced in order to deter future unauthorised arrivals, the main impact of the detention policy was to reinforce the notion of the unauthorised migrant as a threat and to legitimise measures that effectively criminalised those refugees who were unprepared or unable to seek resettlement in Australia. As subsequent events were to show, mandatory detention did little to prevent unauthorised movement into Australia but helped establish the framework for the systemic abuse of unauthorised refugees and non-citizens.

Chapter five examines the events of 2001 and the implementation of the Pacific Solution. It highlights how the institutional consensus that cohered around the concept of border protection was crucial to rationalising the Australian government's 'war on people smuggling'. This war sat at the epicentre of a process of externalisation in which the Australian state sought to extend its authority and border policing practices into the Asia-Pacific region. Moreover, the prosecution of this war reflected a widening disjuncture between border controls and the human rights of unauthorised migrants as the Australian state moved to systematically deny the rights and capacities of unauthorised migrants to enter Australian territory. The alienation, criminalisation and abuse of unauthorised migrants became part of an everyday enforcement culture legitimised on the basis that Australian sovereignty and identity were being undermined by illicit movement.

Chapter six considers the development of the mandatory detention policy; the evolution of the detention regime through the Pacific Solution; and the impact of detention on detainees. Detention has played a defining role in the criminalisation of unauthorised migrants and has led to patterns of systemic violence and abuse for which the Australian state bears primary responsibility. The chapter argues that the mandatory detention policy gave rise to a culture of containment within the Australian state that resulted in the incarceration of not only unauthorised non-citizens, but also those with legal status who were unable immediately to establish their credentials with an officialdom conditioned to the routine use of detention as a first resort. The detention policy also provided the basis for a system of forced and largely unregulated removal of unauthorised migrants by the Australian state, while the increasing resort to offshore detention system raised the prospect of the Australian state being responsible for organised human rights abuses in locations where it is difficult to monitor and challenge its actions.

Reflecting on this, chapter seven analyses the relationship between various sectors of the Australian state and the extent to which they operate in a unitary or co-ordinated fashion. The chapter argues that while the Australian government plays the primary role in devising and implementing border policing policy, it has received substantial legitimacy and support from the judiciary, the civil bureaucracy and enforcement agencies. The chapter further argues that exclusionary measures against unauthorised migrants associated most graphically with the events of 2001 were implemented in the context of an ideological offensive by the Howard government aimed at reshaping popular perceptions of the legitimate migrant by recourse to some of the earlier traditions of White Australian nationalism. This analysis rests on the three focal points I suggest ought to be used as the basis for applying a criminological critique of border protection: the alienation of unauthorised migrants; the criminalisation of unauthorised migrants; and the abuse of unauthorised migrants. Each of these focal points challenges prevailing notions of national sovereignty and highlights the contradiction between the restriction of human movement and the increasingly globalised nature of trade and social activity. Understanding how state crime develops as a consequence of this contradiction provides insights into how state crime can be understood more generally as rooted in the state's exercise of force and legitimised through shifting but ultimately exclusionist nationalist ideologies.

Introduction

The epilogue considers the implications of the election of the Rudd Labor government in November 2007. It argues that while the new government officially abandoned the Pacific Solution and relaxed important aspects of the detention policy, the fundamental dynamics of border policing policy have not changed. Moreover, while policies towards refugees and unauthorised migrants were not centre stage during the Rudd government's first year, the spike in boat arrivals during 2009 has renewed the debates about border policing strategy. This book is offered as a response to those who maintain that draconian policing, criminalisation and deterrence are either necessary or legitimate reactions to this systemic cycle of forced migration. Instead, I hope the arguments raised here will contribute to our capacity to place at the centre of the government's response the life experiences of people like Amal Basry rather than the punitive mechanisms of the Australian state.

Notes

[1] The account here is based on Gordon (2002); Hutton (2006a); Kevin (2004); and Zable (2003).

[2] SIEV is an acronymn for Suspected Illegal Entry Vessel. The term SIEV X was initially coined by former diplomat Tony Kevin, who has campaigned tirelessly for a full inquiry into the incident. The central source of information on the SIEV X is the outstanding website maintained by Margo Hutton at http://sievx.com/. See also Kevin (2004).

[3] In 2007, a temporary memorial was established with the support of the ACT government to mark the anniversary of the sinking. For accounts of the unsuccessful attempts to establish a permanent memorial see Biddulph (2007); Caldwell (2006); Peake (2007); and Towell (2007).

[4] Those whose claims for refugee status failed were mostly granted exceptional leave to remain; a form of leave that has subsequently been abolished.

Chapter 1

Border policing, criminology and state crime

What is state crime?

State crime is a controversial concept amongst criminologists. The main point of contention is whether declaring state acts, such as the detention of a person without a visa, as criminal is appropriate when the acts in question do not specifically breach criminal law. The issue can be posed in a number of ways: Is the concept of state crime useful if it is mainly an interpretive tool or rhetorical device? Are harmful, abusive or immoral actions legally carried out by state agencies capable of being considered criminal if they don't breach domestic law? Does this devalue the concept of crime as it is popularly understood and stretch to breaking point the boundaries of criminology?

The answers to such questions are not straightforward; at a minimum they require criminologists to accept the need to challenge the state's monopoly of force; and they rely upon developing categories of deviance not generally found in domestic criminal codes. Nevertheless, in arguing that Australia's border policing practices often constitute state crime, this book is engaging in more than an internal disciplinary debate. Rather, it is designed as an intervention – first as an addition to the criminological literature on state crime; second, as an attempt to refocus mainstream debate about border controls onto the actions of states; and third, as an argument against viewing recent experience in Australia as an aberration. The focus of this book is not the extreme, but the routine and mundane, and notwithstanding changes to government policy implemented since the 2007 federal election, its aim is to delegitimise organised exclusion by the Australian state.

Border policing, criminology and state crime

Within criminology, the debate about state crime is not new but while there are signs that state crime is becoming a more active area of interest to criminologists[1], it remains fairly marginal to criminology as a whole. Moreover, the literature on state crime tends to deal with subjects such as genocide and torture, rather than border policing.[2] Various explanations are offered for the lack of attention by criminologists to state crime (Ross et al 1999). However, two fundamental conceptual challenges confront any attempt to apply criminological perspectives to state actions: first, breaking from the notion that criminology is principally concerned with the study of individual criminal behaviour as defined and policed by the state; and second, developing a paradigm for analysing how state behaviour can be understood as criminal. While some progress has been made in addressing these challenges, the literature is fragmentary and there is a lack of continuity in the concepts employed. Much work remains in developing an accepted paradigm for state criminality that retains the basic conceptual tools of criminology. This book uses Green and Ward's (2004:2) definition of state crime as 'state organised deviance involving the violation of human rights' but in order to develop this, it is helpful to revisit the arguments originally advanced for focusing on state crime in order to consider their contemporary relevance.

In a landmark article first published in 1970, Herman and Julia Schwendinger (1975:137) threw down a challenge to mainstream criminology by arguing that 'imperialism, racism, sexism and poverty can be called crimes' and that criminology should focus on the 'social relationships or social systems which cause the systematic abrogation of basic rights'. In making such arguments, the Schwendingers (1975: 131–138) sought to intervene in longstanding debates within criminology about the definition of crime, by arguing that it should be redefined according to 'some traditional notions of crime as well as notions organised around the concept of egalitarianism'. They also argued that criminology operated within existing paradigms of social control, rather than as a field of neutral research and inquiry, and that if criminology was to be expanded to include subjects such as the socially injurious activities of the state, human rights must be utilised as the discipline's central conceptual tool (Schwendinger and Schwendinger 1975: 134).

There is much to be commended in the Schwendingers' critique and their call for criminology to re-focus onto some of society's most powerful institutions. However, they did not provide a clear methodological framework. Empirically, their approach would require some concrete assessment of systemic violations of human rights, but they did not explicitly formulate a paradigm for understanding state crime nor, as they acknowledge, did they offer a satisfactory solution to the problem of defining crime. Rather, they hoped to stimulate 'the development of a number of alternative approaches' at a 'time when so many received doctrines (were) being called into question' (Schwendinger and Schwendinger 1975:131). Although the Schwendingers' work formed part of the critical criminology that emerged alongside the radical social and political movements of the 1960s and 1970s, criminologists did not take up their challenge until quite recently.[3] Instead, the study of what we might define as state crime developed within disciplines such as international relations or political economy;[4] or in specific areas of international law, such as war crimes or crimes against humanity.[5] However, the difficulty highlighted in many of these studies is the absence of a clear definition of state crime in either domestic or international law.

State crime as a legal concept

Within the realms of domestic law, state crime is almost a contradiction in terms. The state does not police itself in any collective sense; rather it can target individuals who have broken the laws the state enforces. Thus, while in most domestic jurisdictions it might be possible to charge particular individuals with criminal offences such as murder or assault, the criminal justice process is concerned with the behaviour of the allegedly deviant few within its control. As the recent trials of United States army personnel engaged in torture at Abu Ghraib illustrated, this leaves open the question of how to locate responsibility for the offending acts within the wider culture, policies and practices of the state. Within a domestic legal framework, there is little room for the concept of political accountability (HRW 2005c).

Border policing, criminology and state crime

State crime is perhaps a more coherent concept within international law, where the prospect of international tribunals might remove some of the problems associated with states policing themselves. However, attempts to devise a body of enforceable international law have met with mixed success. From its inception in 1948, the International Law Commission engaged in extensive deliberations on state responsibility for breaches of international law, including 'international crimes and delicts arising from state acts'. Conceptually, such breaches would amount to state crime but no agreement could be reached on how they should be defined (Crawford 1998: pars 76–100; Crawford 2002; Jørgensen 2003).

The commission's draft formulations reflected the growing body of international human rights law in areas such as genocide and racial discrimination and the emerging concept of crimes against humanity, established as a principle by the Nuremburg tribunal. Under the tribunal's principles, these crimes included:

> murder, extermination, enslavement, deportation and other inhuman acts done against any civilian population; or persecutions on political, racial or religious grounds, when such acts are done or such persecutions are carried on in execution of or connection with any crime against peace or any war crime.[6]

The 'logic of the crime against humanity', noted Robertson (2006: xxii),

> ...was that future state agents who authorised torture or genocide against their own populations were criminally responsible, in international law, and might be punished by any court capable of catching them.

However, while the Nuremberg trials might have succeeded in convicting a handful of prominent Nazis, they did not trigger an extensive system of international criminal justice. This not only reflected the paralysing influence of the Cold War, when commitments to the international enforcement of human rights were very much subordinated to geopolitical interests, but also the systemic difficulties in establishing an international legal regime in a world political system characterised by competing nation states and shifting geopolitical alliances. As if to highlight this, the United States, China, Israel and India refused to sign up to the International Criminal Court, established in 2002 to prosecute cases of genocide, crimes against humanity, war crimes and the crime of aggression[7], on the grounds that it represented an unacceptable risk of politically motivated prosecutions (Robertson 2006: 419–467).

While the linkage of a criminological paradigm of state crime with codified and enforceable law is therefore seriously constrained[8], Rothe and Friedrichs (2006: 156) suggest nevertheless that international law and its principles provide a 'foundational basis' for understanding state criminality because they incorporate concepts such as human rights and social harm. However, criminologists have reached no clear agreement on how to draw on such themes.

State crime as a criminological concept

For criminologists, conceptualising the relationship between criminal behaviour and breaches of human rights has always been problematic. From the outset, the Schwendingers (1975: 133–134) created a significant problem by seeking to bring a broad spectrum of rights into the realm of criminology. 'Food, shelter, clothing, medical services, challenging work and recreational experiences' were joined with 'security from predatory individuals or repressive and imperialistic social elites' as rights to be distinguished from 'rewards or privileges'. Such a sweeping approach, criticised by Cohen (1993: 98) as 'a moral crusade', risked blurring meaningful distinctions between social harm and organised human rights abuses (Green and Ward 2000a: 104) and invited the criticism that the notion of state crime provides no basis for coherent criminological perspectives because it is indistinguishable from the state 'doing nasty things' (Sharkansky 1995).

One way of resolving this is simply to ignore human rights as an explanatory mechanism and revert to reliance upon activities already defined as criminal. This is essentially the approach taken by Chambliss (1989) and Kauzlarich and Kramer (1998), who focus on illegal acts by state officials. Similarly, Friedrichs (1995: 74) argues

Border policing, criminology and state crime

state crime should be understood as a sub-type of the larger category of government crime, which in turn, is 'best regarded as a cognate form of white collar crime'. Such descriptive approaches, while incorporating behaviour which may well reflect state crime, leave little scope for analysing the institutional dynamics of state behaviour beyond that of individual state officials or behaviour which the state has declared illegal. They also risk marooning controversial but legal practices, such as the Australian state's mandatory detention and forced removal of asylum seekers, outside of any possible state crime framework. For practices such as these to be understood as state crime, human rights violations must be incorporated into the definition.

As noted above, Green and Ward (2004: 2) argue that state crime should be understood as 'state organisational deviance involving the violation of human rights'.[9] Green and Ward (2004: 4–5) locate state crime as a category of organisational deviance, defined in the following terms:

> ...an act is deviant where there is a social audience that (1) accepts a certain rule as a standard of behaviour, (2) interprets the act (or similar acts of which it is aware) as violating the rule, and (3) is disposed to apply significant sanctions – that is significant from the point of view of the actor – to such violations.

> The relevant actors are state agencies. The relevant rules are rules of international law, domestic law and social morality, as interpreted by audiences that include domestic and transnational civil society...international organisations, other states and other agencies within the offending state itself. The relevant sanctions include legal punishments, censure or rebellion by the state's own population, damage to the state's domestic and international reputation, and diplomatic, economic and military sanctions from other states.

Utilising deviance in relation to the state's treatment of forced migrants is both apposite and confronting given the deviant character bestowed by the state upon the refugee. The official discourse on refugees most of whom have committed no criminal offence, constructs them as dangerous outsiders who potentially threaten national security and identity and therefore deserve the full counter-mobilisation of state resources. This is a conscious and highly organised process, which claims and seeks a high level of popular legitimacy.

In Australia, a wide range of state agencies operate a centrally coordinated, widely publicised, clearly defined, goal-driven immigration control policy aimed at policing 'unlawful non-citizens'. This policy has been the subject of extensive public debate and protest, including by detainees. Particular practices, such as offshore processing and mandatory detention, have been the subject of sustained criticism for breaching human rights norms. However, few legal or formal sanctions have operated against Australian government policy. The Australian judiciary has only sporadically intervened to prevent or delay individual government decisions and has no capacity to over-rule government policy as a whole. Similarly, there is no viable international legal mechanism for challenging Australia's policies, which are consistent with and, to some degree operate as a model for, the exclusionary practices of all the advanced states. Moreover, forced migrants are often stateless and therefore unable to acquire the support of a third party state in demanding their rights in a destination state.

Therefore, the main criminological issue is not so much the potential illegality of the state policy and practice (although that remains a necessary subject to address), or whether formal legal sanctions (desirable as they might be) can be imposed, but whether a paradigm can be developed to allow state activities regarding refugees and forced migrants to be recognised as deviant and subject to sanction from outside the state's formal legal machinery. This book argues that state crime operates through the alienation, criminalisation and abuse of unauthorised migrants. However, before addressing such themes, it is helpful to define the state and outline some of the important dimensions of its activities.

The criminogenic features of the state

With the partial exception of Green and Ward (2004), writers on state crime have paid little attention to theories of the state. This is a serious methodological shortcoming as without a concrete analysis of the state(s) in question, it is difficult to develop a paradigm of state crime that can explain in sociological terms how the state's actions can be condemned as deviant.

All states have certain common features: they exercise power through a combination of administrative and coercive institutions; they seek to control a specified sovereign territory from which they can extract revenue and command loyalty; they can be distinguished from the communal whole, although the extent of the state's autonomy and the nature of the social and class interests it represents are matters of some debate; and all conduct activities which can be declared criminal if carried out by private individuals. However, this does not mean that all states are the same. There are substantial differences between liberal democracies and, for example, the fascist and Stalinist states that provided the basis for modern conceptions of totalitarianism.[10] But in an era when terms such as 'rogue state' and 'failed state' proliferate, acknowledging global linkages is also important; state crime often derives from the economic, social and military relationships between the dominant imperialist states and their weaker geopolitical allies and trading partners. This suggests that distinguishing arbitrarily between 'democratic' and 'totalitarian' norms is highly problematic and that a more subtle differentiation of the continuities and differences between states is required.

Further, the state is not an abstract or fixed entity. States need to be viewed historically in order to understand how and why they acquire power; how and why they exercise and maintain their authority; and the limits to their power and authority. Answering such questions requires us to examine the relationship between wider social interests and the state, and the extent to which the state can be viewed as an autonomous set of institutions, separate from, or acting independently of, the interests of civil society. This has particular relevance to liberal democratic states such as Australia where 'power is shared; rights to participate in government are legally or constitutionally defined; representation is wide, state power is fully secular and the boundaries of national sovereignty are clearly defined' (Hall 1984: 9–10). Within these states, power is exercised through an ensemble of inter-related institutions, incorporating 'the government, the administration, the military and the police, the judicial branch, sub-central government and parliamentary assemblies' (Miliband 1976: 50).

There are a number of conceptual reasons for focusing on contemporary liberal democracies when developing a paradigm of state crime. First, it distinguishes criminology from international law where in the case of war crimes, for example, prosecutions have largely been conducted at the behest of Western states (Robertson 2006). Second, if state crime is to be understood as the organised abuse of human rights, Western states such as Australia that proclaim an adherence to human rights ought to have their records judged. Third, there is often a continuum of abusive practice between liberal democracies and 'rogue states' (Chomsky 2000). This includes practices such as arbitrary detention and torture by Western states (not necessarily conducted within their sovereign boundaries) as well as direct military and financial support for regimes uniformly condemned for abusing human rights norms.

There are also important local variations in the history and dynamics of the advanced industrialised democracies, which have a direct bearing on their responses to forced migration. While the responses of the Australian state typify the operation of three Western zones of exclusion which have consolidated in the post-Cold War period; these zones are neither identical nor homogenous. Thus, Australia's formation and historic role as a Western, colonial settler state in the Asia-Pacific region, and the traditions of forced exclusion this entailed, is pivotal to understanding the Australian state's responses to forced migrants and refugees. Trying to analyse current Australian government policy without, for example, some reference to the history of the White Australia policy, seriously limits our ability to understand the ideological heritage underpinning many of the arguments justifying present policy, and the ways in which the Australian state has been able to legitimise the use of force against unauthorised migrants.

The state's monopoly of force

The state's monopoly of force is central to understanding the dynamics of state crime. Indeed, the concept of the state itself is rendered almost meaningless without institutional expressions of its existence such as standing armies, police forces, prisons and border controls. Force is important to our understanding of the modern state in at least three general senses.

First, force played a crucial role in the creation of the modern state. In Europe, the path from absolutism to the advanced liberal democracies was shaped by revolutions, civil wars, and wars between states. The colonial empires of the European states were forged and sustained by full-scale military mobilisations and in many cases only relinquished after prolonged periods of violent conflict. As part of this process, settler states like Australia were constructed through the establishment of a community transplanted (sometimes forcibly) from the colonising state and the marginalisation or destruction of the indigenous population. Nationalist narratives therefore explicitly justify or at least acknowledge a degree of state violence as a necessary or inevitable precursor to the achievement of contemporary democratic aspirations or norms.

Second, the state's military and policing apparatus is the most potent symbol of its existence and the primary mechanism by which it asserts its capacity to protect its subject population. In a global system characterised by competing nation states controlling territories in which there are often substantial social and economic contradictions, state-sanctioned force in the form of standing armed forces and increasingly militarised police forces becomes a compelling and logical means of protection from internal and external threats.[11] This might not always entail full-scale military mobilisation or the formal declaration of war with an adversary state but the metaphor of war, bestowing the most urgent and resolute character to a state enforcement operation (for example, the 'wars' against drugs and people smuggling), can be mobilised to justify a range of coercive measures.

Third, the modern state comprises a complex set of hierarchical institutions devoted to social control. In particular, the transition from feudalism to capitalism gave rise to separate but reinforcing judicial and penal systems that shifted the locus of state power in relation to individuals away from private ecclesiastical and absolutist sources to a central, public sphere where the rule of law is buttressed not only by 'armed men' but also 'material adjuncts, prisons and institutions of coercion of all kinds' (Engels 1973: 327–328). While the boundaries between the various types of state institution are to some degree inscribed by the separation of powers; the sources of legal authority, chains of command, administrative cultures and social networks underpinning state institutions often overlap. Moreover, in areas like education and welfare the state's exercise of authority has a disciplinary and normative aspect associated with it.

While each of these aspects of the monopoly of force impacts on refugees, state coercion has specific historical relevance to forced migration. The slave trade, the transport of convicts and indentured workers (coolie labour), the forcible enclosure of common agricultural land and the conflicts with indigenous populations in colonised territories were important to the development of industrial capitalism. Many contemporary urban populations owe their existence to processes of displacement and migration shaped by economic and state-organised compulsion. State coercion is also at the heart of the refugee discourse that developed during the twentieth century and permeates all aspects of the refugee experience from persecution and flight though to detention and return. Few images could epitomise the state's coercive power more graphically than children caged in by razor wire and other forms of state-of- the-art security in the South Australian desert.

However, the state's use of violence, while specific to it, is neither the sole nor principal mechanism for maintaining its integrity. Brute force alone is insufficient to sustain a state's authority in the longer term and incompatible with most contemporary conceptions of human rights. Instead, a degree of 'willing compliance', passive acquiescence' or 'ingrained dependence' (Draper 1977: 251) is required; to paraphrase Weber (1977: 78), the state's monopoly of force must be accepted as legitimate.

Legitimacy, hegemony and the state.

Legitimacy is an important theme within criminology. It underpins Merton's (1938) concept of anomie[12] and some of the seminal criminological works on political corruption and corporate crime[13] draw on the concept to locate state organised deviance as a product of a conflict between 'what are believed to be legitimate goals and what can be achieved within the rules' (Green and Ward 2000b: 78).[14] As Cohen (1993: 107–108) points out, whether certain behaviour is legitimate is also central to Sykes and Matza's (1970) identification of particular 'techniques of neutralisation'[15] (denial of injury, denial of victim, denial of responsibility, condemnation of the condemners and appeals to higher loyalty) that are employed to justify acts that the perpetrators acknowledge in part are unacceptable. Cohen's (1993, 2001) application of this framework to human rights violations illustrates its value in highlighting the capacity of the state at both an institutional and individual level to legitimise or morally justify behaviour perceived by various audiences to be abusive and contrary to the state's own policies.

Green and Ward (2000a and 2004) approach the issue of legitimacy by adapting interpretations of Italian Marxist Antonio Gramsci's writings on hegemony, to explain the relationship between the state and civil society and how this 'involves the internalisation, by the ruled and rulers alike, of a complex set of shared beliefs'. Gramsci (1971 and 2000) sought to use the concept of hegemony to explain how ideological control could be maintained within a capitalist state. Having been imprisoned by Mussolini's regime from 1926 until his death in 1937, Gramsci needed no tuition in the state's capacity to exercise force. However, his writings also emphasised the 'interweaving of coercion and consent' (McLennan 1984: 95); the many subtle and complex forms by which non-violent, internal controls enable the state to operate with popular consent or legitimacy. Gramsci's insights were formulated around the twin themes of civil society and hegemony, which he saw as organically linked to the interests of the state and the ruling class. For Gramsci, civil society incorporated a 'range of structures and activities like trade unions, schools, the churches, and the family' that formulate, filter and consolidate 'an entire system of values, attitudes, beliefs, morality, etc. that is in one way or another supportive of the established order and the class interests that dominate it' (Boggs 1976: 39). In the most advanced states, Gramsci (2000: 227) likened the complex 'superstructures of civil society' to the 'trench systems of modern warfare' capable of stabilising and protecting the state during times of economic or social crisis.

However, in Gramscian terms, this process of hegemony, while capable of creating a 'common social-moral language' (Femia: 1981:24) through its operation as an 'organising principle' for the diffusion of ideas which help 'ruling elites perpetuate their power, wealth and status...[as] part of the natural order of things' (Boggs 1976: 39), is not static. While the state's claimed role in, for example, protecting the nation's law and order, borders or national identity might for periods be relatively uncontested or indeed positively embraced, the ideological underpinnings for such beliefs are not fixed or stable. Rather, the state, partly because of the overlap between state and civil institutions, can be subject to challenge from below, or in some circumstances from within. In this sense, civil society comprises sites of contradiction where antagonistic classes and other social formations contest prevailing ideologies. While it can help legitimise the state's activities, civil society (or counter-hegemonic formations operating independently of the state) 'can also play a crucial role in defining state actions as illegitimate where they violate legal rules or shared moral beliefs' and 'label state actions as deviant' (Green and Ward 2004: 4). In this context, human rights provide the conceptual basis for identifying and challenging state crime.

Human rights and state deviance

The contemporary human rights discourse dates back to the revolutionary upheavals in Europe and North America that swept away feudalism and laid the foundations for modern liberal democracy. The 1776 American Declaration of Independence and the 1789 French Declaration of the Rights of Man and of the Citizen spoke of a new world in which natural and universal rights replaced a divine order. In Jefferson's (1939: 13) famous words, 'We hold these truths to be self-evident: that all men are created equal; that they are endowed by their Creator with inherent and unalienable rights; that among these are life, liberty and the pursuit of happiness'. Similarly, the slogan most associated with the French revolution, 'liberty, equality and fraternity', signaled a new concept of the nation state, 'the one and indivisible republic' ruled by an elected government, and in which there was no fixed social order defined by birth. However, this was always a very qualified form of equality that entrenched the political authority of a new class comprised largely of white, property owning men (Callinicos 2000: 20–23). Thus, Jefferson was himself a slave owner and the British, Spanish and French governments all militarily intervened against the slaves of what is now Haiti when they rebelled to demand 'liberty, fraternity and equality' (James 1980). Such interventions illuminated the state's role in suppressing claims to universality, while reflecting how the highly contested concepts of liberty and equality could only be realised through prolonged and continuing political struggle.

The revolutionary implications and limitations of these newly proclaimed rights were the subject of some of the more influential political writings of the time. Edmund Burke's famous polemic in defence of English political institutions against the revolutionary French model attacked the 'rights of men' as 'political metaphysics' (Burke 1961: 71). For Burke (1961: 63–74), the professed ideals of the French revolution were an abstraction, to be contrasted with the nationally rooted 'practical science of government', and the people most suited to undertaking the pragmatic process of governance were those with property. It followed that the state should be primarily concerned with the security of the propertied few (Burke 1961: 262).

Burke's pamphlet prompted his erstwhile friend, Thomas Paine, to draft *The Rights of Man*, in which he sought to generalise the American and French experience by distinguishing natural and civil rights; the latter flowing from the former:

Man did not enter into society to become *worse* than he was before, nor to have fewer rights than he had before, but to have those rights better secured. His natural rights are the foundation of all his civil rights….Natural rights are those which appertain to man in right of his existence. Of this kind are all the intellectual rights, or rights of the mind, and also all those rights of acting as an individual for his own comfort and happiness, which are not injurious to the natural rights of others. Civil rights are those which appertain to man in right of his being a member of society (Paine 1961: 306).

Paine (1961: 308–310) further distinguished between governments that 'arise out of the people' and those that arise 'over the people'. For those arising out of society, a constitution is a marker of its legitimacy and the state a reflection and protector of commonly held rights. The dispute between Burke and Paine thus set the terms of debate about rights around the universal and the particular; that is, about what constitutes universal rights and how these are to be embodied in the states emerging out of feudalism. The polarities established by Burke and Paine still resonate through current debates over migrant and refugee rights, especially in disputes where the formal protection of human rights is counterposed to the exercise of state sovereignty, thus reducing questions of human rights principle to pragmatic balancing acts. However, the Marxist paradigm utilised by Gramsci helps transcend this tension by explaining why the state is unable to consistently protect human rights.

In his essay *On the Jewish Question*, written in 1843, Marx argued that civil rights did not flow automatically from natural rights. In an analysis of the most radical French constitution of 1793, he criticised the concept of universal rights for abstractly representing individual 'egoistic man' and submerging the profound economic and social inequalities of capitalism. Marx (1963: 24) stressed that the 'rights of man' as opposed to the 'rights of the citizen' applied to 'man…as a member of civil society' in which 'individual liberty is determined by law', leaving 'man…as an isolated monad, withdrawn into himself'. In other words, individual rights, while purporting to apply to all people equally, provided an ideological rationale for entrenching the power of the property owning classes, given that one's role in civil society was determined largely by control and ownership and property and the preferential political and legal rights flowing from it.

The central feature of Marx's critique was not the undesirability of rights per se but the nature of rights as 'the outcome of the reason of capital and not of the public reason of society' (Douzinas 2000: 163). The conceptual challenge that flows from this is to consider whether the dynamics of the rights discourse enable human rights to either reflect or be claimed in the name of the 'public reason of society'. Put simply, is it possible to look beyond the normative nature of the rights discourse as the ideology of individual rights to property and trade and instead embrace the role it might play in the further democratisation or radicalisation of civil society? Is there an emancipatory kernel within the rights ideal that can provide a means of confronting state crime?

Critical analyses of human rights suggest a pessimistic response to such propositions, especially when applied to the treatment of unauthorised migrants. Reflecting on the fate of refugees and stateless people in the 1930s, Hannah Arendt (1976: 299–300) concluded:

> The conception of human rights, based upon the assumed existence of a human being as such, broke down at the very moment when those who professed to believe in it were for the first time confronted with people who had indeed lost all other qualities and specific relationships – except that they were still human. The world found nothing sacred in the abstract nakedness of being human....If a human being loses his political status, he should, according to the implications of the inborn and inalienable rights of man, come under exactly the situation for which the declarations of such general rights provided. Actually the opposite is the case.

For Arendt, the failure of non-totalitarian Western states to protect the stateless highlighted the profound contradiction between universal rights and the political organisation of society around the nation state. For those who find themselves outside the protection of or loyalty to a national polity, rights were brutally rendered meaningless in any practical sense. 'The very phrase "human rights"', she wrote, 'became for all concerned...the evidence of hopeless idealism or fumbling, feeble-minded hypocrisy' (Arendt 1976: 269).

Arendt's critique seemed to be confirmed by the immediate post-war experience. The prosecution of war crimes at Nuremburg and Tokyo; the signing of the United Nations Charter; and the adoption of the Universal Declaration of Human Rights and the Genocide Convention were important symbolic moments of the post-war order. However, the newly espoused universality of human rights was inevitably subordinated to national interests and rivalries. Victors' justice, no matter how meritorious in relation to the state organised mass murder of the Holocaust, neatly removed episodes such as the atomic blasts in Japan from the orbit of state criminality, while the Universal Declaration and the Genocide Convention 'proved powerless to move politicians or diplomats to do anything much about genocide, or any other of the multiple or massive breaches of human rights which took place over the next fifty years' (Robertson 2006: 41). Moreover, as the Cold War intensified, instruments such as the 1951 Convention on Refugees were used more as a mechanism for Western European states to criticise their eastern counterparts than to genuinely internationalise the rights of forced migrants.

However, despite such limitations, the rights discourse gained enormous momentum from the popular political movements that developed during the Cold War in both the West and the East. In the United States, Northern Ireland and parts of Eastern Europe, universal civil rights was an important mobilising ideal that challenged the authorities within the dominant states in the 1960s and 1970s. This, combined with mass strikes in countries like France and the movements against conscription and the Vietnam War, helped create the atmosphere of change in which writers like the Schwendingers were able to argue for an alternative criminology based on human rights concerns. It also shifted the terms of mainstream political discourse, so that terms like multiculturalism

Border policing, criminology and state crime

and anti-discrimination became an accepted part of the language of Western states.

Moreover, following the collapse of the regimes in the Soviet Union and Eastern Europe, both the supporters of the emergent neoliberal consensus and those who sought to challenge its imperatives have increasingly appropriated the language of rights. Green and Ward (2000b: 83–84; 2004: 9–10) argue that such contradictory claims to human rights ideals arise from the struggle for 'global hegemony' by the dominant powers. In other words, under the control of the dominant states, a range of international institutions such as the World Bank, the International Monetary Fund and the World Trade Organisation operate to enforce free trade norms which suit the interests of the major economic powers but do so alongside the promotion of universal human rights norms by a range of United Nations agencies and non-government organisations (NGOs). This creates a number of paradoxes, not least of which is that most states formally proclaim standards by which their selective adherence to human rights can be judged. However, the extent to which they can be judged depends on a number of factors, particularly their power relative to those who are criticising them and their capacity to neutralise or co-opt those who oppose them.

While acknowledging these concerns, establishing universal human rights norms by which state behaviour and illegitimacy can be measured is important from a criminological perspective because it highlights the role of an international audience in defining deviance. Whether this audience can be understood in terms of 'transnational civil society' (Green and Ward 2000b: 84) is a complex question. In particular, refugees and forced migrants are not only excluded from their own national polity but often from the less formal, sometimes transnational, networks of civil society. Further, the dividing line between the state and the institutions of civil society is fluid and often indistinct. This is most apparent in relation to non-government organisations that are placed under considerable pressure to conform to the conditions imposed by states in order to secure funding or guarantee a safe and unhindered operational environment and are called upon, or independently deciding to carry out, enforcement or administrative functions traditionally associated with the state. For example, the United Nations High Commissioner for Refugees (UNHCR) and the International Organisation for Migration (IOM), which have always been largely funded by Western states with a view to containing refugees in zones outside of the West, have had direct involvement in the operation of Australia's refugee and asylum seeker policy. This potentially limits their capacity to act as independent advocates for human rights while giving the state scope to distance itself from some aspects of its activities or justify its policies by claiming an imprimatur has been bestowed upon it by the cooperation of such agencies. In such circumstances, the processes by which the state secures legitimacy are integrally connected to the stabilising role of civil society highlighted by Gramsci.

Nevertheless, the fact that most states claim to support the Universal Declaration of Human Rights and the International Covenants on Civil and Political Rights and on Economic, Social and Cultural Rights, illustrates how the idea that all humans share an entitlement to basic human rights is now deeply ingrained in official political discourse. While Cohen (1993: 99) is overstating his case by describing human rights as '*the* normative language of the future' (emphasis in original), the language of human rights is afforded an important, if contested, ideological space. This enables us to develop a criminological paradigm that emphasises the disjuncture between the legitimate expectations of subjects such as unauthorised migrants and the restrictive and abusive policies of 'rights abiding' states. Such disjunctures create the terrain for various social audiences to understand state actions as deviant, with the gap between popular understandings of what constitutes a refugee and the relatively narrow legal definitions that developed in the aftermath of the Second World War providing an important example of how this dynamic works.

Refugees, rights and the state

Thus far, the term refugee has been used quite loosely to describe people whose circumstances force them to move. From a state crime perspective, there are two important reasons for

Border policing, criminology and state crime

adopting this approach and locating the refugee within the broader phenomenon of the forced migrant: It enables us to challenge the hierarchy of legitimacy that operates for forced migrants by including in our consideration of organised human rights abuses, the seekers of refuge whom states have refused to acknowledge as refugees; and it contextualises the refugee as an integral product of the economic, social and political contradictions unfolding within a state system compromised by the growth of transnational networks, rather than someone acting outside the system with a meaningful level of independence or 'deviant' free will. In short, it restores a sense of legitimacy to the whole forced migration experience; and, in the face of an increasingly hostile and criminalising range of state restrictions, challenges punitive state responses to it. The complexities of forced migration are discussed in more detail in the next chapter. At this point, it is useful to establish exactly how refugees are defined by Western states and what relationship this might have to the ways in which exclusionary practices are legitimised.

The 1951 United Nations Convention Relating to the Status of Refugees is the defining instrument for contemporary consideration of refugee status and entitlement (Feller et al 2003).[16] The preamble to the Convention locates it alongside the 1948 Universal Declaration of Human Rights and its affirmation of 'the principle that human beings shall enjoy fundamental rights and freedoms without discrimination'. At its highest point, the 1948 Declaration proclaims a right of free movement within national borders[17], the right to leave and enter one's own country[18], the right to seek asylum from persecution[19] and the right to a nationality[20] but the 1951 Convention was never designed to entrench or normalise wide-ranging universal rights for forced migrants. Rather, by fitting the refugee into the concepts of persecution and nationality, the 1951 Convention, at best, offered limited assistance and protection to a relatively small proportion of forced migrants. It did this by restricting the definition of a refugee and by not according the refugee a generalised right to asylum in line with the 1948 Declaration. Instead, obligations, most notably not to refoule[21], were imposed on the Convention's signatory states.

The political context of the 1951 Convention defined its limits and reaffirmed the dominant role of the nation state within the emerging body of international humanitarian law. The role of key states in drafting the Convention illuminated its fundamentally Western character and the disparity between a notional universality invested in the individual refugee, which might provide some measure for assessing state crime, and the state's power to selectively apply criteria for repatriation and resettlement. As a result of this disjuncture, protection and human rights were applied according to pragmatic geopolitical considerations and conceptions of state security influenced by the basic polarity of the Cold War.

Throughout the 1951 Convention's gestation period, those who had been uprooted and displaced by the Second World War were considered a burden that needed to be moved on and dispersed. There seems little doubt that the scale of displacement during and immediately after the Second World War[22] contributed to the evolution of the burden-sharing principle, which provided a rationale for repatriation and resettlement programs conducted with a high level of state intervention that often had little regard for the wishes of those affected. In 1943, the United Nations Relief and Rehabilitation Agency (UNRRA) was established to work alongside the Allied Military Forces in promoting and overseeing the repatriation of 'prisoners and exiles to their homes' (Holborn 1956: 17). Taking control of refugees and preventing them from hindering the movement of troops and supplies was seen as 'basic for military success' within Europe (Holborn 1956: 19). In this context, the new agency was accused of showing little appreciation of the sensitivities of refugees because it 'devoted a substantial part of its efforts to aiding Allied military forces in identifying displaced persons, separating them into broad national categories, putting them into trucks and boxcars, and shipping them back to the countries from which they had originally come, without regard to their individual wishes' (Loescher 2001: 36).

Consequently, substantial numbers of refugees, especially those facing repatriation to the Soviet Union, resisted return and as East-West relations deteriorated, their circumstances became an emerging Cold War issue (Salomon 1991: 95–164). In 1946, the United States

Border policing, criminology and state crime

instigated the formation of the International Refugee Organisation (IRO), with a view to encouraging resettlement rather than repatriation. This policy shift was endorsed by the UN General Assembly, which declared 'no refugees or displaced persons [with valid objections] shall be compelled to return to their country of origin'[23] . Valid objections included those based on 'persecution, or fear, based on reasonable grounds, of persecution because of race, religion, nationality or political opinions' and objections 'of a political nature, judged by the organisation to be valid'.[24] This definition provided for the recognition of individual refugees for the first time and after the IRO's mandate was expanded to include escapees from the Eastern European regimes after 1948, 'perceiving refugees to be of symbolic and instrumental use in the Cold War...Western governments - especially the United States - prevailed upon the IRO to apply refugee criteria more liberally, to accommodate larger numbers of escapees' (Loescher 2001: 39).

In addition to political considerations, such as the perception of European refugees being anti-communist and white, a number of mainly Western states were willing to accept refugees as labour migrants. Over one million were resettled by the IRO, of whom the United States received 31.7 percent, Australia 17.5 percent[25], Israel 12.7 percent, Canada 11.9 percent, Britain 8.3 percent, western Europe 6.8 percent and Latin America 6.5 percent, through various designated labour migration schemes, mostly in coal mines, road-building and construction work (Holborn 1956: 365– 442; Salomon 1991: 185–213). However, by the late 1940s, with new zones of forced migration emerging on the Indian subcontinent, the Korean peninsula, in China and in Palestine, Western European states, backed by India and Pakistan, argued that the temporary post-war arrangements would not hold. In 1949, with the United States unwilling to continue funding the IRO and with eastern bloc states boycotting proceedings, negotiations began for the establishment of a new UN refugee agency (UNHCR) and the drafting of the United Nations Convention Relating to the Status of Refugees (UNHCR 2000: 18–26).

From the outset, the United States and Britain sought to limit universal and ongoing obligations to refugees. Both successfully argued against the UNHCR having any relief role and insisted on UN General Assembly approval for appeals for voluntary contributions. As a result, the UNHCR 'became totally dependent on a small administrative budget granted by the UN General Assembly and on a small "emergency fund" to which the United States made no contribution at all until 1955' (Loescher 2001: 44). Similar tensions arose over the drafting of the Refugee Convention, particularly regarding the definition of a refugee. Eventually, a compromise formula was reached based on the concept of a 'well founded fear of persecution for reasons of race, religion, nationality, membership of a particular social group or political opinion'[26], but this was limited to events occurring before January 1951, with states also given discretion to limit the convention's application to events in Europe (UNHCR 2000: 24).[27] This definition of refugee entrenched the notion of the individual refugee, upon whom there is a burden to prove refugee status to the satisfaction of the receiving state. Such an obligation immediately questioned the legitimacy of the refugee, rather than the legitimacy of the receiving state's response. Moreover, Article 1 specified that a refugee must be 'outside the country of his nationality'. Internally displaced persons, stranded within the borders of their state of origin or habitual residence, and often the most weak and vulnerable of forced migrants, effectively were penalised for their relative incapacity to move, or for not being aliens (Tuitt 1996: 11–13).

In the post-Cold War era, the changing security context and the growth in the number of refugees seeking entry to the West from the developing world prompted receiving states to take advantage of the latitude provided by the definition to restrict entry to forced migrants. Primarily, this was achieved by reducing forced migrants, many of whom have fled en masse, into individual asylum seekers, who must navigate an increasingly tortuous legal and bureaucratic path before attaining the status and rights bestowed upon the refugee. Increasingly, refugees who have not been officially resettled are provided with only graded or provisional levels of protection, such as temporary protection visas.

Moreover, the absence of an enforceable right to free movement and the requirement that refugees justify their individual claims enables Western states to more easily evade their Convention obligations. Detaining and criminalising unauthorised refugees pending the outcomes of their applications and/or putting in place enforcement measures designed to prevent refugees physically accessing state mechanisms for refugee protection further undermines minimum Convention rights. Such systemic exclusion is legitimised at its most basic level through the acceptance of nationalist ideology and the state's role as the sovereign power but as the narrow constructions of the refugee in the 1951 Convention indicate, labelling a state's activities as sociologically criminal presupposes a generalised right to free movement that goes beyond the limited protections offered by international human rights law.

State crime and refugees: a working paradigm

Analysing every dimension of the contemporary refugee is beyond the scope of any single academic discipline, no matter how broadly defined, and certainly this book. Nevertheless, the application of criminological perspectives to forced and illicit migration provides both valuable insights into the relationship between the state and the refugee and a more nuanced understanding of state crime. In this sense, Green and Ward's definition of state crime provides a conceptual framework that, when broken down thematically, offers challenging lines of inquiry, rather than a strictly legal formula upon which to found a tightly bound black letter solution to the multiple human rights abuses endured by refugees.

This does not mean that solutions, even partial ones, are not important. It does suggest, though, that a much broader conceptual base is required to challenge the systemic nature of human rights abuses and to liberate a commitment to human rights from the institutional strait-jacket of the nation state. In short, a state crime paradigm must provide a framework for identifying and challenging systematic and profound state deviance that defies legal sanction, but routinely impacts on the lives of unauthorised migrants. Such a perspective also challenges norms of border policing we are implored to support and take for granted, and reinforces the contrast between a managerial criminology devoted to the efficient functioning of state sponsored wars against forced and illicit migrants, with a critical criminology that seeks to contest the state's monopoly of force and power in this domain.

A number of recurring themes emerge in developing such an approach, including: the inter-relationships between forced migration, the global economy and the nation state; the role of border policing in legitimising state authority and sovereignty; the state's use of nationalist arguments to justify the exclusion of certain types of migrant; the contradictions and limitations of the human rights discourse, especially in relation to free movement; and the need for a global perspective that goes beyond conventional conceptions of international law. While such themes necessarily overlap, the main working paradigm of this book is that state crime derives from the organised and deviant use of force diffused through the alienation, criminalisation and abuse of unauthorised migrants. This deviance can be measured by reference to breaches of international human rights norms; but more importantly, it can be defined from below, through an understanding of the fundamental disjuncture between the legitimate expectations of unauthorised migrants and the exclusionist responses of the Australian state. In order to establish how the competing concepts of legitimacy have evolved, the next chapter provides an explanation of forced and illicit migration that challenges the deviance bestowed by the state upon the unauthorised migrant.

Notes

[1] See for example Barak (1991); Green and Ward (2004); Kauzlarich and Kramer (2000); Pickering (2005); Ross (1995); Rothe and Friedrichs (2006); and (2005) *British Journal of Criminology* Volume 45, Number 4, a special issue on state crime. Some of the material in this chapter was also used in Grewcock (2008).

[2] The main exception to this is Pickering (2005). See also Weber (2002); Weber and Bowling (2002); Weber and Gelsthorpe (2000); Weber and Landman (2002); and Pickering and Weber (2006).

[3] See, for example, Barak (1991); Cohen (1993); Green and Ward (2000a, 2000b and 2004); Kauzlarich and Kramer (1998); Pickering (2005); Ross (1995 and 2000); and Rothe and Friedrichs (2006). For an account by the

Schwendingers of developments within criminology in the period following their article, see Schwendinger et al (2002).

[4] See, for example, Bayart et al (1999) and de Waal (1997).

[5] See, for example, Bass (2000); Detter (2000); Falk et al (1971); Maogoto (2004); and Robertson (2006).

[6] Principle VI (c), *Principles of the Nuremberg Tribunal*, adopted by the International Law Commission in 1950.

[7] Article 5, Rome Statute of the International Criminal Court, 1998.

[8] This is not to argue that the concept of international criminal justice is solely to be understood as relating to the prosecution of state crime. See Findlay (2008).

[9] See also the development of their argument in Green and Ward (2000a) and (2000b).

[10] The person most associated with developing the concept of totalitarianism was Hannah Arendt (1967) and (1976). While I disagree with two central aspects of her thesis – that Bolshevism led directly to Stalinism and that the Stalinist and Nazi states were roughly comparable – her insights into the limitations of democratic states to uphold the human rights of refugees are quite useful. For critiques of totalitarianism theory, see Ferro (2007); Losurdo (2004); and Traverso (2007).

[11] This does not mean that all threats need to be conceptualised in national terms. For example, within the discourse of anti-terrorism, threats can be state-based, in the form of 'rogue states', or stateless, in the form of international terror networks or transnational organised crime; although some form of state sponsor is normally identified.

[12] Merton's concept of anomie, first outlined in essay form in 1938, was used to describe the social disjunctures arising from the inability of layers of society to attain by legitimate means goals that were encouraged by society. See Merton (1938) and Akers (2000: 139-188).

[13] For example, Merton (1968) and Passas (1990).

[14] See also Kauzlarich and Kramer (1998: 148) for their application of this to their 'integrated theory of organizational crime'.

[15] This study, first published in 1957, challenged the notion of 'juvenile delinquency as a form of behaviour based on the values and norms of a deviant sub-culture', and sought to explain why 'the juvenile delinquent would appear to be at least partially committed to the dominant social order in that he frequently exhibits guilt or shame when he violates its proscriptions, accords approval to certain conforming figures, and distinguishes between appropriate and inappropriate targets for his

deviance' (Sykes and Matza 1970: 294).
[16] For a discussion of the origins of asylum, see Marfleet (2006: 97-119).
[17] Article 13(1).
[18] Article 13(2).
[19] Article 14(1).
[20] Article 15(1).
[21] Article 33 prohibits a contracting state from expelling or returning (refouling) refugees 'to the frontiers of territories where [their] life or freedom would be threatened on account of [their] race, religion, nationality, membership of a particular social group or political opinion…'
[22] For a summary of the various population movements, see Holborn (1956:15) and Loescher (2001: 34-35).
[23] Document A/45, 12 February 1946, incorporated as Annex III of the IRO Constitution.
[24] Annex III(c)(ii).
[25] See chapter 3 below
[26] Article 1A(2).
[27] The temporal and geographical restrictions were lifted by the 1967 Protocol to the Convention.

Chapter 2

Forced migration, refugees and the state

State crime and forced migration

The main focus of this chapter is the role played by Western states in creating and sustaining the global infrastructure for the production and exclusion of forced migrants; and the implications this has for our understanding of individual and state deviance. This approach emphasises that the degree of free choice attributed to unauthorised migrants who make the decision to breach border controls is falsely constructed. Instead, illicit movement should be understood as a product of complex economic and social factors and the imposition of border controls.

There are multiple sources of forced migration. State crime, in the form of organised human rights abuses, is one of them but in many situations, the role of the state is more difficult to determine. Nevertheless, state bodies in the form of governments, troops or border policing agencies usually have some role in determining what meaningful human rights, if any, forced migrants can exercise. From a criminological perspective, the ongoing relationships between the state and the forced migrant – the confrontations along multiple fronts between a complex political economy in which the state often plays a central role, and a human rights regime that routinely fails to provide meaningful protection or avenues for free movement – become the most important sites of inquiry.

An important threshold issue is the extent to which the term 'refugee' can be applied to the much broader sociological phenomenon of the forced migrant. Individual decisions to move are rarely made in isolation and can be shaped by a multiplicity of systemic factors[1], ranging from direct military threats through to economic hardship. Further, shifting location may not always involve crossing an international border. This does not mean that all refugees or forced migrants are the same; for example, there are still meaningful distinctions between voluntary and forced migration and between those forced to cross borders and those who are internally displaced. However, it does highlight the difficulties in defining precisely the point at which migration ceases to be a product of compulsion; the need to further research and understand the complexity and scale of forced migration; and the inconsistent and sometimes contradictory state responses to it. As Marfleet (2006: 216) comments:

> More displaced people are now long distance migrants and more are involved in complex movements across regions and continents. Until recently, however, these experiences hardly featured in migration research. To make sense of them it is necessary to think of changed patterns of movement – global networks within which migrants undertake multiple journeys which may involve repeat, shuttle, 'orbital', 'ricochet' and 'yo-yo' migrations, and attempts at settlement and return. Elaborate patterns of movement suggest *circuits* of migration, accommodating all manner of journeys (emphasis in original).

There are three main, albeit overlapping, types of forced migration: conflict-induced displacement where state authorities are either unable or unwilling to protect people forced to flee armed conflict, generalised violence or persecution; development-induced displacement where, for example, people are forced to move as a result of infrastructure projects, urban clearance or mining and deforestation; and disaster-induced displacement, including both natural and human made disasters.[2] Those compelled to move defy easy classification other than being overwhelmingly from the developing world where they are disproportionately drawn from indigenous and ethnic minorities and the urban or rural poor. They include refugees (as defined by the 1951 Convention); asylum seekers; internally displaced persons; development displacees; environmental and disaster displacees; smuggled and trafficked migrants, stateless people; and refugees who have returned to their homes but require ongoing protection and assistance (Loughna 2005; UNHCR 2005a).

Forced migration, refugees and the state

Estimates vary widely as to the number of forced migrants. The reasons for this are partly conceptual. As Castles (2003: 13–14) points out, sociology and related disciplines have yet to produce 'a developed body of empirical work and theory' in relation to forced migration.[3] There is also a lack of systematic data collection; different methods of counting are used by major agencies such as the UNHCR and the United States Committee for Refugees and Immigrants (USCRI); internal migration is often not recorded at all; and the distinctions between voluntary and involuntary movement and different types of involuntary movement are easily blurred (Crisp 1999: 4–6).[4] Nevertheless, it is clear that refugees as defined by the 1951 Convention (especially given its increasingly strict interpretation by Western states) represent a minority of forced migrants, who as a group constitute a substantial proportion of the growing total of global migration. A recent UN report that estimated that the number of international migrants increased from 100 million in 1980 to 175 million in 2000 of whom, 'about 158 million were deemed international migrants; approximately 16 million were recognized refugees…and 900,000 were asylum seekers' (UN 2004: vii). At the end of 2004, there were also over 1.1 million people, including those who are stateless or of indeterminate nationality, living in 'refugee-like situations' but not meeting the refugee definition (USCRI 2005: 15).

However, the most significant group of forced migrants is the internally displaced (IDPs); that is, those who have not crossed a national border. According to the Internal Displacement Monitoring Centre, the number of people displaced in this way increased from 16.5 million in 1989 to 26 million in 2008 (IDMC 2009a). It is also estimated that 90 to 100 million people were displaced as a result of infrastructural development projects during the 1990s (Loughna 2005); that there were at least 25 million environmental refugees[5] in 1995; and that by 'the middle of the [21st] century, 200 million more people may become permanently displaced due to rising sea levels, heavier floods, and more intense droughts' (Stern 2006: 56). Moreover, events such as the 2004 south Asian tsunami which left 290,000 people dead or missing and more than one million displaced (Hedman 2005a: 4) graphically demonstrated the lack of real choices open to forced migrants; the typically sudden nature of their movement; and the enormous casualties likely to occur when flight is prevented or otherwise impossible.

Significantly, while the number of international migrants in the developed world increased from 42 percent in 1960 to 63 percent in 2000 (UN 2004: 26)[6], the vast majority of forced migrants remain within the developing world. In 2000, refugees accounted for 23 percent of all international migrants in Asia and 22 percent for those of Africa (UN 2004: 26–27). In 2004, 71 percent of the world's refugees were hosted by countries with a per capita income below $2,000; 24 percent where the per capita income was between $2,001 and $10,000; and only 5 percent where per capita incomes were over $10,000 (USCRI 2005: 13). By the end of 2008, developing countries hosted four fifths of the world's refugees, with the largest concentrations in Pakistan (1.8 million), Syria (1.1 million) and Iran (980,000) (UNHCR 2009). Internally displaced persons are similarly concentrated in the developing world. At the end of 2008, 'Sudan, Colombia and Iraq together accounted for 45 percent of the world's internally displaced people' (IDMC 2009b).

This disjuncture between the formal migrant, who can choose or be chosen to move from the developing to the developed world, and the forced migrant stranded in the shanty town, camp or (often illusory) visa queue represents one of the main fault lines demarcating the Global North from the Global South.[7] This does not mean that forced migration is purely a phenomenon of the developing world but it does suggest that any analysis of organised human rights abuses committed against refugees ought to take into account broader questions of political economy and shifting forced migration patterns.

The sources of forced migration

In gruesome contrast to the human rights norms that also evolved, the twentieth century produced unparalleled levels of state violence. One widely quoted study estimates nearly 170 million people, over four times the numbers killed in wars, were murdered by governments between 1900 and 1987 (Rummel 1994: 1–28). It

Forced migration, refugees and the state

was also an era in which interstate conflicts and struggles for state power resulted in unprecedented levels of human displacement and multi-dimensional refugee movements (UNHCR 2000).

During the first half of the century, the restructuring of national boundaries out of the collapsing Ottoman and Czarist empires; the two world wars spilling out from the European continent; and state-orchestrated genocidal campaigns against the Jews and other minorities made statelessness 'the newest mass phenomenon in contemporary history' (Arendt 1976: 277). Further, the Second World War left over 40 million people outside the borders of their homeland (Newman 2003: 13) ensuring that while substantial displacement occurred in parts of Asia and Africa, initial perceptions of the refugee were dominated by the concerns of the Western European states and allied military authorities to control those displaced within or struggling to enter the emerging network of Western European states.

During the latter part of the century, the epicentre of the refugee discourse began shifting towards the developing world. The formation of the state of Israel and the partition of India and Pakistan left unresolved border disputes in Palestine and Kashmir and created refugee populations, which in the case of the Palestinians[8], continue to the present day. More generally, decolonisation often involved lengthy military campaigns for the creation and control of independent nation states that, as in the case of Indo-China, prompted interventions by external imperialist powers seeking to defend or extend their geopolitical interests.

By the mid 1970s, a series of protracted refugee crises emerged 'with the appearance of massive new flows in both Asia and Africa, attributable to complex internationalised conflicts that engulfed entire regions' (Zolberg et al 1989: 228). While many were forcibly moved 'as a result of the formation of new states out of colonial empires, and confrontations over the social order in both the old and new states' (Zolberg et al 1989: 230), the geopolitical dimensions of the Cold War meant many regimes in the decolonised world relied for their survival on aid and military hardware supplied by their superpower sponsors. Thus, prolonged civil wars in various

Border Crimes

parts of Africa, Asia and Central America that resulted in substantial forced movement were sustained by outside intervention (UNHCR 2000: 105–131).

The end of the Cold War produced a further series of seismic upheavals that continue to generate forced migration and systemic threats to human security.[9] Between 1989 and 2003, over 50 states underwent major transformations and over 4 million people were killed as a result of armed conflict or political violence (Troeller 2003: 55). By 2006, the UNHCR had a 'population of concern' of 32.9 million, including some 12.8 million conflict generated internally displaced persons (UNHCR 2007a: 2–13). By September 2007, the UNHCR estimated over 4 million Iraqis had been displaced, with an estimated 60,000 being forced to leave their homes every month by continuing violence' (UNHCR 2007b).

Much of the forced movement during this period was generated by conflict and systematic human rights violations; and in some cases, convulsive bursts of genocidal terror. The recurrent scale of forced migration also coincided with the emergence of changing patterns of warfare and organised violence in the developing world (Duffield 2001: 161–201; Kaldor 2002: 1–2). It is estimated that civilians now constitute up to 90 percent of all conflict casualties (Carnegie Commission 1997: 11) and while there is some dispute over whether this scale of human casualties represents a linear departure from previous conflicts (Newman 2003: 12–15), the experience of the Democratic Republic of the Congo, where an estimated 5.4 million mainly civilians died between 1998 and 2007 makes the case compelling. However, the developed states are not blameless. Not only are they the major suppliers of weapons (SIPRI 2005), but the aerial bombing campaigns favoured by the United States and NATO inevitably create high levels of casualties and displacement; while the use of munitions such as cluster bombs continue to provide a significant threat and source of dislocation to civilian populations following conflicts in Afghanistan in 2001, Yugoslavia in 1999 and both campaigns in Iraq (HRW 2005a: 2).[10]

Further, while the 'new wars can be understood as a form of non-territorial network war that works through and around states…

[and] typically oppose and ally the transborder resource networks of state incumbents, social groups, diasporas, strongmen, and so on' (Duffield 2001: 14), the consolidation of the post-Cold War system of states has been accompanied by extensive rearmament, especially since the promulgation of the 'war on terror' (SIPRI 2005). These trends towards militarisation and warfare reflect attempts by the elites in many developing states (or rival factions within them) to shore up their control, often in circumstances where the state machine is considered to have failed.

The internal divisions that have arisen within a number of states in the post-colonial era reflect partly the arbitrary way the colonial powers drew boundaries with little reference to economic, social and cultural borders. Many of the serious ethnic conflicts that have broken out in countries like Rwanda also reflect the divide and rule policies of the colonial powers that favoured particular social groupings; encouraged ethnic rivalry in areas where it had not previously existed in any organised form; and backed corrupt, violent and undemocratic governments (Melvern 2000; Zeilig and Seddon 2002). Rwanda also provided an extreme example of the linkages between economic liberalisation and forced migration when the undermining of the International Coffee Agreement in 1989 triggered a chain of events that included genocide; ongoing civil and regional warfare; and prolonged, complex refugee movements (Melvern 2000).

The imposition of neoliberal policies has not always had such catastrophic results but it has contributed to a dramatic increase in inequality between the developing and developed world. Between 1960 and 1990, the ratio of the income of the richest fifth of the world's population to that of the poorest fifth increased from 30:1 to 60:1; and to 74:1 by 1997 (UNDP 1999:3). In 2005, UN Secretary General Kofi Annan reported that despite reductions in extreme poverty in China and India, 'dozens of countries have become poorer', ensuring that 'more than one billion people – one in every six human beings – still live on less than one dollar a day, lacking the means to stay alive in the face of chronic hunger, disease and environmental hazards' (UNGA 2005: 7).

Changes in the nature of the market and economic life have also had a significant demographic impact. According to a recent UN report,

> During the next 30 years, the global urban population will increase by more than 2 billion while rural populations will be almost static. The greatest impact will be felt in the developing world, and nowhere more so than through South and South-Eastern Asia and sub-Saharan Africa. During the next 15 years, many large cities in Asia and Africa will nearly double their population (UN-Habitat 2003: 5).

This shift towards the cities is neither the product of freely embraced social mobility nor an invitation to Malthusian prescriptions. In Africa, particularly, it has coincided with ongoing food shortages directly produced by changes in agricultural patterns as rural production shifts to focus on export commodities, profits from which are channelled into debt repayment (UN-Habitat 2003: 46). Moreover, urbanisation has not usually involved industrialisation. Instead, public sector employment typically has been curtailed, basic services privatised and 'fledgling urban industries that might have had a chance for long-term growth eliminated' (UN-Habitat 2003: 46). Consequently, a surplus rural population, disproportionately drawn from young women and children, has migrated to the cities. There they provide a pool of cheap, often bonded, labour for a growing informal sector with multiple pathways into human trafficking and associated illicit activities.

The scale of human trafficking and contemporary forms of slavery gives rise to serious human rights concerns that are of immediate relevance to an analysis of state or institutional crime (Bales 2004; Lee 2007). In West Africa, for example, trafficking includes children being '"sold" by their parents or contracted to agents for work in exchange for cash' (Adepoju 2005: 81); or is a product of large numbers of young people relocating to the streets of shanty towns surrounding major cities such as Addis Ababa, Dakar, Lagos and Nairobi, where, living on the streets, they become highly vulnerable to traffickers (Adepoju 2005: 81). Similar patterns can be observed in South Asia, where trafficking...

Forced migration, refugees and the state

'...revolve(s) around the large scale of undocumented or irregular labour migration...the widespread movement of women as wives and domestic workers, in addition to sex and entertainment work; the trafficking of children for labour, sexual exploitation and adoption; and the strong link between prostitution, sex tourism and militarization' (Piper 2005: 208).

However, the extent to which those living in such areas can rely on protection from the local state is questionable. Most of the growth in the developing world's urban population and the illicit networks arising from it occurs in slums on the edges of established cities; that is, in areas where there is 'overcrowding, poor or informal housing, inadequate access to safe water and sanitation and insecurity of tenure' (UN-Habitat 2003: 28). Many of these conurbations house concentrations of forced migrants and the urban poor and are vulnerable to repressive law and order campaigns designed to force the population into rural or equally untenable urban environments, with little or no regard for their human rights.

The 1990 bulldozing of the Maroko beach slum in Lagos; the 1995 demolition of the squatter town of Zhejiangcun on the edge of Beijing; the mass evictions from the Angolan townships of Boavista, Soba Kapassa and Benfica between 2001 and 2003; the destruction of over 400 structures including homes, schools, churches and a clinic in the Kibera district of Nairobi in 2004; and the forced eviction of 6,000 people by Lagos State authorities in 2005 were operations that officially targeted 'criminal elements' by removing the capacity of whole communities to survive (Davis 2004a: 17; Tibaijuka 2005: 81). Similarly, the Zimbabwean Government's 2005 Operation Murambatsvina ('Get rid of trash') that destroyed the homes or livelihoods of over 700,000 people living in illegal urban settlements throughout the country (Tibaijuka 2005: 7), involved a full-scale military-style mobilisation relying 'on a set of colonial era laws that were used as a tool of segregation and social exclusion' (Tibaijuka 2005: 7–8) and aimed also at undermining political opposition.

Such outbursts of state repression are not the only threat facing those seeking survival in the city. Increasingly, urban landscapes in the developing world operate along an 'urban-rural continuum' in which the inhabitants are 'everywhere forced to settle on hazardous and otherwise unbuildable terrains – over steep hill slopes, riverbanks and flood plains' (Davis 2004:7,16). Here, they enter more precarious circuits of forced migration as a result of their vulnerability to environmental disasters such as floods, landslides and exposure to industrial emissions and waste (Davis 2004a: 7). State activity (or lack of it), encompassing a range of criminal acts or omissions, can have an important influence on the human impact of such disasters. In Turkey, for example, the deliberate stifling of political dissent protected corrupt state practices in the provision of dangerously substandard housing and infrastructure in poor urban areas devastated by earthquakes in 1999 (Green and Ward 2004: 64–67). As the experience of Hurricane Katrina showed, even in the most powerful and economically developed state in the world where there was considerable advance warning of the impending storm system; disturbingly accurate predictions of the devastating impact on poor communities (Davis 2004b); and unimaginable resources compared with developing countries, race and class largely determined who was evacuated and who was abandoned (Lavelle and Feagin 2006), prompting one writer to describe the state response as 'a bipartisan political crime' (Ortiz 2006: 1).

Environmental crises similarly can exacerbate previously existing conflict-induced displacement situations. In Sri Lanka, for example, the 2004 tsunami added approximately one million people to an already serious refugee situation arising from the war between the Sri Lankan state and Tamil separatists, giving rise to allegations that aid was not being distributed fairly to displaced Tamil communities (GIDPP 2005a and 2005b). Likewise, in Aceh, where the Indonesian government declared a state of military emergency and martial law in May 2003, the tsunami compounded a situation in which the destruction of infrastructure and mass displacement of the civilian population was already state policy (Hedman 2005a and 2005b; Ramly 2005).

In summary, forced migration is integrally linked to a matrix of war, social conflict, economic marginalisation and environmental hazards that can often be directly attributed to Western states and

Forced migration, refugees and the state

the economic and social interests they promote and defend, or to local states seeking to protect their own narrow interests. In this context, the multiple acts of survival that constitute forced and illicit migration challenge notions that in attempting to escape their immediate environment, forced migrants are merely self-seeking or pursuing undeserved economic advancement. From a criminological perspective, rather than being deviant, forced migrants are responding to factors and to some degree, conforming to norms, outside of their control.

This throws into question the bases upon which the human rights of various types of forced migrant are differentiated internationally and suggests we ought to focus on how the responses of states in both the developing and developed world systematically threaten those rights. Whether some or all of those state responses constitute specific instances of state crime may lead to significant disagreement and in some senses, is a secondary question. The main conceptual challenge at this point is to recognise that forced migrants are not the primary actors in their decisions to move and that their immediate containment and other restrictions on movement constitute sources of abuse. This becomes apparent when we consider that those who are displaced risk being stranded for lengthy periods in temporary camps or other forms of controlled settlement offering limited personal security or stability. Far from being a humanitarian haven, the camp is emerging as a central institutional component of organised exclusion in both the developing and the developed world.

Forced migration and the camp

The prolonged or indefinite containment of people in camps evokes images from the 1930s and 1940s of some of the most extreme state organised human rights abuses, many of which prompted the development of contemporary human rights norms and would satisfy most definitions of state crime. Indeed, a reduction in the numbers of refugees living in camps was one of the main emphases of the refugee protection regime that developed after the Second World War.[11] The re-emergence of the camp as an almost permanent institution has therefore prompted social theorists to question the rationales provided by states for supporting their use and the limitations of human rights norms.

Giorgio Agamben (1998 and 2000)[12], for example, argues that the stripping away of refugees' rights, especially in the context of the detention camp, is a defining feature of contemporary sovereignty. Agamben (1998: 8) invokes from Roman law the concept of *homo sacer*, the 'sacred man', whose 'bare life' constitutes the 'essential function in modern politics'. For Agamben (1998: 9–11), *homo sacer* is distinguished by a total absence of rights; and the 'realm of the bare life' operates 'at the margins of the political order', where it inhabits a state or 'zone of exception' which, 'actually constituted, in its very separateness, (represents) the hidden foundation on which the entire political system rest(s)'. In this sense, sovereign power, which is invested in or claimed by the state, is principally understood through the processes of inclusion and exclusion. The bare life, that which is excluded and therefore depoliticised, represents the power of the state over the individual, while also defining politics and the state by being their opposite. Accordingly, *homo sacer* is distinguishable from the politicised citizen by the latter's capacity to secure legitimacy and a level of formal protection from the state and the 'the camp' is the ultimate expression of a 'zone of exemption' that produces bare life. It 'is the space that opens up when the stateof exception starts to become the rule' (Agamben 2000: 39); 'the most absolute biopolitical space that has ever been realised – a space in which power confronts nothing other than pure biological life without any mediation' (Agamben 2000: 41).

Agamben's reminder that the extensive use of camps across Europe paralleled 'the new laws on citizenship and on the denationalisation of citizens [that] were issued...by almost all the European states...between 1915 and 1933' (Agamben 2000: 42–43), and was not unique to the dystopian experiences of fascism or Stalinism, is important to remember when looking at the role of the Western democracies such as Australia in legitimising the contemporary use of camps. But while Agamben's imagery is powerful, the conceptualisation of the detention camp as a human rights free zone hinders a more focused analysis of human rights abuses being perpetuated within camps and the border protection

Forced migration, refugees and the state

complex, often in flagrant breach of state policy. Agamben does not provide much insight into the means by which states exercise different degrees and forms of political authority and exclusion over their own citizenry, or those non-citizens (such as refugees on temporary protection visas) who are not absolutely excluded. There is also no recognition that on a global scale, camps take a variety of forms and operate in circumstances allowing sporadic and limited interplays with the broader civil society. This enables the camp to become a potential site of internal and external opposition, particularly in the developing world where, for many refugees, the camp provides, albeit in a perverse and entirely unsatisfactory way, an environment in which social and political solidarity can cohere.

Nevertheless, while the contemporary refugee camp run by an agency such as the UNHCR cannot reasonably be equated with a Nazi concentration camp, the substantial impact of the camp on the human rights of those who have little choice but to remain in them is a significant issue.[13] Detention and various forms of state containment are now central to the border policing strategies of the main Western states, while over the past 25 years, the refugee camp has become a preferred mechanism for accommodating and containing forced migrants in the developing world (Black 1998: 2), often as a result of the way aid operates as an adjunct to the foreign policy interests of the dominant states (Harrell-Bond 1986).

The growing permanence of camps is symptomatic of the wider trend towards warehousing refugees - 'the practice of keeping refugees in protracted situations of restricted mobility, enforced idleness, and dependency…deprived of the freedom necessary to pursue normal lives' (Smith 2004: 38)[14] - in preference to previously promoted durable solutions to refugee flows such as voluntary repatriation, permanent local integration in the country of first asylum or resettlement (Jacobsen 2001: 1–10; Smith 2004: 38). While it can be argued that the practices associated with warehousing reflect both conscious state policies and pragmatic agency decisions in periods of crisis and emergency that by default have turned warehousing into a 'durable' solution;[15] for those who cannot be repatriated, voluntarily or otherwise, being marooned in a camp - often segregated by force from the local host community and with limited capacity to move, work or take advantage of broader civil and cultural rights - is a significant contributing factor to forced migrants losing the ability to claim the protection of another state. In this sense, the camp plays an important institutional role in the conduct of state crime.

As with forced migrants, camps raise definitional issues. The UNHCR defines refugee camps as 'enclosed areas, restricted to refugees and those assisting them, where protection and assistance is provided until it is safe for the refugees to return to their homelands or be resettled elsewhere' (UNHCR 2000: 108). This is quite a narrow definition that mainly refers to arrangements in the developing world, that are intended to be temporary, rather than immigration detention centres in countries like Australia. It also distinguishes camps from self-supporting arrangements such as agricultural settlements or refugee villages (UNHCR 2000: 108). However, such distinctions are not necessarily helpful. Camp arrangements are diverse, ranging from 'tented cities supplied wholly from the outside' through to village type communities less dependent on external aid and control (Black 1998: 4), and many are far from temporary. Moreover, it is the impact of the particular settlement arrangement on the rights of the forced migrant that is the more important issue when interpreting the role of the institution.

One of the most significant features of the camp is its role in segregating refugees from their host community. Host governments often favour this for political or military reasons (Bakewell 2002: 230–231; Smith 2004: 38) but even when this is not the case, refugee camps are often located in remote areas on the borders of war zones[16] or especially in the case of those who are internally displaced, in inhospitable and otherwise dangerous environments. Combined with overcrowding, this contributes to significant health risks, as confirmed by the deaths of over 50,000 Rwandan refugees during a cholera epidemic in Goma, Zaire, in July 1994 (Van Damme 1995: 360–361).

The main argument advanced in favour of camps by agencies such as the UNHCR and Médécins Sans Frontieres (MSF) is that they are the best available practical response to sudden, wide scale displacement or migration. Camps enable refugees to be registered for the purposes of receiving aid, make refugees more easily accessible and enable refugees' status to be monitored (Van der Borght and Philips 1995: 907–908). According to the UNHCR (2000: 108), camps might also 'provide a safer and materially more secure option than self-settlement [given that] refugees and their leaders frequently organise themselves into camp-like settlements before UNHCR or any other humanitarian organisation establishes an assistance programme'.

On the face of it, this appears to be common sense but human rights concerns arise from across the spectrum of temporary settlement arrangements. USCRI (2005: 40–41), for example, argues that warehousing breaches 11 articles of the 1951 Refugee Convention. However, in addition to the time people remain in them, it is the institutional nature of camps that undermines their capacity to protect human rights. While those working for NGOs may well be motivated by very genuine humanitarian concerns and are often working in circumstances of high personal risk (UNHCR 2005b: 13), aid agencies, often with the encouragement of host state governments, take on state-like functions in the camp environment sometimes going to great lengths to ensure that refugees are placed in camps. A number of critical studies of camp life in Africa since the 1980s[17] highlight how this contributes to the disempowerment of refugees by host governments and aid agencies. While forced migrants often require emergency aid, camps can also create a cycle of dependency and a source of further victimisation by denying refugees the means to make independent decisions, develop strategies for survival, integrate or move on (Harrell-Bond 1986: 87–92; Chen 2005: 2–3).

This is partly the product of aid agencies tying protection to aid and viewing refugees as '"victims" to be pitied' rather than 'survivors of adversity' (Harrell-Bond 2002: 52–54). This has an impact on the way refugees perceive themselves and the types of behaviour they feel are appropriate to gain access to further resources (Harrell-Bond 2002: 57–58). In some cases, the mentality of distributing 'handouts' to passive refugees has contributed to

Border Crimes

their complete 'infantilization' (Harrell-Bond 2002: 60), while the marshalling of refugees for the purposes of distributing rations has led to authoritarian practices, including collective punishments, headcounts conducted at gunpoint, and assaults on refugees by NGO staff (Verdirame and Harrell-Bond 2005: 271–339). Other problems associated with aid dependency include vulnerability to food shortages if aid supplies cease or are disrupted and hostility from within the local community to perceived advantages for refugees if aid appears to be sustaining a viable or superior parallel economy. The refusal by host states to allow refugees to work in or integrate into the local community also provides the basis for organised crime, including drug smuggling, human trafficking, illegal logging and gun running, to become a significant means of survival (Jacobsen 2001:13). Increased policing or militarisation does not necessarily reduce the human rights risks arising from this. In the wake of the 2004 tsunami, a UN report on the circumstances of internally displaced persons noted 'there had been an increase in reports of sexual and gender based violence in IDP locations with a marked military presence' (Kälin 2005: 18).

In recent years, the most serious concerns about personal security have arisen from the militarisation of refugee camps. This issue was brought to a head by the flight of Rwandese refugees into Zaire and other neighbouring states in 1994. The refugees included some 30,000 soldiers loyal to the former Hutu regime, who took physical control of the camps, manipulated the distribution of supplies and effectively created a mini-state in exile. There were extensive first hand reports of 'killings, threats, extortions, rape and thuggery', and an estimated 4,000 murders in Goma, within the first month of the exodus (Melvern 2000: 223). The regrouping of the Hutu militias made the refugee camps an important focus of the regional war that engulfed the Great Lakes region throughout the 1990s. This seriously compromised agencies such as the UNHCR and contributed to tens of thousands of refugees being forced to flee back into Rwanda or into neighbouring Burundi when troops from neighbouring states such as Zaire targeted the camps (Lischer 2005: 73–117; UNHCR 1996).

Forced migration, refugees and the state

The intricacies of this conflict cannot be addressed here but experiences such as those in Rwanda have contributed to refugee camps being central to security and sovereignty concerns expressed by host states. At times, this has led to whole camp populations being forcibly moved by state authorities and has included refugees being pushed across borders in violation of the prohibition against refoulement in the Refugee Convention[18] and the forcible relocation of internally displaced persons.[19] Such episodes are facilitated by the fact that camp populations can be rounded up at gunpoint but other forms of coercion also apply such as the refusal to allow forced migrants to work outside the camps, the withdrawal of their protected status, or the withdrawal of aid.[20]

Forced evacuation of camps is consistent with the trends toward the return of internally displaced persons, the repatriation of refugees and asylum seekers, and the introduction of various forms of temporary protection by Western states that implicitly reject linking refugeehood with permanent solutions outside the zone of flight. This pattern dates back to the 1980s and has two immediate material causes: the growing scale, complexity and impact of forced migration in the developing world since the 1970s, and the barriers imposed by developed states against the entry of forced migrants, other than the small minority allowed through resettlement schemes. The turning point came with the complex refugee movements generated by the wars in Indo-China. The Australian state's response to this is discussed in some detail below but the global impact was significant. Between 1975 and 1995, over 1.3 million Cambodian, Laotian and Vietnamese refugees were resettled in the West, including approximately 823,000 in the United States and 138,000 in Australia (UNHCR 2000: 99). However, it also included the repatriation of some 500,000 refugees back to Indo-China (UNHCR 2000: 99) and a prolonged crisis during which 'countless people…drowned…or lost their lives or suffered in other ways from pirate attacks, rape, shelling, pushbacks, and long-term detention in inhumane conditions' (UNHCR 2000: 102).

This somewhat contradictory scenario established a precedent for twinning repatriation with resettlement in a way that allowed for repatriation to gain currency as a preferred solution when Western states became less accommodating during the 1990s. Now, levels of resettlement are far more modest, although they comprise a substantial proportion of the overall intake of key reception states. Thus in 2004, approximately 30,000 refugees, that is, less than one percent of the global total, were resettled in 15 countries with UNHCR assistance. The United States and Canada took 76 percent and Australia, 19 percent. Including those resettled as a result of bilateral agreements not involving UNHCR, the United States resettled 52,900 refugees, Canada 10,500 and Australia 16,000 (UNHCR 2005d: 4).

By contrast, approximately 1.5 million refugees were officially recorded as repatriating voluntarily, but given this included 940,000 to Afghanistan; 194,000 to Iraq; 90,000 to Burundi; 90,000 to Angola; 57,000 to Liberia; 26,300 to Sierra Leone; 18,000 to Somalia; 14,100 to Rwanda, 13,800 to the Democratic Republic of the Congo; and 10,000 to Sri Lanka (UNCHR 2005d: 4), there must be serious doubts whether these people were returning either to conditions of safety or completely of their own volition. As a recent Oxfam report noted, 'many refugees feel compelled to return home prematurely because assistance in a camp or settlement has been reduced, or protection is inadequate' (Oxfam 2005: 11).

The disempowering experiences of camp life and return highlight a fundamental conceptual difficulty arising from the 1951 Refugee Convention and associated instruments – the separation of the concept of asylum from that of non-refoulement (Goodwin-Gill 1984: 114–115). In other words, in the absence of a duty imposed on states to provide long solutions for refugees within the host or destination state, camps emerge as a long-term stopgap measure that reinforces the emphasis on how to return refugees or avoid having to confront the obligations regarding refoulement. This seriously limits the nature of human rights protection available to refugees and provides a potential source of state crime. This and other aspects of the Western response will be discussed in the next section, but in the context of the developing world, the contradictions inherent in the camp being an institution offering aid and protection, and a means by which the majority of forced migrants can be corralled and controlled, suggest that while not necessarily the site of institutional or state abuse, the camp is an integral part of the global processes of organised exclusion operating against refugees.

The Western exclusion zones

In the developed world, state responses to forced migration are neither uniform nor internally consistent. Nevertheless, since the mid 1970s, we have witnessed the emergence of three comparable zones of exclusion – the European Union ('Fortress Europe'), North America (especially the United States/Mexico border) and the southeast Asia/Pacific Rim bordering on Australia. These zones incorporate the main clusters of states consciously asserting a Western identity. While each zone has its own local peculiarities, the Western exclusion zone represents a common strategic response to instability and crisis; and provides Western states with an ideological, territorial and enforcement framework for the identification, control and exclusion of forced and illicit migrants, through measures that systematically violate their human rights.

Common features of this framework include: deliberate government strategies to make border protection a major domestic political issue; a qualified commitment to multiculturalism that emphasises the distinction between the legitimate (legal) and illegitimate (illegal) migrant; the militarisation of border control; a declared war against people smuggling/human trafficking as part of a broader fight against terrorism and transnational organised crime; the externalisation of border control including the creation of buffer zones, the use of transit camps and offshore processing; an increased policing role for a range of state welfare agencies, the private sector and some NGOs; and the routine use of detention, removal and interdiction.

The organised exclusion of forced and unauthorised migrants operates through their construction as a threat to national security and identity. Exclusion also consolidates illicit routes of entry, feeding a cycle of further border policing measures. The extent to which this occurs varies according to immediate political circumstances, but it is indicative of the Western norm that refugee protection functions as a conditional concept applicable only to a minority of forced migrants. This suggests that state crime is built into the border protection regimes of the West and arises from systemic exclusion, rather than individual, episodic deviations from formal commitments to human rights. In order to explore this further, two aspects of the Western response are highlighted here: the externalisation of border controls and the 'war' against people smuggling and trafficking.

The externalisation of border controls

The externalisation of border control, the attempt to enforce border controls beyond the territorial borders of the operating states, is an important manifestation of state power in the post-Cold War era and an indication that sovereignty remains a potent concept despite the inroads of globalisation. From the perspective of Western states, the main purpose of externalising border policing strategies is to take control of the physical and legal routes by which a forced or unauthorised migrant can acquire some form of legitimacy. As Australian prime minister, John Howard, declared at the launch of his party's federal election campaign on 28 October 2001: 'We will decide who comes to this country and the circumstances in which they come....we will decide and nobody else...'[21] Those who fall foul of this mantra, the migrants who fail to comply with the legal and bureaucratic requirements imposed by Western states, risk being detained, turned around en route, criminalised and made to bear responsibility for their fate. State responsibility, let alone state crime, is thus casually removed from official discourse.

Externalisation reinforces the alien character of the unauthorised migrant, who is pushed away or excluded by border controls operating at three separate levels: internally, at the border and externally. Internal measures include the detention of refugees who have entered without authority in order to claim asylum. At the border, exclusionary measures range from restrictive visas through to full-scale military mobilisations. External policing operates through outposts of Western asylum and immigration services that process visa applications in countries of transit or departure; carrier

Forced migration, refugees and the state

liability measures that engage organisations like airlines in immigration policing; multi-agency and multilateral efforts to prevent smuggling and trafficking; and the maintenance of increasingly punitive detention camps and buffer zones.

In short, externalisation amounts to pre-emptive strikes against the entry of forced migrants and refugees into areas where they might gain access to the human rights machinery that was developed explicitly to protect them. It also enables state institutions to extend their coercive power and authority beyond their territorial borders, including through military invasions,[22] with the effect of making forced and illicit migration increasingly dangerous. This is not an abstract issue – the human cost of Western border restrictions, and a tangible measure of state crime, can be inferred from the fatal risks taken by those attempting to enter the West by illicit means. Although there are no absolutely reliable statistics, illicit border crossings are routinely lethal, with indications that record numbers of people are dying attempting to enter North America,[23] the European Union[24] and Australia.[25] Some deaths arise from direct confrontations between unauthorised migrants and state authorities but typically border deaths arise from the means of travel adopted to evade border controls – a point not lost on Western the authorities. As a European Union study on the feasibility of controlling the EU's maritime borders noted:

> When a standard destination is shut off by surveillance and interception measures, attempts to enter tend to shift to another, generally more difficult, destination on a broader and therefore riskier stretch of water.... The ships...are unseaworthy, slow and highly dangerous both for their passengers and for regular navigation (CIVIPOL 2003: 9–10).

Yet, despite a human toll that exceeds the numbers killed and injured by terrorist attacks in the West since September 11, 2001, there is a broad consensus at a state level that militarised border policing, which rarely discriminates between different types of illicit migrant, is legitimate. The broad symmetries in the enforcement methods used is illustrated by the resemblance between the naval interdiction policies employed by the United States government

Border Crimes

against Haitian refugees (Dow 1994; McBride 1999; Taft-Morales 2005); the Australian government against 'boat people' from Asia and the Middle East; and the maritime patrols conducted by various European Union states since 2002. Under such policies, coastguard, navy and other military forces board vessels, sometimes in international waters, with a view to removing them to their state of origin or to a 'safe' third country. Again, the policing methods place those seeking entry at considerable personal risk. In October 2001, the Australian navy towed the dangerously leaking boat at the centre of the 'Children Overboard' controversy away from Australian territorial waters for 22 hours. Almost an hour after it began to sink and barely minutes before it finally went under, the boat's 223 passengers were finally taken on board the Australian navy vessel . There have also been concerns raised that in contrast to the emphasis on surveillance and interdiction, insufficient resources and attention are paid to rescuing those in distress. This is central to the controversy surrounding the sinking of the SIEV X and the drowning of 21 people travelling in boats intercepted by Spanish naval patrols as part of Operation Ulysses in June 2003 (Fekete 2003; Hayes 2003).

Interdiction of this type is also integrally linked to offshore detention and processing. Between 1981 and 1991, the overwhelming majority of Haitian refugees intercepted at sea were returned to Haiti while 'screening interviews' were being conducted on board (Dow 1994). Since then, while their claims are processed, substantial numbers have been detained at the US naval base at Guantanamo Bay (McBride 1999: 4–8). Australia's Pacific Solution replicated this pattern, while the European response has included unilateral actions by EU member states, such as the Italian Government's repeated mass deportations of unauthorised migrants to Libya, a state that is not a party to the 1951 Convention and which operates a network of desert camps where systematic human rights abuses are believed to occur (AI 2005a; BBC 2005a; HRW 2005b; Trucco 2005).

While Italy's actions have been condemned by the European parliament,[26] the general trend within Europe has been to consolidate plans for offshore processing in order to restrict and exclude unauthorised arrivals. Thus in March 2003, the British government initiated proposals for discussion by the European Commission aimed at the 'better management of the asylum process globally' and based on improving 'regional management of migration flows' and establishing 'processing centres, on transit routes to Europe' (Statewatch 2003).[27] Sites for the proposed centres included Albania, Croatia, Iran, Morocco, Romania, Russia, northern Somalia, Turkey and Ukraine – almost all of which have records of human rights violations against refugees (Dietrich 2005; Oxfam 2005: 59; HRW 2003a). Subsequent communications from the European Commission presented these proposals as part of the development of new 'durable solutions' but in essence, such measures further corral and ghettoise forced migrants in the developing world; entrench the 'presumptive refoulement' arising from the establishment of EU buffer zones (Morrison and Crosland 2001: 8–9); and undercut the right to seek asylum within the European Union (Hayes 2004).

Establishing such practices as contrary to the obligations of the 1951 UN Convention and as organised breaches of human rights severe enough to qualify as state crime is complicated by the ambiguous role of key NGOs such as UNHCR and IOM. The UNHCR increasingly is being called upon or taking upon itself to process refugee applications. In some states, such as Egypt, UNHCR does this in the absence of any government machinery for determining asylum claims. Apart from flaws in legal process such as UNHCR being the initial decision maker and reviewer,[28] in such circumstances, a general conflict of interest must arise between this function and the UNHCR's protective and advocacy role on behalf of refugees. This conflict is sharpened in situations such as that on Nauru where, from 2001 to 2008, the IOM, which has no protection mandate, administered the detention facility and UNHCR determined refugees status in circumstances where the government was deliberately removing refugees from within its jurisdiction, in a manner that openly confronted its obligations not to refoule under the Refugee Convention.

Moreover, the UNHCR's response to the British government proposals for external processing, suggested willingness to formalise such arrangements. Indeed, as part of its Convention Plus proposals, it suggested the establishment of an 'EU-based mechanism as a step towards a common asylum system' that would 'target caseloads of asylum seekers that are composed primarily of economic migrants and...reinforce returns of persons not in need of international protection' (UNHCR 2003). Elements of this mechanism would include: closed reception facilities located close to the external borders of the EU where asylum seekers would be required to reside for the duration of the procedure (not to exceed one month); the immediate transfer to these centres from EU member states of asylum seekers of designated nationality; the rapid determination of asylum claims by a consortium of national asylum officers and second-instance decision makers; the 'fair' distribution of persons found to be in need of international protection to the member states; and the rapid return of persons found not to be in need of international protection (UNHCR 2003 and 2004).

Convention Plus was not implemented and represented an attempt to fill protection gaps opened up by the exclusionist policies of various European states. However, the willingness of UNHCR to focus on processing asylum applications in zones outside of the West says much about the political and financial pressures being brought to bear by its dominant Western donors. It also confirms that locating the institutional sources of the exclusion of forced migrants by Western states involves looking beyond the acts of the states themselves to the delegation of enforcement responsibilities and the associated ideological assumptions about issues such as illegitimate and illicit economic migrants. Fundamentally, it means challenging the discourse that has arisen around the concerted attempts to police people smuggling and trafficking.

Declaring war against smuggling and trafficking

The war against human smuggling and trafficking[29] is one of a number of state sponsored wars of enforcement justified by the most powerful states as necessary to combat transnational organised crime. While many of the studies of transnational organised crime emphasise how global illegal markets are associated with globalisation and the collapse of the Soviet Union,[30] enforcement

Forced migration, refugees and the state

efforts and most modes of analysis are predicated on transnational organised crime as a threat to national security. This is achieved by grouping together an eclectic range of illicit activities that have vastly differing social dynamics but share an organised cross-border character. In this context, smuggling or trafficking is threatening by definition – it is illegal, clandestine, well organised, beyond official scrutiny and control. It has a shadowy and dangerous character; the capacity to threaten national security, social integration and racial harmony; and while the moral scruples of human smugglers and traffickers may be questionable, the deviance attributed to their activities as illicit migration agents is made more threatening by an unlikely association between illegal migration and terrorism.

The notion of a war against organised crime was first popularised in the United States during the period of alcohol prohibition. During the 1970s and 1980s, it re-emerged in the form of the war on drugs prosecuted by the United States and various European governments (Andreas and Nadelmann 2006). The invocation of a policing war conducted under pseudo military titles helps legitimise the mobilisation of the state's military forces; the militarisation of policing; the acquisition of exceptional extra-judicial powers; the use of invasive and punitive methods of surveillance and control that invariably over-ride universal human rights; and the engagement of a range of agencies (for example government welfare agencies) with no formal policing role. These developments are underpinned by the fusion of national security and domestic policing issues that has been solidified by the war on terror and resulted in the substantial expansion of the powers and territories of operation of agencies such as the Australian Federal Police.

In each of the three main Western exclusion zones, the war on human smuggling and trafficking is associated with its own catalytic episode or time frame. In Australia, the war against people smuggling emerged alongside the Pacific Solution during the period 2000–2002. In the United States, attention to the subject 'soared...from being a near non-issue, to a national policy topic and issue for the National Security Council' (Beare 1997: 11–12) after a cargo ship carrying 260 Chinese nationals ran aground off the New York coast in June 1993 and 10 people drowned trying to swim

Border Crimes

ashore (IOM 2000). In the United Kingdom, the discovery of the bodies of 58 Chinese nationals in the back of a lorry at Dover in June 2000 generated draconian national legislation and sharpened debates within the European Union regarding anti-trafficking measures.

At an international level, the war against human smuggling and trafficking gained further momentum from launch of the 2000 United Nations Convention Against Transnational Organised Crime (the UN Organised Crime Convention) and its associated Protocol Against the Smuggling of Migrants by Land, Sea and Air (the UN Smuggling Protocol); and the Protocol to Prevent, Suppress and Punish Trafficking in Persons, Especially Women and Children (the UN Trafficking Protocol). From the outset, these instruments were designed to facilitate transnational enforcement measures through the uniform criminalisation of activities related to organised breaches of border controls. Consistent with its stated purpose of 'promot(ing) cooperation to prevent and combat transnational organised crime more effectively',[31] the Organised Crime Convention requires signatory states to criminalise participation in an organised criminal group,[32] money laundering,[33] corruption,[34] and the obstruction of justice.[35] Enforcement measures include sanctions that take into account the gravity of these offences,[36] widespread powers of confiscation, seizure and disposal,[37] increased international co-operation,[38] and greater extradition powers.[39]

As an instrument of enforcement, the Transnational Crime Convention invokes wide-ranging state powers designed to target various forms of criminal association and organisation. The targets can be relatively modest, given the very broad definition of an organised criminal group as 'a structured group of three or more persons, existing for a period of time and acting in concert with the aim of committing one or more serious crimes or offences'[40] and the considerable variation in the types of organisation engaged in activities such as human smuggling and trafficking. The emphasis on group activity was in keeping with enforcement concerns expressed throughout the 1990s in relation to smuggling and trafficking. For example, in 1994, the IOM proposed that in order to identify and understand human trafficking emphasis should be placed 'on the nature of the trafficking organisation per se' (Salt and Hogarth 2000). Similarly, the Budapest Group[41] urged attention to the steps involved in 'breaching the border' and such 'key elements of the smuggling enterprise' as 'recruitment', 'transportation', 'corrupted officials', 'guides', 'support services', 'debt collection' and 'management' (Budapest Group 1999: 33–35).

Within such a perspective, organised crime is broken down into individual, constituent, criminal parts, each of which can be the target of a law enforcement process. This highlights the multiplicity of the criminality and helps sustain an acceptance of smugglers/traffickers as a threat; the separation of smuggling and trafficking from its operational context; the attribution of blame for illicit migration to the agent; and, in some circumstances, where an emphasis is placed on the ethnicity of organisations such as the Mafia or the Triads, suspicion being cast on whole communities.

This process is refined further by the formal distinctions made between smuggling and trafficking. According to the Smuggling Protocol, smuggling of migrants means 'the procurement, in order to obtain, directly or indirectly, a financial or other material benefit, of the illegal entry of a person into a State Party of which the person is not a national or permanent resident'.[42] This definition of smuggling assumes the smuggled person exercises a degree of free will and in practice, is applied mainly to refugees and migrant workers. The Trafficking Protocol also covers illicit workers but emphasises the coercive and exploitative nature of the trafficking arrangement, defined as the 'recruitment, transportation, transfer, harbouring or receipt of persons, by means of the threat or use of force or other forms of coercion, of abduction, of fraud, of deception, of the abuse of power or of a position of vulnerability or of the giving or receiving of payments or benefits to achieve the consent of the person, for the purpose of exploitation'. Exploitation includes, 'at a minimum, the exploitation of the prostitution of others or other forms of sexual exploitation, forced labour or services, slavery or practices similar to slavery, servitude or the removal of organs'.[43]

Border Crimes

The recognition of trafficking does give overdue acknowledgement to contemporary forms of slavery, such as chattel slavery, debt bondage and contract slavery, that many forced migrants must endure (Bales 2004); and the extensive human rights abuses, particularly in relation to women and children, that arise from physical and sexual violence and lack of consent (Lee 2007). The exploitative nature of trafficking therefore raises very legitimate concerns and explains why there has been considerable input by NGOs, such as Anti-Slavery International, Free the Slaves and UNICEF in the promotion and implementation of the Protocol. However, from the perspective of Western states, the main practical thrust of the protocols is to further strengthen border controls. This is most apparent in their implementation of the Trafficking Protocol, which emphasises cooperation between 'source' and 'receiver' states, with signatories required to facilitate and accept the return of their trafficked nationals and permanent residents with due regard to their safety;[44] exchange information aimed at identifying perpetrators or victims of trafficking, as well as the methods and means employed by traffickers;[45] and strengthen border controls as necessary to prevent and detect trafficking.[46]

A European Commission action plan illustrated how such requirements are interpreted:

> Human trafficking has to be converted from a "low risk" – high reward enterprise for organised crime into a "high risk" – low reward one. Law enforcement must use all the resources and capacity available to enforce the prohibition of human trafficking, to deprive it of any economic advantage and…seize and confiscate any assets. The investigation of human trafficking should be afforded the same priority as other organised crime in that specialist investigative techniques and disruption strategies should be employed (CEC 2005a: 4).[47]

The Trafficking Protocol does include a number of optional measures, that have the stated aim of protecting victims of trafficking, but which do not go beyond 'consideration of adopting legislative or other measures permitting victims of trafficking to remain in their territories temporarily or permanently in appropriate cases with consideration being given to humanitarian and compassionate factors'.[48] Signatory states have been reluctant to entertain a permanent migration outcome for victims of trafficking. To the extent that temporary or renewable stays become available, they are dependent on the migrant co-operating with criminal justice agencies, in circumstances where relatives and close associates may be exposed to reprisals.[49] In this context, the measures to police trafficking allow for a cynical manipulation of human rights rhetoric that does little to break the migrant from the cycle of illegality constructed by border controls and the utilisation of illicit means of entry.

Focusing on the role of the individuals or networks responsible for such arrangements also enables the major Western states to use anti-trafficking measures as a vehicle for promoting Western foreign policy, with failure to police traffickers emerging as a rationale for Western sanctions against specific governments that are otherwise considered to be threatening Western interests. Thus, pursuant to the US Department of State's 2005 Trafficking in Persons Report (USDS 2005a), the United States president, George W. Bush determined that sanctions should be imposed on Burma, Cambodia, Cuba, the Democratic People's Republic of Korea and Venezuela (USDS 2005b). How little this had to do with protecting the human rights of trafficked persons was reflected by the president's determination regarding Saudi Arabia:

> The Government of Saudi Arabia does not fully comply with the Act's[50] minimum standards for the elimination of trafficking, and is not making adequate efforts to bring itself into compliance. The President has determined to waive all sanctions...in the national interest of the United States....Over five billion dollars in foreign military sales to Saudi Arabia would have been restricted by sanctions under the Act. A full waiver has been granted in the national interest of providing these sales in order to advance the goals of the Global War on Terror (USDS 2005b).

This stark example of the elision of the war against transnational crime into the war on terror is indicative of the established practice of Western states making development aid and assistance to states that are a source or transit zone for illicit migrants conditional on their compliance with Western border policing priorities.[51] This has been a central feature of the processes of enlargement in the European Union, where policing trafficking is seen as a measure of state competence and suitability for membership of the Western club, and is an important aspect of Australia's relations within the Asia Pacific region.

Overall, the distinction between trafficking and smuggling serves to create a hierarchy of legitimacy, with those migrants who voluntarily engage in arrangements to subvert border controls portrayed as the least deserving and most deviant. This draws attention away from the complex causes of forced migration and, even though the Smuggling Protocol[52] explicitly states 'migrants shall not become liable to criminal prosecution' for the act of being smuggled, helps legitimise the migrant's detention as an illegal entrant and their expulsion or return. It also provides human rights justification for exclusionary processes of border enforcement. Further, the removal of refugees and asylum seekers from the orbit of the trafficking discourse ignores or denies that refugees can be vulnerable through 'political, economic and social insecurity' (Koser 2001:67) and that they might seek to enter a country via means that might allow them to maintain themselves – even in very exploitative circumstances - rather than risk detention, removal or attention being drawn to their whereabouts.

The focus on criminalising smugglers and traffickers, by portraying them as a predominant source of illegal migration, also deflects attention from the fundamental role of the state in excluding migrants and forcing them to utilise illicit networks. Although it was widely reported they were brought into the country by 'snakehead gangs', it will never be known for certain the degree of consent exercised by the 58 Chinese nationals found suffocated in the back of a lorry at Dover in England in June 2000. What is clear is that there was no prohibition on the boxes of tomatoes that surrounded the corpses. Whether it was negligence or malevolence that motivated the driver to seal off the air vents so that no noise could be heard, there is no avoiding the fact that there was no

Forced migration, refugees and the state

formal route these people could have taken into the United Kingdom.

In a global system where the means of communication and travel are increasingly available but where borders for humans are more formidable than for any other commodity, traffickers, regardless of their motives, or involvement in other cross-border criminal activity, increasingly fill a role as migration agents alongside a range of official and semi-official agencies (Koslowski 2001). The migrants they assist may be moving relatively willingly as participants in existing social networks disrupted by border controls or changes to asylum policy, or as pioneers taking part in global forms of movement, opened in part by traffickers. Others may be the victims of deceit and intimidation from the outset, and subject to indefinite bondage and abuse at the point of destination. Whatever the degree of individual consent, the exploitation of the migrant ultimately is contingent upon the migrant's legal status and the availability of a market for the migrant's services, rather than just the motives and behaviour of the agent.

From a criminological perspective, it is therefore important to recognise the common dynamics in the criminalisation of smugglers and traffickers, rather than focus on legal differences devised to help police different types of illicit migration. This is a necessary first step to delegitimising the state's right to appropriate the language and rationale of war to conduct organised human rights abuses against unauthorised migrants. It is also a prerequisite for constructing an alternative methodology that focuses on the ways in which criminalisation by the state is integral to legitimising criminal activity by the state. In locating state crime as a product of the disjuncture between border enforcement and the rights and expectations of migrants, this book argues that forced migration is part of the fabric of the global political economy and is a product both of abusive state practice and social disorder exacerbated by globalisation; Western responses to forced migration are driven largely by wider geo-political considerations and notions of security shaped by the war on terror; the formation of Western exclusion zones and the internationalisation of refugee protection produces systemic human rights violations affecting a wide range of unauthorised migrants;

and these violations are submerged by a state offensive against people smuggling and trafficking that propels border policing into the heart of the national security complex and reinforces a methodology that criminalises migrants and their agents for seeking to subvert border controls.

An alternative discourse of state crime must therefore highlight the multi-dimensional and systemic nature of the human rights violations perpetrated against forced and unauthorised migrants; construct a paradigm that rejects personal responsibility and deviance as the basis for criminalising illicit migrants and their agents; and develop a theory of state deviance around a critique of the legitimacy of border protection. Through an examination of the Australian experience, the following chapters seek to develop this alternate discourse by analysing how the alienation, criminalisation and abuse of unauthorised migrants are core functions of the Australian state.

Notes

[1] Much of the literature on forced migration describes these as 'push factors', which work in tandem with various 'pull factors'. I have not used these terms here as they can be over-mechanical and imply the possibility of an equilibrium being reached if appropriate enforcement procedures are in place. Such a framework also fails to take into account what Marfleet (2006: 216) describes as the 'circuits of migration'.

[2] The distinction between natural and human made disasters is often hard to establish. Ideologically, the acceptance of an event as a natural disaster removes the element of human (including state) responsibility necessary to establish breaches of human rights. See Davis (2001).

[3] For a further discussion of some of the conceptual issues, see Turton (2003)

[4] The data for refugees and asylum seekers is generally considered more reliable than for forced migrants or international migration as a whole (Hovy 2002). On the challenges confronting research into human trafficking, see Salt and Hogarth (2000); Laczko and Gozdziak (2005); and Di Nicola (2007).

[5] There are significant disagreements over the value of employing the concept of the environmental refugee. Compare, for example, Black (2001); Castles (2001); and Myers (2005). Nevertheless, it is clear that

Forced migration, refugees and the state

environmental problems and forced migration increasingly are being drawn into wider policy discourses over national security. See, for example, Schwartz and Randall (2003).

[6] This increase is partly affected by the inclusion of the former USSR among the developed countries.

[7] While not entirely satisfactory, the terms Global North and Global South are used here to distinguish the developed from the developing economies. The developed economies incorporate the European Union, the United States, Canada, Japan, Australia and New Zealand. The developing economies incorporate Africa; Asia and the Pacific (excluding Japan, Australia, New Zealand and the member states of CIS in Asia); Latin America and the Caribbean. Within this very broad division, there are important sub-divisions, including the transition economies of southern and eastern Europe and the Commonwealth of Independent States (CIS). For a full breakdown of states within this framework, see UN (2005: xii).

[8] Palestinian refugees are excluded from most official statistics because they are covered by a separate agency, the United Nations Relief and Works Agency for Refugees, and were not covered by the definition of refugee in the 1951 Convention. It is presently estimated there are 4.3 million Palestinian refugees (UNHCR 2007a: 2)

[9] Human security has become an increasingly contested concept with Refugee Studies. Here, the term is used broadly to describe the vulnerability of forced migrants. See Suhrke (2003).

[10] Notwithstanding 1997 Ottawa Mine Ban Treaty, at the time of writing, only five countries had signed Protocol V of the Convention on Certain Conventional Weapons, which covers unexploded war materials.

[11] See, for example, UN General Assembly Resolutions 925(X), OP2, 25 October 1955; 1166 (XII), OP1(a), 26 November 1957; and 1284 (XIII), PP2, 5 December 1958.

[12] Agamben draws heavily on the work of Michel Foucault and Hannah Arendt. For discussions on Agamben, see Fitzpatrick (2001) and Prem Kumar and Grundy Warr (2004).

[13] See, for example, the debates in (1998) *Forced Migration Review* Numbers 2 and 3; UNCHR (2000: 108-109); and Jacobsen (2001).

[14] This is usually in camps but applies to all situations when refugees for periods of five years or more 'are deprived of the freedom necessary to pursue normal lives' (Smith 2005: 38). Basing its calculations on refugee populations of 10,000 or more, the USCRI estimates that at the end of 2004, there were approximately 7,765,7000 refugees warehoused for five

years or more, of whom 6,911,600 had lived in such conditions for ten years or more (WRS 2005: 2). Merrill Smith is the editor of the USRC publication, *World Refugee Survey*.

[15] The Declaration issued at the conclusion of the Ministerial meeting of the States Parties to the 1951 Convention and or its 1967 Protocol, in December 2001, stated (at paragraph 13): '...the ultimate goal of international protection is to achieve a durable solution for refugees, consistent with the principle of *non-refoulment*, [and commended states to] continue to facilitate these solutions, notably voluntary repatriation and, where appropriate and feasible, local integration and resettlement, while recognizing that voluntary repatriation remains the preferred solution for refugees' (UN doc.HCR/MMSP/2001/09, 16 January 2002, reproduced in Feller et al (2003: 81-84)).

[16] The 1951 UN Convention is silent on this question but according to Article II.6 of the 1969 OAU Refugee Convention, 'countries of asylum shall, as far as possible, settle refugees at a reasonable distance from the frontier of their country of origin'. See also UNHCR (1999: paragraph 61); and UN General Assembly Resolution 56/166, OP8, 26 February 2002.

[17] For example, Kibreab (1990); Verdirame (1999); Harrell-Bond (2002); Verdirame and Harrell-Bond (2005).

[18] For example, approximately 25,000 Rwandese refugees were forcibly repatriated from Tanzania in November-December 2002 (AI 2005a). In June 2005, approximately 5,000 Rwandan refugees were sent back to Rwanda from Burundi, after being arbitrarily reclassified as 'illegal immigrants' (UNHCR 2005c).

[19] For example, approximately 6,000 IDPs living in the Sikhan camp in Khartoum were forcibly relocated by government forces in August 2005 (GIDPP 2005c).

[20] The UNHCR has been accused of complicity with assisting forced repatriation in this way, for example, in relation to encamped Rwandese and Burundian refugees from Tanzania (AI 2005a).

[21] For a full text of Howard's speech, see http://www.australianpolitics.com/news/2001/01-10-28.shtml. .

[22] The Clinton administration used 'the threat of a mass exodus of refugees' as a principal justification for its military intervention in Haiti in 1994. See Newland (1995).

[23] The U.S. Bureau of Customs has confirmed a record 464 immigrants died attempting to cross the U.S/Mexico border during the 2004-2005 fiscal year (Reuters 2005).

[24] The campaign group UNITED has documented over 6300 deaths attributable to 'border militarisation, asylum laws, detention policies, deportations and carrier sanctions', including 3358 drownings, between 1993 and 2004 (UNITED 2004 and 2005). According to the Consorcio Euromediterráneo para la Investigación Aplicada sobre Immigración Internacional (Carim), 'Between 8,000 and 10,000 immigrants died or disappeared as they tried to enter Spain via Morocco from 1989 to 1992' PICUM (2005a).

[25] This provides the context for analysing the sinking of the SIEV X.

[26] Resolution P6_TA(2005)0138, 14 April 2005.

[27] The full text of the Blair-Simitis letter can be accessed at http://www.statewatch.org/news/2003/apr/blair-simitis-asile.pdf.

[28] For an analysis of the UNHCR's determination processes in Cairo, an important filter for refugees from sub-Saharan Africa seeking entry into Australia and other Western states, see Kagan (2002). See also Verdirame and Harrell-Bond (2005: 78-119).

[29] As with the war on terror, this has become an accepted phrase within mainstream policy discourse. I use the term here in its everyday sense, rather than as an endorsement of its validity.

[30] See, for example, Friman and Andreas (1999) and Williams and Vlassis (2005).

[31] Article 1

[32] Article 5

[33] Article 6

[34] Article 8

[35] Article 23

[36] Article 11

[37] Articles 12 and 14

[38] Articles 13 and 18

[39] Article 16

[40] Article 2

[41] The 'Budapest Process' operates under the auspices of the International Centre for Migration Policy Development. It describes itself as follows: 'The Budapest process is a consultative forum of more than 40 Governments (Ministries of Interior) and 10 international organisations, aiming at preventing irregular migration and establishing sustainable systems for orderly migration in the European region'. See http://www.icmpd.org.

[42] Article 3(a)
[43] Article 3(a)
[44] Article 8(1)
[45] Article 10
[46] Article 11(1)
[47] See also Europol (2004a).
[48] Article 7
[49] One important qualification to this argument is that Article 14(1) of the Council of Europe Convention on Action against Trafficking in Human Beings 2005 requires states to issue renewable residence permits to victims of trafficking if (a) 'the competent authority considers that their stay is necessary owing to their personal situation' and/or (b) the competent authority considers that their stay is necessary for the purpose of their co-operation with the competent authorities in investigation of criminal proceedings'.
[50] *Trafficking Victims Protection Act* (2000).
[51] In somewhat opaque language, the European Commission has told EU institutions and member states they 'should intensify efforts to address the issue of human trafficking within the EU and in relations with third countries, eg. by building on efforts to support anti-trafficking initiatives through development co-operation' (CEC 2005b: 4).
[52] Article 5.

Chapter 3

From white Australia to multiculturalism: exclusion, hegemony and unauthorised migrants

Nationalism, white Australia and the colonial settler state

This chapter seeks to identify the various means by which the Australian state historically has sought to legitimise border restrictions. This helps locate Australian policy in the context of the global trends discussed in chapter two and provides the basis for arguing that Australia's contemporary policies towards unauthorised migrants reflect a long tradition of exclusion that conflicts with Australia's human rights obligations.

A central function of the Australian state that has rarely been challenged is the enforcement of border restrictions against 'aliens'. The high degree of legitimacy accorded the state's role in regulating migration has normalised perceptions of unauthorised migrants as a threat, despite the shifting ideological frameworks informing and legitimising the state's migration and settlement policies. Thus, while there are substantial differences between current state responses and those employed under the White Australia policy, there are also significant ideological and practical continuities; that is, there is a relationship between current measures to externalise border control and the organised exclusion associated with the consolidation of the Australian state. The fusion of national security and border policy defines this relationship and produces organised human rights violations through full-scale state sponsored mobilisations that alienate, criminalise and abuse unauthorised migrants.

In order to develop a theory of state crime in its contemporary and historic contexts, four overlapping themes are addressed: the centrality of the White Australia policy to the formation of the Australian state; the official promotion of resettlement as the preferred mechanism for refugee entry; the responses to the first phase of Indo-Chinese 'boat people' between 1976 and 1981; and the development of multiculturalism. The interplay between these different dimensions of Australia's border policies demonstrates that establishing the deviance of Australia's border policing practices is both complex and far-reaching in its implications and cannot be achieved without incorporating a critique of Australian nationalism and the alienation of particular types of migrant that helps sustain it.

Nationalism is a modern phenomenon associated with the development of capitalism and the reordering of global society around competing nation states over the past three centuries (Anderson 2000; Gellner 1998 and 2001). The association of nationalism with the state ensures that despite its recent lineage, nationalism is an extraordinarily pervasive and powerful ideology, continually replenishing itself by reference to external and internal threats. This is particularly evident in relation to migration controls, which invariably are legitimised by the state as protecting the national interest.

Nationalism serves to particularise human solidarities around the concept of the nation state, it confronts notions of class solidarity at both an international and national level, and it divides human society along lines that are often inconsistent with common international experiences and universal rights. Whether expressed in terms of overt racism or cultural difference, nationalism demands loyalty in the name of identity, which is reinforced through state enforced notions of citizenship that disguise class inequality and social difference. Nationalism is also sustained by the concept of 'otherness' which is reinforced by the state at an institutional and ideological level. At the institutional level, the state's capacity to define the external alien through the formalities of passport control and citizenship works alongside its capacity to make particular language, religious, racial or cultural pre-requisites the basis for defining the legitimate migrant. However, as the policy transition from white Australia to multicultural Australia shows, nationalist ideas and the associated concepts of national identity are not fixed. Just as borders can change, so do the official requirements for acceptability within and formal membership of the national entity.

From white Australia to multiculturalism

Nationalism also personalises the sense of identity by blurring the boundaries between public and private life; and reconstituting the family in the image of the nation and the state. Most nationalist narratives are replete with familial language and imagery – the founding fathers of the mother country being those to whom homage is made in the mother tongue and in whose name and memory exclusion, repression and war become acts of duty, honour and protection. This profound personalisation of the national experience leads to an atomisation within civil society by enforcing notions of competition and difference into every aspect of human experience. While nationalism is defined in collective terms, breaching the enclosures of national identity can be analogous to personal defilement as the external invasion becomes internal. Thus, in a trademark piece of racist populism, One Nation leader, Pauline Hanson argued in 1997:

> What a high price we must pay for economic integration [with Asia]. It is like running a shop and having a major trading partner only deal with you if you allow them first to have sex with your children, move into your house and take over (quoted, Hall 1998: 209).

While not all Australian nationalist sentiment is expressed in such explicit terms, the traditions of exclusion that were essential to the development of the original nationalist ideal continue to shape contemporary manifestations of nationalism. Understanding the continuity in Australian nationalism is therefore crucial to understanding and challenging the legitimacy of the Australian state's border policing practices.

The colonisation of Australia led to the construction of a new settler state that drew consciously on its British heritage for its identity and wider nationalist ideology. Exclusion was at the heart of this ideology, whether expressed through a belief in the inevitable extinction of the Indigenous population or as policies directed at keeping out those seen to be of inferior or culturally incompatible status.[1] As the settlements spread from their initial coastal enclaves, colonialism and exclusion were intertwined along multiple internal and external frontiers, where frontier violence and demands for the annexation of neighbouring territories underpinned the formation of a white European outpost in the Asia-Pacific region. Moreover, while the colonies that federated in 1901 were a direct product of British colonialism and British imperial power was seen as essential for the protection of the various settlements,[2] the disparate local elites that coalesced into a nascent Australian ruling class developed strategic interests of their own.

The White Australia policy was an unequivocal expression of these interests (Griffiths 2006) and was an important ideological component of the push to federation. As Edmund Barton, shortly to become Australia's first prime minister and minister for external affairs, told the Australasian Federal Convention in 1898: 'Questions which relate to the whole body of the people, to the purity of race, to the preservation of the racial character of the white population are Commonwealth questions, and should be so exclusively' (quoted, Evans et al 1997: 207). Widespread fears within the colonial elite[3] that substantial Asian immigration would weaken the British character of the Australian settlement drove this policy forward.[4] 'No motive', Attorney-General Alfred Deakin told the new federal parliament in September 1901...

> ...operated more powerfully in dissolving the technical and arbitrary political divisions which previously separated us than the desire that we should be one people and remain one people without the admixture of other races...This was the motive that swayed tens of thousands...this was the note that touched particularly the Australian born, who felt themselves endowed with a heritage not only of political freedom, but of an ample area in which the race might expand, and an obligation...to pass on to their children and the generations after them that territory undiminished and uninvaded (quoted, Evans et al 1997: 209).

Historians have generally attributed a high level of popular legitimacy to such expressions of Australian nationalism[5] and while the hegemonic grip of a white Australian ideal might have declined, Deakin's conception of an Australian nation fundamentally defined by its colonial heritage remains influential. From a criminological perspective, the significance of the White Australia policy therefore

From white Australia to multiculturalism

rests not so much in its affront to contemporary human rights norms and expectations regarding racism but in its role in entrenching ideologies, cultures and measures of control which underpin and legitimise current patterns of state organised exclusion.

The Australian state's capacity to enforce a White Australia policy rested in the federal parliament's constitutional power to 'make laws for the peace, order, and good government of the Commonwealth with respect to naturalisation and aliens'.[6] The main legislative elements of the policy were contained in the 1901 *Immigration (Restriction) Act* - the first substantial legislation to pass through the Australian parliament – and the 1901 *Pacific Island Labourers Act*. Both pieces of legislation were administered by the Department of External Affairs, in co-operation with the Department of Trade and Customs, and reflected successive early parliaments' desire to entrench migration control as an important national security concern.[7]

From the outset, Australia's border control regime invoked significant administrative and coercive powers that underpinned an enduring bureaucratic culture of alienation and exclusion. While aliens were not strictly defined in law, the *Immigration (Restriction) Act* and its associated regulations imposed a duty on customs officers to prevent prohibited immigrants entering the Commonwealth.[8] Customs officers were empowered to refuse entry;[9] detain a passenger for a medical examination;[10] and board and search vessels at any time.[11] Most significantly, the *Immigration (Restriction) Act*[12] gave customs and police officers the power to target potential Asian migrants by prohibiting the entry into Australia of any person failing to write out at dictation, and sign in the presence of an officer, a passage of 50 words in length in a European language.[13] Little discretion was allowed; internal directions issued by the Home and Territories Department reminding customs officers in 1927: 'the test when applied to an immigrant is intended to serve as an absolute bar to such person's entry to Australia, or as a means of depriving him of the right to remain in the Commonwealth if he has landed' (cited Langfield 1999: 34).

Meanwhile, the *Pacific Island Labourers Act* targeted the recruitment of Pacific Islanders, an often violent practice that had begun in the 1860s, as labour for the Queensland sugar industry. No sanctuary was on offer to those who had been brought unwillingly or for whom return would further dislocate or shatter their social world. The legislation heavily restricted further 'recruitment'; banned the entry of Pacific Island labourers completely after March 1904; and required their mass deportation after December 1906, although the actual scale of the forced removals is unclear (Moore 1985: 274–292; and 2000).[14]

The consolidation of the Australian state's national powers of exclusion drew on the pre-existing colonial regulatory infrastructure. The *Immigration (Restriction) Act* consolidated policies and methods of border policing established by the anti-Chinese legislation passed in the various colonial jurisdictions between 1877 and 1888, while by federation, 'the recruitment and employment of Melanesians was governed by no fewer than seven Acts, 18 schedules, 58 regulations and 38 instructions' (Willey 1978: 5). In the case of the anti-Chinese laws, migration and state security policy were fused. In a remarkable parallel with the '*Tampa* crisis' more than a century later, the anti-Chinese legislation of the 1880s was passed amidst a manufactured political crisis that helped create a hegemonic discourse of border enforcement, notwithstanding concerns from within the judiciary and sections of the colonial administrations.

The foundations of white Australia: the '*Afghan* crisis' and the anti-Chinese laws

On 27 April 1888, the SS *Afghan*, one of five vessels carrying approximately 550 passengers of Chinese descent to arrive during April and May 1888, entered the port of Melbourne. The Victorian government acted immediately and unlawfully to prevent the landing of the 67 passengers due to disembark. The following day, the Melbourne *Age* reported that:

> Pending a rigid examination of each man's credentials, and the identification of the bearers as the persons specified therein, not

a soul will be allowed to leave the ship. Two Customs officers and a couple of constables have been placed on board to preclude the possibility of escape, and the captain is held responsible in a fine of £100 per head for every Chinese who eludes these precautions. At the same time communication from the shore is debarred by the effectual method of placing the vessel in quarantine...

Similar methods were used on 30 April when the SS *Burumbeet* arrived in Melbourne. Even though the 14 Chinese passengers on board were legally entitled to enter, having satisfied existing poll tax requirements, they were illegally imprisoned on board for 5 days and quarantined for 19 more. Eventually a threat of habeas corpus proceedings forced the government's hand and they were allowed to land (Britain 1969: 52). However, despite some of them holding naturalisation papers or exemption certificates issued in accordance with the current legislation,[15] none of the *Afghan's* passengers was allowed to land. Instead, after striking a deal with the port authorities that enabled him to avoid the threat of fines imposed under legislation similar to current carrier liability provisions, the captain set sail for Sydney.

The New South Wales government responded with a substantial mobilisation of state resources. Prior to its arrival from Melbourne, New South Wales colonial secretary, Henry Parkes, made arrangements with Burns Philp, the shipping agents for the *Afghan*, for the New South Wales government to pay the return passages for the 62 Chinese passengers with naturalisation papers or exemption certificates, and for Burns Philp to pay for the remainder. On 4 May, under instructions from Parkes, a third boat, the SS *Tsinan*, carrying 45 Sydney bound Chinese passengers, was intercepted in Sydney Harbour by 10 police officers. Customs officers then boarded the vessel 'to make their usual search and to muster all the "celestials" on the deck' (*Sydney Morning Herald*, 5 May 1888). After the chief tide-surveyor found 3 stowaways, who he ordered to be locked in the strong room of the ship, the vessel was quarantined in Watsons Bay with a round the clock guard on board. Two days later, the arrival of the *Afghan* prompted similar measures. Customs officers and a detachment of water police boarded the vessel, refusing to let any Chinese passengers disembark. After they refused to be transferred to a decrepit hulk or into quarantine, the Chinese passengers were subsequently kept under heavy police guard. Parkes refused to yield to representations from the local Chinese community or to formal complaints from the masters of the *Tsinan* and *Afghan* regarding the illegal detention of their vessels. Instead, on 15 May, he ordered the quarantine and fumigation of two further vessels, the *Guthrie* and the *Menmuir*, carrying 218 Chinese immigrants.[16]

Parkes' open flouting of the existing laws was controversial within the legal establishment and sections of the media;[17] but although a successful application to the Supreme Court for habeas corpus by one of the detained Chinese passengers[18] resulted in 50 passengers from the *Tsinan* and *Afghan* and 40 from the *Guthrie* and *Menmuir* being allowed to land under heavy police guard in the early hours of 18 and 19 May, Parkes' main aim was achieved. On 16 May, he introduced into parliament a new bill, which sought to introduce retrospectively to 1 May, a range of additional restrictions on Chinese immigration that included a bar on the issue of any further naturalisation certificates; a requirement for ships' masters to provide Customs with a full list and personal details of their Chinese passengers; financial penalties for carrying more that one Chinese passenger per 100 tons of cargo; and a £100 poll tax for any Chinese passenger. Any vessel breaching these restrictions could be detained. British subjects by birth were the only Chinese migrants exempted from the proposed restrictions. Newly arriving Chinese could only live in designated areas, while those resident prior to the Act had to register with the Police Magistrate within one month and would thereafter be required to produce their licence to a police officer on demand.[19]

With this extensive regime of border control and surveillance in the offing, Parkes convened an intercolonial conference on 12 June that approved uniform legislation virtually ending Chinese migration and criminalising the unauthorised movement of Chinese between colonies.[20] Although reservations voiced at the conference about the extent of Parkes' proposals enabled the New South Wales Legislative Council to remove some of the more draconian and exclusionist aspects of Parkes' original bill, the foundations for the White Australia policy had been laid.[21] While the *Afghan* played a catalytic rather than causative role in the consolidation of anti-Chinese legislation and many aspects of the episode could be more usefully explored,[22] two dimensions are particularly relevant to contemporary state responses to unauthorised migration.

Scale of the state response

The first is the scale of the state response, especially in New South Wales. It seems clear that this was a major policing exercise involving quarantine and customs officers as well as water and local police. At the time, quarantine was an established mechanism for filtering migrants within a quasi detention regime. Associated practices, such as fumigation of vessels, had 'the additional recommendation of being the most effectual method known to the authorities for detecting…stowaways' (*Sydney Morning Herald*, 16 May 1888). Quarantine concerns also provided the basis for early forms of international border policing cooperation. Thus, in November 1887, a report from a Detective Rochaix in New Caledonia warned the Inspector-General of Police in Sydney that '200 Chinamen', some of whom were thought to carry dèngue fever, were possibly moving to Sydney (NSW Legislative Assembly 1888: 207).[23]

However, while the use of quarantine was relatively routine, the deployment of the police to prevent entry was not. A report in the *Sydney Morning Herald* on 16 May 1888 bemoaned the impact of policing 'the Chinese difficulty' on the local force:

> To maintain the close surveillance that is kept over the Chinese immigrants by the Afghan and Tsinan necessitates the employment of something like 102 men. About 56 of these do special duty at Circular Quay, whilst the remainder render similar services at Smith's Wharf. The 102 men are divided into four detachments, two of which confine their attentions to the Afghan and two to the Tsinan. The ordinary duty of a constable keeps him engaged for eight hours, but special guard duty watching Chinese carrying vessels involves continuous vigilance for 12 hours, so that the constable actually renders to the

Border Crimes

Government in every 24 hours one and a half day's service. The work of a constable on street patrol is a quite a tour for recreation compared with that of the man on the Chinese guard.

Moreover, maintaining the policing operation inevitably meant exercising the state's coercive powers. Customs and police forcibly prevented formal attempts by passengers from three of the vessels berthed at Miller's Point to land (*Sydney Morning Herald*, 14 May 1888) while in Newcastle, nine Chinese passengers aboard the SS *Guthrie* 'made a frantic rush for the after gangway' in the belief they would not be returning to Sydney from the vessels coaling run. They were subdued by eighteen police after 'two constables who tried to stop them went down under them'. Two of the passengers 'had to be carried to the ship's doctor' (Rolls 1993: 489).

Incidents such as these encouraged the captains of the *Tsinan* and *Afghan* to demand that special naval guards or armed convoys accompany them to Hong Kong for fear 'of a possible outburst of frenzy on the part of the Chinamen' (*Sydney Morning Herald*, 22 May 1888). Willingness to use force was also accompanied by a state of almost farcical alarm amongst the various enforcement agencies. For example, Rolls (1992: 477–478) recounts the reception for the SS *Albany* when it arrived in Melbourne from Western Australia via Adelaide on 13 May, carrying 44 European passengers a Chinese passenger, William Kinoon, and his two sons. Kinoon had lived in Australia for 35 years, had spent 19 years in Victoria and was a naturalised South Australian:

> A flurry of urgent telegrams directed the Albany into quarantine....A telegram to Russell Street station brought a squad of police on the run, but all the European passengers had disembarked before they got there. At the suggestion of the captain, Kinoon had remained on board. Constable Dunn was stationed on the ship to see that he stayed there. A crowd gathered on the wharf. The next day the authorities relented and Kinoon and his sons began their holiday. But Captain Anthony faced the Williamstown court for unloading his passengers without a customs clearance. He was fined £50, half the maximum penalty.

A pre-modern moral panic

The second relevant dimension of the 1880s legislation was the atmosphere of intense public agitation in which it was passed. In what could almost be described as a pre-modern moral panic (Cohen 2002), the level of hysteria engendered by the arrival of the *Afghan* operated in inverse proportion to the numbers of Chinese aboard or the existing population of Chinese descent.

While the *Afghan* was still en route from Melbourne, over 5,000 people rallied at Sydney Town Hall. Led by the chief magistrate, the mayor of Sydney, they then marched to Parliament House and attempted to 'rush the Legislative Chamber' (Markus 1979: 143; Rolls 1993: 481–482)). The day after the *Afghan* arrived in Sydney, a crowd of over 1,000 attacked Chinese owned businesses and homes in Brisbane. This was not a rampage by a marginal lumpen mob. Evans (1999: 89) describes how '...the so-called 'larrikins' and the so-called 'respectable' here composed an organic whole in an essentially politically based encounter, the latter sooling on the former to outrageous acts, contributing to the menacing chorus of anti-Chinese chanting, and closing in to sample the spoils once a store front had been demolished'. Indeed, one police explanation for not baton charging the crowd was that 'the majority of people in the street were respectable citizens and would probably have been injured if this was done' (quoted, Evans 1999: 90).

The arrival of the *Afghan* also triggered a substantial labour movement mobilisation. Unions played a prominent role in the Sydney demonstrations, with a strike by members of the Seamen's Union demanding the dismissal of Chinese seamen on visiting vessels the centerpiece of a series of union boycotts against Chinese businesses and individuals (Griffiths 2006: 349–402; Markus 1979: 144–149). While this might provide evidence of the perceived legitimacy of the restrictive legislation and the hegemony of anti-Chinese sentiment, this developed within a supportive institutional framework. As the *Sydney Morning Herald* suggested on 26 June 1888, the union leaderships felt emboldened by Parkes' proposed legislation to organise around this issue: 'It is a noteworthy circumstance that that the legislation which Parliament is about to

Border Crimes

adopt for the restriction, if not the prevention of Chinese immigration, should in some quarters have hardened the feeling against the inferior race...it seems curious that just at this time the working man should consider it necessary to boycott the Chinese'.

There was also a sustained campaign by sections of the media to exclude Chinese immigrants. Popular magazines such as *The Bulletin*, *Melbourne Punch* and *Queensland Figaro* attributed multiple forms of deviance to Chinese immigrants who were repeatedly caricatured as immoral, sexually rapacious, opium-smoking, disease-carrying, devious and dishonest.[24] A survey of the main Newcastle papers published between 1861 and 1900, reveals a prolonged and extensive vocabulary of racist abuse targeting 'almond eyed celestials', who were variously described as 'odious pests' with a 'stony heart', 'thick hide', 'obtuse faculties', 'low sensuality' and 'ignoble brutal lusts'....an 'incubus', constituting 'the greatest social evil that [had] stained the annals of civilisation' (Graham 1984: 240). Even the more sober *Sydney Morning Herald*, whose editorials opposed many aspects of Parkes' legislation, acknowledged approvingly 'The determination of the Australian people to preserve their territory from a Mongolian invasion is not to be shaken...'(*Sydney Morning Herald*, 4 May 1888), while one of the paper's correspondents could write of the policing operation on the *Tsinan*: 'A strong guard of ...stalwart custodians of the peace were scattered about the deck prepared for any of those dark tricks and vain ways for which we have it on high practical authority the heathen Chinee [sic] is peculiar' (*Sydney Morning Herald*, 19 May 1888).

A fear of invasion, interwoven with anti-Chinese racism, was also evident within the popular literature of the time (Webb and Enstice 1998: 130–167). Australian literature of the period also popularised a new colonial type; a precursor to the 'Coming Man', a white, robust, independent and resourceful (usually male) individual, who was not restrained by the conservative and overly urbane traditions of the English homeland and ultimately represented the empire's best chance of survival (White 1981: 63–109). As part of this trend, bush literature and imagery (often created by city based artists) and the appropriation of local flora and fauna as national

From white Australia to multiculturalism

symbols played their part in the idealisation of a certain 'Australian type'; a white pioneer for whom the emerging state and its exclusionary practices represented an affirmation of colonisation and the desire of a small population of European descent to control a vast land mass in the Asia Pacific region.

By definition, Chinese migrants were incompatible with such a national stereotype, whether expressed in terms of racial difference, cultural incompatibility or overwhelming numbers. So, even though the movements of the *Afghan* were the subject of public attention for only a matter of weeks and, in that sense, the moral panic subsided quite quickly, the ideological assumptions underpinning the panic were deeply rooted. This helped ensure that the racist legislation implemented in its wake was 'carefully, even harshly administered' (Willard 1967: 94) and had a long-term impact. Between 1888 and 1901, the Chinese population declined from 45,000–50,000 to 32,000 (Willard 1967: 94); between 1901 and 1921, the population of predominantly Chinese 'Full Blood Asians' declined from 40,577 to 25,939 (Yarwood 1964: 163); and by mid-1947, 99.3 percent of Australia's 7.5 million population were of European descent and only 128,000 were born outside of the British empire (Willey 1978: 7).

The grim human impact of these statistics is described in a study of the Chinese population of the Northern Territory in the immediate post-federation period. 'Entire townships were vacant', with farmers and miners forced of their land and their leases. 'Cyanide vats were handy for those who could not face an enforced journey and the swollen remains of 100 men who poisoned themselves dotted the fields' (Lockwood 1968: 86). An engineer, who served on ships trading between Darwin and China at the time, told the study's author:

> We were sometimes little more than a floating hearse. We had dead bodies everywhere. To make it worse, the trip was often too rough for old and fatigued people. Many died on the way. Their bodies were disembowelled and stuffed with oakum…We had contracted to deliver these people, dead or alive, to their homeland. They couldn't be buried at sea (Lockwood 1968: 86–87).

Border Crimes

The forced removal of Chinese migrants and the enduring barriers erected against them and other non-Europeans illustrate how, as a flashpoint, the responses to the *Afghan* were an important measure of the perceived legitimacy of state attempts to forcibly exclude Chinese immigrants. They also reflected broader popular acceptance of notions of racial difference and national identity that in their construction of a particular concept of the alien were a central part of Australian nationalist ideology. This helped legitimise popular perceptions of national security that associated some forms of migration with high levels of risk that should properly attract severe state sanctions. In this context, flare-ups or panics can be expected; but state driven exclusion through the strict regulation of who could enter the country and under what conditions was very much business as usual, if not the core business, by the time of federation. As *The Bulletin* declared on 2 July 1887, 'No nigger, no Chinaman, no lascar, no kanaka, no purveyor of cheap coloured labour, is an Australian'. And the hegemonic role of the Australian state was to ensure that remained the case.

White Australia, refugees and resettlement

Refugees did not figure prominently in the early debates about immigration control or the establishment of the White Australia policy but some of the exclusionary measures, particularly carrier liability and interdiction, developed to police non-white immigration are recognisable in current policies towards unauthorised migrants. The fact the majority of recent refugee boat arrivals would have been refused admission under the White Australia policy suggests the same dynamic of exclusion, if not the actual policy, still operates.

There appear to be no detailed studies of the border policing methods of this period but many of the same concerns about smugglers and traffickers that percolate throughout current border protection discourse seem to have been present.[25] As with current border control policy, the White Australia policy was the subject of continuous legislative and practical amendment as the various agencies fine-tuned and expanded their policing methods against stowaways and others evading immigration controls. Thus, from 1902, shipping companies acquired a de facto border policing

From white Australia to multiculturalism

function by being required to 'refuse passages to coloured persons who lacked documentary evidence of a right to enter' (Yarwood 1964: 53).[26] In 1905 and 1912 amendments to the *Immigration (Restriction) Act* imposed harsh penalties on deserters, who could be arrested on a warrant issued by the ship's master or agent. From 1904, all Chinese vessels were searched for stowaways on arrival. In 1907, an official report by the chief clerk of customs advised that 'a large organisation existed with branches in various Australian states and in Hong Kong that arranged…the smuggling of Chinese into Australia' (Yarwood 1964: 58).

Although in absolute terms, the numbers being smuggled were minimal,[27] state officials were particularly keen to employ a proactive response. In 1908, the Department of External Affairs offered a £10 reward to customs and police officers for securing convictions of prohibited immigrants (NAA: A1, 1908/13342). The chief clerk and various customs and police officers recommended the fumigation of Eastern vessels; the compulsory registration of Asians in Australia; the use of travelling detectives on suspected vessels; increased pay for officers and informers; further attempts to stop the traffic in Hong Kong and Singapore; and increased prosecution powers for the Department of Customs against suspected prohibited immigrants (Yarwood 1964: 58–59). The *Immigration Restriction Act* was also amended in 1908 to increase the carrier penalties for bringing prohibited immigrants into port. At the instigation of the Australian authorities in 1911, the colonial secretary in turn put pressure on the Hong Kong and Straits Settlements governments to further police trafficking. In 1912, a Detective Inspector Gabriel 'was sent to Hong Kong to try and break up the stowaway organisation', while in the same year, a system of identification cards was introduced for 'coloured crew members' (Yarwood 1964: 60–62). There were concerns that overseas agencies could not be relied upon to police Australia's borders[28] and that Australian agencies should follow the lead of Inspector Gabriel and play a more proactive role in the region.

There was also an atmosphere of suspicion affecting many within the local population of Chinese descent that mirrors much of the suspicion cast upon contemporary refugee and immigrant communities. Similarly, the relationship between controls, illegal organisations and the risks taken by some migrants is immediately recognisable. Yarwood's (1964: 62) comment that despite restrictive measures, 'the traffic in stowaways continued, bringing death by suffocation or exposure to a number of Chinese, hard won success to others, and fines (with doubled penalties for frequent offenders) to the masters of vessels' has a desperately familiar ring to it.

Despite the very proscriptive regime and the absence of an international refugee protection framework, small numbers of European refugees still managed to enter Australia as migrants between the 1880s and the Second World War (Neumann 2004: 15–17).[29] However, the Australian state remained more concerned about maintaining its Anglo-Celtic identity than providing protection from persecution. As Price (1981: 99) notes, 'Not even the Evian Conference of 1938, when Australia agreed to consider the problem of refugees from Nazi Germany (and somewhat reluctantly consented to accept 15,000), was sufficient to persuade the Australian government to accept responsibility'. Rather, Australia's delegate, Colonel T.W.White, told the conference, 'It will no doubt be appreciated also that, as we have no real racial problem, we are not desirous of importing one by encouraging any scheme of large-scale foreign migration' (quoted, Blakeney 1984: 130).

Such attitudes began to change after the Second World War, albeit in a haphazard way. During the war, approximately 1,500 refugees from the Asia Pacific region, including 5,473 non-Europeans, were given permission to stay for the duration of the hostilities. Government attempts to force the removal of the thousand who had established personal ties and wished to remain after the war led to successful legal challenges and prompted the Labor government to introduce the *Wartime Refugees Removal Act* 1949 (Neumann 2004: 92–95). A change of government a few months later resulted in the act not being implemented but those who stayed were not allowed 'to become naturalised or bring in wives, children or assistants' (Price 1981: 100).

The Labor government's refusal to allow wartime refugees to stay contrasted with its promotion of migration as a central plank of government policy. The key figure in this was Arthur Calwell, a strong proponent of the White Australia policy who, shortly before becoming Australia's first immigration minister in 1945, published a book in which he argued for an urgent and substantial increase in Australia's migrant intake for reasons of national security and development (Calwell 1945). Calwell's immigration policies prioritised migration from Britain through free and assisted passage schemes. However, it soon became clear that other sources of migration would be required to meet the government's targets. Accordingly, in July 1947, Calwell signed an agreement with the Preparatory Commission of the International Refugee Organisation (IRO) covering the admission to Australia of displaced persons from Europe. Although Calwell made some claim to humanitarianism (CoA 1946: 1050), the protection of refugees was not a major motivation for the resettlement scheme.[30]

Instead, the resettlement agreement gave the Commonwealth 'the full right of selection of migrants' (CoA 1947: 1067) in a situation where there was some competition between the major countries of immigration for 'suitable settlers' (Kunz 1988: 38). Over the next four years, some 170,700 people migrated to Australia under the 'Calwell Scheme' (Kunz 1998: 43). From the outset, their conditions of entry and the activities in which they could engage were subject to strict government control. With no apparent sense of irony, given the circumstances that many of the displaced people had just left behind, displaced persons were initially housed at the Bonegilla Reception Centre.[31] They were to remain at this former military camp near Wodonga until 'settled in employment' (CoA 1947a: 1067–1068), often 'in developmental projects which necessitated camp-type accommodation' (Kunz 1988: 41).

One controversial aspect of Calwell's scheme that has particular relevance to a discussion of state crime is the likelihood that it allowed 'a significant number of persons who committed serious war crimes' to enter Australia (A-GD 1994: 15). Aarons (2001:255) argues that 'Australian officials... not only ignored evidence of racial bigotry, but turned a blind eye to widespread claims that former SS and Nazi police officers were among the migrants'. This applied not only to the relatively ad hoc screening procedures implemented by Australian authorities in Europe but also to the regime at Bonegilla:

> Repeated attacks against Jews, including serious beatings and knifings, were alleged against Nazi migrants...Authorities...were said to be only nominally in charge, the true power being a Baltic migrant, a former Nazi storm trooper who allegedly participated in the destruction of the Riga ghetto in which thousands of Jews were killed. An Australian teaching English...reported that in summer, when the men wore sleeveless singlets while they worked, it was common to see the SS blood group tattoos (or scars where they had been) under many of their armpits (Aarons 2001: 255).

At the time, such allegations were dismissed as potentially undermining the displaced persons scheme or, as the Cold War progressed, the complaints of a vociferous pro-communist minority (Aarons 2001: 244–286). However, while Calwell clearly was not motivated by a desire to recruit war criminals, there is substantial evidence that the Australian government and security establishment were or ought to have been aware that people known to be implicated in, if not directly responsible for, recognised war crimes, were being recruited.[32]

The strict control exercised over the displaced persons and the 'cherry-picking' exercise conducted within the camps in Europe set a precedent for the Australian government to conceptualise refugee resettlement primarily as a form of labour migration, rather than a means of protecting human rights. In 1953, with the IRO scheme over, the Australian government signed up to the Inter-governmental Committee for European Migration (ICEM). Under the arrangements with the ICEM, 199,000 of the 628,000 people who migrated to Australia between 1953 and 1973 were refugees (ABS 1978: 125); while 260,164 refugees migrated to Australia under some form of assisted passage between 1947 and 1973 (ABS 1974: 164).

Australia ratified the 1951 UN Refugee Convention in 1954 but exercised the option to limit its application to events occurring in Europe prior to 1951 and did not did not sign the 1967 Protocol until 1973. Ratifying the convention did not diminish the Australian state's preference for resettlement.[33] Moreover, throughout this period, maintenance of the White Australia policy was fundamental. No non-European refugees were granted entry between 1945 and 1965 and, even after the policy was relaxed in 1966 to allow visas for non-Europeans with special skills that local residents could not provide, European heritage and self-identification were decisive. 'Ceylonese Burghers who identified as white and South Africans of European extraction were considered a "useful supplement" to the predominantly Anglo-Celtic intake. Chinese refugees fleeing to Hong Kong in the late 1950s and early 1960s, and Asians expelled from Uganda in 1972, were not' (Neumann 2004: 51).

The Cold War also shaped government preferences. Two substantial intakes of eastern European refugees (14,000 Hungarians between 1956 and 1958 and 6,000 Czechs and Slovaks in 1968) were resettled via the ICEM;[34] and to the extent that Australian governments were willing to grant asylum to onshore claimants, the largely ad hoc decision making processes were limited to small numbers of high profile defectors such as the Soviet diplomat, Vladimir Petrov or members of the Hungarian 1956 Olympics team, with intelligence or propaganda value (Neumann 2004: 52–64).

Overall, the refugees who settled in Australia between 1946 and 1976 had a contradictory impact on Australian migration patterns. While challenging the Anglo-Celtic norm, and being the subject of some hostility, refugees were not widely regarded as a fundamental threat to the White Australia policy. Instead, they were promoted at a state level because of their contribution to the workforce and were distinguished from other migratory 'threats' from Asia.

Conceptually though, the tradition of subsuming refugee entry to resettlement programs that form part of the larger migrant intake was quite different to a policy based on universal rights to protection or non-refoulement. Consequently, there has never been a period of unfettered access for refugees or a policy determined primarily on humanitarian grounds. This does not make Australia unique but it does suggest any argument that recent Australian state responses are systemically deviant should trace the mechanisms of exclusion back to the ways in which aliens were defined within the established policy distinction between those refugees chosen to come and those who arrived without permission and seeking protection; particularly as the context in which this distinction operated was about to significantly change.

'Boat people' and border enforcement

Australian state responses to unauthorised migrants and refugees were redefined during the 1970s as successive federal governments lifted the restrictions on non-European migration and formally abandoned the White Australia policy. Although the extent of the accompanying ideological shift should not be overstated or the enduring legacy of earlier border policing practices overlooked, the introduction of a formally non-discriminatory immigration policy and the consolidation of new multiculturalist norms removed a significant institutional component for state organised exclusion; and facilitated the development of closer economic and social ties between Australia and the Asia-Pacific region. This marked a serious break from the past and gave official legitimacy to Asian migration, including a high profile resettlement program for Indo-Chinese refugees.

The defeat of the regimes in South Vietnam, Cambodia and Laos in 1975 triggered several phases[35] of forced migration that had far reaching geopolitical implications. While the majority of Indo-Chinese refugees became encamped in the immediate region of flight, eventually to become the focus of prolonged resettlement and repatriation negotiations, a minority managed to undertake unauthorised boat journeys to Australia in order to claim asylum.

The first phase of these arrivals between 1976 and 1981 prompted the Australian government to establish new mechanisms for processing asylum applications and the beginnings of a state infrastructure for monitoring and ultimately detaining and deterring unauthorised refugees. The more exclusionist and abusive aspects of this infrastructure were not developed until after the next phase of boat arrivals in 1989. However, there was always an exclusionist dimension to resettlement. While it played some part in establishing an elite consensus around humanitarian, non-discriminatory norms, resettlement also constituted an important part of the Australian government's strategy of forward containment as the Australian state sought to assert its control over any forms of refugee movement that threatened to challenge Australia's border controls. The evolution of this response provides some insight into how the Pacific Solution later developed, even if there is no absolute continuity in the policies and policing strategies involved.

Faced with the imminent collapse of the Saigon regime in April 1975, the Whitlam Labor government, which had opposed Australia's military involvement in the Vietnam War and had cut the migrant intake, was reluctant to accept Vietnamese refugees (Viviani 1984: 53–65). Initially, it offered temporary entry to only three categories of Vietnamese citizen: spouses and children of Vietnamese students already living in Australia; spouses and the under 21 year-old children of Australian citizens; and Vietnamese with a long and close association with the Australian presence in Vietnam, whose life was to be considered in danger, and whose applications would be considered on a case by case basis (SSCFAD 1976: 6). In May 1975, with many of those eligible under the new criteria unable to reach Australia and the extent of the potential refugee flight becoming apparent, the federal government approached the UNHCR to urge that 'there should be co-ordinated international action under the direction of the High Commissioner for the placement of refugees…in as many countries as possible' (SSCFAD 1976: 31). In the following months, small numbers of refugees were approved for resettlement in Australia but, in general, 'the intention of [Whitlam's] policy was to be as restrictive as possible' (Viviani 1984: 64).

While the Liberal National Party Coalition was critical of Whitlam for excluding Vietnamese refugees on ideological grounds, and was subsequently more disposed to accepting Indo-Chinese refugees out of a declared moral obligation arising from Australia's involvement in the Vietnam War, its first steps on securing office in December 1975 were also tentative. In March 1976, 568 refugees living in camps in Thailand were granted resettlement (DIEA 1976: 8). However, the selection criteria had little to do with their objective human rights situation and required only that 'they be in sound health with no adverse record and that they be able to integrate into the Australian community', a judgment made by immigration officials on the basis of the 'individual's background, previous employment and education' (SSCFAD 1976: 35).

Such ad hoc and inconsistent responses prompted the Senate Standing Committee on Foreign Affairs and Defence (SSCFAD 1976: 89) to recommend the creation of a 'comprehensive set of policy guidelines together with the necessary administrative machinery to be applied to refugee situations'. These guidelines would allow for refugees to be part of a planned migration process that enabled them 'to adjust quickly to life and work within a new environment' and therefore 'make their particular contribution to the country's economic well-being, and to its social and cultural development'. The standing committee's report provides insight into two important themes underpinning government policy at this time: refugees were to be brought to Australia on government terms and on resettlement, they were to be welcomed as part of Australia's developing commitment to multiculturalism. Moreover, this approach was to be seen as an expression of the Australian government's broadly interpreted commitment to the 1951 UN Refugee Convention and the 1967 Protocol (SSCFAD 1976: 90). The standing committee's recommendations formed the basis of the government's refugee policy announced in May 1977. Immigration Minister Mackellar outlined four principles underpinning the policy: Australia fully recognises its humanitarian commitment and responsibility to admit refugees for resettlement; the decision to accept refugees must always remain with the Australian government; special assistance will often need to be provided for the movement of refugees in designated situations or for their resettlement in Australia; and it may not be in the interest of some refugees to settle in Australia (CPD 1977: 1714). This was far from a definitive policy statement but it did reaffirm that a controlled resettlement process was the government's preferred option for managing refugee entry and implied that a more restrictive response might develop towards unauthorised boat arrivals.

From white Australia to multiculturalism

These had begun in 1976, signalling Australia's emergence as a potential first refuge for forced migrants. However, the unauthorised boat arriving in Darwin on 27 April 1976 was greeted with none of the organised hostility that characterised the *Afghan* and *Tampa* episodes:

> The previous evening they had anchored their boat about a mile round the coast off the Darwin suburb of Nightcliff. Although Nightcliff has a sandy, white beach which attracts evening strollers, they were not noticed. A crowd had been drinking in the open near Lim's restaurant...but no-one had been aware of the small alien boat a short distance offshore...
>
> When, the following morning the refugees sailed round to the harbour entrance and spoke with the man near the wharf, the workman scarcely lifted his head and spoke only briefly. None of the refugees understood his words...Only when Hoang added that South Vietnam was their place of origin and that they were here to seek asylum did the Australian stop what he was doing, take Hoang to his car, and drive off to a phone booth to inform the authorities.
>
> Half an hour later the wharf became crowded with onlookers, reporters and cameramen. Two immigration officials boarded a pilot boat and came out to "greet" the refugees on their boat (Tran 1981: 11–12).

There was little media coverage of this event and little state infrastructure designed to obstruct or deter such arrivals. The five men were granted one month's entry and referred to the St Vincent de Paul charity for support. Two more boats, carrying 106 Vietnamese refugees, arrived in November and December 1976. All were permitted to enter and most were flown to the Wacol Migrant Hostel in Brisbane, where they resided while their status was considered (Viviani 1984: 69). Between April 1976 and August 1981, 56 such boats arrived, carrying 2,100 people (DIEA 1982: 59). A range of state agencies developed a relatively low level response for the unauthorised arrivals, who were required to undergo quarantine, health and immigration screening before being officially landed and their cases referred for consideration by the immigration minister (DIEA 1979: 13).

During this period, the 'boat people' constituted a small proportion of Australia's refugee intake, given that 51,780 Indo-Chinese refugees were resettled between April 1975 and June 1981 (DIEA 1981: 47), but the possibility of substantial numbers of unauthorised refugees landing on Australia's northern coastline enabled fears of an invasion to be revived, especially during the federal election campaign of December 1977. Such fears were not necessarily expressed in racist terms, although newspaper headlines such as 'It's the Yellow Peril Again'[36] encouraged such sentiments, but rather were 'couched in terms of the impact on unemployment, health risks and the like' (Viviani 1984: 79). With the 'boat people' dominating the public discourse on refugees, the government sought to restrict the numbers of boat arrivals through a combination of increased surveillance measures and extended opportunities for resettlement (Viviani 1984: 78–80).

At this stage, the pressure to extend resettlement was largely from external sources. After states such as Malaysia began demanding that Australia take 'its share', the government announced in March 1978, 'that there would be an increase of 2000 refugees brought from Thai and Malaysian camps before the end of June 1978, bringing the total of Indo-Chinese refugees accepted since 1975 to about 9000.' However, 'no targets over time were set, nor was there any announcement of a regular intake, indicating that Cabinet was still trying to avoid a long term commitment to resettle substantial numbers' (Viviani 1984: 80).

Government attempts to strictly limit the entry of more than a few thousand Indo-Chinese refugees became increasingly unviable during 1978 as government policy changes in Vietnam triggered an exodus of mainly ethnic Chinese refugees into neighbouring states and created a further spike in the numbers of boat arrivals in Australia (Grant 1979: 51–107). The new phase of departures included the use of large-scale freighters that offered a much safer passage to larger numbers of people. The Vietnamese government's role in encouraging and probably assisting this illicit movement[37] generated increasingly hostile responses from Australia and neighbouring southeast Asian states (Viviani 1984: 89–99). In January 1979, concerned that a large-scale commercial shipping operation involving government officials was moving refugees out of Vietnam, the Australian government announced that it 'could in no circumstances deal with the owners or masters of any such ship arriving in Australian waters, except to re-provision it at a cost to the company concerned'; that it 'would deny entry to any passengers on such ships'; and 'would legislate to introduce severe penalties for those who profiteered by bringing people into Australia without prior authority' (DIEA 1979: 6–7).

In addition to this forerunner to its campaigns against people smuggling, the Australian government entered into a series of 'regional boat holding arrangements' with Indonesia and Malaysia under which the Australian government agreed to prioritise the resettlement of refugees from these states in exchange for them preventing the departure of unauthorised boats to Australia (Viviani 1984: 83–85). The Australian government's commitment to resettle 9,000 refugees under these arrangements was not viewed as especially generous by other states in the region, which accused Australia of choosing refugees who best fitted migration rather than humanitarian entry criteria (Viviani 1984: 87–88).

Nevertheless, the holding arrangements were relatively successful in their own terms and provided a platform for the Australian government to further externalise its response following the decision of the member states of the Association of Southeast Asian Nations (ASEAN) in June 1979 to uniformly 'push back' refugee boats (UNHCR 2000: 84). Approximately 373,000 people were stranded in camps in southeast Asia at the time (DIEA 1980: 46) and, seeking to avoid the possible knock on effect of increasing numbers of boats reaching Australia and in no position to return boats to ASEAN states that would not accept them, the federal government stepped up its efforts to promote an 'international solution' based on extensive resettlement elsewhere (DIEA 1979: 13). As result of such efforts, the UN secretary general convened an international conference in July 1979 at which worldwide resettlement pledges were increased from 125,000 to 260,000; the

Border Crimes

Vietnamese government agreed to police illegal departures from Vietnam and promote orderly and direct routes of exit; and Indonesia and the Philippines pledged to establish regional processing centres to speed resettlement (UNHCR 2000: 84). While the Australian government promoted voluntary repatriation as 'the ideal solution', it agreed to increase its annual intake of Indo-Chinese refugees from 9,000 to 14,000 between 1978 and 1982 (SSCFAD 1982: 9).

The Australian government also continued to develop a containment strategy based on regional policing, external processing and resettlement, notwithstanding concerns that 'third country resettlement carries with it the strong possibility that it can serve to encourage more people to flee the source country' and thus motivate 'some of the boat refugees' (SSCFAD 1982: 10). Such concerns were generally unfounded. For most of the affected states, the 1979 agreement served to stabilise the situation (UNHCR 2000: 84). In Australia, the stabilisation was reflected by a decline in 'boat people' and coincided with more systematic government attempts to question the legitimacy of Indo-Chinese refugee claims. The removal of 146 Hong Kong and Taiwanese nationals, who had arrived by unauthorised boat claiming to be Vietnamese refugees in October 1981 and were detained at Darwin's East Arm quarantine Station, was an early example of boat arrivals being linked with organised forms of illegal migration (DIEA 1982: 63–64).

More significantly, the concept of 'queue jumping' acquired official sanction[38] and was used by Immigration Minister MacPhee in a major policy statement in March 1982, to justify a review of refugee policy 'to ensure that only genuine refugees are admitted under Australia's refugee programs' (DIEA 1983: 27). Changes arising from the review included a tightening of refugee selection criteria to exclude those falling outside the definition of refugee in the 1951 Convention and the determination of refugee claims on an individual basis (CPD 1982: 992). Also under the new procedures, 'people of any nationality outside their country' were able to apply to be assessed for resettlement, with priority going to 'designated programs for regions in which Australia has a particular interest' and in which the UNHCR has sought assistance – 'Indo-China, Eastern Europe and Latin America' (DIEA 1983: 27–28).

The procedures put in place by the 1982 review provided the basis for the resettlement quotas that sustain current policy. While most resettled refugees came from Indochina, the eastern European, Latin American and Timorese programs provided some diversification. In addition to these intakes, the 1982 review consolidated the special humanitarian program introduced in 1981 to resettle 'individual members of minority groups suffering human rights violations or serious discrimination', but who did not meet the 1951 Convention definition of a refugee (DIEA 1983: 27–29). Under these programs, nearly 22,000 people settled in Australia in 1981–1982; the highest figure since 1950–1951 (DIEA 1982: 56–57), and unmatched since. For this reason, the period of the early 1980s is often held up as a high point of inclusiveness and humanitarianism. This might seem reasonable when comparing the records of the Howard and Fraser governments,[39] but at best this can only be a relative judgment. The specific Cold War context of the Indochina conflicts and the willingness of other major powers, such as the United States, to participate in resettlement and to some extent encourage refugee flight as an indicator of the shortcomings of the Vietnamese government, created particular difficulties for those seeking to impose a harsher, exclusionist policies.

One indication of this, which provides a useful point of reference for the *Tampa* events, is the official response to boats carrying refugees rescued at sea. The combination of unseaworthy vessels, overcrowding and piracy made boat travel particularly hazardous for Vietnamese refugees. While 'thousands'[40] are believed to have died, approximately 67,000 were rescued at sea between 1975 and 1990 (UNHCR 2000: 79–87). Long established maritime practice and international maritime law required sea captains to aid vessels in distress. Initially, there were concerted efforts to maintain such norms as an exercise in humanitarianism and to portray the refugees in a relatively positive light. The 1977 *Immigration Department Review* (DIEA 1977), for example, carried sympathetic photos of two wooden fishing boats being escorted by a naval vessel into Broome and a group of refugees being provided with accommodation at the local Christian Brothers College 'after their ordeal' (DIEA 1977: 15). The 1980 *Review* (DIEA 1980: 50) carried a series of Department of Defence photos showing children being lifted on board the *HMAS Swan* with the caption: 'Australia accepted responsibility for the resettlement of seventy-two Indo-Chinese refugees rescued in the South China Sea…[who] had been at sea for two weeks, were low on fuel and water and had run out of food….All aboard for a new life as *Swan* resumes her journey'.

Apart from official rescue exercises, a number of privately sponsored 'international mercy vessels' (UNHCR 2000: 87) operated to assist the refugees. These provoked a mixed response from Australia and other states in the region (Grant 1979: 30–31). In January 1977, confronted by the prospect of an old minesweeper, the *Roland,* one of two boats hired by the World Council for Religion and Peace, bringing several hundred refugees picked up at sea to Australia, Immigration Minister MacKellar warned of a 'get tough' policy and threatened to refuse admission in such circumstances. However, the minister was extensively criticised by sections of the media and the Returned Serviceman's League (RSL) for making such threats (Viviani 1984: 71). Eventually, 74 refugees from the *Roland* and 52 from the second boat, the *Leap Dal* were resettled from Malaysia (DIEA 1977: 15). Similarly, the Australian government agreed to resettle 135 refugees landed by an Australian registered vessel in Singapore in January 1979 (Viviani 1984: 94).

Between 1975 and 1978, 'ships from 31 different countries rescued refugees from a total of 186 boats' (UNHCR 2000: 87) but as the 'pushback' policies of the ASEAN states intensified in 1979, the number of rescues fell significantly. In August 1979, UNHCR convened a conference which established the disembarkation resettlement offers (DISERO) program under which 'eight Western states, including the United States, jointly agreed to guarantee resettlement for any Vietnamese refugee rescued at sea by merchant ships flying the flags of states that did not resettle refugees' (UNHCR 2000: 87). Under this scheme, Australia resettled 330 refugees between 1979 and 1982 (DIEA 1982: 57).

It is clear that throughout this period, the Australian government would have preferred there was no informal boat travel by refugees.

Nevertheless, a number of international factors combined to make unilateral action of a Pacific Solution nature impractical, even if influential sections of Australia's political establishment had advocated it. Australia's involvement in the Vietnam War and the ongoing Cold War context after 1975; the Fraser Government's increasingly hostile attitude to the policies of the Vietnamese government; the central role of the United States in promoting and normalising this particular resettlement program; the regional nature and relative novelty of Indo-Chinese forced migration; and the desire of the Australian government to develop constructive relations with ASEAN states rendered a totally exclusionist policy unviable.

Instead, the Australian government's focus was to secure through a series of multilateral measures the control and containment of forced migration in the region. Refugee resettlement was entrenched as legitimate if it complied with other aspects of the government's migration program. This approach required conscious government efforts to establish an institutional consensus around resettlement and multiculturalism. This went well beyond the immediate institutions of government to include, for example, wide-ranging programs in schools. However, political bi-partisanship was especially important. As Malcolm Fraser later commented, 'If any of the political parties had tried to make politics over the resettlement of the Indo-Chinese in the seventies and eighties, Australians would have found it difficult to support the policy' (quoted, Brennan 2003: 32). While significant as a departure from the White Australia policy, this did little to broaden the universal rights that could be claimed by forced migrants. Rather, refugee policy operated as a form of humanitarian largesse to be bestowed upon its recipients. Whether or not this reflected the motives of the individuals concerned, it left open the possibility of increasingly harsh state sanctions being imposed on later groups of unauthorised boat arrivals. Their subsequent treatment, through measures such as mandatory detention, highlights the sharp disjuncture that developed between official commitments to universal rights and increasingly exclusionist state practice, notwithstanding the implied inclusiveness of multiculturalism.

Multiculturalism and exclusion

The consolidation of multiculturalism changed the official ideological landscape of migration policy. However, despite this being a relatively bipartisan process within the institutions of government, multiculturalism has never been hegemonic to the extent of the White Australia policy. Rather, multiculturalism evolved in a piecemeal fashion, primarily around issues of migrant settlement, and as a relatively amorphous policy ideal intended to reinforce social cohesion, it has been confronted and limited by discourses on cultural homogeneity and conformity that rely on the ideological traditions of the past. In short, the institutionalisation of multiculturalism legitimised a degree of cultural diversity and tolerance and provided a measure for rejecting attitudes and state practices associated with the White Australia policy as deviant.

However, by being conceptualised largely in terms of migrant settlement rather than in more universal human rights terms capable of challenging the Australian state's monopoly over cross border movement, multiculturalism represented a new paradigm within which state organised exclusion and inclusion of migrants could operate. In particular, partly through state contrived moral panics about unauthorised refugees, a new embodiment of the legitimate migrant emerged; one not primarily defined by initial nationality and upbringing but, without such considerations being totally abandoned, one that is entry criteria compliant and legal. In this context, perceptions of what constitutes an alien have shifted but the state's capacity to alienate, exclude, criminalise and abuse certain types of unauthorised migrant has remained intact.

The most significant philosophical aspect of multiculturalism is its formal rejection of assimilation. There were a number of dimensions to assimilation, which provided the ideological cornerstone of the White Australia policy, but essentially assimilationist policies reinforced the white settler identity of the Australian nation though the recruitment of migrants with a designated capacity to 'blend in'. Partly, this meant promoting an Australian physical type, distinguishable from those of Asian and African descent.[41] However, as immigration from central and southern Europe made the Caucasian cohort more diverse and a trickle of non-European migrants began in the 1960s, there was a growing emphasis on integration; a policy described by Immigration Minister Snedden as 'aiming to maintain a predominantly homogenous population neither exclusive nor multi-racial' (quoted, Jacubowicz et al 1984: 40).

The accompanying expectations of cultural assimilation, of first and second generation migrant families complying with cultural norms derived from a British or European heritage, were measured by practices such as speaking English, deferring to Christianity and wearing conformist dress (Jupp 2003: 22–23). In this context, cultural difference was conceptualised as a problem to be overcome or as a point of distinction from other more acceptable migrants. This approach was never fully negated by multiculturalism and has resurfaced in many of the officially sanctioned responses to Muslim asylum seekers or those of 'Middle Eastern appearance' targeted for practising deviant and dangerous 'cultural practices' or for simply 'failing to integrate' or accept 'Australian values'(Poynting et al 2004). The recourse to integrationist or neo-assimilationist thinking, particularly under the Howard government, suggests that multiculturalism has never been absolutely embraced at an official level and that the absence of a clearly articulated multiculturalist paradigm in the early 1970s left the new policy vulnerable to constant challenge.

The abandonment of the White Australia policy was a drawn-out process that can be traced back to the 1950s (Tavan 2005). The Whitlam government brought the policy to an official end in 1973 by announcing that all migrants, of whatever origin, would be eligible to obtain citizenship after three years of permanent residence. The government also issued policy instructions to overseas posts to disregard race as a factor in the selection of migrants and confirmed its intention to ratify all international agreements relating to immigration and race. Whitlam's government gave some of these measures a formal rights basis through the introduction of the *Racial Discrimination Act* 1975. This completed Australia's ratification of the UN Convention on the Elimination of All Forms of Racial Discrimination, which it had originally signed in

1966. However, there was no clear policy of 'multiculturalism' at that stage. The expression gained some currency during the tenure of Whitlam's immigration minister, Al Grassby, who defined it in terms of an inchoate concept of the 'family of the nation', where 'the overall attachment to the common good need not impose a sameness on outlook or activity of each member, nor these members deny their individuality and distinctiveness in order to seek a superficial and unnatural conformity' (Grassby 1973).

For Grassby, 'the important thing [was] that all are committed to the good of all'. Such vaguely expressed sentiments, although consistent with Whitlam's reforms and much of the global human rights language of the time, did not offer a detailed institutional paradigm of multiculturalism. Rather, in practice, multiculturalism evolved as a consequence of both the Whitlam and Fraser governments applying through state intervention a more inclusive philosophy for migrant settlement. At one level, this represented predominantly pragmatic responses to demographic changes, given that postwar migration had resulted in significant changes in the ethnic composition of the Australian workforce, particularly in major industrial centres such as Sydney and Melbourne.[42] In the early 1970s, a range of reports into the social conditions of migrant workers from non-English speaking backgrounds demonstrated the discrimination and disadvantage arising from assimilationist practice[43] and pushed issues such as migrant poverty and welfare onto Labor's wider reform agenda. Meanwhile, the growing engagement of migrants in unions and cultural and community organisations opened a political space for migrant or 'ethnic' issues, with flashpoints such as the bitter strike by the largely migrant workforce at Ford's Broadmeadows plant in 1973 highlighting the centrality of migrants to the blue-collar workforce and the potential consequences of their exclusion from a narrowly defined political and cultural mainstream (Lever Tracy and Quinlan 1988).

At the ideological level, the Coalition developed a more clearly articulated notion of multiculturalism that in redefining Australian nationalism provided a framework for the state to promote national stability.[44] In practical terms, this involved the provision of specific services for migrants. In broader policy terms, this involved the federal government and various state institutions actively engaging in an attempt to create a new hegemony to replace the White Australia policy. The 1978 Galbally Inquiry into Migrant Services and Programs played an important part in this process. Its report established as policy principles: '(a) all members of our society must have equal opportunity to realize their full potential and must have equal access to programs and services; (b) every person should be able to maintain his or her culture without prejudice or disadvantage and should be encouraged to understand and embrace other cultures; (c) the needs of migrants should, in general, be met by programs and services available to the whole community but special services and programs are necessary at present to ensure equality of access and provision; (d) services and programs should be designed and operated in full consultation with clients, and self-help should be encouraged as much as possible with a view to helping migrants to become self reliant quickly' (Galbally 1978: 4).

These principles reflected an obvious departure from the earlier tenets of assimilation that denied or downplayed the difficulties confronting migrants from non-English speaking backgrounds and philosophically rejected the desirability of cultural diversity. Instead, the report urged the adoption of cultural diversity as a means of developing the sense of nationalist loyalty amongst migrants (Galbally 1978: 91). Galbally's report was especially influential in consolidating a state sponsored institutional framework for multiculturalism. Along with bodies such as the Australian Institute of Multicultural Affairs, the reconstituted Department of Immigration and Ethnic Affairs, and the Independent and Multicultural Broadcasting Corporation, it contributed to the development of a multiculturalism that was conceptualised primarily as mechanism for consolidating national unity. This was also sustained by officially recognised and financed ethnic organisations that helped legitimise government policy (Foster and Stockley 1988: 30–33).

The envisaged role of multiculturalism in staving off social fracture was central to Malcolm Fraser's legitimisation of the policy. 'By responding to the fact of Australia's diversity' he commented in 1981, 'we have not created, and will not create, situations where particular ethnic communities form exploited, alienated, separate groups within our nation' (Fraser 1981: 4). While narrowly construed as a means of managing population composition, this construction of multiculturalism was never hegemonic to the extent of the White Australia policy and was vulnerable to challenge by those who argued for competing concepts of nationalism that emphasised colonial and European heritage. The extent to which this occurred was a matter of degree, rather than principle. Challenges to Indo-Chinese refugees took a variety of forms, from frequent and inflammatory newspaper references to an 'invasion' by an 'armada' (Viviani 1984: 75); through to the speeches and writings of historian, Geoffrey Blainey (1991: 26–30), who triggered an extensive public debate about Asian immigration in 1984 by claiming,

> I do not accept the view, widely held in the Federal Cabinet, that some kind of slow Asian takeover is inevitable. I do not believe we are powerless. I do believe that we can, with good will and good sense, control our destiny....
>
> I do not accept the view, widely held in the Federal Cabinet, that some kind of slow Asian takeover of Australia is inevitable. I do not believe that we are powerless....
>
> The fact that we are one of the world's seven biggest lands does not give us an obligation to take in a disproportionate number of refugees (Blainey 1991: 26–30).

Such arguments, with their sub-texts of 'us' being taken over by 'them', relied heavily upon the legitimacy of fears of an invasion and generated a revival of anti-Asian racist activity;[45] and while Blainey's interventions were generally opposed by the Labor Party they touched 'a nerve-centre of discontent...within non-Labor politics' (Kelly 1992: 134). Following Blainey's speech, Coalition MPs began voicing concerns in parliament about the racial 'mix' or 'balance' in the immigration intake, before retreating once the extent of the opposition from within the Liberal Party and the political establishment became apparent (Kelly 1992: 124–134). Nevertheless, Blainey and others associated with the 'new conservatism' had succeeded in returning to the mainstream assumptions that multiculturalism was potentially divisive because it accorded special privileges to minorities and undermined cultural homogeneity (Markus 2001: 49–81). In particular, Blainey was influential in labelling multiculturalism as the product of a powerful minority lobby and an 'industry' that had captured the ear of government.

This theme gained further currency following the publication of the Fitzgerald Inquiry report in 1988 (Fitzgerald 1988). This inquiry was established by the Hawke Labor government and asked to undertake 'a broad ranging look at its immigration policies' (Fitzgerald 1988: ix). It made 73 recommendations and produced a model Migration Bill that included express statutory provisions setting out the exclusive rights of Australian citizens and permanent residents to enter and remain in Australia (Fitzgerald 1988: Volume 2). While the committee was not specifically directed to examine multiculturalism, its call for a 'coherent philosophy of immigration' and its suggestion that immigration policy should be in the mainstream of government decision making, rather than operate for the benefit of 'sectional interest groups' (Fitzgerald 1988: xi), was widely interpreted as a critique of multiculturalism and fuelled debates that were developing during the official bicentenary of European settlement about the nature of Australian identity.

The report's critique was based partly on its contradictory findings regarding attitudes to multiculturalism. Despite finding there was widespread institutional support for non-discriminatory policies, the report concluded multiculturalism 'is seen by many as social engineering which actually invites injustice, inequality and divisiveness'. '[E]vidence of [this] failing consensus', it declared, 'is most evident in discussion of the compassionate and economic aspects of immigration, which is polarising between those who see the program as inhumanely preoccupied with economics and those who see it as foolishly charitable' (Fitzgerald 1988: 3). The overall thrust of the Fitzgerald report was that a formally non-discriminatory immigration policy should be entrenched but that the intake should not be determined by a desire to develop a multicultural populace. Leaving aside whether that was ever the function of multiculturalism, the report's emphasis on economic migration necessitated a selective entry process and provided scope for restrictive interpretations of who would be appropriate migrants. This reinforced the state's role in excluding unauthorised migrants, including by implication, 'boat people'.

The federal government accepted much of the report (CPD 1988: 3753–3760) and announced its immigration program would be based on three main streams – family reunion, economic and humanitarian – and a small special eligibility category that would balance the 'economic, social and humanitarian imperatives of the program. And while not fully endorsing the Fitzgerald recommendations, there was as a strong policing motivation behind the review system. The immigration minister explained:

> The Committee's Model Bill provided for many of the enforcement functions relating to prohibited non-citizens to be carried out through state law enforcement and justice systems. This so-called criminalization of enforcement has been widely opposed as harsh and out of step with criminal law policy. It places a potentially heavy burden on the state, police, court and penal systems. While the Government will not be taking this course, it is concerned to ensure that the deportation process is both just and effective. The introduction of the new review system will ensure that a person's claims to stay in Australia…will be rigorously and impartially tested. If those claims are found to be wanting, then departure should follow. If the person fails to depart within the time provided, deportation will be mandatory (CPD 1988: 3759–3760).

The wider implications of the legislative changes for unauthorised migrants are discussed in chapter four below. At this point, the main impact of the inquiry to be noted is that alongside its conceptualisation of immigration as essentially an economic project, multiculturalism was presented as an ideological vehicle for reducing barriers to the recruitment and settlement of 'suitable' migrants, rather than an expression of migrants' or refugees' rights of entry, or a challenge to the state's capacity to alienate particular categories of 'unacceptable' migrant. For the Labor government, migrant suitability and access to official legitimacy was to be determined on a largely pragmatic basis but there was also a commitment to solidify the institutional and philosophical basis of multiculturalism. Thus, it established the Office of Multicultural Affairs within the Prime Minister's Department in 1987 and in 1989, it produced an *Agenda for Multicultural Australia* (OMA 1989), 'a policy for managing the consequences of diversity' and containing eight goals:

All Australians should have a commitment to Australia and share responsibility for furthering our national interests

All Australians should be able to enjoy the basic right of freedom from discrimination on the basis of race, ethnicity, religion or culture

All Australians should enjoy equal life chances and have equitable access to an equitable share of the resources which governments manage on behalf of the community

All Australians should have the opportunity fully to participate in society and in the decisions which directly affect them

All Australians should be able to develop and make use of their potential for Australia's economic and social development

All Australians should have the opportunity to acquire and develop proficiency in English and languages other than English, and to develop cross-cultural understanding

All Australians should be able to develop and share their cultural heritage

All Australian institutions should acknowledge, reflect and respond to the cultural diversity of the Australian community.

An important aim of these goals was to help 'set the limits to multiculturalism' (Lack and Templeton 1995: 248). They explicitly did not apply to migrant selection, thus allowing restrictive policies and practices towards certain types of potential migrant to continue.

This was significant given the ideological battles unfolding within the Coalition. In 1988, opposition leader John Howard had mounted a generalised 'critique of the ideas that guided Australian conservatism during the Fraser era' (Kelly 1992: 419). A key part of

Border Crimes

Howard's *Future Directions* strategy (The Liberal Party 1988) was the promotion of 'One Australia' as the central theme of the Coalition's immigration and ethnic affairs policy. Although the policy affirmed the non-discriminatory principles established under the Whitlam and Fraser governments, Howard foreshadowed cuts to the intake of Asian migrants should the Coalition be elected on the grounds this would be 'supportive of social cohesion'. Echoing the sentiments of Geoffrey Blainey, he revived earlier attacks on multiculturalism:

> The objection I have to multiculturalism is that multiculturalism is in effect saying that it is impossible to have an Australian ethos, that it is impossible to have a common Australian culture. So we have to pretend that we are a federation of cultures and that we've got a bit from every part of the world. I think that is hopeless (quoted, Markus 2001:87).

Such arguments antagonised influential sections of the Liberal Party and contributed to Howard losing the party leadership in May 1989. He subsequently reasserted non-racist credentials and regained the leadership of the Liberal Party in January 1995 (Markus 2001 89–91). However, the views he expressed at the time and their divisive impact within the Australian establishment illustrated that despite surviving as an official tenet of government policy, multiculturalism formed the basis of a fragile, contested hegemony that left room for the reassertion of some of the Australian state's most exclusionist traditions. This was most apparent from the 1990s onwards when, despite the government claiming its adherence to the formalities of non-discrimination, the nature of multiculturalism was increasingly challenged, while the criminalisation and organised abuse of unauthorised migrants became commonplace. The dynamics of this are discussed in the following the chapters but the historical overview provided here informs a theory of state crime in a number of ways.

First, the hegemonic role of the White Australia policy gave the exclusion of non-white migrants a high degree of legitimacy. However, while exclusion on this basis could be judged as deviant by contemporary standards and to some degree in conflict with multiculturalism and formal human rights obligations, many of the assumptions and exclusionist practices associated with the White Australia policy remain.

Second, because the dominant practice of refugee resettlement has been legitimised by considerations not specifically related to the rights of refugees, claims that Australia has been historically generous towards refugees on a humanitarian basis deny or overlook the important role of resettlement in excluding refugees by externalising state responses to them.

Third, the evolution of multiculturalism represents only a partial shift to a more inclusive refugee policy and does not preclude exclusionist measures being implemented against refugees the state defines as unauthorised.

Fourth, for a state crime paradigm to be applied to Australia's treatment of unauthorised migrants, it must take into account the way in which organised and abusive practice is legitimised by ideologies associated with mainstream Australian nationalism.

In summary, the strands of history highlighted by this chapter suggest that the Australian state's responses to unauthorised migrants in the post-Cold War era are not entirely aberrant. While these responses have been implemented in a context where the overt racism of the White Australia policy is no longer officially acceptable, they also draw on lineages of exclusion that date back to the foundation of the Australian state. Moreover, the continued capacity of the Australian state to alienate certain types of non-citizen provides the basis for and develops with the state's capacity to criminalise and abuse unauthorised migrants.

Notes

[1] For a discussion of racist ideas applied to the Indigenous population, see Reynolds (2005). For a discussion of racist ideas developed during the 19th century, see Haller (1975) and Hannaford (1996: 235-324). Griffiths (2006) makes an original and compelling contribution to this subject by arguing that the key concern of the colonial ruling class regarding immigration was the creation of a culturally homogenous society, an ideal that drew more on the writings of J.S.Mill than on contemporary racial theorists.

[2] For example, in order to strengthen British influence in the region the Queensland government unsuccessfully sought British annexation of the non-Dutch parts of New Guinea in 1883. See Thompson (1980: 51-86).
[3] Until quite recently, there was near unanimity amongst historians of the period that the White Australia Policy was principally a product of labour movement agitation. A persuasive challenge to this orthodoxy can be found in Burgmann (1978) and Griffiths (2006).
[4] Particular fears about the impact of Chinese immigration included the establishment of Chinese colonies in the north, the consolidation of a potential fifth column in the event of a war with China and/or a gradual process of Chinese domination or influence. In relation to fears of invasion, I am indebted to the work of Phil Griffiths (2006). See also Burke (2001).
[5] See, for example, the studies of Markus (1979); Palfreeman (1967); Willard (1967) and Yarwood (1964).
[6] *Australian Constitution*, Article 51(xix).
[7] Immigration was administered by the Department of External Affairs between 1902 and 1916, by the Department of Home and Territories between 1917 and 1932, and by the Department of Interior between 1933 and 1945 (Palfreeman 1967: 4).
[8] Regulation 2.
[9] Regulation 2.
[10] Regulation 3.
[11] Regulation 4.
[12] Section 3 (a). Section 5(2) extended this provision to include immigrants who had entered Australia within the previous year. See also Palfreeman (1967: 81-85); Willard (1967:120-125).
[13] The language test provision was amended in 1905 to '50 words in any prescribed language'. The reference to European was removed at the request of the Japanese Government. However, this diplomatic gesture appears to have had little impact on the arbitrary and complex wording of the test. For example, Willard cites the following test used in Western Australia in 1908: 'Very many considerations lead to the conclusion that life began on sea, first as single cells, then as groups of cells held together by a secretion of mucilage, then as filament and tissues. For a very long time low-grade marine organisms are simply hollow cylinders, through which salt water streams' (Willard 1967: 126). See also Langfield (1999: 29-35); and Yarwood (1964: 45-52).
[14] Another, little documented group of non-European migrants targeted by

the restrictive legislation was the Afghans, who were predominantly recruited to work as cameleers. Those who remained after federation lived in increasingly segregated 'Ghantowns' on the outskirts of regional centres where they operated. See Stevens (2002).

[15] See also *Ah Toy v Musgrove*, Victorian Parliamentary Papers, 1888, Volume 1, Number 23.

[16] A further vessel, the *Changsa*, was also quarantined on arrival from Hong Kong on 27 May.

[17] The *Sydney Morning Herald's* editorial policy during this crisis was especially critical of the refusal to allow those with the appropriate documentation to land.

[18] See *Ex Parte Lo Pak*, 1888 NSWLR 221.

[19] For the full text of the proposed Chinese Restriction Bill, see *Sydney Morning Herald*, 17 May 1888.

[20] For the full minutes of the conference, including the correspondence and debates between the various delegates and colonial administrations, see NSW Legislative Assembly (NSWLA 1888: 173-212).

[21] Parkes' views regarding national security and the relative unanimity of the intercolonial conference signalled a turning point in longstanding debates amongst the colonial authorities, major business figures and landowners about how to develop the sparsely colonised regions of northern Australia. See Griffiths (2006: 137-190; 459-536).

[22] As far as I am aware, no extensive study of border policing, as we now understand it, for this period has been undertaken. Existing accounts of the *Afghan* crisis are also fragmentary. The more thorough studies include Britain (1969); Evans (1999: 79-94); Lewis (1970); Markus (1979: 143-144); and Rolls (1992: 456-508). In addition to these accounts, I have drawn on reports in the *Sydney Morning Herald*, 1 May 1888 to 31 July 1888, and the Reports of the New South Wales Legislative Assembly and Legislative Council during the same period.

[23] It is unclear whether these people ever did seek to travel to Australia but the prospect was considered serious enough for the notice of the report to be published by the New South Wales Legislative Assembly.

[24] For samples from these publications, see Evans et al (1997). For a study of the negative association between the Chinese and opium use, see Manderson (1993: 15-36).

[25] This account draws mainly from Yarwood (1964) but I have also examined some of the fragmentary customs reports in the National Archives of Australia (NAA). Some of the more useful material includes

Border Crimes

'Report of Inspector Lewis', 30 December 1907, NAA: A1, 1908/1320; Memoranda from the Secretary of the Department of External Affairs on rewards, October 1908, NAA: A1, 1908/13342; and confidential Customs and Excise Memoranda on the fumigation of boats coming from China, November 1912, NAA: A1, 1912/19251. See also Langfield (1999: 19-46).

[26] Pursuant to the *Regulations under the Immigration Restriction Act* 1901, ships masters were required to provide Customs with a list of all passengers from non-Commonwealth ports, specifying the name, nationality, place of shipment and calling and occupation of such passengers (Regulation 11). Customs Officers could require masters to provide details of the crew and their nationality (Regulation 12); and masters were required to provide details of all crew members of non-European race or descent (Regulation 13).

[27] The number of Chinese stowaways discovered increased from 16 in 1904 to a peak of 55 in 1908 (*Commonwealth Parliamentary Debates*, 3 September 1909, cited in Yarwood 1964: 177).

[28] The *Age*, for example, cast doubt on the role of British Officers 'on board the British and Australian vessels', who it suggested 'either actively or passively oppose themselves to the "white Australia" legislation of the Commonwealth' and whose 'laxity' was largely responsible for stowaways being allowed to escape (*The Age*, 28 December 1907).

[29] Because they were subsumed within the migrant intake, there are no definitive statistics. The National Population Council's Refugee Review notes 'some 3,500' refugees were settled in Australia between the World Wars (NPC 1991: 65)

[30] Indeed, humanitarian gestures were met with considerable hostility by sections of the establishment. For example, a scheme approved by Calwell in 1946 to allow entry to 2,000 Jewish survivors of concentration camps with close relatives in Australia was opposed by virtually all the major newspapers; the New South Wales Council of the Returned Servicemen's League; and leading figures in the Liberal, Country and Labor parties. Announcing the abandonment of the policy in January 1947, Calwell declared: 'the government has gone as far as it can reasonably be expected to go…on purely humanitarian grounds' and subsequently imposed on shipping companies a 25 percent limit on the numbers of refugee passengers allowed to sail from Europe (Blakeney 1985: 290-306).

[31] For a description of the very rudimentary conditions and dangerous circumstances in this camp, see Sluga (1988).

[32] The failure of successive Australian governments to pursue those named

by Aarons and the Special Investigations Unit report not only says something about Australian government attitudes to war crimes, but throws into sharp relief much of the national security rhetoric directed at unauthorized refugee arrivals today, with the unlikely scenario of potential terrorists seeking to enter Australia on overcrowded and unseaworthy boats standing in sharp contrast to the likely selection by successive Australian governments of refugees with histories of violating human rights.

[33] Indeed, throughout this period, Australian governments resisted attempts to provide a general right of asylum in instruments such as the 1948 Universal Declaration on Human Rights and the 1966 International Covenant on Civil and Political Rights.

[34] Australia's support for the ICEM, which the United States preferred to fund and support as an alternative to the UNHCR (Loescher 2001: 57-66), is also indicative of the priority given to Cold War allegiances over moves towards more universal systems of protection.

[35] The word 'phase' is consciously used here as a neutral description of a period of movement. Nearly all the literature on this topic, including that which is critical of government policy, refers to various 'waves' of boat people arriving in Australia. Apart from my not wanting to accept the implied threat of a wave, any reasonable analysis of the statistics would show that in relation to the overall migrant intake and the official human movement in and out of Australia, the boat people barely constituted a ripple.

[36] Brisbane *Courier Mail*, 29 November 1977.

[37] Grant (1979: 108-133) devotes a chapter to this subject entitled 'trafficking', an indication that distinctions between smuggling and trafficking had yet to develop in relation to refugees.

[38] The term 'queue jumping' was routinely used in sections of the media at the time and had been used periodically in federal parliament since 1978 when Labor's spokesman on Immigration and Ethnic Affairs, Moss Cass, wrote an article for *The Australian* entitled 'Stop this unjust queue jumping' (*The Australian*, 29 June 1978).

[39] Malcolm Fraser, for example, strongly promotes this interpretation. See Love (2001: 39).

[40] See also Viviani (1984: 95) for a discussion of the widely varying statistics.

[41] It also excluded those of Aboriginal descent and underpinned the policy of forcibly removing 'mixed blood' Indigenous children from their families.

See HREOC (1997).

[42] By 1976, '61 percent of male employed Greeks were tradesmen and labourers, 63 percent of Italians, 77 percent of Yugoslavs, 69 percent of Maltese and 61 percent of Poles. This compared with 37 percent of the Australian born and 45 percent of British' (Jupp 2003: 30).

[43] See, for example, Henderson et al (1971: 119-145).

[44] For example, the Coalition Immigration and Ethnic Affairs Policy for 1975 declared a commitment to 'the preservation and development of a culturally diversified but socially cohesive Australian society free of racial tensions and offering security, well-being and equality of opportunity to all those living there' (The Liberal and National Country Parties, 1975).

[45] My memory of living in Sydney at the time is of small far-right, neo-Nazi groups engaging in extensive graffiti campaigns; conducting physical attacks on political opponents and Asian students; and attending public meetings addressed by Blainey to show him their support.

Chapter 4

State of denial: the creation of the illegitimate refugee

Enforcing resettlement

The previous chapter highlighted that the 1970s was a period of continuity and change during which ongoing contradictions within migration and refugee policy were generated and certain threshold points reached. First, the White Australia policy was abolished, allowing permanent migration from non-European sources. Second, multiculturalist norms developed at an institutional and state level, although these were limited and contested. Third, while the federal government formally acknowledged responsibilities under the 1951 UN Refugee Convention and the 1967 Protocol and incorporated these into an onshore determination system for asylum applications, resettlement was firmly established as the preferred mechanism for refugees securing legitimate entry into the country. Each of these developments had a bearing on Australian state responses to the arrival of unauthorised asylum seekers between 1976 and 1982, when Australia resettled significant numbers of non-European refugees for the first time and became a first claim destination for refugees.

This chapter examines the further development of those responses as successive Australian governments introduced measures to enforce offshore processing and selection, while limiting the scope and availability of an onshore protection system. This occurred in the context of two further phases of unauthorised boat arrivals. The first, from 1989 to 1992, coincided with an increase in onshore applications arising from the suppression of the Tiananmen Square protests in China, and culminated in important changes to the *Migration Act*, including the introduction of mandatory detention of 'unlawful non-citizens'. The second, from 1994 to 1998, witnessed the consolidation of Australia's strategy of regional containment, as the Australian government sought to enforce the final dispersal of Indo-Chinese refugees and neutralise further forced migration in the region. Throughout this decade, official representations of the acceptable refugee narrowed as the state moved to exclude unauthorised arrivals through the introduction of measures that increasingly delegitimised and criminalised them. This was a continuous but often subtle process that incorporated the defence of the offshore selection system with the integrity of migration controls and Australian sovereignty. The methods employed by the Australian state during this period and the ideological rationales advanced for them allowed organised human rights abuses against forced migrants to become systemic and ultimately paved the way for the way for the development of the Pacific Solution.

After winning office in 1983, the Hawke government maintained a broadly similar approach to migration and refugee policy to its predecessor. In May 1983, Immigration Minister Stewart West, outlined a set of guiding principles for immigration policy that maintained the over-riding policy principle of migration being carefully controlled and engineered by the state:

> The Australian government alone decides who can enter Australia.
>
> Migrants must provide some benefit to Australia, although this will not always be a major consideration in the case of refugees and family members.
>
> The migrant intake should not jeopardise social cohesiveness and harmony in the Australian community.
>
> Immigration policy and selection is non-discriminatory.
>
> Applicants are considered as individuals or individual family units, not as community groups.
>
> Suitability standards for migrants should reflect Australian law and customs.

The creation of the illegitimate refugee

Migrants must intend to settle permanently.

Settlement in enclosed enclaves is not encouraged.

Migrants should integrate into Australia's multicultural society but are given the opportunity to preserve and disseminate their ethnic heritage (CPD 1983: 662).

While this framework was subjected to criticism (Parkin and Hardcastle 1990: 334–335), it established the broad parameters of bi-partisanship that characterised the immediate post White Australia policy period (Kalantzis 2003). Within this framework, Labor focused on family reunion and skills as determinants of migrant suitability in accordance with its fluctuating views on the needs of the national economy and the stability and integration of the migrant intake.

The new government also maintained a refugee resettlement program for Indo-Chinese refugees[1] but diversified the intake to include greater numbers from Latin America and the Middle East.[2] The first appreciable resettlement of African refugees (106 from Ethiopia) also occurred but given there were over one million Ethiopian refugees in surrounding states at the time (DIEA 1984: 36,118), this was more important for its symbolism than its impact on the situation in the Horn of Africa. Labor's maintenance of a more diverse resettlement system during the 1980s was set against a 50 percent cut in the numbers of people accepted under the offshore refugee and humanitarian program.[3] Within the program, the humanitarian component grew substantially;[4] reflecting the Australian government's selective application of the 1951 Convention and the transformation of the humanitarian program into 'a quasi family reunion category' (Crock 1998: 125).

This reinforced the pattern of the Australian state choosing which refugees it wanted and was accompanied by consistent attempts to question the legitimacy of those continuing to flee Indo-China. In May 1986, Immigration Minister Hurford stated that while the Indo-Chinese already in Australia were genuine refugees, a large proportion of those now leaving could not establish any claim of persecution and were 'migrants pure and simple'. 'It was', he continued, 'unfair on so many queued up elsewhere if there was a 'fast track' for some who were not political refugees' (DIEA 1986: 137). This signalled the government's likely hostility to future boat arrivals at a time when the ongoing conflicts in Indo-China, especially within Cambodia, were continuing to produce substantial forced migration that was of growing concern to states within the region.

Stemming the displacement and illicit movement arising from these conflicts and securing a 'Cambodian settlement' were major foreign policy priorities for the Hawke government (Frost 1997). 'As early as 1985', writes Robinson, Australian policy makers had produced what came to be known as the "Canberra Paper", which outlined the idea of a regional screening program, with third country resettlement for those who were screened in and repatriation for the screened out' (Robinson 1998: 155). By June 1989, the Australian government was playing a central part in the UN conference to draw up a comprehensive plan of action to provide a durable solution to the refugee outflow (DILGEA 1989: 25–26). A few months later, Foreign Minister Gareth Evans instigated a plan for the UN to become directly involved in the civil administration of Cambodia (DFAT 1990). This was designed to facilitate implementation of an earlier peace plan that included as a core component, the mass repatriation of Cambodian refugees (Evans and Grant 1991: 200–220; Mathew 1994: 66–76).

The conference that drew up the comprehensive plan of action was convened by the UN secretary general in Geneva and was attended by representatives of 78 governments, including those of Vietnam and Laos. The plan targeted mainly Vietnamese refugees and had five main objectives: a reduction in clandestine departures; the provision of temporary asylum by first asylum countries to all asylum seekers while their status was determined and a durable solution found; the determination of claims in accordance with international standards under the guidance of UNHCR; the resettlement of those recognised as refugees and those in camps prior to regional cut-off dates; and the return of those found not to be refugees and their reintegration in their home countries (Robinson 1998: 187–230; UNHCR 2000: 64). At the conference,

The creation of the illegitimate refugee

the Australian government committed to resettling 11,000 people over three years (JSCMR 1992: 83); but although the plan was designed to speed up the processes of resettlement and persuade some of the larger Western states to increase the numbers they were willing to take, it also signalled a more restrictive approach to those fleeing the region. In particular, there was an emphasis on policing clandestine departures. Article A (1) of the plan declared:

> Extreme human suffering and hardship, often resulting in the loss of lives, have accompanied organised clandestine departures. It is therefore imperative that humane measures be implemented to deter such departures, which should include the following:
>
> Continuation of official measures directed against those organising clandestine departures, including clear guidelines on these measures from the central government to the provincial and local authorities
>
> Mass media activities at both local and international level, focusing on:
>
> The dangers and hardship involved in clandestine departures;
>
> The institution of a status-determination mechanism under which those determined not to be refugees shall have no opportunity for resettlement;
>
> Absence of any advantage, real or perceived, particularly in relation to third country resettlement, of clandestine and unsafe departures;
>
> Encouragement of the use of the regular departure and other migration programs;
>
> Discouragement of activities leading to clandestine departures;
>
> In the spirit of mutual co-operation, the countries concerned shall consult regularly to ensure effective implementation and co-ordination of the above measures.

While some of these provisions could be justified by the hazards of informal boat travel, seeking to eliminate clandestine travel removed from refugees their 'autonomous right to disengage from an abusive society and to seek protection abroad' (Hathaway 1993: 687). Moreover, making immigration-based resettlement the sole means by which refugees could exercise their rights reflected the implicit stigmatisation of Vietnamese refugees as economic migrants and undermined their legitimacy as asylum seekers, despite there being no 'substantive shift in the nature of the protection claims advanced' (Hathaway 1993: 686, 689).

Fundamentally, the comprehensive plan was an assertion of sovereign authority by regional and resettlement states that disempowered and excluded unauthorised refugees in a number of ways.

First, the institution of regional asylum procedures was largely predicated on resettlement of successful applicants. Without promises of resettlement elsewhere, refugees would be afforded few rights in the region and limited access to neighbouring states. Of the six participating states in the region, only four preserved some form of asylum system. Malaysia and Singapore made no commitments to accepting future boat people and as of 2004, only Cambodia, China, Japan, South Korea and the Philippines had signed the Refugee Convention or Protocol (Robinson 2004: 323–324).

Second, the screening and processing of asylum seekers within the region lacked consistency and was often quite discriminatory (LCHR 1992). The variable approval rates suggested 'humanitarian objectives [were] compromised by migration control priorities' (Helton 1993: 558); while 'the substantive interpretations of refugee status...failed to be consistent with its explicit human rights mandate' and at times fell 'short of accepted international standards' (Hathaway 1993: 691).

Third, the asylum that was offered in the region consisted mainly of detention in worsening conditions, especially after arbitrary cut-off dates were imposed for the consideration of claims (Lawyers Committee for Human Rights 1989). 'In Hong Kong', notes Robinson, there 'was a rising tide of tension and violence in detention centres, sparked by the overcrowded, prison like conditions; the in-camp rivalries and conflicts...and cutbacks in camp services'. Some of these cutbacks were enforced by UNHCR

The creation of the illegitimate refugee

and included 'reductions in medical and counselling services, new restrictions on movement in and around some camps, elimination of income generating activities and reductions in employment opportunities, and limits on monthly remittances from overseas' (Robinson 2004: 323).

Fourth, under the auspices of its 'orderly return program', forced repatriation of 'screened-out' refugees became routine after December 1989. It accelerated after the signing of the UN sponsored peace agreement for Cambodia in October 1991 and the subsequent decision of the US government to normalise relations with Vietnam. By the end of 1995, over 2,100 people were forcibly removed from Hong Kong. This often involved the deployment of heavily armed riot police 'amidst threats of widespread demonstrations and mass suicide attempts'. In November 1991, 'Hong Kong police and security officers forced 59 Vietnamese, including two women injected with sedatives, onto a transport plane bound for Hanoi' (Robinson 1994: 330). Such calculated exercises in encouraging 'voluntary' repatriation were conducted about six times per year, creating in the camps 'a cycle that one UNHCR official described as "two months of silence, one day of violence, two months of silence, one day of violence"'(Robinson 2004: 330). Overall, of the post-cut-off date Vietnamese, 32,200 were granted refugee status and resettled, while 83,300 had their claims rejected and had to return (UNHCR 2000: 85).

The widespread international backing for the comprehensive plan, the central role in its implementation played by UNHCR notwithstanding the human rights implications for many of the refugees,[5] and Australia's high profile intervention in the Cambodian peace negotiations gave high level institutional authority to the coercive methods employed to enforce the agreements. Maintaining the functional integrity of these agreements became the dominant policy imperative shaping the relationship between Indo-Chinese refugees and the various receiving states. There was no special quality that could be claimed for the human rights principles of the Western liberal democracies engaged in this process. The methods used to expel the Vietnamese from Hong Kong were as

Border Crimes

much the responsibility of the Australian state as the local Hong Kong authorities.

In the shadow of these events, the Australian government mounted a sustained campaign to question the legitimacy of any Indo-Chinese whose unauthorised movement and claims for protection represented an objective challenge to the agreements. The deviance vested in the boat people arose from their continued movement in defiance of preferred orderly migration and resettlement models. The Indo-Chinese were to be targeted not because their circumstances of dislocation and flight had changed but because they were coming into conflict with Australia's shifting strategic priorities.

When the comprehensive plan was signed in June 1989, no unauthorised boats had arrived in Australia since 1981, leaving the government to regard the dispersal of Indo-Chinese refugees largely as an external issue. However, on 28 November 1989, a boat carrying 26 Indo-Chinese refugees[6] arrived at Broome. Unlike earlier boat arrivals, those on board were detained pending consideration of their claims; a policy that was retrospectively declared mandatory. Two similar boats, carrying 119 and 79 people respectively, arrived on 31 March and 1 June 1990 (DILGEA 1990: 15, 48). Despite media reports that several more were on their way,[7] no further boats arrived until March 1991. At the time, there remained serious doubts whether the political circumstances in Cambodia had altered sufficiently to deny Cambodian asylum seekers refugee status, given the 'intense fighting between the Cambodian factions, the practice of conscripting even 14 year-old children to fight...fear that the Khmer Rouge would again take power...the corruption that had grown with economic liberalisation, and the often violent prejudice against those of Vietnamese or Chinese origin' (Hamilton 1993a: 24). Moreover, the Cambodian peace agreement had not yet been finalised and refugees returning from Thailand faced serious hazards such as land mines and severe economic hardship (Robinson 1998: 238–250).

The creation of the illegitimate refugee

Nevertheless, the government's disdain for those on board the boats was summed up in a television interview given by Prime Minister Hawke on 6 June 1990:

Q. We woke up this morning to read that we're asking the Cambodian government to take back some of the Cambodian boat people who came to our shores. Why are we doing that?

A. For the obvious reason. I mean we have…a compassionate humanitarian policy, which will stand comparison with any other country in the world. But we're not here with an open door policy saying anyone who wants to come to Australia can come. These people are not political refugees.

Q. How can you be sure of that, Mr. Hawke?

A. Simply there is not a regime now in Cambodia, which is exercising terror, political terror, upon its population.

Q. What do you make then of these hundreds of people…Who get on their tin boats and travel across

A. What we make of it is that there is obviously a combination of economic refugeeism, if you like. People saying they don't like a particular regime or they don't like their economic circumstances, therefore they're going to … pull up stumps, get in a boat and lob to Australia. Well, that's not on.

Q. And risk their lives to do it?

A. Their lives…we have an orderly migration program. We're not going to allow people just to jump that queue by saying we'll jump into a boat, here we are, bugger the people who've been around the world. We have a ratio of more than 10 to 1 of people who want to come to this country compared to the numbers that we take in.

Q. And you personally have no qualms about that?

A. Not only no qualms about it, but I will be forceful in ensuring that that is what's followed.[8]

Immigration Minister Hand distanced himself from these comments when they became the subject of litigation before the

Federal Court[9] but the prime minister's responses, along with similar sentiments expressed by the foreign minister (Cockburn 1990), encapsulated the reasoning behind the Labor government's evolving policy of detention and removal and its hostility to legal challenges to the policy.

That enforcing the comprehensive plan was a predominant motive of government policy became even more apparent when the next phase of boat arrivals began. On June 1994, a boat carrying 51 refugees from southern China arrived in Darwin. These were Sino-Vietnamese refugees who had been resettled in the southern Chinese province of Behai under the comprehensive plan but who continued to face substantial persecution and hardship (Crock 1995: 42–43). As more boats from southern China began to arrive, an atmosphere of crisis was generated.[10] By the end of December, a month in which 342 people arrived in six boats, 'emergency discussions' were taking place between the Australian and Chinese governments. On 29 December, *The Age* reported, 'The Chinese Government is effectively refusing to take back hundreds of people who have recently arrived...leaving Australia facing its worst refugee crisis in 15 years'.

Immigration Minister Bolkus sought to make this a policing issue for the Chinese authorities and effectively denied the legitimacy of any prospective asylum claim from the region. 'To the Chinese authorities', he said, 'the message is very strongly that these people have no right to come and impose themselves on Australian shores in the way that they have...we're saying "Look, there is a responsibility to ensure those who are profiteering from this racket don't continue to do so"'. Clearly disturbed by the expanding use of the language of rights, he further accused 'refugee support groups of coaching the boat people and said some had been able to spell "refugee" and "asylum" in English' (Middleton 1994). On the same date, the Chairman of the New South Wales Ethnic Affairs Commission was quoted as demanding 'decisive and immediate action' to meet 'the emergency'. Indicating the emerging ideological demarcation between the official and unofficial migrant, he promised the migrant population of Australia was as committed as

The creation of the illegitimate refugee

those born here to seeing the 'integrity of the borders' was maintained (Hill 1994).

The other source of unauthorised boat arrivals during this period was the network of refugee camps in Indonesia and Malaysia. On 7 July 1994, a boat carrying 17 Vietnamese asylum seekers who had left the refugee holding centre in Galang, Indonesia, having previously been screened and refused refugee status by the UNHCR, arrived in Broome. Three of this group were granted refugee status on the basis of new information, which the government argued would have enabled their claims to be re-examined had it been available to UNHCR. In order to prevent the failed applicants from appealing, the immigration minister issued conclusive certificates denying them access to the Refugee Review Tribunal, claiming that to do otherwise would 'prejudice...our international relations' (CPD 1994: 2831). Along with the refugees from southern China, those who had left camps were accused by the Australian government of 'forum shopping' and were made the target of legislation explicitly preventing subjects of the comprehensive plan or those leaving 'safe' third countries such as China, from applying for protection visas in Australia.

On 17 November 1994, two days after the first amendments were enacted,[11] 58 Vietnamese refugees were forcibly removed without warning from the Port Hedland detention centre in North Western Australia. In a widely televised episode, they were handcuffed, and in some cases had their feet bound, before being put on a charter flight back to Indonesia with the full support of UNHCR (Gregory and Middleton 1994; O'Brien and Walker 1994). Such public exercises of state force and deterrence had an important symbolic and ideological impact. The belittling of the boat people's status, the implicit criminalisation arising from their treatment and the institutional closing of ranks to secure their exclusion ensured that as a group, Indo-Chinese boat arrivals were stripped of their remaining official legitimacy as refugees and unambiguously redefined as economic migrants. Such labels were routinely employed to discredit and denigrate all those who failed to satisfy refugee determination and selection procedures that were increasingly biased against on-shore applicants (Hamilton 1993b).

They were also designed to reinforce the government's attempts to alienate and exclude asylum seekers other than those being resettled.

Debasing on-shore asylum

The legislative changes made during the early 1990s were an important first step in creating the legal framework for the Pacific Solution. Although the Howard government was directly responsible for the consequences of its policies, the organised abuse of the human rights of unauthorised migrants was a bipartisan political exercise that began with domestic enforcement measures targeting Indo-Chinese boat arrivals that were subsequently applied to all such arrivals and extended into the Asia-Pacific region. These changes occurred over a ten year period, with Labor's initial legislative changes having the enduring ideological impact of entrenching in public consciousness an equation between the unauthorised asylum seeker and the 'queue jumper'.

The conversion of the queue into the primary means by which a refugee was expected to exercise rights to protection was routinely attributed hegemonic community support and became part of the common sense of mainstream political discourse. For example, the Senate Joint Standing Committee on Migration Regulations (JSCMR) declared in 1992:

> In addition, while the Australian community for some time has been willing to accept persons in genuine need, there is a growing concern that many of those applying for refugee status within Australia may not be actual refugees, but may be seeking to stay on in Australia to improve their economic prospects and general lifestyle. This belief can create a degree of community antagonism. There is a general consensus that persons should not be able to 'jump' the immigration queue and obtain settlement simply because they have managed to reach Australia (JSCMR 1992: 46).

Beginning with particular groups of refugees, such as the Indo-Chinese subject to the comprehensive plan, but extending to all unauthorised arrivals, the assertion these people were jumping a queue transformed them into objects of suspicion: cheats who were

The creation of the illegitimate refugee

immediately distinguishable from the legitimate, resettled refugee and who took up valuable resettlement places ahead of more genuine refugees.[12] This imposed an otherwise absent sense of order on the forced migration experience and transferred responsibility for the impact of a restrictive entry policy for refugees away from the government's arbitrary imposition of quotas back on to individuals for whom a queue was a legal and political fiction. Indeed, given the absence of an orderly departure program from Cambodia, there was not even a notional administrative queue for Cambodian refugees to join.

The multiple amendments to the *Migration Act* made between 1989 and 1994[13] facilitated this conceptual transfiguration. As part of a wider policy shift towards the increased regulation and policing of migration, they consolidated the distinction between unauthorised asylum seekers and resettled refugees. The 1989 *Migration Legislation Amendment Act*, for example, was devised as a response to the Fitzgerald inquiry and aimed to formalise immigration procedures by replacing discretionary decision making with a more rigid system of statute and regulation. The new legislation introduced a points system for the assessment of visa applications and created a system of immigration appeal tribunals for the review of migration decisions. It also targeted 'illegal migrants' by introducing mandatory deportation after 28 days; providing the immigration department with the power to sell illegal entrants' possessions with a view to recovering costs relating to detention and deportation; and setting a 12 month deadline for those without visas to apply to regularise their status (MILGEA 1989a).

The government's promotion of these 'tough' measures had widespread institutional support. An *Age* editorial on 16 December claimed that 'up to 75 percent of Australians want the government to make more effort to detect and deport illegal immigrants' because 'illegal immigration...undermines an orderly immigration program by encouraging others to jump the queue.' Such language contributed to suspicion of all unauthorised migrants and clearly drew on and reinforced suspicions of unauthorised boat arrivals, although they were not the main focus of the new legislation. This changed following a sudden and substantial increase in the numbers of on-shore asylum applications. Until 1989, the number of on-shore asylum claims had been relatively low, increasing from 170 in 1982 to 564 in 1988–1989 (JSCMR 1992: 38). This figure jumped to 3,370 in 1989–1990 and peaked at 13,954 in 1990–1991 (JSCMR 1992: 38). There were a number of reasons, which had little to do with boat arrivals or people smuggling, for these developments.

First, and most important, was the impact of political developments in the People's Republic of China (PRC). The Australian government responded to the violent suppression of the Tiananmen Square protests by announcing in June 1989 that PRC nationals presently in Australia would have their visas extended until 31 July 1990. This was further extended in June 1990, when the government announced that 'PRC nationals in Australia on 20 June 1989, whether legal or illegal, would be able to stay in Australia for four years under a special category of temporary residence permit (JSCMR 1992: 187–188)'. These concessions, combined with the tone of the prime minister's rhetoric against the actions of the Chinese government, were interpreted as a signal that asylum claims by PRC nationals would be viewed favourably (JSCMR 1992: 38–41).[14] The government also put in place special arrangements to maintain the lucrative recruitment of fee paying Chinese students (JSCMR 1992: 183–186). Between 1 July 1989 and 30 September 1991, over 52,000 PRC citizens arrived in Australia, approximately 17,000 of whom applied for refugee status (JSCMR 1992: 190).

The 1989 legislation effectively removed the immigration minister's discretion initially to allow entry on compassionate or humanitarian grounds, therefore forcing those wishing to remain who did not meet the criteria for the general migration class of visas to go through the refugee determination system (Crawford 1990; Germov and Motta 2003: 39).[15] The reduction in the resettlement intake from 20,216 in 1981–1982 to 10,411 in 1989–1990 (JSCMR 1992: 3) also may well have been interpreted as a signal that official resettlement opportunities were likely to be limited.

Although there was a broad institutional consensus that the on-shore determination system should be brought under stricter state

The creation of the illegitimate refugee

control, the exact response to the exponential increase in on-shore claims was a hotly contested political issue. The government hoped that the introduction of a special permit would provide PRC nationals with a breathing space and reduce the numbers lodging individual asylum claims. The opposition parties opposed 'blanket approvals' and 'preferential treatment' and argued that PRC nationals should have their claims to stay assessed individually (JSCMR 1992: 190–191). While there was argument over the resource implications of the opposition's stance, the broad consensus that the on-shore asylum system was being manipulated or abused made those applying for refugee status in Australia vulnerable to distinction from the more legitimate resettled refugee.

In June 1990, the government announced it was separating its obligation to protect refugees from its practice of granting automatic permanent residence to those deemed to be refugees (MILGEA 1990a). In future, on-shore refugee claimants would be given a four year temporary entry permit (TEP). On expiry the TEP holder could apply for permanent residence under the migration program, subject to the availability of places, or a further TEP if protection was still required (NPC 1991: 133). This decision effectively created two classes of refugee: resettled refugees who were granted permanent residence; and those who came to Australia first and were subsequently subjected to an additional and prolonged period of uncertainty regarding their future. Although this visa was replaced by the protection visa system introduced in March 1994, its rationale confirmed that from the perspective of the Australian state, compliance with migration policy and border controls was more important than an objective need for protection as a criterion for official inclusion.

The changes to the visa regime for on-shore applicants were accompanied in December 1990 by changes to the determination process (JSMCR 1992: 120). A new three-stage procedure was introduced: a primary stage for applications to be assessed and decisions taken quickly on the grant of refugee status; a review stage, including an examination by a new refugee status review committee of a negative assessment; and in the event of a failed application, ministerial discretion to grant temporary stay on humanitarian grounds in exceptional and compelling circumstances[16] providing 'the applicants were not prohibited entrants or, after 1 July 1991, unlawful non-citizens' (Crock 1998: 257). The review committee was comprised of representatives from the Department of Immigration, the Department of Foreign Affairs and Trade, and Attorney General's Department. Its function was to review, on the papers, cases rejected at first instance and to recommend to the minister the grant or refusal of refugee status (Crock 1998: 257). A notable feature of the committee was that it included for the first time a non-government representative nominated by the Refugee Council of Australia. It also continued the practice of having an observer from UNHCR. Such NGO involvement was justified as a means of ensuring that 1951 Convention requirements were broadly applied within the decision making process. However, as part of a closed bureaucratic system, it also gave added imprimatur to refusals and more importantly, the delegitimisation and physical consequences that followed for those who were refused.

In any event, the review committee was short-lived. In July 1992, the minister announced the establishment of the Refugee Review Tribunal (RRT), which would be similar to the Immigration Review Tribunal and operate as a 'quasi inquisitorial body with sweeping powers to set the parameters of any appeal'; would provide an oral hearing but no right to representation; and would conduct its hearings in private (Crock 1998: 257–259). The RRT's decisions were to be final and its jurisdiction was limited to hearing appeals against adverse determinations by the immigration department. It had no authority to consider other aspects of the refugee's situation such as detention, delays in decision-making or possible entitlement to social benefits and no power to recommend that the minister grant entry on humanitarian grounds for those who failed to meet the Convention definition of refugee. Appeals against the tribunal's decisions to the higher courts could only be made by way of judicial review on points of law.

While the RRT was intended to provide an independent and transparent system of review, it was also designed to substantially reduce, if not eliminate, judicial intervention in the decision making process. The role of the courts in reviewing and in some cases overturning departmental and ministerial decisions on refugee claims clearly irritated the government and provoked sustained attacks in parliament against the legal profession for unnecessarily interfering in and delaying the decision-making process for their own benefit,[17] especially in the case of the Cambodian asylum seekers (Hamilton 1993a and 1993b). In this context, the introduction of the RRT was an attempt to consolidate the state's exclusionary powers within the executive and the bureaucracy. And although the government's reforms of the determination system were criticised by the opposition for not going far enough,[18] the trajectory towards a tighter state response was clear.

The strict limitations imposed on the scope of humanitarian entry to those who failed in formal asylum applications further curtailed the entitlements of forced migrants and reinforced the state's decision making monopoly. Prior to 1989, the minister's discretion to grant permanent residence on humanitarian and compassionate grounds was broadly defined and liberally interpreted by the courts (Crock 1998: 130–134; Brennan 2003: 34–35); with applicants able to receive humanitarian status if they could 'show that if they were forced to leave Australia, they would face a situation that would invoke strong feelings of pity or compassion in the ordinary member of the Australian public'.[19]

The 1989 changes sought to prevent the issue of humanitarian protection visas 'to persons fleeing a natural or ecological disaster, or a general situation involving a political or social upheaval'; and to limit the exercise of the minister's discretion to persons facing a 'significant threat to personal security on return as a result of targeted actions by persons in the country of origin' (Crock 1998: 131; 257), with no review to the courts. The changes separated the concepts of compassionate and humanitarian entry and by forcing those seeking protection visas to first apply for refugee status, tied them to the notion of the failed refugee. This contributed to the hierarchy of legitimacy that was operating in relation to various categories of forced and unauthorised migrant. Meanwhile, the government streamlined the refugee claim procedures to impose stricter time limits on when applications should be lodged; requiring all relevant information to be lodged at the application stage; and restricting repeat applications (JSCMR 1992: 122–123).

The thrust of these changes was to impose a greater onus on applicants to prove their case and to relieve pressure on the state in the enforcement of border controls it had created. This further highlighted the developing double standard in the treatment of those asylum seekers who, having applied while legally on-shore were able to live in the community and access some welfare services pending consideration of their claims; and border claimants, such as the boat arrivals, who were detained. The method of entry and the level of compliance with border control was becoming the defining factor in the state's response to claims for protection.

Mandatory detention and the new legal regime

The detention, pending consideration of their claims for asylum, of those on board the unauthorised boat that arrived in November 1989, was emblematic of the Australian government's determination to enforce its authority over the entry process and laid the basis for the mandatory detention policy formalised by the 1992 *Migration Reform Act*. The legal basis on which unauthorised boat arrivals were detained in 1989 was more complicated than under the present regime. At the time, the *Migration Act* distinguished between those who arrived by sea and by air (JSCM 1994: 73–74) and gave immigration officers the power to detain boat arrivals pending the departure of their vessel from the last port of call in Australia; the grant of an entry permit; or 'until such earlier time as an authorised officer directs' (JSCM 1994: 73).

Determined to enforce the comprehensive plan of action, the immigration department made a conscious policy decision from 1989 to detain the mainly Indo-Chinese boat arrivals for the duration of the refugee status determination process rather than exercise any discretion to release. The department decided that because the unauthorised boats were burnt or confiscated for quarantine purposes, it had the authority to enforce an indefinite period of temporary custody (JSCM 1994: 73), despite the *Migration Act* provisions upon which it relied being intended originally to apply only for short periods. That particular rationale was subsequently rejected by the High Court of Australia, which declared continued detention on that basis as unlawful.[20]

However, the High Court did not challenge the main thrust of the government's detention policy. Under the 1992 *Migration Amendment Act*,[21] which was designed to retrospectively justify the detention of the Cambodians and was introduced because of ongoing litigation initiated by them in the Federal Court,[22] all 'designated persons' had to be kept in custody after 6 May 1992. A designated person was defined as a non-citizen, who *inter alia* has been on a boat in the territorial sea of Australia after 19 November 1989 and before 1 December 1992; has not presented a visa; is in Australia; and has not been granted an entry permit. It also included a non-citizen born in Australia whose mother was a designated person.[23] Custody was defined as being held in a detention centre established under the act; a prison or remand centre; a police station or watch house; or in another place approved by the minister in writing.[24] The length of detention was nominally limited to 273 days but this could be extended for the duration of legal proceedings.[25]

The precedent established by the detention provisions for the Cambodians soon formed the basis of a uniform legislative framework. Five months later, the 1992 *Migration Reform Act*, which came into operation in September 1994, abolished the distinction between visa and entry permits, replacing them with a single visa document; and introduced a distinction between lawful and unlawful citizens[26] to replace the previous categories of unprocessed, prohibited, designated, illegal and legal non-citizens. Under the act, unlawful non-citizens included undocumented border arrivals; overstayers; non-citizens whose visas have been cancelled; and those who were illegal entrants at the commencement of the act.[27]

The centrepiece of the legislation was the introduction of 'a detention regime based on the principle that detention will be mandatory for all persons who have no authority to be in Australia' (JSCM 1994: 87). Under the act, an immigration officer must detain a person in Australia's migration zone who is known or suspected to be an unlawful non-citizen, or a person seeking to enter the migration zone who on entry would be an unlawful non-citizen.[28] As with the Cambodians, detention was defined in the act as a detention centre established under the act; a prison or remand centre; a police station or watch house; or another place approved by the minister in writing.[29] Unlawful non-citizens detained by such means cannot be released, even by a court, otherwise than for removal or deportation, unless the unlawful non-citizen has made a valid application for a visa and has satisfied all the criteria for the visa.[30]

The nature and extent of the policing powers conferred by this legislation and the human rights implications of the evolving mandatory detention regime for those imprisoned by it are discussed in chapter 6. At this point, it is important to note how the official rationale for mandatory detention drew on the historical imperatives advanced for border controls and how mandatory detention contributed to a continuum of exclusionary measures that systematically nullified the very right to be a refugee, by removing any sense of independent free movement from its meaning.

First, mandatory detention was justified as a means of the state maintaining control of the migration process. As Immigration Minister Gerry Hand told parliament when introducing the retrospective provisions in May 1992:

> I believe it is crucial that all persons who come to Australia without authorisation not be released into the community. Their release would undermine the Government's strategy for determining their refugee status or entry claims. Indeed, I believe it is vital to Australia that this be prevented as far as possible. The Government is determined that a clear message be sent that migration to Australia may not be achieved by simply arriving in this country and expecting to be allowed into the community (CPD 1992a: 2372).

Second, maintaining control of the migration process was an elemental expression of national sovereignty. Using language similar to that later employed to great effect by Prime Minister Howard during the 2001 election campaign, Labor senator, Jim McKiernan

The creation of the illegitimate refugee

(1993: 4), chairman of the Joint Standing Committee on Migration, commented bluntly, 'I believe it is the government...that should determine who should be admitted to Australia...To concede that right to foreign nationals...would be a direct attack on Australia's national sovereignty'.

Third, detention would be a form of deterrence against organised criminality. Pre-empting the much greater focus on people-smuggling that developed in the latter part of the 1990s, and expressing some misplaced triumphalism, McKiernan (1993: 5) claimed Australia was avoiding the problems arising from

> '...the more liberal-minded policy of the United States' and that the 'firm government policy on detention of non-documented arrivals has...already paid dividends. The gangs who benefit from the business of carrying human flesh for profit appear to have received the message'.

Fourth, mandatory detention was a buttress for resettlement. 'Another reason', for its introduction added McKiernan (1993: 4–5), 'is my support for Australia's refugee and humanitarian program'. The 13,000 people to be chosen in the next financial year 'will be chosen for resettlement by the government and the Immigration Department in accordance with criteria established under Australian law, government policy, international conventions and protocols'. At this stage, physically turning people away from the border was not being contemplated but there would be an organised process of internal exclusion. Promised Immigration Minister Hand:

> Australia, will of course, continue to honour its statutory obligations as it has always done. Any claims made by these people will be fully and fairly considered under the available processes, and any person found to qualify for Australia's protection will be allowed to enter. Until the process is complete, however, Australia cannot afford to allow unauthorised boat arrivals to simply move into the community (CPD 1992a: 2370).

Fifth, the exclusion imposed by detention served more than the efficient operation of administrative due process. It would, according to McKiernan (1993: 4–5), reduce social conflict: 'Order will be maintained and all steps will be taken to ensure social cohesiveness and harmony of Australian society is not jeopardised'.

Sixth, detention was intended to prevent queue jumping. It was not about locking up forced migrants seeking protection in Australia but about protecting those stranded in the camps elsewhere, no matter how few would ever be offered resettlement. 'We must remember', McKiernan (1993: 7) reiterated, 'there are millions of people living in appalling refugee camps in many parts of the world. Let's not forget them. You can be assured your government will not'.

Such arguments dominated the bipartisan political discourse that surrounded the legislation. Deploying some of the state's most visible, coercive and damaging powers against small numbers of unauthorised asylum seekers became a norm of government policy; and a defining part of the routine, complex, culture of control within an immigration department committed to maintaining the integrity of a universal visa system. And while the department distanced itself from some of the more bellicose political pronouncements about the deterrence value of mandatory detention,[31] the incorporation of wide-ranging, non-discretionary policing measures into the refugee determination process impacted on state responses to asylum seekers and any other person whose immediate lack of authorised migrant status rendered them suspicious.

Although there had not been a great clamour for the use of mandatory detention, possibly because of the way it had been informally introduced in 1989, its introduction was routinely justified by the government as a response to public sentiment. In the circles of official politics, there was a widespread view that elite opinion in relation to refugees was far more accommodating than that of the public at large (Kingston 1993; McAllister 1993). Leaving aside the vagaries of what actually constitutes public opinion and how best to assess it, the historical role of the Australian state in legitimising the exclusion of unauthorised migrants should not be ignored. Nor should the conscious arguments of politicians who promoted the policy as a necessary act of sovereign interest or who

The creation of the illegitimate refugee

promoted detention and offshore processing as an act of self defence against an organised threat to national security and identity.

The inquiries conducted by the Joint Standing Committee on Migration Regulations into Australia's refugee and humanitarian system in 1990 and 1991 (JSCMR 1992), and the Joint Senate Committee on Migration into the government's detention policy in 1993 (JSCM 1994), also helped legitimise mandatory detention as a long term bipartisan strategy. These cross-party parliamentary committees played a similar role to the earlier Galbally and Fitzgerald inquiries in providing a hegemonic rationale and bipartisan institutional support for policy shifts within the politically volatile migration area.

The JSCMR Inquiry located detention as an important element of an on-shore refugee and humanitarian system committed to 'achieving a balance between refuge and control'.[32] Control, in the eyes of a committee seemingly devoted to better systems management, was interpreted according to its administrative rather than human impact. Concerned by the 'confusing array of provisions' the committee recommended that:

> The provisions in the Migration Act 1958 relating to the detention arrangements for border claimants be rewritten in a simplified and comprehensible manner. The rewritten provisions should not make legal distinctions concerning custody of border claimants based on the mode of transport which they have used to travel to Australia or their method of arrival in or at Australia. The rewritten provisions also should not use a variety of terms ... Rather the provisions should use...a single descriptive term for border applicants (JSCMR 1992: 159–160).

Such streamlining, which was implemented in the second round of changes, was tied explicitly to the maintenance of the Port Hedland immigration detention centre, which had opened in October 1991:

> As for the facilities at Port Hedland, a number of Committee members have visited this centre and other refugee processing centres in other parts of the world. These Committee members

Border Crimes

were struck particularly by the high standard of facilities at Port Hedland. The problems experienced by those detained at Port Hedland appear to derive from the term of detention rather than the location of or conditions at the facility (JSCMR 1992: 178).

The 'problems' to which the committee referred were manifested by the transfer of ten Chinese boat arrivals from Port Hedland to the equally remote state prison in Roebourne following escapes and unrest in April 1992. While the escalating protests by immigration detainees, which included hunger strikes and attempted suicides, were partly a response to the length of detention, more fundamental questions about the nature and impact of the detention regime also arose.[33] The committee did not consider these, although arguably this would not have been outside the terms of reference. Instead, the committee promoted detention, along with restricted access to legal assistance, as a means of more efficiently processing the refugee applications and recommended that:

> '...the Government retain the policy of holding border claimants for refugee status in detention until such time as their applications can be processed; the detention facility at Port Hedland be maintained to ensure that processing targets in relation to border claimants for refugee status are met; priority to be directed to the expeditious processing of border claimants, with adequate resources to be directed to the Department...to ensure that processing targets are met; and public funding be available through the Department...for the provision of legal advice and assistance to border claimants in relation to the preparation of primary applications...[and] thereafter...to refugee claimants seeking review of a refusal decision...via the legal Aid Commission, based on the merits of the particular case' (JSCMR 1992: 179–180).

The legitimisation of mandatory detention on such a utilitarian basis was continually reinforced by a range of practices and policies conceived almost exclusively within the paradigm of maintaining the integrity of the processing system. Contributing to this, the Joint Standing Committee on Migration inquiry into detention practices rejected the alternative responses to unauthorised arrivals put before

The creation of the illegitimate refugee

it. Within quite narrow terms of reference, the committee undertook a comprehensive survey of the legislation relevant case law and international human rights obligations to which the Australian government was formally committed including the Refugee Convention and Protocol; the interpretive UNHCR Executive Committee Conclusions on detention; the International Covenant on Civil and Political Rights; the Convention Against Torture; and the Convention on the Rights of the Child. It compared Australia's unique detention regime with the practices of other Western states; received 94 written submissions (most of which opposed essential aspects of the policy and its arbitrary nature); and heard extensive oral evidence.

Despite the diverse range of critical material before it, the committee's report contained only a limited discussion of the human rights implications of detention. The 'best interests of the child' requirement in the Convention on the Rights of the Child was interpreted as meaning children should be kept in detention with their parents, rather than provide a reason for releasing entire families (JSCM 1994: 155). Assurances from the immigration department and Australian Protective Services that concerns, such as those raised in reports produced by the Human Rights and Equal Opportunity Commission and the Australian Council of Churches about the quality of staff and services in the centres, were being addressed were presented in a positive light along with a recommendation for the establishment of an Immigration Detention Centres Advisory Committee (JSCM 1994: 169–194).

The committee rejected comparisons made between immigration detention centres and prisons; and even more so comparisons between detention centres and refugee camps in countries such as Hong Kong, Indonesia, Malaysia, Pakistan and Thailand (JSCM 1994: 189–190). It adopted the general thrust of the evidence provided by the Department of Immigration and Ethnic Affairs and Attorney General's Department, concluding that:

> As a basic principle, the Committee asserts that Australia must retain its sovereign right to determine who may enter, the conditions under which a non-citizen's entry may be permitted,

and the circumstances under which a non-citizen may be permitted to stay or may be removed from Australia...

In this regard, the Committee is of the view that those who arrive in Australia without authorisation or with invalid authorisation should be detained upon arrival. To do otherwise would compromise Australia's system of immigration control. In addition, detention of unauthorised arrivals ensures that the community is not exposed to unknown or undetected health or security risks. In the Committee's view, Australia's immigration control system must be upheld (JSCM 1994: 148–149).

While the one dissenting voice on the committee, Senator Christabel Chamarette, argued that the government should base its policy on its 'right *not* to detain' (JSCM 1994: 201–214, emphasis in original), the overwhelming emphasis in the committee majority's report on maintaining state control over entry was punctuated only by concerns about the length of time people should remain in detention, an issue raised following investigations by the Australian Institute of Criminology, the Human Rights and Equal Opportunity Commission and the Australian Council of Churches (JSCM 1994: 166–170). The committee reiterated the view of the Joint Standing Committee on Migration Regulations that the new procedures must prevent a repetition of the lengthy detention experienced by the Cambodians (JSCM 1994: 147). Senator Chamarette addressed this by proposing a limit of two months detention for 'preliminary identity, security and health checks' (JSCM 1994: 212); but the committee's report asserted that 'previous lengthy detention should not serve as an indication of what will happen in the future' and pointed to the 'important changes' aimed at 'minimising delays in the determination process' (JSCM 1994: 148).

The committee proposed that under the immigration minister's power to 'prescribe certain classes of non-citizens as being eligible to apply for the grant of bridging visa', 'unprocessed border detainees who have been held in detention for more than six months' should be eligible pending consideration of

> ...whether the applicant has a special need on the basis of age, health or previous experiences of torture or trauma; whether the

applicant has satisfied appropriate health, character and security checks; the likelihood that the applicant would abscond if granted a bridging visa; whether there is a reasonable basis for the applicant's claim to refugee status; the timeliness of the lodgment of the application for refugee status; the extent to which the applicant co-operated with the DIEA in the provision of information relevant to the applicant's claims; whether there will be adequate support arrangements if the applicant is released into the community; and Australia's international obligations' (JSCM 1994: 154).

It is unclear from the committee's report whether it was envisaged that many people would be released under these provisions. The committee's assertion that the 'Cambodian situation' was relatively unique certainly was proved wrong and also avoided consideration of the implications of detention per se. The regulations that came into force with the detention provisions in September 1994[34] adopted the thrust of the committee's recommendations but as the Human Rights and Equal Opportunity Commission (HREOC 1998: 20–21) subsequently found:

> It should be noted that these classes are very limited in practice. For example, only two children arriving as boat people or born in detention have been released of a possible total of 581 since bridging visas were introduced. Where it is thought to be in the child's best interests to stay with his or her parents, release will be denied.

> The release of people on the ground that they are elderly is rare since few people of 75 or more travel by boat or otherwise without authority. Even in the case of people affected by past torture or trauma, the presumption is in favour of continued detention. Finally, cases in which a primary decision has not been made within six months of application are increasingly rare. It should be noted that the Minister has no discretion to release people, other than in the prescribed classes, where the primary decision was made (in the negative) within six months but the applicant has instituted an appeal.

The committee's confirmation that the detention policy was compliant with human rights obligations became a recurrent justification of the policy in response to subsequent and escalating criticisms of the impact of detention. Having been refined by the parliamentary inquiry process, official discourse became a form of doublespeak that ignored or denied a fundamental disjuncture between even the baseline protections of international conventions and the Australian government's assertion of its sovereignty. Ideologically, this disjuncture was subsumed by the normalisation of detention as a legitimate exercise of arbitrary state power, paralleled in Australian history only by the use of internment during the two world wars and as with those experiences, ensuring the alienation and criminalisation of those detained.

Detention and the criminalisation of unauthorised migrants

The use of a blanket (as opposed to mandatory) detention policy by the Australian state is not unprecedented. During World War One, the 1914 *War Precautions Act* gave the Australian military authorities extensive powers to intern 'enemy subjects with whose conduct they were not satisfied', including from 1915, 'disloyal natural born subjects of enemy descent and...persons of hostile origin or association' (Fischer 1989: 65). A total of 6,890 people were interned under these provisions in camps administered by the Australian army (Fischer 1989: 77). About 4,500 had been resident in Australia at the outbreak of war; the rest were either taken off ships arriving in Australia or transported to Australia from other parts of the Commonwealth at the request of the British authorities (Fischer 1989: 77). The majority of the internees were of German descent, many of them vulnerable and socially marginalised. They also included political and labour movement activists, whose opposition to Australia's participation in the war, the government regarded as a threat to national security. At the conclusion of the war, most were deported (Fischer 1989: 77–120).

During World War Two, the 1939–40 *National Security Act* provided similar powers for the internment of 'enemy aliens' and prisoners of war held by the allied forces (Saunders 2000: 114).

The creation of the illegitimate refugee

Japanese nationals were especially targeted; 97 percent of all registered aliens of Japanese descent were interned, compared with less than one third of aliens of Italian or German descent (NAA 2004: 2–3). In total, approximately 7,000 Australian residents and 8,000 transported prisoners of war, including substantial numbers of refugees, were interned, although many were able to remain at the conclusion of hostilities (NAA 2004: 2–4).

Unlike the current detention policies, wartime internment was enforced under specific legislation associated with actual full-scale military conflicts in which enemies or potential threats to national security were defined in relation to a particular hostile state. In the case of the Second World War, there was also a strong racial bias in the policy, consistent with both the intensity of the conflict between Australia and Japan and the operation of the White Australia policy. Notwithstanding such distinctions, internment was an important means by which the state segregated specific social groups, regardless of their individual activities. As Fischer (1989: 66) comments in relation to German-Australian detainees during World War One, 'by one stroke of the pen, they had been transformed from citizens with full civil rights to outcasts who could be treated like criminals by the military authorities, worse off in fact than criminals who at least could enjoy the protection of the law'.

A similar dynamic can be observed in relation to the mandatory detention policy, although the concept of enemy alien operates as a more amorphous ideological construct in the current context. Introduced as a specific response to the Cambodian arrivals but generalised as a response to all unauthorised non-citizens, Australia's mandatory detention policy was from the outset an arbitrary and coercive measure of institutional containment. The indeterminate deprivation of individual liberty the policy necessitated gave visible expression to the processes of criminalisation it entrenched. Leaving aside the numerous human rights issues that arise, the locking up of unauthorised migrants in prison like conditions, often in very remote locations, exacerbated their physical separation from the wider Australian community and contributed to their stigmatisation as deviant outsiders, whose individual circumstances were concealed. Mandatory detention also operated as a normalising form of punishment, meted out with little accountability, officially to exorcise and deter the multiple forms of deviance that the policy itself helped to sustain. Beyond the routine administrative and political decision making processes, the separation of detainees is both physical and ideological. The legal framework imposed by the Australian state marginalises and isolates detainees outside the social borders of the national polity and undermines the refugees' claim to a sense of a social solidarity. The subtle legal distinctions between the unauthorised, the unlawful and the criminal are blurred by the certainty that these people are alien non-citizens, with questionable loyalties and claims to protection from the Australian state. The unlawfulness of their entry enables them to be associated with various forms of moral deviance such as dishonesty, cheating and queue jumping.

Moreover, the growing focus on people-smuggling during the 1990s and terrorism since 2001 has drawn more sinister associations between unlawful entrants and the most dangerous forms of organised crime. Specific forms of protest such as hunger striking and lip sewing have been presented as manipulative. Rioting and demonstrating have been condemned as wanton and ungrateful vandalism; while escape attempts generated calls for even greater security. Allegations such as those arising from the 'Children Overboard' episode, even though they were subsequently proven to be unfounded, were used to great effect to discredit the moral scruples of the refugees concerned and to justify the government's decision to intercept unauthorised boats and detain those on board.

The alienation of refugees by the state on such bases enables the punitive consequences of detention to be rendered secondary to the primary imperatives of deterrence and sovereignty. The criminality of the refugee rests not in legal fact or due process but in the metaphoric impact of terms such as 'criminal' and 'illegal' to describe persons whose personae as refugees rightly attract the disciplinary powers of the state. Further, the automatic incarceration of such people removes any ongoing public process of acknowledging or evaluating the detainee's individual circumstances. Instead, a self-fulfilling cycle of locking people up because they represent a risk helps maintain a public perception that they are in

The creation of the illegitimate refugee

fact just that. Such an analysis of mandatory detention is clearly at odds with official justifications advanced for it. But as is discussed in the next chapter, even in its own terms, mandatory detention failed to operate as a deterrent to further unauthorised arrivals or to deny the legitimacy of the refugees' claims.

Notes

[1] Approximately 95,000 were resettled between April 1975 and June 1985 (DIEA 1985: 68-69).

[2] Of the 14,769 people resettled under the Refugee and Special Humanitarian Programs in 1983-1984, 10,092 were Indo-Chinese; 1,964 were from Eastern Europe (mainly Poland); 982 were from the Middle East (mainly Lebanon) and 838 were from Latin America (mainly El Salvador) (DIEA 1984: 35-36). Refugees from more than 60 countries - about half of whom were Indo-Chinese - were admitted in 1987-1988 (DILGEA 1988: 184).

[3] The numbers granted entry declined from 21,917 in 1981/1982 to 10,411 in 1989/1990 (JSCMR 1992: 3, 35-36)

[4] The humanitarian component grew from 1,701 in 1981/1982 to 10,411 in 1989/1990, while the refugee component decreased from 20,216 to 1,537 (JSCMR 1992:3, 35-36).

[5] UNHCR's role in implementing the plan was heavily criticised. For example, James Hathaway, a leading authority on international refugee law, concluded: 'Overall, the UNHCR has unfortunately been co-opted into legitimizing the tacit pact between first asylum and resettlement states, relegating the explicit human rights mandate to the realm of pure symbolism....The final result is that no party to the ...Plan...has been both willing and able to seriously champion a human rights inspired interpretation of the Convention refugee definition' (Hathaway 1993: 702).

[6] Although generally referred to as Cambodian refugees, their nationalities were a mixture of Cambodian, Vietnamese and Chinese. See DIMIA (2004).

[7] For example, the *Sunday Age* warned of an 'invasion in the north' by 'a wave of boat people and illegal Indonesian fishermen' (Graham 1990). *The Australian* quoted an immigration department official expecting more such boats but ruling out 'mass arrivals on the scale of Darwin 10 years ago' (AAP 1990). *The Age,* also carried a front page report on 24 April 1990 claiming a syndicate in Phnom Penh was selling boat passages to Australia for up to $5,000 and that eight fishing boats had recently left the port of Kompong Som (Murdoch 1990).

[8] Extract from interview on *A Current Affair*, cited in *Mok Gek Bouy v The Minister for Immigration, Local Government and Ethnic Affairs and Malcolm Patterson* (1993) 47 FCR 1.

[9] During his evidence in *Mok Gek Bouy*, Hand described Hawke's statements as 'ill advised, improper and that for someone who ought to have known better, stupid'. He later described the term 'economic refugees' as 'a nonsense term' and 'a contradiction in terms' before concluding 'Evans and Hawke were wrong, and I think they now appreciate that they were wrong (transcript 1686-87; 1705-1706).

[10] For example, *The Age* ran a series of articles between 29 December and 6 January under the collective heading 'The Refugee Crisis'. Prominence was given to a 'worst case scenario' envisaged by immigration officials of '5,000 boat people' heading for Australia (Hill 1995).

[11] Migration Legislation Amendment Bill (No.4) 1994.

[12] For example, at a function to mark the tenth anniversary of the Community Refugee Settlement Scheme in December 1989, immigration minister, Robert Ray, told the audience Australia shared concerns about 'the large numbers of people seeking a better life who presented themselves as asylum seekers' and that 'if we use valuable resettlement places to help them, we may deny freedom and security to a corresponding number of genuine refugees in precarious circumstances' (MILGEA 1989b).

[13] The regular and complex changes to the legislation and regulations during this period are outlined in Germov and Motta (2003: 65-75). Here, I am primarily interested in drawing out the main trends, rather than analysing the intricacies of the changes.

[14] The Immigration Minister was quoted on 8 June 1989 as acknowledging that 'Australia will have to accept any of the 15,405 Chinese nationals in the country who can prove they have a genuine fear of persecution in their country' (Peake 1989).

[15] The government also sought to restrict humanitarian claims 'by introducing a requirement that countries from which humanitarian flows emanated had to be gazetted before a person could be considered for humanitarian resettlement' (NPC 1991: 132-133) . This system was extensively criticized and not implemented (Crawford 1990; NPC 1991: 133).

[16] The minister's discretion was only to be exercised when a person the person faced a 'significant threat to personal security on return as a result of targeted actions by persons in the country of return' (Crock 1998: 257).

[17] See, for example, the debates in the House of Representatives on the Migration Amendment Bill 1992 on 5 May 1992; and the Migration Reform Bill 1992 on 4 and 11 November 1992.

[18] An example is the amendment moved by the Shadow Immigration Minister, Philip Ruddock, to the 1992 Migration Reform Bill, deploring 'the Government's failure to control the refugee determination process'; noting 'the lamentable time delays in moving to reform the refugee determination system'; and regretting 'that the further proposals put by the Coalition to limit judicial appeals, to require leave to access review procedures and to redeploy staff to the refugee screening process have been ignored' (CPD 1992b: 3145).

[19] Dr.Arthur, Director of the immigration department's asylum policy branch, quoted Crock (1998: 134).

[20] See *Chu Kheng Lim v The Minister for Immigration, Local Government and Ethnic Affairs* (1992) 176 CLR 1.

[21] See Section 54 *Migration Act* 1958, introduced by *Migration Amendment Act* 1992.

[22] The context of the legislation is discussed in the *Lim* case, cited above. See also Crock (1995: 37-39) and Penovic (2004).

[23] Section 54(k) *Migration Act* 1958.

[24] Section 11(a) *Migration Act* 1958.

[25] Section 182 *Migration Act* 1958.

[26] Section 54W *Migration Reform Act* 1992.

[27] Section 15 *Migration Reform Act* 1992.

[28] Section 54W *Migration Reform Act* 1992.

[29] Section 4 *Migration Reform Act* 1992.

[30] Section 54ZD(3) *Migration Reform Act* 1992.

[31] In its submission to the Senate inquiry into detention the department described mandatory detention as 'only one component in efforts to discourage unauthorised arrivals. Australia's universal visa system and other border control measures are of greater significance' (JSCM 1994: Vol 3: 655).

[32] This was the subtitle of the JSCMR Report (JSCMR 1992).

[33] See chapter 6 below.

[34] Section 72(2) *Migration Act* 1958 and *Migration Regulation* 2.20.

Chapter 5

Declaring war in the Pacific

The birth of 'border protection'

On 26 August 2001, the captain of a Norwegian container vessel, the MV *Tampa,* answered a mayday call and rescued 433 mainly Afghan asylum seekers en route to Australia aboard an overloaded fishing vessel, KM *Palapa 1*. The 438 passengers on board this profoundly unseaworthy vessel were extremely vulnerable and included two pregnant women, 43 children and a man with a broken leg. Upon being rescued, between 'a dozen and twenty adults had collapsed unconscious on the deck' (Marr and Wilkinson 2003: 19). But far from being lauded as an act of humanitarianism, the *Tampa's* actions provided the catalyst for a federal election contest that in the wake of September 11 was subsumed by a national security panic over refugees and terrorism.

Leaving aside the government's use of the episode for electoral purposes, the *Tampa* events were a turning point in Australian state responses to unauthorised refugees. Determined to channel all refugee entry into Australia through its selective resettlement program, the Howard government instituted a 'Pacific Solution' that took established methods of exclusion to a new level. Ideologically, the full-scale military mobilisation triggered by the actions of the *Tampa's* captain placed preventing a small number of unauthorised boats from reaching Australian territory at the centre of the government's national security agenda. In more practical terms, the interception of unauthorised boats was an exercise in state force designed to entrench offshore processing and detention as the core components of Australia's response to unauthorised asylum seekers.

The *Tampa* events were a defining moment of the 'border protection emergency' of the late 1990s when, despite the established practice of mandatory detention, unauthorised boat

Declaring war in the Pacific

traffic carrying refugees from the oppressive regimes and civil conflicts in Afghanistan, Iran and Iraq suddenly increased. From a criminological perspective, the most important feature of this period was the rapid evolution of a continuum of abusive and exclusionary measures, based on the policies and practices established by various Australian governments since the late 1970s that demonstrated the Australian state's systematic alienation, criminalisation and abuse of unauthorised migrants.

For much of the 1990s, there were very few unauthorised boat arrivals in Australia. The numbers fluctuated from a low of 78 people on 3 boats in 1991–1992; to a sudden peak of 1,171 on 21 boats in 1994–1995; before declining to 157 on 13 boats in 1997-1998 (DIMIA 2004). However, this pattern began to change in 1998–1999 when 920 people arrived on 42 boats; and spiked suddenly over the next two years with 4,174 arriving in 75 boats during 1999–2000 and 4,141 in 54 boats during 20002001 (DIMIA 2004). Set against the numbers of overstayers who had legally arrived in Australia and the numbers seeking asylum at the borders of Europe, these were negligible statistics. Nevertheless, once the boat traffic started picking up, the imagery of waves, floods and tsunamis to describe boat arrivals flourished within mainstream political discourse and across the full spectrum of the media. Providing a flavour of the supposedly more serious and objective coverage of the time, ABC radio's *PM* program introduced its story on 2 November 1999, by commenting: 'If the latest arrests of illegal immigrants is a wave, the next one could be a Tsunami. Three hundred and fifty illegal immigrants, mostly Iraqis, are being detained in Western Australia, more than double the previous record' (Vincent 1999).

While the language used in this piece came straight from the genre of crime reporting, the refugees in question had not been arrested in formal terms, nor had they illegally entered, given that it is not an offence under the Refugee Convention to cross a border without authorisation in order to claim asylum. Moreover, the fact that detention numbers had doubled was a product of a detention policy that had plainly failed to fulfil its stated aim of deterrence, rather than any criminality on the part of the refugees. However, there seemed little room for such legal niceties within the collective mindset of the mainstream media. By the following week, *PM* utilised an extravagant mixture of metaphors to opine that the 'wave of illegal immigrants...appears to be spiralling out of control' (Lowth 1999). By 18 November, 'Refugee crisis warning' was emblazoned across the front page of the *Age* (MacDonald 1999). Three days later, its Sunday edition carried a profile of Immigration Minister Ruddock under the banner 'Holding back the tide...It's his job to stop the human flow'; while in case the point was lost, the photo caption had the minister 'contemplating King Canute' (Heinrichs 1999).

Such emotive and misleading language often came direct from the federal government. On 18 November, a ministerial media release warned 'We are facing the biggest assault to our borders by unauthorised arrivals ever' (MIMA 1999a). On the same day, the *Age* quoted minister Ruddock's estimate based on unsourced 'intelligence reports' that 10,000 people were trying to come to Australia this way, including 'whole (Middle East) villages'. 'If it was a national emergency several weeks ago', the Minister claimed, 'it's gone up something like 10 points on the Richter scale since then' (MacDonald 1999). The minister's intelligence sources were never seriously interrogated and his predicted levels of unauthorised boat traffic never materialised; but the perception that Australia's borders were being targeted by unscrupulous smuggling gangs and devious 'forum shoppers' became mainstream political parlance during late 1999.

This was largely a manufactured crisis, constituted solely within the established border-policing paradigm. Already conceptualised around resettlement and the earlier responses to unauthorised boat arrivals, refugee policy underwent a further ideological recalibration to become inseparable from 'border protection', a defining concept that invoked reformulated fears of a foreign invasion. In such an atmosphere, border protection became an existential imperative in defence of Australian sovereignty and a social order fatally vulnerable to informal travel; while the parameters of official discourse were stultified by the focus on the 'illegality' of the refugees' entry, the threats this posed to the integrity of the state's refugee program and the collateral risks to national security. In pursuit of this perverse inversion of the concept of protection, the government embarked upon a determined offensive against people smuggling, the removal of permanent refuge and the denial of family reunion. As a result, boat arrivals were further marginalised as a deviant sub-class of 'illegal' refugees, despite the overwhelming validity, in moral if not convention terms, of their claims to protection.

The government's focus on people smuggling operations was a reaction to the prospect of continued unauthorised arrivals by refugees from states, notably Iraq and Afghanistan,[1] with human rights records consistently criticised by the Australian government,[2] international institutions such as the United Nations, and NGOs such as Amnesty International. Those claiming asylum from these countries could not simply be rejected as economic refugees,[3] although efforts to undermine their legitimacy were routinely made (Stani 2000).[4] Instead, the involvement of 'organised people smugglers forming a chain from the home nation areas through Southeast Asia (especially Thailand, Malaysia and Indonesia) to Australia' (Hugo 2001:31) became the central emphasis of government policy and was cohered at the institutional and legislative levels around the *Migration Legislation Amendment Act (No.1)* 1999; the recommendations of the Coastal Surveillance Task Force; and the 1999 Border Protection Legislation Amendment Bill.

The *Migration Legislation Amendment Act (No.1)* entrenched people smuggling at the most serious end of the criminal justice spectrum and targeted people involved at all levels of the smuggling enterprise. Under the legislation it became an offence punishable by up to 20 years imprisonment for organising or facilitating the entry of a group of five or more unlawful non-citizens into Australia; presenting false or forged documents; making false or misleading statements; or passing documents to assist in gaining unlawful entry. Within this legislative framework, being associated with unauthorised boat arrivals was tantamount to committing murder or rape.

The wider policy implications were spelt out by the Coastal Surveillance Task Force that was established in April 1999 to make recommendations on the strengthening of coastal surveillance procedures and systems (ANAO 2002: 77). The task force was chaired by Max Moore-Wilton, the Secretary to the Department of the Prime Minister and Cabinet, a senior hand-picked official who was to play a key role in formulating the Australian state's response to the *Tampa*. When the task force reported in June, the prime minister accepted all of its recommendations and announced a '$124 million boost for the fight against illegal immigration' (Prime Minister of Australia 1999). The package included plans to increase the levels of coastal surveillance; strengthen liaison between Coastwatch, Defence and other state agencies; post Australian immigration officers in major source and transit countries; conclude bilateral agreements with source and transit countries for co-operation on people smuggling issues and to provide for the return of illegal arrivals; push for the conclusion of the protocol on people smuggling to the UN Convention on Transnational Organised Crime; and establish a high level Information Oversight Committee, chaired by the Office of National Assessments, to coordinate information and intelligence on people smuggling operations (PMA 1999). A further series of budget allocations in May 2000 committed $64.7 million for the consolidation of enforcement measures in source and transit regions (ANAO 2002: 79).

Although not expressed in such terms, these measures indicated the government's intention to develop a Pacific Solution. The 1999 Border Protection Legislation Amendment Bill authorised a significant extension of state power by giving Australian customs and defence force officers legislative authority, including outside of Australian territorial waters, to board, chase, search, move and destroy ships and aircraft believed to be involved in people smuggling operations to Australia (Grimm 1999: 5–16). The granting of extra-territorial jurisdiction foreshadowed the naval interdiction efforts central to the *Tampa* events; and helped shift the policy paradigm for unauthorised arrivals solidly into the realm of policing operations designed to 'maintain the integrity of Australia's borders against attempted intrusions of the criminal elements behind most people smuggling operations' and 'ensure that the organisers of this criminal activity are not beyond the reach of our laws' (CPD 1999a: 10147, 10151).

These attempts to reduce forced migration to a policing and security issue were reinforced by the government's decision to remove the possibility of unauthorised arrivals claiming immediate permanent protection. In October 1999, the immigration minister announced that unauthorised arrivals found to be 'genuine refugees' would only be given a three year temporary protection visa or a short term safe haven visa[5] (MIMA 1999a), at the expiry of which the refugee would have to re-apply for protection. The minister claimed that the introduction of temporary protection visas 'would…remove incentives to forum shoppers who might otherwise have considered Australia as their country of protection over closer and more logical alternatives' (MIMA 1999a). Whether this was a successful form of deterrence is highly questionable but the introduction of temporary protection visas and further restrictions in 2001 did formalise the hierarchy of legitimacy that Australia's preference for resettlement had established in the preceding period.

There were now two classes of refugee in Australia: resettled refugees, who were granted permanent residence with access to the full range of government services and benefits and, importantly an entitlement to family reunion; and unauthorised arrival refugees, with limited access to services and benefits, no rights to family reunion and in contravention of the 1951 Convention,[6] no right to re-enter the country should they leave for any reason. The Australian government justified this demarcation of refugees according to their mode of entry on the basis of a narrow reading of the Refugee Convention that precluded any obligation on the part of the receiving state to provide permanent protection. Convention requirements not to refoule refugees became the baseline for a policy of total state discretion over which refugees would enter the country and on what basis. This not only allowed for unauthorised arrivals to be singled out for exclusionary and discriminatory measures, subjected to prolonged periods of uncertainty about their futures and vulnerable to return,[7] but also reinforced an attitude that all refugees derived their legitimacy from the government's selective humanitarianism, rather than their individual rights to movement and protection.

The Australian state's shift towards a temporary protection regime contravened a number of established refugee rights and was clearly deviant in relation to international practice. No other country granted temporary status to refugees who had been through a full asylum determination system and been assessed as refugees in accordance with the 1951 Convention. The requirement that refugees re-prove their claims in light of new circumstances, several years later, in order to obtain a renewal of their protection visas, had 'no justification in international law' and was a *misuse and distortion* of temporary protection' (HRW 2003b, emphasis in original); a status historically used in circumstances of sudden, large scale movement and which included mechanisms for accessing permanent protection and family reunion. Moreover, the burden imposed on refugees to re-prove their claims defied international practice and case law that required 'host authorities…to show that an apparent change of circumstances in the country of origin is significant, effective, durable, substantial and clearly removes a fear of persecution from the individuals concerned' (HRW 2003b).

As an exercise of state power, the temporary protection regime operated as a form of punishment to an already traumatised cohort of refugees (Leach and Mansouri 2004; Steele et al 2006:63). As the awful experiences of Amal Basry and her fellow passengers on the SIEV X demonstrated, temporary protection also prolonged the separation of family members and acted as an incentive for some refugees to take extreme risks to try and bring their families together. The shift towards temporary protection also provided an insight into the political bi-partisanship that characterised and helped legitimise the Pacific Solution. While there were sporadic spats between the government and the Labor opposition over specific details, Labor's support for the key legislation and policy thrust of the government's response to unauthorised migration enabled an institutional consensus to cohere within the Australian state that fixed the terms of public debate within an exclusionist and punitive framework. There were a number of dimensions to this.

Declaring war in the Pacific

First, the fact that the previous Labor government had introduced mandatory detention made it easier to argue that measures such as temporary protection were an important adjunct to the policy of 'defend, deter and detain'. Labor had also used a form of temporary protection for Chinese nationals following the events at Tiananmen Square. Second, Labor's critique of government policy was pragmatic, inconsistent and based on the fear that it would be electorally damaging to be caricatured as 'soft' on refugees.[8] Third, the consensus between the Coalition and Labor was shaped by the far-right One Nation Party's policy pledge in 1998 to replace the humanitarian program with 'a program of temporary refuge of those who meet the UNHCR definition of a refugee, with repatriation when the situation resolves' (ON 1998). Moreover, the mainstreaming and legitimisation of One Nation's policies presaged a political bidding war over which party was 'toughest' on people smugglers and, by implication, refugees.

Such developments demonstrated that prior to 2001 the bipartisan consensus on unauthorised refugees was shifting in a more exclusionist direction. How this connected with Australia's history of state sponsored racism and the ideological trajectory of the Howard government is discussed in chapter 7. Here, the point to emphasise is that by the time the *Tampa* picked up the passengers of the *Palapa 1*, the Australian state was already geared for organised human rights abuses, with the border, not refugees, the concern of state and official discourses on protection.

The military response

The entry of the phrase '*Tampa* crisis' into Australia's political lexicon was the result of conscious decisions by the federal government and various organs of the state to mount a highly co-ordinated military-style operation to physically prevent unauthorised refugees gaining access to Australia's on-shore refugee determination system. In the process, some of the most vulnerable asylum seekers were exposed to considerable further risk, subjected to a sustained campaign of demonisation and unwillingly pitted against the state's overwhelming force. While Australia's impending federal election played its part in the timing and political theatre of these events, the government's capacity to transform the *Tampa's* rescue mission into a national security crisis derived not from the intrinsic nature of the hapless rescuees, but from deeply rooted policy imperatives and enforcement practices. This was not a crisis waiting to happen; but when the opportunity arose, it was choreographed with unremitting purpose.

The decision to deploy members of the elite Special Air Services (SAS) to board and seize control of the *Tampa* on 29 August 2001 was the culmination of an extraordinary stand-off between the Australian government, the *Tampa's* captain and the Norwegian government under whose flag the *Tampa* operated. Having responded to a somewhat belated mayday call from the Australian authorities on 26 August,[9] the *Tampa*, which was registered to carry 50 people and only had safety equipment for 60, found itself in the middle of a major rescue operation. The rescue took place in international waters about four hours from the Australian territory of Christmas Island. However, the Australian government was determined the passengers should be returned to Indonesia, going so far as to warn the *Tampa's* captain that he could be prosecuted for people smuggling should he attempt to enter Australian waters (Marr and Wilkinson 2003: 25).

Accordingly, the *Tampa*, which was en route to Singapore, initially set course for the Indonesian port of Merak, twelve hours away. Faced with the prospect of being returned to Indonesia, a group of distressed refugees, who had already risked their lives to claim asylum in Australia, confronted the captain and made threats that included jumping overboard unless the *Tampa* turned back. Ill-equipped, outnumbered, and faced with the possibility of the crew being overwhelmed, the *Tampa's* captain and owners agreed to change course and head for Christmas Island (Marr and Wilkinson 2003: 19–29). However, having followed maritime convention by prioritising the safety of the crew and the survivors, the *Tampa* was refused permission by the Australian government to enter Australian territorial waters. On 27 August, Christmas Island's only port was closed indefinitely, while the *Tampa* languished 12.5 nautical miles from the island, just outside the territorial zone. While conditions worsened on board the ship, the Australian government argued that where those rescued disembarked was a matter for the Indonesian or Norwegian authorities and directed its energies instead to devising means by which the *Tampa* could be prevented from entering Australia and its passengers accessing the Australian refugee determination system.

By 28 August, the Royal Flying Doctor Service (RFDS), prevented by the Australian government from providing direct medical assistance but in radio contact until the *Tampa's* satellite phone was jammed, advised:

> *Tampa* indicated 438 persons on board, 15 unconscious patients, 1 sick child, large number of people with open sores and skin infections and a broken leg. Adults have started a hunger strike, suffering from abdominal pains and diarrhoea. RFDS thought situation might worsen, possibly rapidly… Confirmed there was a mass situation medical crisis and that medical attention was urgently required (AMSA 2001).

In such circumstances, something had to give. The Australian government was not providing immediate aid and its offers of humanitarian assistance were contingent upon the *Tampa* remaining in international waters. On 29 August, the *Tampa* sent a mayday message indicating it had 'no alternative but to declare a distress situation and move close to shore for assistance' (AMSA 2001) but was again forbidden to enter Australian territorial waters. Later that morning, the 'Master indicated that he had tried to accommodate the wishes of Australian authorities but [was] unable to wait and must proceed to nearest shore immediately' (AMSA 2001). Shortly after entering Australian territorial waters, the *Tampa* was boarded by 45 members of the SAS (SSCCMI 2002: 2). Upon seizing the *Tampa*, the SAS demanded that the ship return to international waters before any medical assistance would be provided,[10] even though the number of passengers on board meant the *Tampa* 'was not seaworthy and could not lawfully sail' (Marr and Wilkinson 2003: 82). A further stand-off ensued, during which the foreign minister publicly threatened to have the *Tampa* towed out to sea. Every movement of the refugees was now strictly controlled and their conditions deteriorated.

Border Crimes

Meanwhile, the full range of Australia's state agencies was mobilised and the ship effectively sealed off from the outside world. A no-fly zone was imposed and media access prevented. The Defence Signals Directorate (DSD) unlawfully monitored conversations between the *Tampa's* owners and their lawyers, in the course of reporting to the government on all outside communications with the ship, while the Australian Security and Intelligence Organisation (ASIO) was granted a warrant to 'assist with foreign intelligence collection activity that the DSD was not empowered to conduct' (Marr and Wilkinson 2003: 85–86).

As the government hastily began putting into place its Pacific Solution, it maintained its position that the *Tampa* and the refugees were free to leave Australian waters at any time. On 3 September, the refugees were transferred to an Australian troopship which eventually removed them to detention facilities in Nauru. This was despite the Federal Court of Australia finding the refugees were detained without lawful authority and ordering that they be released onto the Australian mainland.[11]

The use of the SAS and the Royal Australian Navy (RAN) to police the *Tampa* episode signalled the beginning of a major military interception exercise. From 3 September, the Australian Defence Force (ADF) was mobilised as the central agency responsible for Operation Relex, which aimed 'to conduct surveillance and response operations in order to deter unauthorised boat arrivals from entering Australian territorial waters' (SSCCMI 2002: 14). This determined attempt to externalise border policing involved an unprecedented deployment of 25 RAN major fleet vessels that between September and December 2001, implemented a 'forward deterrence strategy' (SSCCMI 2002: 14). During the operation, the RAN blocked the entry of 2,390 asylum seekers by intercepting twelve 'Suspected Illegal Entry Vessels' (SIEVs), four of which were escorted back to Indonesia and three of which 'sank at some point during the interception or tow-back process'. (SSCCMI 2002: 14–27). The fact that the navy was now removing refugees, rather than towing their boats to the Australian mainland, substantially increased the refugees' levels of desperation and risk. There were 'numerous' threats and instances of violence and self-harm

(SSCCMI 2002: 29) and for many, prolonged periods of detention aboard unseaworthy boats.[12]

Operation Relex was a wartime level deployment that legitimised the political rhetoric of war and invasion through the mobilisation of the state's coercive powers. The military mobilisation also provided the catalyst for high levels of co-ordination between different state agencies. During Operation Relex, the ADF was backed up by 'an extensive inter-agency intelligence capability' that included the immigration department; the Australian Federal Police; the Australian Customs Service and Coastwatch; the Defence Department; the Department of Foreign Affairs and Trade; ASIO; the Office of National Assessments; and the Office of Strategic Crime Assessments (SSCCMI 2002: 19–30). As part of this pattern of consolidation and an indication of the direct political lines of control at play, the government established its People Smuggling Task Force (PST) on 27 August chaired by a senior public servant from the Department of the Prime Minister and Cabinet. This brought together the Australian Federal Police, the Australian Defence Force, Customs, Coastwatch and a number of other agencies and departments (SSCCMI, 2002: 7–8). The lack of written records makes the PST's exact role and responsibilities somewhat opaque (SSCCMI, 2002: 160–173) but it clearly 'provided advice on policy and operational issues' (SSCCMI, 2002: 161).

This centralisation of government decision making raised important questions of accountability and culpability; reflected the rise in the role and influence of unelected ministerial staff; and was a central theme in the investigation into the 'Children Overboard' affair (SSCCMI, 2002: 173–194). Overall, the PST operated as a quasi war cabinet,[13] the political role of which was to co-ordinate and centralise an agenda of border protection at the highest levels of government. This 'war' was no longer to be left as a series of potentially fragmented administrative or political decisions or ad hoc policing operations. It was to be high profile, core state business without margin for inconsistency or ambiguity. Similarly, while Operation Relex was intended to be a show of 'non-lethal force', its symbolic value outweighed the actual scale of the force imposed. Any residual suggestions that the Australian state could offer a welcoming response to unauthorised arrivals were effectively rebuffed; boats bearing refugees were to be repelled at all costs. The sense of national emergency and crisis engendered by the government ensured that future policy debate was locked into a very narrow national security discourse, institutionalised by the Pacific Solution and a government-controlled media strategy designed to dehumanise and physically isolate the refugees.

Dehumanising the 'enemy'

The government's escalation of the *Tampa*'s rescue efforts into a full-blown military confrontation was accompanied by a carefully devised media strategy designed to conceal, demonise and alienate the refugees from the wider Australian public. The jamming of the *Tampa's* satellite phone and the no-fly zone imposed in light of the SAS operation prevented journalists gaining physical access to the vessels caught up in Operation Relex. Instead, they were expected to rely upon carefully vetted information released by the defence minister. This was both a departure from the normal procedure for activities involving defence personnel force and an indication of the high level of direct political control being imposed (SSCCMI 2002: 22–24). The censorship also extended to visual images of the refugees. The government forbade the involvement of staff from the Department of Defence Public Affairs, which recalled its photographer from Christmas Island (SSCCMI2002: 24). ADF personnel involved in Operation Relex could take photographs but were subject to strict guidelines. A senior defence official explained:

> Essentially, we were told to concentrate on the ADF activities at the time – so the work of ADF personnel in relation to Operation Relex, first of all, as targets of opportunity for photographers. We were then given instructions in regard to photographing SUNCs [suspected unauthorised non-citizens] – or whatever the latest term is. We were certainly aware that Immigration had concerns about identifying potential asylum seekers, so we got some guidance on ensuring that there were no personalising or humanising images taken of SUNCs (quoted, SSCCMI 2002: 24).

Declaring war in the Pacific

The reduction of the refugees' humanity to bureaucratic, double-edged acronyms such as SUNC was part of a conscious attempt to ensure that 'no imagery that could conceivably garner sympathy or cause misgivings about the aggressive new border protection regime would find its way into the public domain' (SSCCMI 2002: 25).

Before the SAS took control, some direct contact had been made with the *Tampa* and images of the type the government opposed released. A widely published series of photos taken by a member of the *Tampa's* crew showed the exposed asylum seekers corralled by containers on the ship's deck and plainly in a vulnerable state. However, some of the refugees later complained that subsequent video shot by the SAS, that included footage of hungry people squabbling over a pot of jam and later, dozens of others queuing for overflowing latrines following a bout of food poisoning, was intended 'to show we are wild people, we are inhuman, we are not worth accepting into civilised society' (quoted, Marr and Wilkinson 2003: 103, 119–120, 123). Such measures could not prevent all critical media commentary[14] but the developing culture of control, which in 2001 ensured the legitimacy of the refugees was under sustained attack and every media release carefully constructed to suit the government's agenda, enabled two themes to dominate representations of the asylum seekers as dangerous, desperate, alien outsiders: the association of asylum seekers with Islam and specifically with terrorism following the events of September 11; and the 'children overboard' affair.

The fact that the majority of the 2001 boat arrivals were Muslims from Iraq, Afghanistan and Iran was already a dominant theme in the media coverage prior to September 11. After September 11, the government made the linkage between terrorism, Islam and asylum seekers explicit even though the perpetrators of the September 11 attacks were lawfully resident in the United States and those attempting to enter Australia were fleeing the Taliban and Baathist regimes accused of backing the attacks. In a radio interview on 13 September, Defence Minister Peter Reith, disingenuously commented:

But there is a simpler, broader point to make and it was a fact made by...the [US] Assistant Secretary of State... responsible for our region when he said...look you've got to be able to manage people coming into your country, you've got to be able to control that otherwise it can be a pipeline for terrorists to come in and use your country as a staging post for terrorist activities. Now that's in no reference to anybody's background, ethnic background, the Middle East or anything else. But you know that, you couldn't get a clearer message and that is that if you can't control who comes into your country then that is a security issue.[15]

On the same day, the solicitor general told the Federal Court:

'Today, invasions don't have to be military...They can be of diseases or unwanted migrants...[the Government must have the power to protect Australia from the sort of people]...who did what happened in New York yesterday' (quoted, Marr and Wilkinson 2003: 145).

By chance, Prime Minister Howard was in Washington D.C. on September 11, having met with President Bush the previous day. Howard pledged immediate and full support to the United States and on 4 October, a day before announcing there would be federal election on 10 November, provided details of Australia's military contribution to the 'war on terror'.[16] It was in this heightened pre-election environment that the indefensible and untrue accusation that some of the refugees aboard a boat (codenamed SIEV 4) intercepted by the navy on October 7, threw their children overboard. Photos allegedly confirming this subsequently turned out to have been taken during the rescue procedures the following day. The origins of the allegations and how they came to be recycled by the government, even after it was made aware or should have been aware of their lack of veracity, are covered extensively elsewhere.[17]

The real scandal surrounding the SIEV 4 was the delay caused by the imperatives of Operation Relex in rescuing the crew and 223 Iraqi asylum seekers from their dangerously leaking boat.[18] Instead, a succession of ministers, including the prime minister, used the allegations to remove all moral legitimacy from the refugees.

Declaring war in the Pacific

Immigration Minister Ruddock accused the refugees of a 'clearly planned and premeditated act', while Prime Minister Howard in slightly more calculated language, declared: 'I don't want in this country people who are prepared, if these reports are true, to throw their children overboard. That kind of emotional blackmail is very distressing' (quoted, Kelly 2002). The 'Children Overboard' affair was a clear example of a government relying on deep-seated prejudices and established practices of institutional exclusion to further deny the experiences or rights of targeted groups of forced migrants. The lies characterising this episode were systemic; a product of highly controlled lines of communication, little accountability, and government ministers interpreting information to suit their primary political purpose: the externalisation of border controls through the Pacific Solution.

The Pacific Solution

Following the seizure of the *Tampa* on 29 August 2001, Prime Minister Howard made an urgent statement to the Australian parliament in which he declared:

> The government was left with no alternative but to instruct the Chief of the Australian Defence Force to arrange for Defence personnel to board and secure the vessel...Every nation has the right to effectively control its borders and to decide who comes here and under what circumstances, and Australia has no intention of compromising that right...The problem lies in the ease of entry of many people from Middle Eastern and other countries...
>
> Something has to be done to stop that flow of humanity (CPD 2001a: 30516–30518).

In response, the Labor opposition leader, Kim Beazley, joined 'the Prime Minister in the first instance in expressing gratitude to the members of the Australian armed services engaged in this very difficult situation' before declaring that in 'these circumstances, this country and this parliament do not need a carping opposition' (CPD 2001a: 30518). No further debate about the legality or morality of the exercise, or even questions about the welfare and circumstances of the refugees and the *Tampa's* crew, ensued.

The prime minister quickly moved to exploit such unambiguous bi-partisanship by introducing into parliament the same evening retrospective legislation[19] intended to 'put beyond doubt the domestic legal basis for actions taken in relation to foreign ships within the territorial sea of Australia' (Hancock 2001: 1). This was sweeping legislation that did not just apply to the *Tampa*. Under the bill, any authorised immigration, customs, police or defence force 'officer' could direct a ship to leave Australian territorial waters and in the event of a refusal, detain the vessel and forcibly remove it. The proposed power extended to '*any* ship within the territorial sea, regardless of whether it is carrying persons seeking asylum or is otherwise engaged in any activity which is "prejudicial to the peace, good order or security" of Australia' (Hancock 2001: 12, emphasis in original). Such actions were not to be reviewable in any Australian court, while total immunity from any civil or criminal proceedings was to be provided for individuals involved in enforcement action on behalf of the state. No applications for a protection visa could be made by any person aboard a vessel subject to the legislation.

This extraordinary attempt to enable the Australian state, without impunity, to forcibly remove refugees or any other unauthorised person and dump them unaided in international waters was too much even for the Labor Party, which blocked the legislation in the Senate, but offered to support specific legislation to cover the *Tampa* (CPD 2001b: 30572). With an election looming, the government's proposal was driven more by ideological and political considerations than practical necessity,[20] especially given *Tampa* specific legislation was passed within four weeks. The government's strategy of making Labor look 'soft' on refugees, while simultaneously introducing an unprecedented range of restrictions on unauthorised entry, certainly paid electoral dividends but it also had very deleterious long term implications for refugees attempting to enter Australia and other Western states.

On 26 September, with Labor support, the Senate passed a series of six bills,[21] which retrospectively locked in place the Pacific

Solution. In addition to validating the seizure of the *Tampa*, key elements of the legislation included: restrictions on refugees applying for protection in Australia if they have already stopped in a 'safe' third country for seven days; minimum prison terms for people smugglers – five years for a first conviction and eight years for a second conviction; the exclusion of certain territories from Australia's migration zone; unauthorised arrivals to the excised territories lost the right to apply for a visa; the possible detention and removal from those territories of unauthorised arrivals to declared third countries where their claims for asylum will be processed; a narrower statutory interpretation of the Refugee Convention; further limits to the grounds for judicial review; the prohibition of class actions in migration litigation; and the possibility that adverse inferences may be drawn when visa applicants fail to provide supporting information including documentation, without reasonable explanation. Each of these pieces of legislation had implications for the rights of unauthorised arrivals. However, with refugees already in the process of being removed to extra-territorial detention centres, the novel and defining provisions of the new legislation were those relating to excision and offshore processing.

Excision

Excision of Australia's offshore territories provided a surreal dimension to a discourse emphasising the primacy of physical borders. Nearly 5,000 islands, including important landfalls such as Christmas Island, Ashmore and Cartier Islands and the Cocos (Keeling) Islands, were simply removed from Australian territory for the purposes of the *Migration Act* (Coombs, 2005). Any person arriving at these places without a visa thus became an 'unlawful non-citizen'; unable to make a visa application; subject to mandatory detention and liable to removal to a declared country such as Papua New Guinea or Nauru. The government justified excision purely in terms of security and deterrence. People smugglers were targeting islands close to the mainland and removing *Migration Act* coverage, it was claimed, would reduce the incentives for people to make hazardous journeys to Australian territories and make it harder for people smugglers to escape detection and arrest (Coombs 2005).

However, the process created a dynamic of its own. Once migration excision had begun, it was only a matter of time before additional excisions were announced, usually in response to further boat arrivals.[22]

The arrival of 43 West Papuan refugees on Cape York in January 2006 triggered the inevitable endgame when, as part of its efforts to ease the diplomatic tensions with Indonesia arising from Australia's decision to grant the refugees temporary protection visas, the Australian government announced in April 2006 that 'all unauthorised boat arrivals will be transferred to offshore centres for assessment of their claims' (MIMA 2006).[23] Despite the high likelihood that other governments would refuse to accept refugees who had initially landed in Australia, and the refusal of the PNG government to process West Papuan asylum seekers on PNG territory (Rheeney 2006), the Australian government arranged with the (IOM) and the Nauru government to upgrade Nauru's detention facilities. Thus, while the proposed legislation was ultimately withdrawn, it signalled the government's willingness to remove any avenue for unauthorised asylum seekers to access Australia's domestic legal machinery. Ideologically, by denying any political obligation pursuant to the Refugee Convention to provide an operative system of refugee protection, the government effectively declared that forced migrants should be corralled and processed entirely in the developing world.

Offshore processing

Having taken the decision to intercept the *Tampa*, the Australian government was compelled to find an offshore location where the refugees could disembark. Indonesia was under no legal obligation to accept the refugees, who had made their preference for Australia clear.[24] Furious and secretive negotiations ensued between the Australian government and the French authorities, in relation to French Polynesia; and a range of Pacific states including East Timor, Kiribati, Fiji, Palau, Tuvalu and Tonga (SSCCMI 2002: 293). To the chagrin of many states in the region, the Australian government sought to use its economic power and the prospect of economic aid to lever a deal (SSCCMI 2002: 294–295). Eventually, agreements were struck with the governments of Nauru and Papua New Guinea to host detention facilities.

The agreement signed with Nauru on 10 September 2001, coincided with 'severe cash flow problems' in the island state (Hughes 2004: 5). Under the agreement, the Australian government committed to funding significant local infrastructure and to reviewing 'options to provide advice or assistance on, but not limited to, telecommunications and aviation infrastructure, the protection of economic resources and any other matters as jointly determined through administrative arrangements' (SSCCMI 2002: 296). Overall, Australia's 'development assistance' to Nauru under this agreement and a subsequent memorandum of understanding totalled 26.5 million dollars between 2001 and 2003 (SSCCMI 2002: 298). A further 22.5 million over two years was allocated in March 2004 (Hughes 2004: 5), while in October 2004, $200,000 was promised for 'nutritional advisers...to address ailing food supplies and diet-related health problems' and an Australian Federal Police officer was committed to be the Director of Police in Nauru (ABC Online 2004b). In 2005, 'Australia's foreign minister...reported that some $70 million had been spent since 2001, but much of this went to the Australian companies providing services to the camps' (Gordon 2005: 82). In July 2007, a further memorandum of understanding was signed but the details were not disclosed. However, concerns were raised about the continued 'blowout' of the funding from 17.7 million to 29 million dollars during the 2005–2006 financial year. A former Ausaid official, who was responsible for the agency's Nauru program, 'described the aid payments as an "unmitigated bribe" to retain the centre', which at the time held 90 Sri Lankan and Burmese refugees (Skehan 2007).

The agreement signed with Papua New Guinea on 11 October 2001 to allow the establishment of a processing centre in the Lombrum Naval Patrol Base at Manus Island was not tied so directly to additional aid payments, although it did result in the fast tracking of previously committed aid projects (SSCCMI 2002:300–302). The common characteristic of the various agreements was that it locked in economically vulnerable regional states to Australia's border policing strategy. This entrenched neo-colonial relationships and had important foreign policy implications.[25] It also had immediate human rights implications for the refugees, over and above those associated with the coercive practices of Operation Relex. Nauru was not a signatory to the Refugee Convention and Papua New Guinea had only signed on a restricted basis (Crock and Saul 2002: 49; SSCCMI 2002: 305). Neither state operated its own refugee determination process. Moreover, the remoteness of the locations and the different jurisdictions meant access for lawyers, human rights monitors, journalists and independent observers was extremely difficult (Gordon 2005).

Legally devolving detention arrangements also enabled the Australian government to try and avoid responsibility for them.[26] While the Australian government was committed to funding the operational costs of the detention centres and considerable ADF resources were devoted to their construction, the International Organisation for Migration was responsible for their management and security in cooperation with the immigration department, Australian Protective Services[27] and local police forces (SSCCMI 2002: 306–312). The role of the IOM in facilitating the offshore detention system not only put the Australian government at arm's length but also incorporated the resources and authority of the major Western backed international institution concerned with migration control in the establishment of Australia's exclusion zone.

The Australian government also sought to incorporate the UNHCR in its official consensus building exercise. The government had managed to break the impasse over the *Tampa* by September 1, when it announced the initial arrangements for Nauru and the agreement of the New Zealand government to process 150 of those aboard the Norwegian ship (PMA 2001a). New Zealand also undertook to settle those of the 150 whose claims were accepted but the Australian government made no similar undertakings to those on Nauru. UNHCR, which was generally critical of the Australian government's actions throughout this period and questioned the lawfulness of the agreements with Nauru and Papua New Guinea (SSCCMI 2002: 302–305), nevertheless agreed to a formal request from the Nauruan government to process a group of approximately 500 refugees, including those from the *Tampa*, who were taken to

Declaring war in the Pacific

Nauru. The remainder of those taken to Nauru and all those taken to Manus Island, were to be processed by Australian officials in accordance with processes 'modelled' on UNHCR guidelines (SSCCMI 2002: 317–319).

It would be wrong to engage an argument of moral equivalence or to attribute comparable levels of complicity to the Australian government and UNHCR in the institutionalisation of the Pacific Solution, especially given UNHCR's criticism of the government's role in the *Tampa* episode and subsequent refusal to assist with attempts to institute a blanket offshore processing system (Fitzpatrick 2006a; Kirk 2006). However, government ministers repeatedly used the fact that UNHCR was in some way associated with the initial arrangements on Nauru to try and legitimise offshore processing, highlighting the somewhat contradictory role of major NGOs in the normalisation of state practice.

The agreements with the governments of Nauru and Papua New Guinea to host detention and processing sites and the subsequent decision of the Australian government to construct a purpose built centre on Christmas Island, effectively created across thousands of kilometres of ocean an offshore gulag, to be opened, shut or extended as the government saw fit and where the inhabitants were cut-off from independent scrutiny; timely and proper legal advice; the norms of Australia's judicial process; and nearly all meaningful social interaction with the outside world. Moreover, the processing and dispersal of the refugees aboard the *Tampa* set a precedent for the Australian state to establish the Pacific region as buffer zone for Australia's border control policies, within which unauthorised arrivals lose all control over their movements. Thus, 43 West Papuan asylum seekers who arrived at Cape York on the Australian mainland in January 2006 were removed to the Christmas Island detention centre before being granted temporary protection visas. In February 2007, 83 Sri Lankan Tamils who were intercepted en route from Indonesia were also detained on Christmas Island before being transferred to Nauru.[28] There they became the subject of an extraordinary arrangement whereby their claims for asylum would be processed by Australian immigration department officials, with successful claimants then being subject to resettlement in the United

States under a special exchange agreement covering up to 200 refugees intercepted by the respective countries each year (Dastyari 2007; Topsfield 2007a). This bizarre, final phase of the Pacific Solution never came to fruition, but it formed part of a wider pattern of forced transfers and questionable repatriation practices.

Expulsion and repatriation

The removal of 'failed asylum seekers' is the ultimate sanction that can be imposed under Australia's border policing regime. Force is often involved, including the use of techniques that would constitute a serious assault in other circumstances. Abdul Khogali, a Sudanese refugee detained for seven years in Australia before being removed in 2005, described an earlier attempt to deport[29] him in 1999, which failed after the plane's captain refused to carry him:

> Soon the doctor entered the cell carrying an injection with four tablets asking me to choose either the injection or the tablets. I refused them both. He the doctor, ordered the security guards to do their job and he and the officers laid me down on the floor and sit, both of them, on my back. So then I accepted to receive the tablets....The doctor told me how those tablets are only tranquilisers. But they didn't work. So they force me to take a fifth tablet at the airport when they got me on the airplane with a wheelchair accompanied by a nurse, two companions and three ACM officers. All that continued for about five to six hours with three types of handcuffs and ties of leather, plastic and steel around my hands and belly and trunk....I stood screaming and asking for help from the passengers there. I immediately regretted that for those companion escort officers started to hit me and beat me fiercely and cruelly with kicks all over my body....The nurse on trying to inject in my leg missed my body to hit the plane seat where the needle got bent. But he didn't change the needle and injected me again...in a completely odd side on my leg....I continued to scream and ask for help until a few passengers cried and combined to come and relieve me of my oppression...So the officers got me to the prison.[30]

Declaring war in the Pacific

The use of such removal techniques reflects the systemic use of force within the detention and removal process. All persons removed must be accompanied by escorts trained in the use of restraint and in possession of equipment such as handcuffs (SLCAC 2000: 305–306). Despite the accounts of Mr Khogali and many others,[31] the immigration department's official policy is 'that medication (including sedatives) must not be used for the purposes of restraint in removals' (SLCAC 2006: 275). The issue is clouded by the overlap between migration and navigation law. According to the Senate Legal and Constitutional Affairs Committee (SLCAC 2000: 322),

> As a general principle, everyone on the aircraft is under the authority of the captain, regardless of whether the removal is being contracted by the airline carrier or DIMA [immigration department]

Subject to this principle, DIMA has stated that:

> ...escorts...are permitted to use reasonable force to restrain passengers being removed and ensure the safety of the aircraft, passengers and crew in accordance with international conventions relating to aircraft and passenger security.

The availability of 'reasonable force' allows for quite extreme forms of physical restraint. An international flight passenger on a stopover in Sydney in December 2005 recalled:

> On re-boarding the plane...a very officious man bustled in and cleared some space in the overhead luggage compartment, reassuring passengers that disturbance would be minimal....But then there was an alarming sound – metal scraping on metal, banging and clattering...and then our fellow passenger was on the plane. Squeezed between two security officers I can only define as goons, the man was handcuffed, with a chain leading to a restraint on his waist, and to cuffs at his ankles. But perhaps the most shocking was the gag. The man had layers of black gaffer tape around his mouth, bound so tightly that it was cutting into his face. Above the tape his eyes were wildly panicked. They

locked onto mine briefly before he was manhandled into the seat, and a blindfold placed over his eyes.[32]

There is little readily available data to indicate how routinely such methods of restraint are used.[33] What is clear is that such expulsions are intended to be a one-way process that removes the unauthorised person from the immediate jurisdiction of the Australian state, which then absolves itself of any further responsibility. There is no monitoring by the Australian government of the circumstances into which 'failed asylum seekers' and others are returned. This failure by the Australian state was already an issue when the Pacific Solution was implemented. In its submission to a Senate Inquiry in 2000, the Human Rights and Equal Opportunity Commission had urged unsuccessfully that the Australian Government institute a system of monitoring for returned asylum seekers. Instead, the committee took 'the view that, while there is scope for further development of the informal representations and monitoring currently undertaken by Australian overseas missions and local and international human rights organisations, the operation and funding of a formal monitoring system would be impractical and may also be counter-productive' (SLCAC 2000: 331–332). The committee did however recommend that 'the Commonwealth Government place the issue of monitoring on the agenda for discussion at the Inter-Government/Non-Government Organisations Forum with a view to examining the implementation of a system of informal monitoring' (SLCRC 2006: 296). Asserting the 'impractical and possible counter-productive' nature of monitoring, the government dismissed the committee's recommendation, adding: 'Where it is assessed as part of the determination process that there is no real chance of persecution of the applicant on return, Australia is not responsible for the future well being of that person in their homeland merely because at some stage they spent time in Australia'. As a result of the government's stance, it has been left to independent researchers to monitor the repatriation process and the fate of those removed.[34]

The government's disinterest in the fate of returnees was given greater institutional expression by the establishment of an offshore detention regime designed to deter and disperse refugees. For the

Australian government, the repatriation or resettlement of those it had forcibly diverted to Nauru was to be a measure of the Pacific Solution's success. The overthrow of the Taliban regime in November 2001 therefore prompted the Australian government immediately to negotiate with the Afghanistan interim government for the return of Afghan refugees. In May 2002, following the signing of a memorandum of understanding by the two governments, 'the Australian Government announced details of a reintegration package available to Afghan asylum seekers who volunteer to return to Afghanistan' (DIAC 2007c). The package applied to 'all asylum seekers offshore, including persons not from Afghanistan', whose claims were still being processed, and 'to those who have been found not to be refugees'. It included 'failed asylum seekers who were located in Australia, Nauru and the regions excised from the Migration Zone on or before 16 May 2002' (DIAC 2007c). Under the package, those who volunteered to return would be eligible for cash payments of $2,000 Australian per individual or up to $10,000 per family. The International Organisation for Migration played a key role in the implementation of the repatriation program. Its 'services' included 'help in obtaining passports, arranging air travel to Kabul, reception upon arrival, facilitating access to vocational training and help with transport from Kabul to other destinations within Afghanistan if required' (DIAC 2007c).

The Australian government's decision to begin a formal repatriation program for Afghan refugees was also given some legitimacy by the UNHCR, which launched a major repatriation program, mainly from Pakistan, in March 2002. In July 2002, the UNHCR announced that 'the time is now ripe for Afghans – wherever they are and at whatever stage they may be in the asylum process – to be offered the option of voluntary repatriation' (quoted, Corlett 2005: 61). UNHCR's apparent belief that Afghanistan was a safe place to which refugees could return was immediately contested (HRW 2002; Corlett 2005: 61–62). Not only did it run contrary to recent UNHCR assessments of the situation, but it also contradicted an extensive body of evidence from humanitarian non-government organisations and others with direct knowledge of the situation on the ground, especially in areas outside of Kabul (ERC 2006: 7–9). In June 2002, for example, a coalition of

160 NGOs in the United States had written to senior United States government officials:

> The people of Afghanistan continue to be victimized by crime, banditry and factional fighting. Displaced populations and ethnic minorities in particular are being subjected to increased harassment, intimidation and theft of their property. The women of Afghanistan, who suffered gross violations of their rights under the Taliban, continue to be subjected to violence and coercion. Homes have been burned, families displaced and camps looted (quoted, ERC 2006: 7).

Despite such concerns, extensive pressure was brought to bear on Afghan refugees to accept the package. Those who were eligible initially were only given 28 days to accept, or risk being returned anyway. A clear message was also being promoted by the camp authorities. One Afghan refugee rescued by the *Tampa* claimed 'the Afghans...were told by UNHCR and IOM staff that they must go back to Afghanistan: because it is now the policy of Australia to send refugees back. However much your life will be in danger, you won't be accepted' (quoted, ERC 2006: 15). Another described how 'every week there would be meetings in the camps to tell Afghans that Afghanistan was now safe and to encourage them to return' (Corlett 2005: 61). Others spoke of being forced to leave as a result of 'threats...about being sent to other camps', 'of not communicating with family if we did not leave', and of being dropped 'in a camp where we would not be free for many years' (ERC 2006: 57).

The pressure being applied to detainees occurred in circumstances where requests for legal advice were routinely 'refused by Nauru, Australia and the International Organisation for Migration' (Amor and Austin 2003: 76). This became especially perverse after the *Migration Act* was amended in 2002 to enable the forcible transfer of detainees to Australia for 'temporary purposes'.[35] Lawyer, Julian Burnside QC, recalls that:

> These provisions were used in early September 2002 to bring six Afghans to Australia from Nauru...The Commonwealth wanted them to give evidence against the people smugglers who had

brought them on their ill-fated journey. They were forced to give evidence on 19 and 20 September, and (despite the efforts of lawyers in Australia) on 21 September they were taken back to Nauru. Once back in Nauru, they had just eleven days in which to make the agonising decision: should they accept the government's 'repatriation' package...or stay in Nauru and face the possibility of life imprisonment without trial....As they left the Perth detention centre on 21 September, they were weeping with fear and anguish, convinced that their lives were, at last, irretrievably blighted (Amor and Austin 2003: 76–77).

In such an intimidating environment, the Australian government's repatriation program had an immediate impact. By January 2003, 274 Afghans detained on Nauru had returned under the scheme, in addition to 40 from mainland centres (Dastyari et al 2006: 148); and eventually, of the 785 Afghans held on Nauru, 420 were returned (ERC 2006: 58). However, in 2004, following prolonged hunger strikes by the remaining detainees and an indisputably deteriorating security environment in Afghanistan (Corlett 2005: 66–67; Maley 2006: 30–77), the Australian government 're-examined the cases of the remaining 197 Afghans and accepted...168 of them as genuine', although there was 'no evidence that the refugee claims of those who "chose" to return under conditions of extreme hardship, fear and stress, were different or less compelling than the claims of those who stayed' (ERC 2006: 58).

In May 2005, the Australian and Afghan governments signed a further memorandum of understanding regarding the repatriation of Afghan refugees. In announcing the arrangements, the immigration minister emphasised the substantial financial outlay by the Australian government in assisting Afghanistan to develop 'its border management capacities'. This included providing $21 million to UNHCR and $6 million to the IOM since 2001 to support the 'management of returnees and displaced people' (MIMA 2005). In the context of the Pacific Solution, the refugees were at best, passive participants in this process. Those who accepted return packages were subjected constantly to reminders of the exclusionary force of the Australian state. One described how on his 'long and difficult' journey back to Kabul, 'the police on the plane threatened them with handcuffs if they moved about and showed them guns to back up the threat' (ERC 2006:25). Moreover, on arrival, in many cases, the inducements to return, such as jobs and accommodation did not materialise, while 'several...were soon robbed of up to $1,000 from the money given them to return (ERC 2006: 57).

Such difficulties on return masked the serious consequences of danger in which many of the returned asylum seekers and their families found themselves (ERC 2006). But the failure of the Australian government to monitor the fate of those whose return from Nauru to Afghanistan it engineered was entirely consistent with the sustained efforts it made to repel unauthorised migrants. The logic of border protection meant that notwithstanding formal commitments to non-refoulement, unauthorised migrants should be removed as uncompromisingly as possible. Routinely, this involves the use or threatened use of force to put people on planes. But the Edmund Rice Centre study (ERC 2004) also included allegations that such removals involved Australian officials providing returnees with false documents; or documents that were confiscated or expired soon after return; and that in some instances, corrupt payments were made to border officials in receiving countries. The Australian government denied these allegations and dismissed the Edmund Rice Centre studies. It also refused to accept a further senate committee recommendation for increased monitoring and review of its removal and deportation processes (SLCRC 2006: 303–304). However, the government's reticence to investigate what was happening in receiving states contrasted sharply to its attitude to interfering in transit states seen to be facilitating illicit movement into Australia. In those circumstances, proactive policing interventions have become the norm on the basis that the Australian state has a legitimate right to combat people smuggling.

The 'war' on people smuggling

Combating people smuggling constituted the core of official border policing discourse from 1999 and gained particular momentum with the Pacific Solution. The Australian government's determination to establish people smuggling as the primary cause of forced migration into Australia was fundamental to the delegitimisation of refugees; led to a considerable expansion of state agencies such as the Australian Federal police; and was an important driver of geopolitics as the Australian state sought to extend its direct influence over policing in the region.

The centrality of the anti-people smuggling offensive was made plain in September 2001 when the immigration minister published an 'unauthorised arrivals strategy' (MIMA 2001) comprising 'three major elements':

Prevention of the problem by minimising the outflows from countries of origin and secondary outflows from countries of first asylum;

Working with other countries to disrupt people smugglers and intercept their clients en route to their destination, while ensuring that those people in need of refugee protection are identified and assisted as early as possible; and

Developing appropriate reception arrangements for unauthorised arrivals who reach Australia, focusing on the early assessment of the refugee status of the individual, the prompt removal of those who are not refugees, or who are refugees but can access effective protection elsewhere, and the removal of additional benefits not required by the Refugee Convention to minimise the incentive for people to attempt illegal travel to Australia.

The government sought to develop 'a broad international consensus' (MIMA 2001) in the implementation of this agenda. This involved increased cooperation between agencies such as the AFP and their regional counterparts, particularly in Indonesia, that aimed to directly disrupt people smuggling activities. Prior to the highly visible interception activities of Operation Relex, the AFP and Indonesian policing agencies were already involved in an extensive and largely secret disruption program. In his evidence before the Senate inquiry (SSCCMI, 2002: 1923–1984), AFP Commissioner, Mick Keelty, confirmed that since September 2000, the AFP was under a ministerial direction 'to give special emphasis to countering and otherwise investigat(e) organised people smuggling'. He also

Border Crimes

claimed that the AFP's efforts were 'successful in bringing people responsible for organised people smuggling before overseas and Australian courts' and that 'since February 2000, the Indonesian authorities ha(d) diverted over 3,000 people suspected of intending to enter Australia illegally into legitimate migration processes under the auspices of the United Nations conventions'(SSCCMI, 2002: 1922–1928).[36]

Keelty's defence of his organisation's work overlooked the fact that many of those diverted found themselves stranded indefinitely in camps or informal settlements such as those on the Indonesian island of Lombok. It also sidestepped serious allegations regarding some of its disruption activities. These were conducted under the auspices of a protocol agreed between the AFP and the Indonesian National Police (INP) in September 2000 in accordance with a memorandum of understanding signed in October 1995 to co-operate in the investigation of transnational organised crime. Under the protocol, the INP established five special intelligence units dedicated to people smuggling operations, with the AFP providing training in investigation and surveillance techniques (SSCCMI, 2002: 10).

The undercover operations conducted by the AFP and INP included INP operatives, under AFP direction, tracking the onshore movements of smugglers and attaching tracking devices to their boats before they set out for Australia (Marr and Wilkinson, 2003: 41). There are also claims that the police were sabotaging, or encouraging the sabotage of smugglers' boats; that one of the agents recruited to assist with their operations 'was paid "expenses" [by the AFP] to travel around West Timor buying information on passengers which the INP then used to arrest them on minor visa and passport charges'; that he 'also robbed asylum seekers by promoting himself as a people smuggler and taking their money which, according to the police, he then handed to the INP'; and that at one stage, he boasted to Australian journalists 'that he and two confederates "had paid Indonesian locals on four occasions to scuttle people smuggling boats with passengers on them"…and that "he was unrepentant saying the boats were sunk close to land so everyone got off safely"'(Marr and Wilkinson, 2003: 41–43). These

Declaring war in the Pacific

claims were flatly denied by the AFP, which referred some of them to the Australian Broadcasting Authority (ABA) (AFP 2002). While the ABA found that some 'unreliable material' had been presented 'as factual material without making adequate attempts at verification' (ABA 2003: 13), few operational details about the disruption program were made public. The nature of the disruption activities and the secrecy surrounding them is clouded further by the sudden suspension of the protocol by the Indonesian authorities in September 2001 for reasons that neither the AFP nor the Australian government were willing to disclose (SSCCMI 2002: 10–12).[37]

What is clear is that the disruption activities, combined with more aggressive policing, increased the risks for asylum seekers. The sinking of the SIEV X should be viewed in this context. The survivor accounts[38] of this tragedy make harrowing reading. One recalled:

> I boarded the boat with 15 other family members, 9 drowned and 6 remained. We clung onto a plank of timber for 20 hours drifting in the water. Something I witnessed left a very strange impression, a baby with umbilical cord still attached to the mother was amongst those who drowned.

Another described how

> 'wherever you look you see the dead children like birds floating on the water, those who survived 22 hours in the water saw the dead bodies of the women and children with cuts from the nails on the boat and with scars from where the fish were biting them in the water and saw blood.'

The survivor accounts also indicate that when the boat sank, 'there were 100 to 120 passengers still alive' (Kevin 2004: 81). However, by the time a fishing vessel began rescue operations the following day only 44 had survived. Testimony that military vessels were in the vicinity and indications that Australian and Indonesian officials had aerial photos of the SIEV X and intelligence that ought to have enabled them to know the boat's whereabouts has led to considerable speculation about what knowledge the Australian authorities had of the boat's movements (Kevin 2004: 70–86).[39] A subsequent Senate inquiry, which did not challenge the fundamental thrust of government policy, examined whether RAN vessels could have been deployed 'with a view to reaching the vessel before it sank or saving more survivors while they were in the water' (SSCCMI 2002: 259–290). While not finding 'grounds for believing that negligence or dereliction of duty was committed in relation to the SIEV X' (SSCCMI 2002: 287), the committee found it

> '...extraordinary that a major human disaster could occur in the vicinity of a theatre of intensive Australian operations and remain undetected until three days after the event, without concern being raised within intelligence and decision making circles' (SSCCMI 2002: 288).

From the outset, the Australian government refused to accept any responsibility for this tragedy and ignored repeated calls to hold a full inquiry into the matter (Kevin 2004: 14–21). On 10 December 2002, in light of 'apparent inconsistencies in evidence...by Commonwealth agencies in relation to the People Smuggling Disruption Program and in relation to Suspected Illegal Entry Vessels...including....SIEV X', the Senate passed a motion calling on the government

> ...to immediately establish a comprehensive, independent judicial inquiry into all aspects of the People Smuggling Disruption Program...including...the circumstances and outcomes of all departures from Indonesia of all boats carrying asylum-seekers, including the circumstances of the sinking of the SIEV X' (CPD Senate 2002: 7401–2; 7562–3).[40]

The government rejected the resolution, instead preferring to use the tragedy as an example to prospective asylum seekers of the risks associated with using smugglers (SSCCMI, 2002: 195–290). No effort was made by the Australian authorities to provide special assistance to the survivors.[41] Their attempts to engage in secondary movement were sufficient in the government's eyes to justify their continued exclusion and return to Indonesia. Few were offered resettlement in Australia.[42]

Most public debate about the SIEV X tragedy remains framed by the illicit nature of the smuggling enterprise, particularly the role played by the alleged organiser, Abu Quassey. Notwithstanding Quassey's apparent lack of moral scruples, many questions about the SIEV X remain unanswered, especially regarding its potential link to the disruption program (Kevin, 2004). Abu Quassey was not tried in Australia where his contact with Australian agencies and the possibility that he acted as a 'sting' agent could be more easily examined; instead, he was extradited to Egypt where in a closed court he was convicted of homicide through negligence and for aiding illegal immigration[43].

The Australian government also used the sinking to pressure the Indonesian authorities to accept the return of illicit vessels and convene intergovernmental discussions on how best to combat people smuggling in the Asia-Pacific region (Kevin, 2004: 3–7). Foreign Minister Downer justified these measures as a means of preventing smugglers and traffickers 'selling their false hope and abusing human rights'.[44] However, this only served to consolidate throughout the various state agencies devoted to border protection a culture of policing and removal that was systemically inimical to protecting human rights. This not only impacted on asylum seekers, like those aboard the SIEV X who were at the centre of the border policing effort, but to trafficked migrants, who could not be caricatured as queue jumpers and whose human rights border policing was supposed explicitly to protect.

The Alvarez Solon case

The case of Australian citizen Vivian Alvarez Solon, who was unlawfully detained by Australian immigration officials and removed to the Philippines just weeks before the *Tampa* was intercepted, gives some insight into the immigration department's treatment of trafficked migrants at the time. After her removal on the completely unfounded basis that she was a trafficked sex worker, three senior DIMIA staff were made aware of what happened but failed to follow it up (Comrie 2005: 81). Vivian Solon remained stranded in the Philippines for over four years and was one of over 200 cases investigated in 2005 as a result of errors made by the department.

The unlawful detention and removal of Vivian Solon raised important questions of accountability for the culture of exclusion within state agencies. For the purposes of this discussion, the most significant feature of the Solon case was the minimal impact of the *Criminal Code Amendment (Slavery and Sexual Servitude) Act* 1999, which codified the offences of slavery and sexual servitude but did not include a specific offence of people trafficking or any meaningful protection for potential witnesses. In practice, this meant that the immigration department routinely removed people found working illegally in the sex industry, regardless of whether those people were consenting to their working arrangements and notwithstanding any formal commitments the government had to protect further violations of the victims' human rights. Clearly, the merest hint that Vivian Alvarez Solon might have been trafficked was enough to have her immediately removed in the most negligent manner without any consideration of the impact this might have on her.

Subsequent legislative and policy developments neither removed the possibility of such a 'mistake' occurring again nor dissociated the victims of trafficking from the exclusionary realm of policing. Australia signed the UN Trafficking Protocol in December 2002 and ratified it in September 2005. In October 2003, the federal government announced a $20 million anti-trafficking package (Phillips 2004) that it consolidated in June 2004 in an 'action plan to eradicate trafficking in persons' targeting 'the four key areas of prevention, detection and investigation, criminal prosecution and victim support' (A-GD 2004). While references to victim support suggested a shift in emphasis, and the immigration department implemented a new protocol for the referral of potential trafficking victims to the police,[45] an indication of the plan's focus was provided by the *Criminal Code Amendment (Trafficking in Persons Offences) Act* 2005. Under this legislation, the attorney-general may issue a 30 day bridging visa to a suspected trafficking victim pending an initial investigation.[46] A victim willing to assist the police might then be granted a criminal justice stay visa that includes the right to work for the duration of the criminal justice process. When that visa expires, a witness protection (trafficking) visa may be issued, allowing for temporary or permanent residence.

Declaring war in the Pacific

There is a lack of consistent and detailed data on the nature and extent of trafficking into Australia (Putt 2007) and a potentially distorting focus on sex trafficking (Segrave et al 2009). The new visas also have serious limitations. Not only has the attorney-general been reluctant to issue them (Carrick 2008) but the insistence that they only be issued on the basis of compliance with the criminal investigation overlooks the consequences such cooperation might have for the victims or their close personal networks. In this regard, the support measures for victims are very much an optional extra, reflecting that conceptually, references to rights protection camouflage a more exclusionary impulse.

The changes at a domestic level also beg the question: What happens to those who are intercepted on their way to Australia? Presumably, they are turned around or detained en route outside Australia's jurisdiction. Given that a substantial portion of the AFP's resources in this area are devoted to regional policing measures and the Australian government is involved at a number of levels in trying to establish mechanisms for the prevention of illicit travel into Australia's contracting migration zone, it is difficult to see how Australia's policing of trafficked migrants is fundamentally different to its response to other types of unauthorised entry.

The acceptance of the anti-smuggling and trafficking agenda within mainstream Australian politics provided a hegemonic rationale for extending Australian state influence in the Asia-Pacific region. The dominant perception that smugglers are dangerous, deviant and criminal was reinforced by the appointment of an Ambassador for People Smuggling Issues, while Australian attempts to integrate regional policing operations were complemented at the diplomatic level through mechanisms such as the Bali Process, which grew out of a ministerial conference, co-chaired by Indonesia, in February 2002.

Participants in the Bali Process include representatives from virtually all governments in the region bordered by Turkey, China, Kiribati and New Zealand, as well as the IOM and UNHCR. Its stated purpose is to develop bilateral, regional and multilateral responses that emphasise regional cooperation in the fight against people smuggling, trafficking in persons and related transnational crime. Specific agreed objectives include:

> ...the development of more effective information and intelligence sharing; improved cooperation among regional law enforcement agencies to deter and combat people smuggling and trafficking networks; the enactment of national legislation to criminalise people smuggling and trafficking in persons; provision of appropriate protection and assistance to the victims of trafficking, particularly women and children; enhanced cooperation on border and visa systems to detect and prevent illegal movements; increased public awareness in order to discourage these activities and warn those susceptible; enhanced effectiveness of return as a strategy to deter people smuggling and trafficking through conclusion of appropriate agreements; cooperation in verifying the identity and nationality of illegal migrants and trafficking victims; enhanced focus on tackling the root causes of illegal migration...and assisting countries to adopt best practices in asylum management' (Millar 2004).

The implementation of an agenda so exclusively focused on control and enforcement consolidated the Australian exclusion zone and devolved many of the enforcement functions beyond Australia's borders. It was also integrally related to the expansion of the Australian Federal Police, which on the basis of combating smuggling, trafficking and other forms of transnational organised crime, was delivered record budgets to establish posts in most South-East Asian countries; undertake extended deployments in the Solomons and Papua New Guinea; oversee the establishment of the Indonesian Transnational Crime Coordination Centre; and extend its Law Enforcement Cooperation Program. Increased AFP activity and the development of ties between the AFP and particularly its Indonesian counterparts also have a wider foreign policy dimension. Combined with measures implemented in the wake of the terrorist attacks on Australian targets in Bali and Jakarta, the growing level of formal contact and informal interagency networks has facilitated the rebuilding of links between the Australian and Indonesian governments that had been strained by the Australian-led intervention in East Timor in 1999. At the enforcement level, cooperation has now extended to Australia renewing training and operational ties with Kopassus, the Indonesian Army Special Forces Unit, widely believed to have been responsible for orchestrating militia attacks in East Timor around the 1999 elections and human rights abuses in areas such as Aceh and West Papua (Dodd 2007; HRW 1999).

Significantly, given the tensions that arose from Australia's decision to grant protection visas to 43 West Papuan refugees in February 2006, the two states signed a framework agreement in November 2006 committing them to co-operate 'in preventing and combating transnational crimes, in particular crimes related to people smuggling and trafficking in persons; money laundering; financing of terrorism; corruption; illegal fishing; and cyber crimes' (DFAT 2006). An indication in the agreement that the Australian government was even less likely to be sympathetic to future West Papuan refugees was the mutual undertaking to 'respect and support...the sovereignty, territorial integrity, national unity and political independence of each other' and not to interfere 'in the internal affairs of one another' (DFAT 2006). As the tensions over the West Papuan refugees illustrated, the assertion of Australian state authority in the region was sometimes problematic. Nevertheless, as the AFP's international activities continue to grow, it seems likely the Australian state will continue to press for its policing priorities in the Asia Pacific region. Targeting human smuggling and trafficking remains a high profile and legitimising focus, with serious implications for unauthorised migrants.

The Pacific Solution and state crime

The nameless, faceless refugees targeted by Operation Relex found themselves at the centre of a military mobilisation that belied their needs for survival, protection and safety. Of the 433 picked up by the *Tampa* and incarcerated on Nauru, 186 agreed to return to their places of origin, although not necessarily in circumstances of their own choosing. The remainder were resettled, mainly in New Zealand, although 29 were eventually allowed into Australia (UNHCR 2005g). For some, the Pacific Solution threatened indefinite detention, despite being found to have genuine fears of persecution. In December 2006, UNHCR eventually managed to negotiate resettlement in an unspecified Scandinavian country for the last of the 2001 detainees, an Iraqi refugee who had been given an adverse security assessment by ASIO (Gordon 2006a). And in February 2007, the immigration department granted a permanent protection visa to another Iraqi, whose adverse ASIO assessment had been reassessed following the man's transfer in a suicidal state from Nauru to a psychiatric facility in Brisbane in 2006 (Gordon 2007).

The Pacific Solution was formally ended by the newly elected Labor government in 2008. Nevertheless, its legacy remains, with the *Tampa* episode representing the point where the fundamental right to enter Australia in order to seek protection was systematically removed. In the place of policies that begrudgingly accepted unauthorised migrants and promoted measures to deter their entry, an over-arching ideology of border protection was enshrined that located preventing illicit entry as entirely a national security concern. Interdiction, offshore processing and the dispersal of refugees consequently established exclusionary norms of state practice that reinforced the deviance of free movement. Within this paradigm, the act of people smuggling and the role played by illicit migration agents in facilitating refugee movement remains the primary state concern. The invocation of the Pacific Solution as a mechanism for the neutralisation and punishment of people smuggling consolidated a multi-tiered exclusion zone and contributed to a developing, long-term Australian policing presence in the Asia-Pacific region.

The fundamental criminological dynamic of the Australian exclusion zone is its systematic assault on the movements and by definition, the rights, of forced migrants. This operates at a number of levels: unauthorised arrivals are alienated by their lack of legal status; they are denied access to a full refugee determination process; their status as refugees is subordinated to that of the resettled refugee; their experiences are denied and delegitimised through their construction as queue jumpers; they are criminalised through their participation in smuggling enterprises; they are punished and abused through the use of detention, dispersal and forced removal; and they are put at greater personal risk by the measures employed to enforce the zone. In the Australian context, these are the systemic components of state crime. The next chapter considers in more detail how the use of detention perpetuated this form of state criminality, particularly through the criminalisation and abuse of unauthorised migrants.

Notes

[1] Of the 4175 boat arrivals in 1999-2000, 2297 were from Iraq and 1263 from Afghanistan. Of the 4141 arrivals in 2000-2001, 2269 were from Afghanistan and 994 from Iraq (MIMA 2001).

[2] Australia was, of course, and active participant in the 'coalition of the willing' and sent troops to both Afghanistan and Iraq in 2002 and 2003 respectively.

[3] In the year ended 30 June 1999, approximately 97 percent of Iraqis and 92 percent of Afghans who applied on arrival in Australia were granted refugee status by either the Department of Immigration or the Refugee Review Tribunal (RCOA 1999). See also Maley (2001) for a discussion of the Afghan refugees entering Australia at this time.

[4] For example, Immigration Minister Ruddock used his second reading speech to Federal Parliament on the Border Protection Legislation Amendment Bill to claim: 'The people being smuggled are, in most cases, not genuine refugees seeking haven in the first available country. They are instead young migrants from less developed countries who are seeking to work in developed countries'. He went on to criticize the unreasonable expectations of the refugees: 'I was disturbed to hear reports of some of these arrivals asking for Pert 2-in-1 shampoo immediately upon arrival in Australia. Some of them have arrived with details of medical treatment that they wanted to receive whilst in detention, including dental work, and often asking to see orthodontists-something I think many Australians would like to be able to do free of charge' (CPD 1999a: 10147-10151). No evidence was ever provided to substantiate these oft repeated claims.

[5] The safe haven visas are not discussed in this book. They were introduced to provide short term stays in 1999 for refugees from Kosovo and East Timor and, as with the temporary protection visas, diminished access to Australia's protection for those non-citizens entitled to protection under the Refugee Convention, the Convention Against Torture and/or the International Covenant on Civil and Political Rights (Taylor 2000).

[6] Article 28.

[7] The state's capacity to return 'failed' refugees was clearly envisaged as a punitive measure. Phillip Ruddock spelt this out in an interview in 2003, commenting on the suicide of a tpv holder: '...there was a right way to come and a wrong way to come and the temporary visa is about saying yes, we honour our obligations but if things change at home, and you can go back, then you'll be going back' (quoted, Sexton 2003).

[8] Thus, Labor's shadow immigration minister, Con Sciacca, justified support for temporary protection on the unprincipled basis that: "I don't think for one moment that it will stop one illegal immigrant from coming into this country. In fact, I think it's a diversion... But the point is that I don't believe the Labor Party...should become...the bunnies for this incompetency of government in handling the issue. I would hate to think that I as Shadow Immigration Minister would be in a position where every time another boat came in that somehow he would be able to say 'Oh, it's the fault of the Labor Party'"(Sara 1999b).

[9] Marr and Wilkinson (2003: 1-13) argue that 'Australia had known for days the 20 metre Indonesian fishing boat with an ancient engine and an incompetent crew was on its way' and that the call could have been made at least 18 hours earlier. Evidence provided by the Australian Maritime Safety Authority (AMSA) to the Senate Select Committee shows that AMSA was informed 'the vessel appeared to require assistance' on 25 August (AMSA 2001).

[10] The medical assistance provided was extremely rudimentary. After the *Tampa* was boarded, an SAS doctor conducted medical assessment of 483 survivors in 28 minutes. A Red Cross team, consisting of a doctor, a nurse and a 'tracing' officer was also refused access to the ship by the Department of Prime Minister and Cabinet (Marr and Wilkinson 2003: 83, 115).

[11] See *Victorian Council for Civil Liberties Incorporated v Minister for Immigration and Multicultural Affairs and Ors; Eric Vardalis v Minister for Immigration and Multicultural Affairs and Ors* [2001] FCA 1297.

[12] For example, 'SIEV 3 was intercepted on 12 September near Ashmore Island with 129 people on board. They included 54 children and a heavily pregnant woman who subsequently gave birth while being transported to Nauru....These people were held in custody on their crowded vessel in Ashmore Lagoon for ten days before being transferred to the *Tobruk* (SSCCMI 2002: 28).

[13] Between 27 August and 9 November 2001, the Committee met at least 53 times, sometimes two or three times in a single day (SSCCMI 2002: 7)

[14] For a discussion of the critical coverage of the Government's actions in relation to the *Tampa* in the *Australian* and *Sydney Morning Herald*, see Kelly (2002). For a discussion of the tabloid coverage, which overwhelmingly and vociferously supported the Government's actions, see Lygo (2004: 34-77); Manning (2004: 34-39); and Poynting et al (2004: 11-51).

[15] Transcript of the Hon Peter Reith MP Radio Interview with Derryn Hinch - 3AK, 13 September 2001, http://www.defence.gov.au/minister/2001/1309013.doc, accessed 6 February 2007.

[16] See Transcript of the Prime Minister the Right Hon John Howard MP, Press Conference, Parliament House, Canberra, 4 October 2001, http://www.pm.gov.au/news/interviews/2001/interview1269.htm, accessed 6 February 2007.

[17] See Kelly (2002: 34-45); Marr and Wilkinson (2003: 181-210, 252-265); SSCCMI (2002: 31-194); and Weller (2002).

[18] The commander of HMAS *Adelaide*, which intercepted the SIEV 4, did not initiate the rescue until the SIEV was sinking and several people were in the water because his mission aim was to deter the entry of the vessel into Australian territorial waters (SSCCMI 2002: 32-39)

[19] Border Protection Bill 2001

[20] According to Marr and Wilkinson (2003: 88), Howard commented privately to Kim Beazley, 'I don't really need it'.

[21] *Migration Amendment (Excision from Migration Zone) Act No.127* 2001; *Migration Amendment (Excision from Migration Zone) (Consequential Provisions) Act 128* 2001; *Migration Legislation Amendment (Judicial Review) Act No.134* 2001; *Migration Legislation Amendment Act (No.1) No.129* 2001; *Migration Legislation Amendment Act (No.6) No.206* 2001; and *Border Protection (Validation and Enforcement Powers) Act No.126* 2001.

[22] Under the 2001 legislation, this could be done by Regulation, thereby avoiding the need for parliamentary debate. For a chronology of the changes from 2001 to 2005, see Coombs (2005).

[23] See Migration Amendment (Designated Unauthorised Arrivals) Bill 2006.

[24] The text of the note handed by the Afghans aboard the *Tampa* to the Norwegian Ambassador is reproduced in *Victorian Council for Civil Liberties Incorporated v Minister for Immigration and Multicultural Affairs and Ors,* as cited, at par.28.

[25] In the case of Nauru, one politician recently argued that much of the aid

money 'was spent "propping up a corrupt and inept government"...Power was still unreliable despite commanding three quarters of the Australian aid money, only one classroom had been built and the port facilities could break down at any moment' (Gordon 2005: 83).

[26] For example, the Government directed the relevant Departments not to cooperate with the 2002 Senate Select Committee.

[27] The APS is an arm of the Australian Federal Police.

[28] One of the Sri Lankan men transferred was initially referred for medical treatment in Perth. Despite suffering mental health problems and having shrapnel embedded in his brain from a bomb, he was subsequently declared fit to travel in June 2007. The Immigration Minister refused the man's request to be processed in Australia (AAP 2007a).

[29] The words 'remove' and 'deport' have precise meanings within the migration legislation but are used interchangeably in this section.

[30] Copy of transcribed statement dated 3/10/04 provided by Ian Rintoul of Refugee Action Collective.

[31] See for example ERC (2004) and (2006).

[32] Statement of Sonia Chirgwin, dated 28/12/04, circulated by email by Rural Australians for Refugees, 10 January 2005.

[33] For an insight into the experiences of security staff engaged in such removals, which suggests that multiple forms of restraint were common, see *Cork and Australasian Correctional Management Pty Ltd* [2003 NSWIRComm 1056 (7 October 2003).

[34] See, for example, Corlett (2005); and Edmund Rice Centre (2004) and (2006). See also Nicholls (2007) for a history of forced removal practices.

[35] See sections 198B and 494B *Migration Act* 1958.

[36] There is a substantial disparity between the often highly publicised allegations of people smuggling and actual prosecutions. Out of approximately 1,000 allegations there were 19 prosecutions and 17 convictions between June 2000 and June 2005 (DIMIA 2005a: 95).

[37] It was formally re-adopted with the renewal of the MOU in June 2002.

[38] I have used accounts taken from a transcript of a videotape made of the survivors in the week following the shipwreck. They have been translated from Arabic into English and are reproduced at http://sievx.com/articles/distaster/KeysarTradTranscript.html. A range of other accounts can be found at http://sievx.com.

[39] See also the extensive reading guide on this subject at http://sievx.com/ReadingGuide.shtml.

[40] See also resolutions to the Senate dated 11 December 2002; 15 October 2003; 16 October 2003; and 22 June 2004.

[41] On the sixth anniversary of the sinking, the Australian Federal Police still refused to release its list of the names of those who died, 'citing continuing investigations into people smuggling' (Peake 2007). See also Kevin (2004: 17-18).

[42] The immigration department has not published details of what happened to the various survivors. According to Margo Hutton, editor of the SIEV X.com website, who is writing a PhD thesis at Latrobe University on the SIEV X, 'five who survived the sinking are living in Australia and several who got off the boat before it sank are also here. Countries the others were resettled to include New Zealand, Finland, Canada, Sweden and Norway' (email from Margo Hutton, dated 12 February 2007).

[43] For the curious tale of how Quassey ended up in Egypt, see Kevin (2004: 201-213). In December 2003, Quassey was sentenced to five years imprisonment for homicide and two years for aiding. The latter sentence was later reduced on appeal to three months. See http://sievx.com/chronology/.

[44] Alexander Downer, MP, Speech to the Bali Process Senior Officials' Meeting, 8 June 2004, at http://www.foreignminister.gov.au/speeches/2004/040608_bali_process.html., accessed 29 March 2006.

[45] See Migration Series Instruction (MSI) 391: 'People Trafficking'. My thanks to Jennifer Burn of the University of Technology, Sydney, for providing me with this.

[46] This framework was amended in June 2009, when the term of the visa was extended to 45 days.

Chapter 6

A system of abuse: the Australian gulag[1]

Detention and criminalisation

The mandatory detention policy is central to the Australian state's systemic exclusion of forced and illicit migrants. The policy consolidated the alienation and criminalisation of unauthorised arrivals, provided the ideological and institutional foundations for the Pacific Solution, and remains the state's first response to unauthorised entry. Detention contributes to the systematic criminalisation of unauthorised migrants at two levels. Ideologically, it reinforces the deviance attributed to unauthorised migrants through the state's persistent association of unlawful entry with illegality; the use by unauthorised migrants of people smugglers; the association of people smuggling with transnational organised crime; and the construction of refugees, especially those from Muslim backgrounds, as threatening outsiders. Physically, refugees have been criminalised through their incarceration in prison-like institutions, where the daily imperatives of control and management systematically undermine detainees' decision making capacity; their ability to engage with the wider polity; and their access to proper legal advice, care and protection.

Punishment is the inevitable corollary of criminalisation. By definition, a system designed to deter unauthorised entry invests in unauthorised migrants a capacity to make free, calculated choices. According to this logic, those who choose to risk being detained are receiving their just desserts. However, this extends beyond the deprivation of liberty and its numerous disciplinary consequences. Detention has exacted a heavy toll on the physical and psychological well-being of many detainees, often exacerbated by existing vulnerabilities arising from age, histories of torture and abuse, and the stress associated with the indeterminate nature of detention. The

A system of abuse: the Australian gulag

serious acts of self-harm, hunger strikes and other forms of protest which detainees have used also illustrate the perverse forms of self-punishment generated by prolonged incarceration.

The notion that unauthorised migrants are so deviant they need to be locked up has driven elaborate bureaucratic processes that have blurred the lines of responsibility for indefensible state behaviour such as the unlawful detention of permanent resident Cornelia Rau and the psychological damage inflicted upon 7 year-old Shayan Badraie. The Howard government's attempts to explain these episodes as mistakes typified the techniques of neutralisation and denial it deployed in response to critiques of the detention regime. These included straight out denial of allegations, denigration of critics, attributing abusive state acts to lapses in management practice, isolating such lapses to the activities of particular individuals or groups of individuals, and where possible, refusing to accept overall political responsibility. The implementation of such techniques was evident in the narrow, politically determined terms of reference given to inquiries such as that investigating the unlawful detention of Cornelia Rau (Palmer 2005). As a result of that inquiry and others it generated, the government committed itself to implementing a number of internal administrative changes aimed at avoiding future enforcement errors involving detainees with a legal right to live in Australia. However, the Howard government continued to promote the theme that unauthorised entry is fundamentally illegitimate and that 'genuine' refugees ought to be accessing formal resettlement processes. In this way, unlawful, negligent or abusive state behaviour was rationalised as an unfortunate consequence of a necessary deterrence policy.

The scale of the abuse in detention centres ultimately damaged the Howard government and since its election in 2007, the Rudd government has attempted to re-frame detention as a short-term administrative necessity that operates primarily to facilitate initial screening or removal. Nevertheless, by the end of 2009, hundreds of refugees were languishing in potential long-term detention on Christmas Island, while the mainland centres were still holding people who had been detained in highly damaging environments for over two years (Grewcock 2009).

This chapter challenges understandings of abuse within the immigration detention system as exceptional or avoidable and will argue that instead abuse is an operational and systemic norm. There are a number of intersecting themes: the impact of detention on detainees; the institutional dynamics of detention; the symbolic and ideological functions of detention; and the fundamental role of the Australian state in its operation.

The detention complex

Although various forms of detention have always been allowable under the *Migration Act*, the current network of immigration detention centres is intimately associated with the development of the mandatory detention policy. During the 1990s, most of those detained under the policy were held in immigration reception and processing centres near Port Hedland and Derby in north Western Australia and Woomera in South Australia. Existing immigration detention centres such as Villawood in Sydney and Maribyrnong in Melbourne, were used as back up while in Queensland, detainees were held in designated prison facilities.

The three regional centres were hastily commissioned on sites previously used as mineworker or military barracks in response to sudden increases in the numbers of unauthorised arrivals. These centres, surrounded by razor wire, were little more than desert prison camps. The Curtin, Port Hedland and Woomera centres are now closed. They were replaced by the purpose built Baxter Immigration Detention Facility near Port Augusta, South Australia, which has subsequently closed; a network of purpose built or upgraded centres in Darwin, Perth, Adelaide, Melbourne, Sydney and Brisbane; secure residential housing centres attached to the Baxter, Sydney and Perth centres; and a purpose-built detention centre on Christmas Island, operating alongside a smaller, makeshift centre. In practice, the various centres constitute a national prison estate for immigration detainees, who are quarantined from the outside world and reduced to mere objects within a wider bureaucratic process. With the Australian state bestowing upon itself the automatic right to detain, maintaining the integrity of that

A system of abuse: the Australian gulag

process, rather than claims to liberty and protection by individual detainees, became the major managerial concern.

As the volume of long term detainees increased during the 1990s and the immigration department was confronted by an increasingly desperate, self-harming and restive detainee population, preventing escapes and maintaining control over individual and collective movement became a priority (SLCRC 2006: 152). For example, in 1995 at Port Hedland, 'a number of internal fences topped with razor wire were installed which, when the gates [were] shut, [fenced] off each accommodation block. In addition, double and triple fences covered in hessian [were] erected around parts of the centre preventing visual contact between detainees and members of the community' (HREOC 1998: 87). In 2002, Port Hedland's isolation block was refurbished even though the centre was soon to close. 'No expense has been spared in transforming Juliet block into a maximum security prison within a prison', wrote Labor parliamentarian Carmen Lawrence (2003) following a visit to the centre. 'The majority of the thirty plus cells are identical with cells normally reserved in the prison system for the most serious offenders. They are complete with massive, soundproof doors, peepholes, toilets and video surveillance and have been designed to eliminate hanging points'.

The refinement of such isolation units was part of a wider strategy of containing and dispersing 'non-compliant' detainees. 'When you are managing a more difficult case load', explained Immigration Minister Ruddock in April 2002, 'splitting the population between a number of centres is a preferable way of ensuring that you're able to maintain order and certainly manage any disturbances and other inappropriate behaviour with much more relative ease' (Griffiths 2002). The drive to physically control detainees produced new centres modelled on high security prisons. Although razor wire did not feature on its perimeter fences, Palmer (2005: 67) described Baxter as a 'corrections style facility' with an 'unavoidably severe' appearance. Gaining access to such facilities was not much easier than getting out. One visitor to Baxter described:

Border Crimes

> The sign in procedure was very thorough...Firstly, you hand over your ID...and they check it off on the list that has been previously approved for visitors. You then are asked to place all your personal possessions into a locker...except the food you are taking in to the detainees. You are wrist banded and then stamped with an ultra-violet sensitive ink-stamp....After the first group had been stamped and banded, we were led over to the main gates of the compound.Each gate is under constant guard, and no one guard can allow people through on their own. The gate is buzzed from one end and opened from the other. The main gate opened and we were led into the cage in between the first and second gate. We waited for our small group to all be inside this cage and then the first gate was closed. Then the buzz was sent from the second gate to the room next door and we were led into the second checkpoint.The fence that joined the second gate to that little room was referred to as the "Courtesy" Fence – it carries a 9,000 volt charge. In this next room, we had to place all the food onto a conveyer belt, where it went through an x-ray machine....We had to individually walk through an airport style metal detector gate ourselves, and then have hand-held scanner passed over our person front and back with arms spread. The guard then checked every bag and food item individually....From here we were led outside to another door where we waited to be buzzed in (Whitten 2005).

The new Christmas Island centre was designed with similar levels of security. It has electric fences and microwave probes for detecting movement; there are camera systems posted under eaves, on roofs and in every room; and the whole camp can be linked by CCTV to a remote control room in Canberra. Detainees can be electronically tagged and tracked within the centre by locator beacons. There are cameras and microphones in every room, wall mounted behind heavy metal grilles. The doors to the rooms are electric and centrally controlled, requiring detainees to use 'request to exit' buttons. Cars accessing the centre must go through airlock systems and electric doors. Between the multi-layered fence systems there are checkpoints for human guards on patrol and outdoor security cubicles for them to sit, sited at short intervals all around

A system of abuse: the Australian gulag

the perimeter of the centre. Each of these security cubicles is wired with duress buttons and microwave probes (Black 2007a).

The maintenance of such expensive, large-scale, purpose-built immigration detention facilities indicates an ongoing commitment to detention. Even when it was empty during 2008, the Christmas Island centre operated as a public symbol of the government's border policing armoury that could be immediately commissioned in the event of another cycle of unwanted illicit migration. Moreover, when called upon by the federal parliament's Joint Standing Committee on Migration to reduce the levels of security at Christmas Island in 2009, Immigration Minister Evans refused on the basis of cost and the centre's role as 'an integral part of Australia's border protection regime' (quoted, Salna 2009).

The Christmas Island centre also provides the possibility of establishing a Guantanamo Bay type installation that can be adapted to holding 'terrorism suspects' and others whom the state might seek to isolate from the Australian community at large. Even if this does not eventuate, the consolidation of Australia's immigration detention infrastructure has normalised the incarceration of unauthorised migrants. And the acceptance of detention as a routine state activity has enabled decisions about its operation to be conceived as largely administrative and thus subject to prevailing fashions, such as privatisation, that affect the provision of public services.

Detention for profit

Australia's detention complex has been privately operated since 1997 (ANAO 2004: 45–46). Allowing private companies to operate immigration detention centres further neutralises the exceptional and deviant nature of blanket mandatory detention. It also raises important additional issues regarding accountability and responsibility for the impact of detention on detainees (Harding 1996; Moyle 2000).

The organisations responsible for privately running Australia's detention centres have been offshoots of multinational 'security' corporations involved in the operation of prisons and detention centres in the United States and Britain (Molenaar and Neufeld 2003). This is a profitable 'industry' with its own peak trade association, the Chicago based Association of Private Correctional and Treatment Organizations, and substantial backing from major financial institutions (Welch and Turner 2004 and 2007). Between 1997 and 2004, Australia's mainland detention centres were run by Australasian Correctional Management (ACM) the operational arm of Australasian Correctional Services, a partnership between the Australian construction giant, Thiess Constructions, and the United States based Wackenhut Corporation (Hooker 2005; Mares 2001:69–78). According to a recruitment advertisement published in the *Australian* on 20 January 2001, ACM was 'an international icon in the area of correctional rehabilitation'. However, the company's management of the detention centres, particularly Woomera, was the subject of extensive criticism, which included 'allegations of racial abuse and heavy-handed treatment by ACM officers' (Molenaar and Neufeld 2003: 130). The damning critiques of the Woomera regime by the Human Rights and Equal Opportunity Commission (HREOC 2004a) and to a lesser extent, the government instigated Inquiry into Immigration Detention Procedures (Flood 2001) probably played their part in ACM losing the contract in 2003 (PPRI 2001).

Between 2004 and 2009, the centres were operated by Global Solutions Limited (GSL), a subsidiary of the British based GSL, initially owned by Group 4 Falck (ANAO 2004: 47). Group 4's operations in the UK, especially at the Campsfield House and Yarl's Wood detention centres where major disturbances took place in 1997 and 2002 respectively, had been heavily criticised (Molenaar and Neufeld 2003: 131–134; PPOEW 2004). In May 2004, Group 4 Falck sold GSL to two European venture capital funds, clearly attracted by the 'growth prospects' of the detention industry. 'Start with a growing market' a television commercial for one of the funds began, 'swim in a stream that becomes a river; be a leader in that market, not a follower' (quoted, Morton 2004). Such corporate interest in detention underscored both its potential profitability and the way in which the commercialisation of immigration detention has contributed to a reinvention of the carceral relationship between the state and the detainee.

A system of abuse: the Australian gulag

With the advent of private prisons, locking someone up is no longer framed as the state exercising its direct authority and force over the individual. For private corporations, detainees fundamentally are a commodity that generates profits. For the state, the contractual process enables detention to be characterised as a service analogous to schools and hospitals; and within neoliberal orthodoxy, contracting out the operation of such institutions is essentially a financial matter. Thus, the federal government's decision to contract out 'detention services' was announced in its 1996 federal budget, without any reference to the wider ethical issues such as public accountability for the actions of the state or whether it is morally defensible to detain someone for profit.

It is left to the private sector to promote the ethical virtues of providing such 'services' but this often takes the form of a self-aggrandising corporate idealism that substitutes for concrete commitments by governments to the proactive enforcement of human rights. GSL's website[2] provided an almost sublime example of this, describing the company's operation of immigration removal centres in the UK as 'essentially managing communities' and 'guided by respect for human rights and personal dignity…and understanding and respect for cultural difference and diversity'. Rather than dwell on the somewhat chequered experience of its mainland centres, GSL's description of its Australian operations focused on the 'exotic' Christmas Island, where the company boasted that it had been able 'to provide professional services – including health, psychology, catering education and recreation – to the same standard that it delivers in the capital cities'. 'Some newcomers', it continued, presumably not referring to detainees, 'find the remoteness of Christmas Island and the unfamiliar experience of living on a small island, difficult to come to terms with, but for most GSL employees, living and working on this exotic tropical island is a place that rest [sic] firmly in dreams'.

Such glib corporate publicity provided an interesting case study of neutralisation. The fact that the UK centres institutionalise forced removal by the British state of unauthorised migrants prompted the silky acknowledgement that GSL was 'sensitive to the fact that many of the people in our care are concerned at the uncertainty of their future, as they await determination of their application to remain in this country'. Such language contrasted with independent assessments of the behaviour of Group 4 staff during the 1997 disturbances at Campsfield House. Nine detainees were charged with riot and violent disorder offences on the basis of evidence about these incidents given to police by Group 4 staff. However, the subsequent trial collapsed within one week when it became clear that some of these witnesses 'were "shown to have fabricated their evidence"' and 'questions were also raised with respect to "the integrity of their conduct during the disturbances"'(Molenaar and Neufeld 2003: 133).

GSL's practices were also strongly criticised in Australia (HRCOA et al 2005; SLCRC 2006: 213–244). In 2005, the company was fined $500,000 for breach of contract by the immigration department after it was revealed that five detainees transferred by GSL security van from the Maribyrnong detention centre in Melbourne to Baxter in September 2004 were 'assaulted, deprived of food and water, denied toilet breaks and subjected to sensory deprivation over an extended period of six hours' (ASRC 2006: 34).[3] GSL was further fined in 2005 after admitting that 'unregistered psychologists were used on 15 occasions to provide services at the Baxter and Christmas Island …centres, in breach of state and immigration laws' (AAP 2005).

In December 2005, a detainee at Villawood applied to the Federal Court to prevent GSL illegally employing detainees under a 'merit system' that enabled the company to pay detainees the equivalent of one dollar per hour, usually in the form of phone cards and cigarettes, for tasks nominally assigned under GSL's contract with the Department to kitchen hands, cleaners, gardeners and similar services (Robinson 2005; SLCRC 2006: 175–178). The case failed[4] but the government changed the Migration Regulations so that 'detainees may lawfully perform work in detention centres whether for reward or otherwise provided that the detainee requests the allocation to him of the work'.[5] This effectively enshrined a system of forced labour as 'detainees had no choice but to work because visitors could not bring them more than $10 per visit, there was no ATM within the detention centre to withdraw their own

A system of abuse: the Australian gulag

money and the federal Government charged detainees about $130 per day to stay there' (Robinson 2005).

GSL was also subjected to close scrutiny by the Palmer inquiry (2005: 57). Palmer prefaced his extensive criticisms of the Baxter regime with the blunt, if understated, 'much is wrong at Baxter'. It also appears from the inquiry into detention conducted by the Australian National Audit Office (ANAO 2004) that many of the shortcomings highlighted by Palmer were inherited from the previous contractual regime (ANAO 2004). However, both the ANAO and Palmer inquiry reports illustrate how privatisation obfuscates public understandings of state accountability. The reports devote considerable space to the administrative detail of detention centre operation without throwing clear light on it. The reports refer repeatedly to 'the contract'; although much of this document is not public and its contents can only be inferred. Nevertheless, it seems clear that the contract process was inherently damaging to detainees. The Palmer Report (2005: xiii) found the contract to be 'fundamentally flawed' and incapable of delivering 'the immigration detention policy outcomes expected by the Government, detainees and the Australian people'. Moreover, its 'unduly rigid, contract-driven approach has placed impediments in the way of achieving many of the required outcomes' (Palmer 2005: 61); and could 'never deliver to the Commonwealth the information on performance, service quality and risk management that DIMIA was confident it would' (Palmer 2005: 70).

Despite its contrary policy in opposition, the Labor Party has maintained private operation of detention centres. In June 2009, the Rudd government contracted Serco Australia; part of the UK based Serco Group, to operate the immigration detention centres for five years. GSL, now operating as G4S, won a separate contract to operate immigration residential housing and transit accommodation. Serco greeted the successful bid with the now familiar corporate-speak, pledging to provide 'the best possible environment for those in our care', while also congratulating itself on its 'ability to successfully leverage our world-leading home affairs capabilities to further broaden our presence in Australia' (Serco 2009). Nothing was said in the press release about the almost contemporaneous report issued by the Children's Commissioner for England, strongly criticising the impact of detention on children held at the Serco operated Yarl's Wood immigration detention centre (11 Million 2009).

At a basic forensic level, private operation multiplies lines of responsibility for state actions. Describing his visit to the Curtin detention centre in 2001, the Western Australian Inspector of Custodial Services observed:

> What soon emerged...is that the DIMA representatives and the ACS personnel see themselves as part of a unitary team. There is absolutely no differentiation in the day-to-day behaviour of their roles. As I walked around the facility, I was accompanied by two representatives of ACS and two of DIMA. In asking questions I found that they deferred to each other on operational and policy matters quite indiscriminately. There was absolutely no role differentiation apparent between them. When I probed about this, I was informed that DIMA was not at liberty to discuss monitoring or accountability arrangements as these were dealt with in Canberra, and were in any case, commercial-in-confidence. In other words, accountability consisted of little more than tick-a-box checks of documentation, supposedly talking place 2,500 kilometres south-east of Curtin (Harding 2001).

The removal of direct ministerial control over the daily operation of detention centres not only allows governments to distance themselves from practices that might be condemned as abusive but also has a deadening effect on public discussion. Private detention centre staff are prevented from publicly disclosing information regarding their employment, while GSL relied on the commercial confidentiality of its contract with DIMIA to avoid any public disclosure of its policies and procedures (SLCRC 2006: 215).

The process of privatisation also raises serious issues about the implementation of the government's obligations under international human rights law. International legal instruments such as the International Covenant on Civil and Political Rights and the Convention on the Rights of the Child impose a range of obligations on the Australian government regarding the 'humane' treatment of prisoners and detainees. Yet the Human Rights and Equal Opportunity Commission noted in 2004 that 'the contract between the Department and ACM did not fully incorporate the rights which the Commonwealth owed children in immigration detention' and that 'the Department's monitoring systems [failed to] reliably record or assess whether children were fully enjoying their rights under the CRC' (HREOC 2004a: 10).

While the detention service contracts have also imposed specific duties of care on the Commonwealth for each individual detainees and detainees as a whole (SLCRC 2006: 214), following litigation arising from the Campsfield House disturbances in 1997, the British High Court held

> ...that is was within the power of the Secretary of State to delegate the running of an immigration detention centre to an independent contractor, and given that the Secretary of State had exercised all reasonable care in the selection of such a contractor, he could not be liable for the torts of that contractor's servants or agents' (Molenaar and Neufeld 2004: 133).[6]

The Australian courts do not appear to have gone that far. In the case of 'S', a Baxter detainee who received inadequate psychiatric care, the Federal Court of Australia held that civil and criminal liability could attach to individual officials who abused or mistreated a detainee; and might also attach to those who manage a detention centre if they failed to comply with their duty of care to detainees.[7] Surprisingly, during the course of the hearing, the Commonwealth conceded that it was subject to a non-delegable duty of care concerning immigration detainees, although the legal issue has yet to be fully tested.

Overall, the private operation of detention centres further complicates the task of analysing state responsibility for the abuses that occur within the detention complex. In addition to the largely false separation the government constructs between itself and the administrative bureaucracy responsible for implementing its detention policy, private operators provide a further organisational tier to the structural chain of command. From a managerial perspective, it may well be possible to attribute responsibility for specific decisions and activities to the private operators, rather than state officials or representatives. However, the private operators do not operate in a vacuum. The 'service' they provide, while structured around the profit motive, is conditioned by both government policy and the culture of compliance driven by that policy throughout the immigration department and the government bureaucracy. As the inquiries generated by the unlawful detention of Cornelia Rau demonstrated, that culture of compliance was deeply rooted, resulting in systemic practices that were highly abusive and largely subordinated to maintaining the organisational integrity and uniform application of the detention process.

The culture of containment

The 'discovery' of Australian resident Cornelia Rau in the Baxter detention centre in February 2005 triggered a series of formal investigations into immigration department 'mistakes' that had resulted in the unlawful detention of 247 people during the years 1993 to 2007. Some of these decisions had profound consequences: Cornelia Rau was detained for ten months; after being wrongly detained and peremptorily removed, Australian citizen Vivian Alvarez Solon was stranded in the Philippines for four years; Australian citizen Mr T was detained on three separate occasions for a total of 253 days (CO 2006a); and East Timorese refugee Mr G, who was entitled to a form of permanent residence,[8] was detained for 43 days having legally lived in Australia for over 25 years (CO 2006b).The reports of the various inquiries provided substantial insights into the decision making processes and the culture of containment operating within the department. Because the reports deal with decisions to detain that clearly were unlawful under the terms of the *Migration Act*, the department was forced to acknowledge its errors and in some cases agree to pay compensation.[9] Nevertheless, in highlighting the routine, systemic resort to detention of anyone immediately unable to prove their identity, the reports provided a valuable body of source material on an administrative culture generally closed to independent scrutiny.

Cornelia Rau

Cornelia Rau was a permanent resident of Australia who was unlawfully detained under section 189 of the *Migration Act* 1958 in March 2004. She spent six months in the Brisbane Women's Correctional Centre (BWCC) and a further four months at Baxter, before she was correctly identified and released. Cornelia Rau arrived in Australia with her family from Germany, aged 18 months, in 1967. She spoke 'fluent Australian-accented English' and according to her sister, could not engage in 'a sustained or very complex conversation in German' (Palmer 2005: 1–2). In about 1996, Cornelia Rau began suffering from mental health problems, including psychotic episodes. In March 2004, she disappeared from a Sydney hospital but because this had happened before, she was not reported missing by her family for five months. In late March, she turned up in north Queensland where, having given conflicting accounts of her identity to the police, she was detained at the request of the immigration department. Following an interview with immigration officers in Cairns, during which she maintained she was German and gave her name as Anna, she was detained in the BWCC. As a result of her behaviour in prison, Cornelia Rau was transferred to the Princess Alexandra Hospital in Brisbane on 20 August for a psychiatric assessment. She was returned to prison after six days, after being diagnosed as not suffering from a mental illness. She continued to have difficulty coping at BWCC, where she was placed on four separate occasions in confinement cells used for prisoners who have breached discipline.

On 6 October, Cornelia was sedated, placed in restraints and transferred against her will to Baxter detention centre. There, she underwent an erratic series of psychological and psychiatric assessments. A psychologist initially diagnosed her as having a personality disorder and her behaviour was regarded as 'attention seeking'. On 6 November, a psychiatrist recommended a further assessment at a psychiatric facility but this was not properly followed up. A further assessment at Baxter on 7 January 2005 suggested she was schizophrenic. Eventually, on 3 February she was committed for further assessment under the South Australian *Mental*

Health Act but later the same day, as a result of a chain of events triggered on 21 January by the circulation of details about her plight that appeared on the Baxterwatch website,[10] Cornelia was identified by her family and transferred to hospital for urgent psychiatric treatment. During her time at Baxter, Cornelia's behaviour was considered 'disruptive and non-compliant ... and she persisted in the attitude that she had done nothing wrong' (Palmer 2005: 207). She spent only fourteen days in normal 'open' conditions. The rest of her detention was spent in 'behaviour management' units, where she had little privacy; was often under the surveillance of male officers; and restrictions on the regime included limiting time out of her room to four two-hour blocks per day.

The inquiry into the detention of Cornelia Rau, chaired by former Australian Federal Police Commissioner, Mick Palmer, was established on 9 February 2005. On 2 May 2005, the immigration minister asked Palmer to also examine the circumstances of the removal of Vivian Alvarez Solon, which had subsequently come to light. Some provisional findings regarding Vivian Alvarez Solon were incorporated into the Palmer Report (Palmer 2005: 183–193), which was published in July 2005. Responsibility for the Alvarez Solon investigation was then passed to the Commonwealth Ombudsman, who had been referred the first batch of the further 247 cases whose unlawful detention the department was forced to concede. The Ombudsman published the Alvarez Solon Inquiry's report, conducted by former Victorian Police Commissioner, Neil Comrie, in September 2005 (Comrie 2005). The remaining reports relating to the outstanding 247 cases were published in 2006 and 2007. These included two detailed case studies of refugees suffering from mental health problems (Mr T and Mr G) (CO 2006a and 2006b); and six consolidated public reports dealing with 'systemic issues' associated with mental health and incapacity, children in detention, detention process issues, data problems, notification issues and other legal issues (CO 2006c, 2006d, 2007a, 2007b, 2007c and 2007d).

The common theme of the various inquiries was that the repeated unlawful decisions to detain by individual immigration officers were the product of an internal immigration department culture motivated by the imperatives of removal (Comrie 2005:31) and that 'urgent reform is necessary' (Palmer (2005: ix). In relation to 70 of the 247 additional cases, the Commonwealth Ombudsman (CO 2007a: 20–21) concluded:

> ...that in many of these cases [immigration department] officers did not have an adequate basis on which to form a reasonable suspicion that the person being detained was an unlawful non-citizen.

Recurring deficiencies included:

> ...failure to consider legislative and policy requirements; failure to take reasonable action to identify a person prior to the person being detained; failure to take reasonable steps to resolve conflicting information about a person's immigration status prior to the person being detained; failure to conduct appropriate checks of [immigration department] systems and other available information, prior to making a decision to detain a person; failure to interview or speak to a person prior to their detention; reliance on information provided by the police, which was not questioned by [immigration department]; and failure to weigh up all the available evidence and justify the detention decision in appropriate records.

Emphasising the automatic resort to detention, the Ombudsman (CO 2007a:21) further noted:

> A particular deficiency is that there was a tendency by officers to rely upon one small piece of information that may have indicated a person was an unlawful non-citizen, even where there was other ample evidence to show that the person was lawful. This was evident in cases where a compliance officer noted that the decision to detain a person was because the person had an accent, was not of Anglo-Saxon appearance or could not be located on DIAC's systems. Overall, the deficiencies in these cases point to a culture amongst compliance officers at the time of exercising the detention power either carelessly or prematurely.

Such 'deficiencies' were clearly the product of an organisational culture conditioned by a rigid and exclusionary public policy and the high degree of administrative power conferred on individual immigration officials. The ways in which the assumptions of illegality are able to take on a momentum of their own and extend to other state agencies are demonstrated clearly by the Vivian Alvarez Solon case, where the wrong decision to detain facilitated and was compounded by unlawful removal.

Vivian Alvarez Solon

Vivian Alvarez Solon was born in the Philippines but became an Australian citizen in 1986. Between 1995 and 2000, she had contact with various mental health services in Queensland and in 1999, was diagnosed as suffering from 'a paranoid psychotic illness complicated by alcohol and illicit substance misuse' (Comrie 2005: 10). On 17 February 2001, Vivian Alvarez Solon failed to collect her son from a Brisbane day care centre. Six weeks later, she was found late at night seriously injured in a park in Lismore, northern New South Wales. Her injuries, combined with recurring mental illness, meant she was not interviewed by immigration officers until 3 May, when she was wrongly assumed to be an 'unauthorised, undocumented arrival who might have been manipulated by certain people for sexual purposes' (Comrie 2005: 13).

Vivian Alvarez Solon was interviewed again following her discharge from hospital on 12 July. During the course of the interview, the record of which she was unable to sign, she told the officers she was an Australian citizen and that she wanted to remain in Australia. Although it should have been possible, DIMIA officers could not find a record of her under the name of Vivian Alvarez and failed to properly pursue the information she gave them. She was detained and placed under guard at a motel where she had little privacy and no access to medical facilities, despite one of the guards logging her condition as 'basically immobile/she requires assistance for walking, dressing and all basic hygiene needs' (Comrie 2005: 15). On 16 July, on the basis of no obvious evidence other than her presumed nationality, an undated, unauthorised note was placed on her file: 'Smuggled into Australia as a sex slave. Wants to return to the Philippines. Has been physically abused' (Comrie 2005: 15). On 19 July, a locum doctor, with no access to her medical records, declared Vivian Alvarez fit to travel. She was removed from the country the following day accompanied by a Queensland Police officer. Despite concerns raised earlier by the Philippines Consulate General in Brisbane, no arrangements were made for Vivian's care on arrival in Manila and she was simply left at the airport. By chance, she was supported by a charity that cared for her until she was 'discovered' by Australian officials on 12 May 2005, nearly four years later.

During the intervening period, and as early as July 2003, three senior immigration department staff were made aware of the unlawful removal but failed to follow it up. A number of more junior staff also knew. Vivian Alvarez Solon's name and photograph were broadcast on a television program about missing persons on 20 August and 'the unlawful removal of Vivian Alvarez was the subject of much discussion in [DIMIA's] Brisbane Compliance and Investigation Office in September and October 2004' (Comrie 2005: 30). In September 2003, the Queensland police notified the Department of Foreign Affairs and Trade (DFAT) that Vivian Alvarez Solon had been removed but neither the police nor the two DFAT officers concerned pursued the legality of the removal. Following the revelations regarding the detention of Cornelia Rau, Vivian Alvarez Solon's former husband, Robert Young, who had persistently contacted the immigration department after being told by the Queensland police in 2003 that Vivian had been removed, emailed the immigration minister's office in April 2005. This triggered the chain of events that uncovered her unlawful removal and led to the Ombudsman's subsequent investigations.

The lack of accountability

The Solon case illustrated clearly the ease with which the Australian state, with little or no accountability, could detain and expel even its own citizens. Had it not been for the publicity attached to the Cornelia Rau case, it is possible Vivian Alvarez Solon would still be in the Philippines.

Border Crimes

However, despite providing very detailed accounts of the internal culture within the immigration department and associated agencies that gave rise to such acts, the Palmer, Comrie and Ombudsman's reports failed to draw any systemic link between government policy and the activities of state officials. This created a conceptual vacuum in which unlawful state acts became the responsibility of errant individuals or unnecessary systems failures. Such a methodology was sustained in two principal ways.

First, the reports focused substantially on organisational and operational matters such as better inter-agency co-operation; more efficient and coherent information systems; improved systems of decision making and review; more staff training; and more oversight and review of the detention contract process. Partly, this approach reflected the government's tight control over the investigation process. Palmer's terms of reference, for example, limited recommendations to 'necessary systems/process improvements' (Palmer 2005: 196); while his report was also prefaced by stating that:

> Australia's immigration policy is deliberately directed at achieving a number of clear policy objectives...This policy was introduced in 1992 and has been maintained by successive governments. The Inquiry's comments in this report are not intended to call the policy into question (Palmer 2005: i).

Producing a report so explicitly designed to maintain existing policy could only be achieved within a narrow managerial framework. This was facilitated further by the method of inquiry. Palmer's inquiry was conducted as a quasi-police investigation, closed to the public. Palmer refused to disclose to lawyers representing Cornelia Rau or her family any of the evidence he collected. The immigration department refused funding requests from Cornelia Rau's lawyers for an independent psychiatric assessment and to take statements from Baxter detainees regarding her conduct and some of the key incidents in which she was involved.[11]

Second, the reports argue that immigration officers failed to properly interpret the relevant legislation or diligently follow internal departmental instructions. Thus, in relation to Cornelia Rau, Palmer (2005: 21–29) found the original decision to detain was lawful pursuant to Section 189 of the *Migration Act* because at the time, the immigration officer reasonably suspected she was an unlawful non-citizen.[12] However, because of a failure to subject that suspicion to ongoing review, the detention subsequently became unlawful.

A similar analysis was applied to Vivian Alvarez Solon's case where Comrie (2005: 68) found the suspicion that led to the original detention was not reasonable, specifically because of 'the failure to test the information Vivian provided in circumstances in which her poor mental health was readily apparent, the inadequacy of the investigation, and the lack of rigorous analysis of the available information'. The lack of reasonable suspicion was also central to the Commonwealth Ombudsman's (CO 2006a) critique of the detention Mr T., an Australian citizen since 1989, whose detention once in 1999 and twice in 2003, 'was a product of cumulative administrative deficiencies and systemic failures within DIMA' (CO 2006a: 18–19). Mr. T's detention suggested more than just sloppiness on the part of individual officials. The lack of care shown in dealing with someone with profound mental health problems was replicated in the case of Mr G (CO 2006b) and the nine other cases involving mental health and incapacity the Ombudsman considered (CO 2006c). Moreover, the consistent pattern emerging from the Ombudsman's reports was that the assumptions and decisions made by immigration officers were shaped by the availability of detention as an option and a belief that it was organisationally and politically expected that the power to detain would be exercised.

The mentally ill are particularly vulnerable in such an environment but others are affected as well. Thus the Ombudsman (CO 2007a: 18) in developing the argument for a more careful application of section 189 emphasised in relation to the 70 referred cases highlighting 'detention process issues' that there is 'no power conferred in the Migration Act to place a person in immigration detention in order to establish the person's identity or immigration status'; 'no power…to require Australian citizens to prove their citizenship'; and a requirement for 'DIAC officers [to] carefully consider and weigh up all the available and relevant information'.

It is a moot point whether the proper application of the *Migration Act* would have prevented the unlawful detention cases in question. However, the failure by individual immigration officers to exercise the minimal discretion allowed under Section 189 ought to be seen in the context of the repeated amendments to the *Migration Act* since the introduction of mandatory detention that have increased arbitrary administrative power; reduced judicial scrutiny; and been central to a government driven political discourse on border protection that has enforcement at its core. Vivian Alvarez Solon, for example, was removed from the country only a few weeks before the *Tampa* events and the subsequent construction of the Pacific Solution. The Palmer and Comrie reports gave some hints of the atmosphere within the department at the time. One of the staff who failed to act on the information that Vivian Alvarez Solon had been wrongly deported told the Comrie inquiry: 'There was a lot worse things going on than this particular case'. He then elaborated:

> We were trying to deal with a huge amount of complex and difficult removals cases, etcetera, at the time...But that's not an issue I can resolve. His is bigger than me. This is huge. As I said, there were - I'd begin to think about it and I couldn't even think of a way out of it, insofar as how you could even begin to resolve it (Comrie 2005: 81).[13]

However we interpret this convoluted explanation, the reports into such cases provided a snapshot of the relationship at a micro level between the state and those who were marginalised and disempowered by the border policing regime. Many of the critical decisions in these cases were made in a highly charged political atmosphere when excluding unauthorised migrants was a central political goal of government.

From the government's standpoint, it was important to neutralise the impact of unlawful decisions on this goal. The focus on departmental organisation and process enabled successive immigration ministers to accept the thrust of Palmer's recommendations and all of the Ombudsman's recommendations as part of its 'reform program' (DIAC 2007b), without being too challenged by wider questions of political accountability for the department's internal culture. Although Comrie (2005: 77–83) found that three senior immigration officers, one of whom subsequently resigned, who ignored information about Vivian Alvarez Solon's removal might have breached the Australian Public Service Code of Conduct, little direct responsibility for these cases was accepted at a senior state level. On the release of the Palmer Report, a new departmental secretary was made responsible for the implementation of the post-Palmer regime, while the secretary in place at the time of the unlawful detention cases was appointed Australia's ambassador to Indonesia; hardly a demotion given the centrality of the Australia-Indonesia relationship to the Australian state's strategy for policing unauthorised migration.

The culture of containment highlighted by the above cases resulted in a significant number of very vulnerable individuals being incarcerated or otherwise physically controlled by the immigration department. The unlawfulness of the department's actions caused a degree of political embarrassment and focused attention on a cohort of detainees who might otherwise have been ignored. However, perceptions of state deviance arising from such cases should not be shaped by the unlawfulness of the decisions to detain alone. Rather, it is the systemic impact of detention upon those who the state can claim some lawful right to detain that requires the detention system to be understood as form of state criminality in criminological terms.

A system of abuse

For many, the indeterminate nature of immigration detention has meant years of imprisonment. In June 2005, the longest serving detainee, Peter Qasim, was granted a bridging visa after seven years in detention. A month earlier, he had been transferred from the Baxter centre to a psychiatric hospital due to severe depression (Kerr 2005). By July 2007, reports tabled by the Commonwealth Ombudsman (CO 2007e) included investigations into four people detained for six years; 12 for five years; 31 for four years; 37 for three years; and 60 for two years or more.

Despite this, the voices of detainees have rarely been heard; indeed, to give some official space to the anxieties, frustrations and sheer rage of those subjected to detention would somewhat undermine the purpose of containing and isolating them. Even when allowed access to detention centres, journalists have been systematically prevented from speaking to detainees (APC 2002). So, we are left with fragments: snatches of evidence from independent inquiries; accounts by former employees with pixelated faces; submissions from concerned professionals and committed activists; sporadic reports by persistent journalists; and occasionally, the letters and recollections of those who have survived the detention experience. It is clear from all such sources that immigration detention entails a debilitating and disempowering daily routine. The younger of two Cambodian brothers detained when they were 16 and 18 years old, told the Human Rights and Equal Opportunity Commission:

> During the last couple of months of the five and a half years we spent in detention we were really depressed as we heard that the Australian Government was going to send us back to Cambodia. Mentally we felt sick and we had no lawyers and no-one else we could talk to about how we felt. I was so depressed at that time that I had nightmares every night. I also had headaches from worrying about what might happen to us and these would last for days... I took medicine like sleeping pills and anti-depressants for my problems but this didn't help me. I took medication every night for the last few months I was in detention (HREOC 1998: 219).

One of the many letters from refugees compiled by Amor and Austin (2003) observed:

> I am talking about a true prison, where thoughts are killed and death is always knocking at the door. The look of the security guards towards a detainee can be exactly compared with the look of a master to a slave, and when a detainee fighting for his self-respect opposes the guard, there is very cruel treatment (Anonymous, quoted Amor and Austin 2003: 38).

Such correspondence from detainees gives human voice to the extensive criticisms of the detention centres made by various inquiries. The Human Rights and Equal Opportunity Commission

A system of abuse: the Australian gulag

1998 report on the detention of unauthorised arrivals, which focused particularly on the Port Hedland detention centre, noted that the complaints the commission received prior to its inquiry focused on:

> 'the length and indefinite nature of the period of detention and the effects this has on detainees' physical and mental health; people not being told of their right to request access to legal advice when they are taken into detention; delays in people receiving responses for legal assistance to make applications to stay in Australia; people being held in isolation from other parts of the detention centre and the world outside; the use of force to control disturbances and restrain people; and the general conditions of detention such as food, medical services, education, recreation facilities, the level of security, privacy, sleeping arrangements and accommodation of detainees of different religions' (HREOC 1998: 4).

The inquiry's major finding was 'that the mandatory detention for almost all unlawful citizens who arrive by boat breaches Australia's human rights obligations under the International Covenant on Civil and Political Rights and the Convention on the Rights of the Child'. These breaches occurred as a result of 'the conditions of detention; detainees' restricted access to services, including legal advice and representation; the practice and effects of long term detention; [and] restricted access to judicial review of detention (HREOC 1998:13–14). The 'human cost' of detention the report noted, 'is apparent in the evidence of mental distress such as depression, boredom, sleeplessness, psychotic episodes, self-harm and suicide. The high level of physical complaints such as headaches, body numbness, dizziness and stomach and digestive disorders also reflects the degree of mental distress experienced by detainees'. 'In addition', the report continued, 'evidence of violence between detainees, especially within families, as well as between detainees and custodial officers suggests considerable tension created by the regime of control necessary to implement the policy of mandatory detention' (HREOC 1998: 218).[14]

The relationship between detention, mental health disorders and violent and repressive techniques of control was highlighted by the inquiry into the unlawful detention of Cornelia Rau. Palmer (2005: 119–158) made extensive criticisms of the arrangements in place at Baxter for the assessment, care and treatment of mentally ill detainees as did the Federal Court in *S v Secretary, Department of Immigration and Multicultural and Indigenous Affairs*.[15] In addition to the profound lack of proper medical care afforded Cornelia Rau, the significant issue to arise from her case was the routine use of isolation units for difficult or uncooperative detainees. Cornelia Rau spent all but two weeks of her detention at Baxter in the two isolation units, Red One and the Management Unit. These units were designed for 'behaviour management'. According to the submission lodged on behalf of Ms Rau by her legal team to the Palmer inquiry:

> The Management Unit (MU) is a punishing unit. It had conditions that would not be permitted in the prisons in South Australia. The features of the MU are as follows: a mattress on the floor; no window that you can see out of; camera surveillance 24 hours a day that offers no privacy; a shower and toilet area also visible on camera; no shower curtains; no reading material; no writing material; no change of clothes; no personal items; no recreational facilities; locked in the room 20 hours per day;[16] no independent monitoring of the unit; no statutory, contractual or regulatory maximum period – there have been reports of detainees kept for months in these environments; and used for detainees with behavioural problems that could…emanate from a mental illness.

The submission continued:

> Ms. Rau talks of times at Baxter when she had her allocated hours outside a cell and she was being moved back into isolation. She says on one occasion she was thrown on the ground with her arm twisted behind her back. She says she thought her ribs were broken she hurt so much. She also talks about another occasion when a number of guards were responsible for detaining her in a rough fashion…
>
> The two regimes of Red One and Management are the precise environments where a person with mental illness would always

fail to modify their behaviour through no choice...[Cornelia Rau] would not have been able to meet behavioural standards required to move through the four stages and out of the units because of her mental health issues. There is the danger in immigration detention that symptoms seen by others as being clear indicators of mental illness are seen by those who work in DIMIA and for GSL...as misbehaving and acting out.[17]

The use of behaviour management techniques against Cornelia Rau reflected both a specific strategy for pacifying her and a general institutional response to those unwilling or unable to comply with a prison regime. In the case of Ms.Rau, this response targeted someone who was already seriously ill when she was forced into the detention system. For many others, the experience of detention either generated mental illness or exacerbated conditions arising from the trauma that many unauthorised migrants have already experienced.

Such reactions to detention were not conditioned by the quality of the facilities. Psychiatrist Jon Jureidini,[18] who conducted a number of psychiatric assessments at the Woomera and Baxter centres, recalled his first visit to Baxter:

A man I have not met before invites me into his room at Baxter to meet his wife. Baxter was described as an 'improvement' on Woomera - en-suites, computers, playing fields. For this man, his wife and three children there were two rooms, each a 3 metre cube, with a bunk bed and just enough space to enter. I have never been in this room before; it is dark and I am disoriented. It doesn't feel right for a room to be so dark in late morning in the desert. As my eyes adjust, I see the man stooping over the bunk, a woman's face, eyes closed but finally opening at his insistence. She looks around, frightened, and within seconds she is keening, half scream and half moan. It builds and continues unrelentingly. Her husband tries to quiet her, looks to me, appealing, a little challenging...The moaning scream continues...I don't want to compound the harm that has been done to this woman who has not spoken for two years, not walked for two months, who crawls to the toilet, is carried to the shower, screams when anyone but her husband approaches her, keeping even her children away. I leave and she screams on (Jureidini 2007: 150–151).

This single encounter throws light on a world far removed from the bellicose state rhetoric about border policing or the neutralising managerial doublespeak about immigration compliance or contractual obligations to meet immigration detention standards. Like Cornelia Rau, the woman observed by Dr.Jureidini was not an exception produced by administrative failures. In his submission to the Senate Inquiry into the Migration Act (SLCRC 2006), Dr Jureidini (2005) wrote:

> The implementation of immigration detention over the last 5 years has caused severe psychological damage to detainees. I know of no other cohort where such universal mental ill-health has been demonstrated. Parents have been crippled by their experiences to a point that they could not protect their children, and all children have been damaged by having witnessed frightening violence and adult self-harm. Most single men who have been in detention for longer periods of time are grossly damaged. Their characteristic coping methods (eg, working, camaraderie, exercise) collapse after 1 or more years. Gradually protest and self-harm emerge, only to be replaced by withdrawal, with men isolated to their rooms, ruminating unproductively about their misfortune or the future and with grossly disrupted sleep and other bodily functions.
>
> Better mental health services in detention will not help, because the environment is so toxic that meaningful treatment cannot occur. It is not clear to what degree the detainees will recover, but some show significant signs of continued traumatisation a year after release.

Dr. Jureidini's submission was consistent with the views expressed to the Senate committee by the Royal Australian and New Zealand College of Psychiatrists (RANZCP 2005) and encapsulated the findings of a growing body of research into the impact of detention, which emphasises the systemic link between immigration detention and mental ill health.[19] This research is not limited to high profile centres such as Woomera and Baxter, or to refugees from

A system of abuse: the Australian gulag

particular states such as Afghanistan and Iraq. A seminal 'participant-observer study'[20] based on 33 detainees who had been held at Villawood detention centre for more than nine months found:

> All but one of the detained asylum seekers displayed symptoms of psychological distress at some time. At the time of the survey, 85% acknowledged chronic depressive symptoms, with 65% having pronounced suicidal ideation. Close to half the group had reached the more severe tertiary depressive stage. Seven individuals exhibited signs of psychosis, including delusional beliefs of a persecutory nature, ideas of reference and auditory hallucinations. Due to the severity of their psychological symptoms, hospitalisation has been recommended for some of these people by the centre health staff, but authorities have not approved this, except in medical emergencies after incidents involving self-harm. A few have been deported without receiving any appropriate care (Sultan and O'Sullivan 2001:595).[21]

The systematic use of confinement techniques within the detention environment intersected with the widespread resort by detainees to acts of self-harm. The Howard government did little to acknowledge or address the scale of self-harm in immigration detention centres acts of self-harm by immigration detainees were not systematically monitored or recorded. Chair of Suicide Prevention Australia, psychiatrist Michael Dudley, noted in 2003, 'Men's and women's rates of suicidal behaviours [in immigration detention], while imprecise, are calculated as 41 and 26 times the national average, respectively, and male IDC rates are 1.8 times the male prison rates' (Dudley 2003). Moreover, figures obtained from the department through a freedom of information request in 2005 indicated there were 878 acts or threats of self-harm, involving approximately one in 20 people in detention, between July 2002 and June 2005 (Topsfield 2005b).

The government consistently argued that such figures misrepresented the extent and gravity of self-harm amongst detainees (Topsfield 2005b) but government's response to self-harm and suicide amongst this group was directly at odds with its relatively proactive suicide prevention policies in the wider community (Dudley 2003). Rather than focus on early intervention strategies that address systemic factors and directly engage with those considered vulnerable, state authorities routinely dismissed self-harm by detainees as manipulative behaviour. Asked whether he accepted self-harm showed desperation by detainees, Immigration Minister Ruddock declared 'in many parts of the world, people believe that they can get outcomes in this way... [i]n part, it's cultural' (Whitmont 2001). While not resorting to such unsubstantiated and racist caricatures, Ruddock's successor, Amanda Vanstone, described self-harm as 'a very unattractive type of protest' (Topsfield 2005b); but as unpalatable and confronting as it might have been for the minister, self-harm was a reflection both of the vulnerability of detainees and the limited, if desperate, forms of protest available to them. The stitching of their own lips by detainee hunger strikers, for example, symbolised a lot more than a desire not to be force fed and stands out as one of the most compelling and damning images of the detention process. The dual nature of self-harm as both a sign of vulnerability and a desperate form of protest was particularly acute in the case of the children locked up under the mandatory detention policy.

Children in detention

The mass incarceration of thousands of children is arguably the most abusive legacy of the mandatory detention policy, which until 2005 did not discriminate between adults and children. It is clear that many children were seriously damaged as a result of their experiences in detention; and that the treatment they received at the hands of, or as a consequence of the decisions of, the Australian state seriously breached international law and would have constituted serious criminality in any other context. Although many of the adverse effects of detention on children apply to detainees generally, the particular vulnerabilities of children arising from their age and recognised by instruments such as the Convention on the Rights of the Child, made their detention especially deviant.

The Human Rights and Equal Opportunity Commission report into the detention of children (HREOC 2004) considered the detention of 2,184 children[22] during the period 1 July 1999 to 30

A system of abuse: the Australian gulag

June 2003 (HREOC 2004: 9). The ages of this group ranged from children born in detention through to 17. A snapshot of those detained on 30 June 2001 showed that 144 were aged 0 to 4 years; 210 aged 5 to 11 years; 278 aged 12 to 17 years (HREOC 2004a: 73–74). These children overwhelmingly were found to be refugees (HREOC 2004a: 66–70), although some had to endure over five years in detention (HREOC 2004a: 9).

The incarceration of such young children clearly confronted all social and legal norms. The inquiry found that the detention system was 'fundamentally inconsistent with the Convention on the Rights of the Child' (HREOC 2004a: 5–6). It recommended the release with their parents of all children in immigration detention centres and residential housing projects within four weeks; urgent amendments to Australia's immigration laws to ensure compliance with the Convention on the Rights of the Child; the appointment of an independent guardian for unaccompanied children;[23] legislative codification of minimum standards of treatment for children in immigration detention; and a review of the impact on children of the Pacific Solution (HREOC 2004a: 2–3).

The federal government immediately rejected these findings and recommendations. On the day the report was published, Immigration Minister Vanstone told journalists: 'What it says to people smugglers is if you bring children, you'll be able to be out in the community very quickly, and that is a recipe for people smugglers to in fact put more children on these very dangerous boats and try to bring them to Australia. We think that is a mistake and we won't be adopting that policy' (quoted, ABC Online 2004a). The minister's standard juxtaposition of the rights of children and the war on people smugglers was extraordinarily glib given the report's detailed catalogue of widespread institutionalised child abuse. Had such abuse occurred in any other institutional setting such as a children's home or school, it would almost certainly have caused a major public and political scandal and may well have led to criminal charges.

This abuse took many forms including: referring to children by their number rather than name, verbally abusing them and treating them like adult prisoners. It was experienced in a range of ways from the anxieties produced by indefinite detention in harsh conditions through to serious physical and psychological damage. The testimonies of the children reproduced in the report repeat many of the frustrations and fears expressed by adults. Some of those interviewed in a group said:

> A feeling of darkness came on me in the detention centre, and all my hope disappeared. My world has been dark ever since....
>
> It was like a desert...It felt like we were in a cage. We could not go anywhere with all the fences and stuff...It was like a jail and there was no care...[M]any of the people were angry because of the time they were in detention. The children were crying. My father is so angry and I don't know why...It was a bad experience. There were no times when we were happy there....
>
> The whole camp is really, really bad, people are really stressed. Those people they are for a long time they get really agitated (quoted, HREOC 2004a: 169).

Such comments reflected the report's emphasis on the 'connection between long-term detention and the declining psychological health of certain children' (HREOC 2004a: 360). Some children were found to be suffering depression and post traumatic stress disorder, either caused or aggravated by ongoing detention. Little attempt was made to shield these children from acts of violence and self-harm. One child detained at Curtin told the Inquiry:

> My world has become like upside down, because I have never seen things like this, I see people who bury themselves alive one day. I wake up in the morning, I see people have buried themselves, I see people go on the tree and just jump down just like that and I see people who cut themselves, I see officers hit woman and children with batons, or use tear gas. I just, it's too much for me, I don't know why and sometimes I wonder you know, it is very stressful to me (HREOC 2004a: 406).

A psychologist who worked at Woomera in early 2002 described similar conditions:

A system of abuse: the Australian gulag

The self-harming was so prevalent and so pervasive that no child would have avoided seeing adults self-harming....There was very visible self-harm, constant talk of it. The children for example when I arrived would have seen people in graves...Some of the children – it was their parents or people they knew. They knew why the parents were doing this. They knew that the parents were talking about possibly dying. They were on a hunger strike. There was visible self-harming on the razor wire. People were taken to the medical centre at regular intervals having slashed. People taken to hospital. There were attempted hangings that these children would have seen (quoted, HREOC 2004a: 405).[24]

In addition to the oral testimony of detained children and professionals, primary records confirmed that as result of detention, children exhibited a range of problems including, 'anxiety, distress, bed wetting, suicidal ideation and self-destructive behaviour including attempted and actual self-harm' (HREOC 2004a: 359). Internal documents disclosed the range of methods considered by 11 Afghani unaccompanied children to implement a suicide pact: 'throwing themselves into razor wire; drinking shampoo or other products they could obtain; slicing skin with razor blades; hanging themselves; banging rocks into their skulls' (HREOC 2004a: 408). A snapshot of self-harm involving children detained at Woomera in January 2002 revealed seven cases of lip-sewing (two children sewed their lips twice); three case of body slashing (one 14 year-old boy who sewed his lips twice also slashed 'Freedom' into his forearm); two cases of ingesting shampoo; one attempted hanging; two unspecified acts of self-harm; and 13 threats of self-harm (HREOC 2004a: 408–409). A quoted report on Woomera by the South Australian Department of Human Services in August 2002 noted, 'Since January 2002, a total of 50 reports of self-harm have been raised on 22 children, ranging from 7 to 17 years...60 percent of these reports related to children 12 years or less' (HREOC 2004a: 410).

The Shayan Badraie case

Perhaps the most extreme example of the damage inflicted by detention is the case of Iranian boy, Shayan Badraie, who having been detained at the age of five, was diagnosed with acute post traumatic stress disorder as result of his experiences in the Woomera and Villawood detention centres between March 2000 and January 2002 (Everitt 2008; HREOC 2002; HREOC 2004a: 343–348). These experiences included exposure to major disturbances and acts of self-harm involving adult detainees; witnessing his mother and father being verbally abused and his father being assaulted by detention centre staff; and being isolated for nearly two months in Woomera's security compound. His symptoms at Woomera included 'bed wetting; sleep disturbance, including waking at night crying and at times gripping his chest and saying "they are going to kill us"; repeatedly drawing fences with himself and his family portrayed within them; social withdrawal; nail biting; and more aggressive behaviour at school' (HREOC 2004a: 344). Shayan's father recalled of their time in Woomera:

…and he doesn't move four or five days at a time.

He's very fearful and anxious, and he just sits in a corner not speaking.

We go to the medical service two or three times a day.

Then after four or five days they take him to the hospital.

Sometimes they tell us the child can survive for five days, meaning that only when he is about to totally collapse will they take him to hospital (quoted, Whitmont 2001).

Having been diagnosed as suffering from post-traumatic stress disorder, Shayan was transferred with his family to Villawood detention centre in March 2001, but after witnessing further fights and self-harm incidents he became increasingly withdrawn and mute. Medical records indicated that following the self-harm incident, 'Shayan would not leave his parents, hid under a blanket, wet himself, would not eat, would only drink small amounts of milk, would not speak and could not sleep' (HREOC 2004a: 346). After three days, Shayan was admitted for the first of eight occasions to Westmead hospital, where the Head of the Department of Psychological Medicine noted that 'his symptoms recur if he is

A system of abuse: the Australian gulag

returned to the environment that he has found traumatic' (quoted, HREOC 2004a: 347). In total:

> Shayan was seen 70 times by the Villawood detention centre medical services and…between March and August 2001, ACM health staff and Westmead Hospital specialists wrote 13 letters setting out the seriousness of Shayan's case and urging the Minister and the Department to remove Shayan from the detention environment in order to prevent further harm' (HREOC 2004a: 348).

Eventually, in August 2001, Shayan was transferred into foster care, while his family remained in detention. His mother and sister were released on bridging visas in January 2002 before his entire family were finally recognised as refugees and granted temporary protection visas in August 2002. The Human Rights and Equal Opportunity Commission conducted a separate investigation into Shayan's case in 2002 and recommended that the immigration department formally apologise and pay compensation to the family (HREOC 2002). The department resisted this but eventually made an offer of $400,000 during proceedings before the New South Wales Supreme Court in 2005.[25]

A new regime?

The shocking facts of the Badraie case and the HREOC report helped ensure that the detention of children remained a focus within parliament for those campaigning to change or overturn the government's mandatory detention policy. By July 2004, the minister seemed to be retreating from her initial response to the HREOC report when she announced that all but one child 'associated with illegal boat arrivals' had been released from detention (Banham 2004). However, including those still detained on Christmas Island and Nauru, 96 children remained in alternative detention while the legal regime so heavily criticised by HREOC remained entirely intact.[26] Amendments to that regime eventually were made in June 2005 when, in response to pressure from sections of its own back-bench, the government announced changes to the *Migration Act*[27] designed to ensure that children should only be detained as a measure of last resort; and that all families with children in detention would be placed under community detention arrangements (Phillips and Lorimer 2005: 10).

While seen as a retreat by the government, the impact of these reforms was limited. The secure residential housing facilities were still a form of detention, the amendments did not create enforceable rights and the new accommodation conditions were entirely at the discretion of the immigration minister. The amendments also had limited impact in the context of the Pacific Solution. Children diverted to other jurisdictions such as Nauru were not covered by the amendments, while the new Christmas Island detention centre was built with 'a compound with an eight cot nursery, childcare centre, play area and class rooms' (Black 2007), leaving open the prospect of the future imprisonment of children. In 2008, the Rudd government finally declared a policy of not detaining children in detention centres and moved to legislate this in 2009.[28] As with the previous amendments, other forms of community detention were not precluded, nor in practice the detention of children on Christmas Island.[29]

The detention of children highlighted the systemically abusive nature of immigration detention. The findings of the Human Rights and Equal Opportunity Commission demonstrated that abuse is fundamentally not the result of bureaucratic errors, aberrant behaviour by staff or administrative processes in need of fine-tuning or reform. But while the systemic impact of detention on children was severe, children should not be viewed as a special case; rather their experiences need to be viewed alongside those of the adults detained with them. The uniformly abusive nature of the detention regime and the shared experiences of detention require a unitary approach. This is particularly evident when considering the forms of resistance offered by detainees and the state's response to it.

Resistance and control

The isolation of immigration detainees from the wider community, readily available legal advice, the media and the routine forms of social interaction associated with civilian life reflects clearly

A system of abuse: the Australian gulag

the exercise of state force. This was compounded by a set of social relationships within the detention centres in which there was almost a total monopoly of power held by department and detention centre staff and no meaningful culture of participation or complaint. Referring to detainees he met at the Curtin centre, the Western Australian Inspector of Custodial Services commented:

> Their sense of being cut off from any kind of proper communication is profound. Nor was this helped by the presence of a scruffy little 'complaints box' in the dining area. There was nothing to indicate that their complaints were given any credence nor that letters to the Ombudsman or the Human Rights Commission necessarily got through – in fact, detainees believed that for the most part they did not get to their destination (Harding 2001).

The Palmer inquiry (2005: 70) similarly found that at Baxter:

> GSL and DIMIA staff attach no importance to communication with detainees and the provision of feedback on the progress of actions and requests. The present approach is, in effect, a one way communication system that does not recognise the importance of ensuring that the 'message' is properly conveyed and understood.

There have been many allegations of immigration and detention centre staff verbally abusing detainees.[30] However, the power relationships within detention centres cannot be understood purely in terms of the systems, levels or nature of communications. Ultimately, it is the state's total control over the fate of the detainee's attempt to enter or remain in the country that shapes the relationship and many of the flashpoints for the protests involving detainees derived from the delays in the state's immigration decision making process or the actual decisions.

Despite the open-ended, one-sided nature of the detention process, the government's attempts to entrap and quarantine detainees in a timeless exclusion zone have not been entirely successful. For detainees, disempowerment has not meant passivity. There have been numerous individual and organised acts of resistance involving various forms of non-cooperation, hunger strikes (including the sewing of lips), militant protests and escapes. These have occurred at all the main detention centres, including on Nauru and Christmas Island, and were escalating as the government moved to implement the Pacific Solution. Many of these protests were led by people with histories of dissident political activity in dangerous and repressive environments and an acute awareness of the political implications of Australia's detention policy. Mares (2001: 10) described a 'well-organised' hunger strike he witnessed at Curtin in 2000:

> Occasionally, before the heat of the day had peaked, or after it had eased, men would rise from the ranks of the crowd to speak, or rouse protestors with the chant 'Where are human rights? Where is freedom? We want freedom!' There was also a large, professionally drawn banner which depicted the dictator Saddam Hussein expressing gratitude to DIMA for its cooperation in locking up his critics.

The extent of the organisation behind detainee protests was also evident from the ways in which the protests were organised across different ethnic and social groups, the election of strike committees, the publication of camp bulletins, the speed with which protests spread between centres, the replication of protest methods, the use of escapes as a means of conducting protests in nearby towns before detainees mostly returned to the detention centres and sustained attempts to link up with activists in the community.[31] The scale of the protests indicated that detainees were able to maintain some sense of collective identity, despite the efforts of the Australian state. In February 2000, over 300 people took part in a hunger strike at Curtin detention centre, where 'a core group of about a dozen or twenty men had sewn up their lips' (Mares 2001: 10). In June 2000, almost 500 detainees broke out of the Woomera detention and staged protests in the nearby town. The same month, 150 detainees broke out of Curtin and 100 from Port Hedland. In November 2000, ten detainees were hospitalised after a hunger strike at Woomera. In January 2001, 'riots' at both Curtin and Port Hedland involved detainees using 'rocks, bricks, tree branches and bathroom fixtures' (Weber 2001). In March 2001, 14 detainees escaped from Villawood. Three days later, 60 detainees 'rioted' at

A system of abuse: the Australian gulag

Port Hedland after three Iranians were told they were going to be returned to Iran. A week later, 200 detainees were involved in disturbances at Curtin, while more protests occurred at Port Hedland throughout May.

There were further protests at Curtin in June, where some buildings, including part of the mess, were burnt down. In July, 46 people escaped from Villawood in two separate break-outs (Whitmont 2001). In August, 39 detainees went on a hunger strike at Curtin, five of these detainees sewed their lips. Another round of protests broke out at Port Hedland in January 2002 and at Port Hedland and Curtin in April. Meanwhile protests both inside and outside the Woomera detention centre over the Easter weekend led to the escape of over 50 people. Hunger strikes followed at Woomera in June 2002, when with the assistance of protestors another 35 people broke out. Although the number of refugee detainees in mainland centres began to decline from this point, there were violent protests at five centres in December 2002. Hunger strikes and similar actions also continued at Baxter in 2004, 2005 and 2006 and Villawood between 2005 and 2008.

This less than exhaustive list indicates the regularity with which detainees have engaged in protest actions. Many of these combined detainees inflicting harm upon themselves with more outward forms of individual and collective protest. Human Rights and Equal Opportunity Commission inquiry staff observed during their visit to Woomera in January 2002:

> ...hunger strikers, including a man being removed by stretcher from the Main Compound; people with lips sewn together; the aftermath of a man jumping onto razor wire; demonstrations (people climbing onto the top of dongas and calling out for freedom, people dragging mattresses and bedding into the compounds); an extremely distressed woman screaming hysterically for an extended period, apparently after a dispute with an ACM officer; actual and threatened self-harm; and smashing of windows' (HREOC 2004a: 303).

The protests that followed a few months later at Woomera, when 50 people escaped, are described in similar terms in ACM's records:

> Amongst other occurrences, detainees climbed on the rooves of dongas, waved banners and shouted chants of freedom. Some children climbed onto rooves with their parents, although they were quickly convinced to come down...Some detainees threatened to set themselves on fire if detention staff did not leave the compounds. Internal and external fences were brought down and some detainees used the dismantled fencing, bricks and rocks as weapons (HREOC 2004a: 308–309).

As video footage[32] of these protests shows, the protestors outside the centre were also involved in pulling down some of the perimeter fencing, allowing some detainees to escape. Protestors also intervened to prevent detainees being physically restrained and assaulted by Australian Protective Services and ACM staff.

There were significant repercussions for the protesting detainees. One account based on an interview with an Iranian detainee claims detainees 'had been warned that those who remained would be punished if anyone escaped'. Accordingly,

> [g]uards trashed rooms, beat inmates with batons, handcuffed the men and forced them to kneel all night on the dirt floor of the compound, teargassed people who had nowhere to run, and used pepper spray on women and children at close range' (McKay 2002: 3).

Drawing on ACM's records, the Human Rights and Equal Opportunity Commission noted:

> Tear gas was deployed on four different occasions. Water cannons were also used to subdue detainees and stop escapes. There were also some instances in which ACM officers used pieces of fencing and rocks as weapons in exchanges with detainees, a practice not condoned by ACM management. The disturbances continued throughout the day and night. Seventeen staff and 14 detainees were treated for minor injuries (HREOC 2004a: 308–309).

A system of abuse: the Australian gulag

Such responses by the detention centre authorities to protest activity appear to have been common. At Port Hedland, detainees working in the kitchen went on strike on 11 May 2001 to demand 'an increase in their rate of pay...a minimum of eight hours work, a proper roster of available work and paid overtime after eight hours' (AHRC 2001). The strike leaders were removed to prison, triggering further protests and a hunger strike. On 26 May, at 4am, '170 police officers and guards, armed with guns batons and shields, made a surprise raid', during which 'men, women and children were handcuffed, and women were hit with batons to force them to sit or kneel on the ground' (AHRC 2001).

In April 2002, ABC television broadcast a video taken by ACM staff of the disturbances at Curtin in June 2001 (O'Neill 2002). The tape showed a group of ten Afghan Hazara[33] hunger strikers placed in an isolation block after refusing to end their strike, which they had undertaken to demand access to legal advice. One of the men is shown to have climbed a tree, prior to being moved. Another group of Hazara refugees is seen outside the isolation block. More than 17 minutes after the tape began recording, the doors are opened. One of the men in the cells has collapsed and is wrongly believed by the outside group to have died. No medical assistance is offered at that point. The transcript read:

> With no effective communication with security or medical staff, their grief turns to anger.
>
> At some point after this tape finishes, other Hazaras push over the fence to get their friends out of isolation.
>
> Fires are set and property is smashed.
>
> The man in the tree, the first man who was seen covered in blood at the start of this tape, is eventually found guilty of four charges related to the riot and sentenced to five years jail.

The government responded to that video and the protests generally by stating that it would not be 'blackmailed'. The decision to charge one of the hunger strikers was also indicative of a general policy to process through the courts detainees believed to have broken the criminal law. The absence of civil rights as detainees and residence rights as unauthorised entrants was not a bar to being drawn into the civilian criminal justice process, where ironically detainees were admitted into a more formalised institutional process.

As can be seen, resistance by detainees was met with a range of control practices such as the deployment of special response teams dressed in 'riot gear, consisting of dark padded suits, helmets batons and shields' (HREOC 2004a: 319); the use of tear gas, water cannons and other forceful dispersal techniques; the use of isolation blocks and solitary confinement; and transfer of non-compliant and troublesome detainees into the prison system or across the detention centre complex (HREOC 1998: 101–119).

From the earliest operation of the detention policy, the government also moved to introduce additional control measures to confront particular forms of protest. In 1992, the Migration Regulations were amended, without any debate in parliament, to allow medical treatment to be given to detainees without their consent.[34] Designed largely to enable the forced-feeding of hunger strikers, the provisions probably breached International Covenant on Civil and Political Rights (HREOC 1998: 102) and clearly breached World Medical Association guidelines prohibiting 'non-consensual force feeding of hunger strikers who are mentally competent' (Kenny et al 2004). Under the guidelines, doctors are not compelled to enforce treatment if such action is contrary to their 'ethical, moral and religious convictions'. As a result, the regulation has been unenforceable.

In 2001, the government introduced legislation[35] that increased the penalty for escaping from immigration detention from two to five years; created an offence of making, possessing or distributing a weapon; established a regime for the strip searching of immigration detainees as young as 10; and introduced new screening measures for visitors to detention centres. At the same time the immigration minister foreshadowed laws to permit detention centre guards to use chemical restraints without the authorisation of a doctor. Following opposition from the Labor Party, the measure was not enacted (Dastyari et al 2006: 193) but such restraints continued to be used. On 11 June 2005, the *Australian* reported on a protest by

A system of abuse: the Australian gulag

Virginia Leong, a Malaysian national whose daughter Nancy was born and spent over the first three years of her life in detention:

> About a year ago, [Virginia Leong] climbed on to the roof of the detention centre with the child. The videotapes show what happened next. When she came down from the roof, Leong, a slight-built woman hardly larger than a child, was dragged along with her head held down by two large detention centre officers. When they reached the management unit, Leong was pushed face-down on the floor and a male officer about twice her size sat astride her, tightly holding her hands behind her back as a nurse instructed Leong, who was crying, to take Valium. In the world of DIMIA rules and regulations, Valium is a form of chemical restraint. Before administering it, detention centre officers must obtain the permission of Bill Farmer, the head of DIMIA. That's the theory, at any rate. In the real world, where Leong was being courteously restrained by detention centre officers engaging in an excessive use of force, the video shows a distressed Leong calling out: "I don't want the Valium." "Virginia, are you going to take the tablets?" says a nurse and, none too surprisingly, Leong, who still has the big officer sitting astride her tiny form, holding her hands behind her back, consents and takes the drugs.

Overall, the Australian state's response to acts of resistance by detainees has been to further punish them through formal criminal justice processes; the imposition of internal centre sanctions often involving force; or the denial of visas even if they are accepted as refugees. To the extent that such responses bestow upon a detainees formal associations with criminality, this only compounds the deviance the detention system inherently attributes to them.

The fact that detainees have resisted the extreme exclusion detention imposes upon them demonstrates a resilience that has not been welcomed by the authorities, and has also been used to justify the development of an even more elaborate security apparatus. Detainees cannot be blamed for this but it underlines the highly systemic and consciously controlled nature of immigration detention and the direct linkages between detention, criminalisation and abuse. This abuse is measured by egregious breaches of international human rights standards and a range of social norms, especially relating to the care and protection of children. It has been sustained by organisational cultures, which are shaped by political policies that reduce interactions between unauthorised migrants, immigration officials and detention centre staff to imperatives of control. That control is maintained by the physical restrictions detention entails, the necessarily regimented regime, and the ability to 'restore order' through overwhelming force. It is also maintained by the state's control over the refugee determination process and the mechanisms for formal inclusion into civil society.

We cannot abstract these broader sources of control from the face-to-face confrontations, or individual decisions that immediately trigger abusive episodes, if we are to avoid limiting conceptions of state crime to the acts or omissions of errant state officials or representatives. The next chapter therefore develops further a criminological perspective on state responsibility for the human cost of mandatory detention and links this to the ideologies of exclusion used to legitimise the state's alienation, criminalisation and abuse of unauthorised migrants.

Notes

[1] The term is taken from a comment by the Inspector of Custodial Services in Western Australia: 'I went to Curtin…and two people shinned straight up a tree and put rope around their necks, threatening symbolically, to hang themselves….clearly, these people are at the end of their tether because they are in limbo, they are in gulag conditions' (quoted, Jones 2002).

[2] http://www.gslglobal.com/sectors/secure_environment/immigration_removal_centres.html, accessed 4 June 2007.

[3] See also DIMIA (2005b) and Hamburger (2005).

[4] See *Hussein v Secretary of the Department of Immigration and Multicultural and Indigenous Affairs* [2006] FCA 286; and *Hussein v Secretary of the Department of Immigration and Multicultural Affairs* [No.2] [2006] FCA 1263.

[5] Hussein [No.2], as cited at par.5.

[6] See *Quaquah v Group 4 (Total Security) and the Home Office*, QBD (High Court of Justice), Case No. TLQ 340/01, 23 May 2001.

[7] See *S v Secretary, Department of Immigration and Multicultural and Indigenous*

Affairs (2005) 216 ALR 252.

[8] Under S.34 of the Migration Act Mr G was entitled to an Absorbed Person Visa, that was deemed to have been granted from 1 September 1994.

[9] In December 2006, it was announced that a 'significant' payout, the details of which would not be disclosed but are believed to be worth several million dollars, was made by the government to Vivian Alvarez Solon (Hart 2006). In March 2008, the New South Wales Supreme Court approved a $2.6 million compensation settlement to Cornelia Rau (Evans 2008b).

[10] See http://baxterwatch.net/

[11] Submission by Cornelia Rau Regarding her Unlawful Detention in Immigration Detention. Copy of submission provided by Claire O'Connor of the Legal Services Commission SA, who acted for Ms Rau.

[12] Section 189 of the Migration Act imposes an obligation upon an authorised officer to detain any person 'reasonably suspected' of being an unlawful non-citizen. See also *Goldie v Commonwealth*(2002) 188 ALR 708 and *Ruddock v Taylor* [2005] HCA 48 (8 September 2005).

[13] For a further account by an anonymous Immigration Officer of the atmosphere within the department at the time, see O'Neill (2005).

[14] One form this violence took, which was clearly linked to the conditions of detention, was sexual abuse. According to psychiatrist, Louise Newman, head of the Alliance of Health Professionals for Asylum Seekers, 'there is a culture of abuse and voyeurism within the system, especially at Baxter' (ABC Online 2006b); but there were also allegations of rape, attempted rape and other forms of sexual abuse at the Curtin (HREOC 2006) and Villawood centres (ABC Online 2006b), typically arising from women being placed in isolated circumstances amongst relatively large groups of male detainees. However, to the extent that action was taken in such cases, it was by way of referral to the police, rather than attempts to address issues related to the regime. In not confronting the context of control within the centres, investigations into sexual violence have remained episodic, including in the Villawood case, interviewing people who may have been abused in the presence of those who may have been abusing them (ABC News 2006; Cubby 2006).

[15] (2005) 216 ALR 252.

[16] In relation to this point the submission also notes that 'this used to be up to 23 hour per day, but Baxter now claim that at least 4 hours a day are now spent outside the cell area. It is unknown if Ms Rau was in

management at the time when the lock up was 23½ hours'.
[17] Extraordinary scenes taken from CCTV footage recorded at Baxter of Cornelia Rau being forcibly removed from her cell and strapped to a bed after her correct identity had been established were broadcast on the ABC Four Corners program on 15 September 2008. The program, including a transcript, can be accessed at http://www.abc.net.au/4corners/content/2008/s2362098.htm.
[18] Dr.Jureidini is one of South Australia's foremost psychiatrists. In his written submission to the Senate Inquiry into the Operation of the Migration Act in 2005, Dr.Jureidini lists his positions as Clinical Senior Lecturer, Department of Psychiatry, University of Adelaide; Senior Research Fellow, Department of Philosophy, Flinders University of South Australia; and Head, Department of Psychological Medicine, Women's and Children's Hospital, North Adelaide.
[19] See, for example, Dudley (2003); Silove and Steel (1998); Steel (2002); Steel et al (2004); and Sultan and O'Sullivan (2001).
[20] One of the authors of this study, Iraqi doctor Aamer Sultan, was himself detained for over three years at Villawood before being granted a 3 year temporary protection visa in July 2002. Following the publication of this study, he was awarded a special commendation in the 2001 Human Rights and Equal Opportunity Commission awards. He was refused permission by the immigration department to attend the awards, even with two escort guards.
[21] See also RANZCP (2005).
[22] These figures exclude the children detained on Manus Island and Nauru, where the Commission was refused access on the grounds that it had no jurisdiction.
[23] Approximately 14 percent of the children discussed in the report came to Australia alone (HREOC 2004a: 9).
[24] For a further account by the same psychologist, see Bender (2007).
[25] See *Shayan Badraie by his tutor Mohammad Saeed Badraie v Commonwealth of Australia and Ors* [2005] NSWSC 1195 (22 November 2005); and Everitt (2008: 273-288).
[26] These statistics were produced by the campaign group, Chilout, based on information provided by the Minister for Immigration, the Federal Senate and Nauruwire.
[27] See *Migration Amendment (Detention Arrangements) Act* 2005.
[28] See Migration Amendment (Immigration Detention Reform) Bill 2009.
[29] See Epilogue.

[30] See, for example, the incidents described by Harding (2001) and Parish (2000).
[31] See also Bailey (2007), which provides excerpts of interviews with former detainees with histories of political activity in their home country.
[32] I have a copy of a video entitled 'Woomera 2002' filmed by those involved in protests outside the centre.
[33] The Hazaras were a persecuted ethnic minority under the Taliban regime. Most of the group involved in these protests were eventually granted refugee status (O'Neill 2002).
[34] Regulation 5.35.
[35] *Migration Legislation Amendment (Immigration Detainees) Act* 2001.

Chapter 7

State crime and the ideologies of exclusion

Lineages of state crime

In order to consolidate a state crime paradigm, this chapter examines how the authority of the Australian state is exercised and maintained in relation to the border policing. Attributing criminality to the state is not an abstract process; the various institutions comprising the state have different levels of involvement and complex inter-relationships. Although the elected government plays a pivotal role and the Australian state does not comprise a monolithic set of institutions, there is a high degree of consensus within the main institutions that provides an internal coherence to border policing policy, a high level of organisation in its implementation and a shared culpability for its consequences.

There are a number of common ideological assumptions that underpin this consensus. The most enduring of these is that Australian sovereignty or the authority of the Australian state is threatened by unauthorised migration. However, the ideologies of exclusion associated with mandatory detention and the Pacific Solution were also symptomatic of a period of contested hegemony in relation to immigration and race. In particular, the Howard government sought to subsume the relatively fragile institutional consensus on multiculturalism to more traditional and racist frameworks of Australian nationalism that emphasised a European or Western heritage; a higher level of cultural homogeneity, for example, by prioritising the speaking of English; and a focus on loyalty to the Australian state through, for example, the new citizenship laws. Within this paradigm, cultural difference is associated with risk and considered a potential threat to social cohesion. Inclusion at an official level was therefore made dependent on the willingness of migrants to comply with Australian

State crime and the ideologies of exclusion

law and embrace cultural norms increasingly defined by government.

Refugees and unauthorised migrants constituted an important part of this discourse. Those who attempted unauthorised entry provided an embodiment of the potential risk, and were only made more deviant by associations between unauthorised entry, Islam and terrorism. The promotion of such associations was central to the construction of contemporary forms of racism based on fear of and distaste for the 'Arab Other' (Poynting et al 2004), while simultaneously drawing on more historically rooted fears of invasion. Such associations had wide public purchase but were far from hegemonic. There remain serious tensions within the Australian political establishment over the nature and role of multiculturalism; an enduring formal opposition to racism (notwithstanding the actuality and impact of many government policies); and a virtual consensus that white Australia is an ideal that can no longer be meaningfully pursued. A diverse range of political activists also built a substantial opposition campaign to mandatory detention and other aspects of the government's border policing policies.

These tensions between what can broadly be described as the state and sections of civil society provide the ideological space for developing notions of state deviance built around the three focal points emphasised in this book: the alienation, the criminalisation and the abuse of unauthorised migrants. These focal points operate within the fundamental contradictions between the primacy of national sovereignty and the tendencies towards, and aspirations for, free movement.

The Australian experience of border policing demonstrates that even within liberal democracies, where there is a formal adherence to the separation of powers, a supposedly non-discriminatory rule of law, and a degree of democratic control exercised through an elected parliament, systemic and violent human rights abuses can occur. Not surprisingly, the policies and practices that generate such abuses are not conceptualised by the various state institutions in such terms. Instead, within official discourses on border policing, the emphasis is on the maintenance of sovereignty and the regulation of cross-border movement. These are posited as matters of national interest and popular concern, which the government of the day is addressing in the exercise of its democratic mandate. This book has questioned the extent to which the state's border policing practices are driven from below. As previous chapters have discussed, an extensive institutional consensus developed around the policing of unauthorised migrants and was crystallised in the concept of border protection. Successive governments were central to the construction of this consensus through the introduction of legislation and the direction of public policy, but the civil administration (mainly the immigration department), enforcement agencies such as the Australian Federal Police, sections of the military during the events of 2001 and the judiciary all had important roles to play.

This was not been an entirely uniform process. There have been tensions within governments over the nuances of policies, for example over the detention of children, and occasionally between the main opposition parties and the government over aspects of the Pacific Solution. As the fallout from the Cornelia Rau case demonstrated, the relationship between the government and the immigration department was also problematic, especially around the issue of the departmental culture. Prior to the 'war' on people smuggling, the Australian Federal Police played a relatively minor role in border policing practice but is now central to the maintenance of Australia's exclusion zone and, with considerably expanding resources, is proactively engaged in the promotion of border policing as a major national security issue. With some misgivings amongst its senior command, the navy was drawn into the events of 2001 when it dutifully conducted the forced removal of the unauthorised asylum seekers to Papua New Guinea and Nauru. Finally, the judiciary, while critical at times of the government's efforts to limit its independence and reduce access by unauthorised asylum seekers to the Australian courts, nevertheless approved the key legislative measures taken by the government, notwithstanding their evident abusive effects.

The involvement of such a broad range of state institutions highlights the need to examine how the interplays between and within these different institutions established the basic trajectories of border protection and the highly organised and goal-oriented nature of its implementation. Australia's border policing practices have not been the product of rogue agencies or elements within them. Moreover, while none of the relevant state institutions has operated autonomously from the other, the events of 2001 exemplified the primary role of governments in dictating the thrust of the policy and seeking to micro-manage its operation. Two key dimensions of the government's role are examined here: the bipartisan approach to refugees and its impact on the goals and organisational culture of the immigration department; and the role of the judiciary in legitimising the government's exercise of its administrative powers to exclude and detain.

The parliament, bi-partisanship and the bureaucracy

The political consensus between Australia's two dominant mainstream political blocs provides a starting point for understanding the evolution of state crime. The formal bi-partisanship over refugee policy between the Coalition and the Labor parties at a parliamentary level developed with the arrival of Indo-Chinese refugees in the 1970s and was consolidated around the mandatory detention policy. Although the events of 2001 strained the consensus, and the Labor Party voiced reservations about aspects of the Pacific Solution, a high level of agreement on mandatory detention and the war on people smuggling remained throughout the Howard years.

Moreover, while the Rudd government has made some modifications to the Howard framework, the basic elements of the border protection paradigm remain intact. Labor's historic commitment to this policy framework can be observed through the operation of the parliamentary committee system. These committees provide some scope for debating and reformulating government policy and often allow for public submissions. But since 1994, a range of Senate inquiries have produced successive reports re-affirming the essential elements of border policing policy. Even when critical of aspects of government policy, the parliamentary committee reports have made limited recommendations aimed at reforming the ways in which the policy is implemented. In many cases, even these recommendations were ignored by the government.

For example, the Senate inquiry into the administration and operation of the *Migration Act* (SLCRC 2006), which had a majority of Labor members, made detailed recommendations requiring a more flexible interpretation of the detention policy. The Coalition government (CG 2007) accepted many of these but rejected even fairly modest proposals to expand the rights of unauthorised migrants, such as informing detainees of their right to legal advice and granting visa applicants the right to have legal representatives participate in primary interviews by immigration officers. The government also bluntly rejected the recommendation to limit the initial period of mandatory detention to 90 days 'for the purpose of initial screening, identity, security and health checks' after which 'a formal process, such as the approval of a Federal Magistrate' should be instituted to approve continued detention 'where there is suspicion that an individual is likely to disappear into the community to avoid immigration processes; or otherwise pose a danger to the community' (SLCRC 2006: xx). The government argued that there had been 'bipartisan support since 1994' for the detention policy and that 'detention also ensures that if applications are unsuccessful [detainees] are available for removal from Australia' (CG 2007: 23-24). Given Labor's commitment to the mandatory detention policy, there was little scope for a sustained or principled opposition to the government's response.

Bi-partisanship over issues such as mandatory detention, and the consolidation of border policing as a matter of national security, provided the political bedrock for the conduct of border policing and affected the culture within the immigration department and wider civil bureaucracy. This started from the top down. As noted in chapter five, senior public servants played a key role in the events of 2001 through bodies such as the people smuggling taskforce. The centralisation of the decision-making structure and the direct political control over the decision-making processes this entailed fitted into a broader pattern of politicisation within the Australian public service (Barker 2007). While the extent to which this

State crime and the ideologies of exclusion

represented a new trend should not be overstated, the strategic placement of government appointees reinforced government attempts to assert more direct control over the senior workings of the civil service. The implications of this were apparent with the 'Children Overboard affair', in which senior civil servants such as the Howard appointed secretary of the prime minister and cabinet department, Max Moore-Wilton, and the chair of the People Smuggling Task Force Jane Halton, played prominent roles (SSCCMI 2002: xxi-xl).

It seems clear there was a high level of direct political intervention during this episode. The Senate's inquiry into this matter criticised 'ministerial staff' for 'inserting themselves into both the military and administrative chains of command' and deplored 'the tendency of ministerial staff to act as quasi-ministers in their own right' (SSCCMI 2002: xxix). The inquiry noted the repeated attempts by Max Moore-Wilton to ensure that the boat in question (the SIEV 4) did not land on Christmas Island. These included Mr.Moore-Wilton personally instructing defence force chief, Admiral Barrie, 'to make sure everyone rescued went on board HMAS *Adelaide*', even though Admiral Barrie 'could not guarantee any such outcome', and told the defence minister that the 'safety of life was to be the paramount consideration' (SSCCMI 2002: xxv). The core finding of the Senate inquiry was that Defence Minister Peter Reith and members of his staff were collectively informed on seven separate occasions prior to the 2001 federal election that the allegations of asylum seekers throwing their Children Overboard as an act of defiance were untrue (SSCCMI 2002: xxiii). However, Reith refused to give evidence to the inquiry and ministerial staff members were prevented by the government from testifying. It also seems that high level officials within the public service and the military made little or no attempt to publicly disclose the truth once it became clear the allegations were false and that conscious attempts were made from within the highest ranks of the military and public service to prevent those with knowledge of the truth speaking out (Weller 2002: 8–91). The committee criticised Admiral Barrie for 'protecting the Minister's position [regarding the veracity of photographs] in the face of various findings and assessments to the contrary'; and also the defence department secretary for 'failing to press Minister Reith on the question of whether he intended to correct the public record in relation to the photographs' (SSCCMI 2002: xxviii).

It may never be entirely established exactly who knew what about the 'Children Overboard affair'. The Senate was not given full access to the people involved and the Coalition government resisted repeated calls to have a full judicial inquiry. But while it was certainly advantageous to the government not to have the truth revealed prior to the 2001 federal election and for Prime Minister Howard to claim that he was not informed the allegations were false, the 'Children Overboard affair' highlighted the blurring of the boundaries between various state institutions in circumstances where the government controlled, in highly organised ways, the political strategy for responding to unauthorised arrivals; the civilian mechanisms by which the strategy was promulgated; and the mechanisms of force by which it was implemented.

Moreover, while this episode and the events of 2001 provided a high profile example of state institutions combining to forcibly exclude unauthorised migrants, the departmental cultures criticised by the Palmer and Ombudsman inquiries developed and operated at more subterranean and subtle levels. As discussed in chapter six, these inquiries highlighted the routine and systemic resort to detention and removal of unauthorised non-citizens, with little serious investigation into possible legal routes for legitimising entry or residence. This internal culture was clearly driven by the political imperatives of the time, notwithstanding government attempts to distance itself from it. Further, the acceptance of detention as a normal and necessary administrative practice contributed to a contracting process that overlooked basic safeguards for the welfare of detainees and a state of denial emanating from immigration officials regarding the abusive impact of detention.

In the wake of Palmer, the government embarked on a conscious strategy to avoid future embarrassing 'mistakes' such as the detention of Cornelia Rau and committed itself to an extensive five year reform program (DIAC 2007b). Aspects of the new regime were welcomed by previous critics of the department but this was tempered by the government's decisions to detain all asylum seekers on Christmas Island and Nauru and the attempt to excise the whole of the mainland for the purposes of the *Migration Act*. More importantly, the hegemonic policy imperatives of border protection ensured that immigration compliance remained a central and defining departmental function. Compliance has many connotations. It implies the existence of a department abiding by and enforcing clearly defined rules; it gives a role to the concerned and legitimate citizenry through measures such as the confidential 'Dob-in Line', via which information about people working or living illegally in Australia can be anonymously passed on (DIMIA 2005c:101); and it reinforces the importance of policing.

The centrality of compliance to the department's operational ideology was reflected by its practice of publishing regular reports and statistics on its compliance activities. These activities include preventing unlawful entry into Australia; regulating entry and departure; intercepting unauthorised air arrivals; detecting unauthorised boat arrivals; dealing with overstayers; cancelling visas; locating unlawful non-citizens; preventing illegal work; combating student non-compliance; detaining unlawful non-citizens; removing unlawful non-citizens; combating fraud; and combating people smuggling and trafficking (DIMIA 2005c). Focusing on such activities was seen as a measure of success in the implementation of the post-Palmer reforms, which include the establishment of a College of Immigration, Border Security and Compliance where all immigration staff can be trained 'in the key areas of compliance, investigations, detention management, intelligence and border security' (DIAC 2007a). This continued emphasis on compliance, even when framed in terms of a renewed emphasis on the fair treatment of clients, is fundamentally at odds with unfettered rights of entry into Australia for the purposes of claiming protection or an internal administrative culture based on inclusive interpretations of human rights. Better training, planning and record keeping may well contribute to more regulated and better managed case flows for immigration staff but this does not fundamentally alter the abusive impact of government policy or the lack of judicial intervention that helps sustain it.

The judiciary and the stamp of legality

The role of the judiciary was especially important in reinforcing the legality of the government's border policing policies. However, the formal legitimacy the courts cumulatively bestowed upon the state's exclusionary practices has not always taken the form of a judicial rubber stamp. Rather, there has been a history of tension between the government and the judiciary, reflected in practical terms by the preparedness of the Federal Court and a minority of the High Court to offer some limited censure of the government and within broad political discourse by the governments attacking and seeking to minimise the involvement of the courts in the area of border policing and refugee determination. This experience was not unique to the Coalition government. In introducing the Migration Amendment Bill 1992, the first piece of legislation underpinning the mandatory detention policy, the then immigration minister Gerry Hand declared:

> 'The most important aspect of this legislation is that it provides that a court cannot interfere with the period of custody. I repeat: the most important aspect of this legislation is that it provides that a court cannot interfere with the period of custody' (CPD 1992a: 2370).

At the time, the minister's particular concern was a recent Federal Court judgment allowing for the release of people seen as unlawfully detained under the *Migration Act*[1] and the legal action taken by a group of 36 detained Cambodian asylum seekers seeking, inter alia, release from detention pending reconsideration of their asylum applications. The Federal Court adjourned the matter of their release to 7 May 1992 by which time the new legislation explicitly prevented courts from ordering the release from custody of such 'designated persons'.[2]

The High Court considered this legislation in the case of *Lim*,[3] and focused on when exceptions might occur to the principle that courts, rather than the executive, have the power to impose involuntary detention. One exceptional circumstance, the High Court determined, is when the detainee concerned is an alien vulnerable 'to exclusion or deportation'. In such circumstances, the power to detain administratively could be exercised in order 'to receive, investigate and determine an application by that alien for an entry permit and (after determination) to admit or deport'.[4] The decision in *Lim* provided a lengthy and authoritative articulation of the powers of the state to arbitrarily detain. These arguments were carefully calibrated within a framework of constitutional law that exceptionalised such powers being used by the state in abstract legal terms but normalised their application during periods of substantial or high profile levels of unauthorised entry. This normalising function, taking the form of the rule of law in circumstances where perversely the government was seeking to exclude the involvement of the courts, enabled the executive to operate an almost unfettered detention policy. In performing this function, the court's main concern was to legitimise and delineate the state's constitutional powers, rather than dwell on the punitive impact their exercise might have.

The court declined to consider submissions that the detention provisions conflicted with the International Covenant on Civil and Political Rights and the Refugee Convention. Rather, it developed reasons for why immigration detention was not essentially penal or punitive in character. Thus, Justice McHugh stated:

'...imprisonment of a person who is the subject of a deportation order is not ordinarily punitive in nature because the purpose of the imprisonment is to ensure that the deportee is excluded from the community pending his or her removal from the country.'

While conceding that 'if the imprisonment goes beyond what is reasonably necessary to achieve the non-punitive object, it will be regarded as punitive in character', and that a 'designated person can be detained for at least nine months for the sole purpose of enabling the department to consider the application for entry and make its own examination and investigation', the judge continued:

'Inordinately long as the potential period of detention may be, it has to be evaluated in the context...that...there are approximately 23,000 applicants for refugee status in Australia at the present time. The appropriateness of the period of detention for the individual cannot be isolated from the administrative burden cast on the department in investigating and determining the vast number of applications by persons claiming refugee status'.[5]

While not entirely blaming the applicants for their own plight, the High Court's subjugation of Cambodian refugees' liberty to the administrative process utilised notions of choice that denied or downplayed the reality of forced migration. 'A person is not being punished', Justice McHugh concluded, 'if after entering Australia without permission, he or she chooses to be detained in custody pending the determination of an application for entry rather than to leave the country during the period of determination'.[6] Such philosophical contortions were clearly of little use to the detained Cambodians, although as part of a political compromise, they did return to Cambodia on a government stipend for one year before being granted resettlement in Australia (Crock 1995: 41).

In many respects, the ideological impact of this decision was more significant than the jurisprudential. The legal construction of the alien refined by the High Court in *Lim* placed detention and removal as routine imperatives for the liberal state. Faced with the exercise of these powers, the alien subject is afforded no formal recourse to over-riding rights. Within this ontological framework, deviance can only be vested in the migrant, whose transgression of national borders and the imputed sovereignty of the state triggers the exercise of the state's powers. This relationship between statelessness and rightlessness, reminiscent of Arendt's (1976) observations of the 1930s, is particularly acute in the case of refugees. In response to the political and social persecution that defines the refugee, additional levels of exclusion are imposed by receiving states that are designed to protect the integrity of the state. This has the potential to condemn refugees to a permanent state of statelessness, where perpetuated by notions of border protection, state sanctioned abuse is cumulative.

The courts were fundamental to integrating this routinised exclusion into the fabric of the liberal democratic response to unauthorised refugees, especially given that the High Court subsequently reaffirmed the legality of detention even in

State crime and the ideologies of exclusion

circumstances where it was indefinite and/or the conditions were so harsh as to constitute violations of civil rights. Nevertheless, while definitive, the High Court's sanction of administrative detention did not reflect an entirely monolithic legal response. In the case of *Al Masri*,[7] the Federal Court considered the situation of a Palestinian refugee from the Gaza Strip, whose claim for protection in Australia had been refused. Having subsequently requested removal to Gaza but been told that the authorities in Gaza, Israel, Egypt, Syria and Jordan had refused entry permission, Akram Al Masri sought release from detention.[8] The practical question before the court was whether a person could be detained, even when there was no realistic prospect of removal. The court found that the power to detain under the *Immigration Act* was 'limited to such time as the removal of the person from Australia is "reasonably practical" in the sense that there is a real likelihood of removal in the reasonably foreseeable future'.[9] In the absence of 'the bona fide purpose of removal',[10] the detention was unlawful and impliedly punitive. Moreover, the legislation should be interpreted in accordance with Australia's treaty obligations under the International Covenant on Civil and Political Rights; the determinations of the United Nations Humans Rights Committee; the Convention on the Rights of the Child; and the jurisprudence of the European Court of Human Rights, all of which prohibit the use of arbitrary detention.[11]

While consideration of international legal obligations distinguished the Federal Court's approach to detention from that of the High Court, the Federal Court's decision in *Al Masri* did not confront the exclusionary thrust of the detention policy, nor the constitutional validity of the immigration minister's extraordinary administrative powers. Rather, it sought to limit the potentially indefinite nature of detention in situations where the state was confronted with significant practical difficulties in the exercise of its removal powers. Rights not to be detained and mistreated[12] were not derived from the fact of being a refugee but were contingent upon temporal limits the court sought to impose on the department. The practical implications of this were very limited. Ahmed Al Kateb, another stateless Palestinian, and Abbas Mohammad Hasan Al Khafaji, an Iraqi recognised as a refugee from Iraq but refused

Border Crimes

protection on the grounds that he could reside in Syria, successfully applied for release from detention for similar reasons. However, 13 others, including an asylum seeker who had been detained for six years had their applications for release refused and the High Court soon removed such limitations on the executive's power to exercise its detention policy.

In the *Al Kateb* [13] and *Al Khafaji*[14] cases, the High Court, by a 4–3 majority, effectively nullified the *Al Masri* decision by ruling that the *Migration Act* could only be interpreted as authorising mandatory detention of unlawful non-citizens and that the government had the constitutional power to enact such legislation. Taken to their logical conclusions, these cases substantially expanded the power of the federal government to impose indefinite detention without trial. By steadfastly separating the impact of detention on detainees from the declared purposes of the empowering legislation, the High Court facilitated the state's exclusionary operations. Reflecting this very narrow legal approach in *Al Kateb*, Justice Hayne emphasised the enforcement rationale for detention:

> The questions which arise about mandatory detention do not arise as a choice between detention and freedom. The detention to be examined is not the detention of someone who, but for the fact of detention, would have been, and been entitled to be, free in the Australian community.[15]

Justice Hayne further elaborated:

> The present legislation, prescribing the period of legislation as it does, may therefore be read as providing for detention for the purposes of processing any visa application and removal. But that does *not* decide the point of how long that detention may persist. It does not decide when that purpose (of detention for removal) is spent. It does not decide that the time during which a person may be detained is "a reasonable time". Here the period of detention is governed by the requirement to effect removal "as soon as reasonably practicable"(emphasis in original) .[16]

Eventually, according to the judge, the purpose of detention would be fulfilled:

State crime and the ideologies of exclusion

> What follows is that the most that could ever be said in a particular case where it is not now, and has not been reasonably practicable to effect removal, is that there is now no country which will receive a particular non-citizen whom Australia seeks to remove, and it cannot now be predicted when that will happen. Nor is it to say that the time for performing the duty imposed by S.198 has come. The duty remains unperformed: it has not yet been practicable to effect removal. That is not to say that it will never happen (emphasis in original).[17]

Even when detention drags on for years, this does not alter its supposedly non-punitive nature:

> It is essential to confront the contention that, because the time at which detention will end cannot be predicted, its indefinite duration (even, so it is said, for the life of the detainee) is or will become punitive. The answer to that is simple but must be made. If that is the result, it comes about because the non-citizen came to or remained in this country without permission. The removal of an unlawful non-citizen from Australia then depends upon the willingness of some other country to receive that person. If the unlawful non-citizen is stateless, as is Mr Al Kateb, there is no nation state which Australia may ask to receive its citizen. And if Australia is unwilling to extend refuge to those who have no country of nationality to which they may look for both protection and a home, the continued exclusion of such persons from the Australian community in accordance with the regime established by the Migration Act does not impinge on the separation of powers required by the Constitution.[18]

The implications of this judgment were particularly perverse for those, like the Palestinians, who have no functioning state entity through which they can formally gain migration and citizenship rights or with which the receiving state can engage. In many ways this epitomised the refugee experience of the late twentieth century, when protracted crises and 'failed states' characterised many of the major source areas of forced migration, rendering return either impossible or highly dangerous. For people like Ahmed Al Kateb, failure to successfully navigate Australia's refugee determination process resulted in their statelessness being reinforced through incarceration by another state. It was little consolation to them that the experiences of detention did not constitute punishment on the grounds that their imprisonment was not been sanctioned by a criminal court.

The *Al Kateb* and *Al Khafaji* decisions provided a legal rationale for the state to impose its absolute authority over an individual without the requirement of due process or the fear of sanction. Their implications were not lost on some of the dissenting judges. Justice Kirby described the majority view as having 'grave implications for the liberty of the individual in this country which this court should not endorse'.[19] With Justice Gummow, he argued that when there was no reasonable prospect in the foreseeable future of effecting deportation, then continued detention would amount to punishment. Moreover, the concept of executive power ought to be interpreted in accordance with international legal principles that reinforce strong presumptions in favour of liberty. As Justice Gummow noted, the reasoning of the majority theoretically could allow for the detention of 'bankrupts' or 'of all persons within their homes on census night'.[20] While the dissenting judgments offered some hope of a more lenient interpretation of the detention powers evolving in the longer term, the unanimous judicial support for detention as a legitimate mechanism for enforcing removal ensured the state retained the capacity to systematically abuse unauthorised migrants.

In the case of *Behrooz*,[21] which the High Court considered alongside *Al Kateb* and *Al Khafaji*, it was also held that such abuse was incapable of providing a defence to escaping immigration detention. Mahran Behrooz was an Iranian refugee, who with two others was charged with escaping from the Woomera Detention Centre, an offence carrying a maximum penalty of five years. The procedural issue before the court was whether evidence regarding the conditions at Woomera should be admissible. Behrooz argued that 'the conditions at Woomera, in their harshness, go beyond anything that could reasonably be regarded as necessary for migration purposes'. Therefore, 'detention at Woomera was not valid "immigration detention" and escaping from it could not constitute escape from immigration detention'.[22] In a 6–1 decision, the court rejected Behrooz's submission, with Chief Justice Gleeson commenting, 'It is one thing to challenge the lawfulness of conditions of confinement, or of practices adopted by those in charge of prisons; it is another thing to assert a right to be freed by court order; and it is another thing again to assert a right to escape'.[23] At the root of this reasoning was the government's claim, reinforced by the decision in *Lim*, to a constitutional power to detain for the purposes of processing and removal. According to Chief Justice Gleeson,

> That being the nature of the power of detention, there is no warrant for concluding that, if the conditions of detention are sufficiently harsh, there will come a point where the detention itself can be regarded as punitive, and an invalid exercise of judicial power. Whatever the conditions of detention, the detention itself involves the involuntary deprivation of liberty. For a citizen, that alone would ordinarily constitute punishment. But for an alien, the detention is an incident of exclusion and deportation to which an alien is vulnerable. Harsh conditions of detention may violate the civil rights of an alien. The alien does not stand outside the protection of the civil and criminal law…But the assault or the negligence does not alter the nature of the detention. It remains detention for the statutory purpose identified above. The detention is not for a punitive purpose.[24]

Within this framework, detainees were neatly and comprehensively trapped by the rule of law. The High Court's concern to maintain the form of constitutionalism exhibited judicial denial of its practical content. The designated legal status of 'non-citizen' or 'alien' removed any legitimate agency from the detainee and rendered the notion of a legal remedy for the conditions of detention as little more than a legal abstraction. Only in exceptional cases, such as that of Shayan Badraie has a detainee managed to obtain some compensation through the courts, and only after irremediable damage to the child concerned. The government's sustained denial of access to lawyers, human rights monitors or any other agency capable of systematically seeking redress on behalf of detainees could only be fortified by the legal fiction that the conditions at centres such as Woomera were not punitive.

The High Court's willingness to license broad powers of detention was further reinforced two months later in *Re Woolley*[25]. In that case, the court unanimously dismissed submissions on behalf of four Afghan children that mandatory detention did not apply to children. Even Justice Kirby felt duty bound to concede that given the history of the detention policy, 'the suggestion that there has been some oversight, mistake or a failure to consider the immigration detention of children in Australia is fanciful'.[26] Significantly, although it was not an issue the court was explicitly required to consider, Justice McHugh revisited the question of whether detention is penal or punitive by commenting that this 'must depend on all the circumstances of the case'.[27] He went on to develop an argument for the legitimate use of 'protective' detention:

> The most obvious example of a non-punitive law that authorises detention is one enacted solely for a protective purpose…The dividing line between a law whose purpose is protective and one whose purpose is punitive is often difficult to draw. This is particularly so where a protective law has acknowledged consequences that, standing alone, would make the law punitive in nature. Protective laws, for example, may also have some deterrent aspect which the legislature intended. However, the law will not be characterised as punitive in nature unless deterrence is one of the principal objects of the law and the detention can be regarded as punishment to deter others. Deterrence that is an intended consequence of an otherwise protective law will not make the law punitive in nature unless the deterrent aspect itself is intended to be punitive.[28]

Justice McHugh's endorsement of protective detention clearly intersected with the wider political discourse on border protection, the government's emphasis on deterring people smuggling, and debates about the use of detention as part of the 'war on terror'. As a legal construct, protective detention may well be narrowly restricted by the Australian constitution but Justice McHugh did suggest that the 'defence and quarantine powers' were 'probably

State crime and the ideologies of exclusion

exceptions' to the principle that detention should not be 'divorced from a breach of the law'.[29] Combined with the power to detain aliens, these exceptions gave the state potentially very broad scope for the use of administrative detention of unauthorised migrants in circumstances where ideologically they are presented as a threat.

There is little in the above judgments to suggest the High Court will offer any principled form of censure to the government's immigration detention policies. With the Baxter detention centre now closed, it is conceivable the new Christmas Island centre will develop into a Guantanamo Bay type facility largely immune to external monitoring. For those who were moved even further afield by the Australian state, the High Court was unwilling to intervene. Thus, despite Nauru being a site excluded from the jurisdiction of the Australian courts for the purposes of the *Migration Act*, in two related cases in 2005, the court used its appellate jurisdiction from the Supreme Court of Nauru[30] to confirm the power of the Director of Police in Nauru to detain refugees transferred to the island state under the Pacific Solution.[31]

The role of the High Court in upholding the legality of the government's response to unauthorised migrants reflected both the judiciary's narrow, literal reading of the constitution and the nature of the constitution itself. More specifically, the High Court's contribution highlighted that the preservation of formal constitutional arrangements, especially the over-riding, decision-making power of the executive, concentrates responsibility for the abusive acts of the state with the government, so long as that government continues to be the primary decision maker in relation to border policing policy. While the formal absence of rights from the constitution and the lack of a Bill of Rights are likely to remain obstacles to the High Court altering the general line of reasoning generated by *Lim*, the fundamental point remains that the judiciary played an essential role in legitimising the abusive behaviours of the Australian state.

The ideologies of exclusion

By itself, the legal power to exclude 'aliens' that successive Australian governments have used with the imprimatur of the High Court does not explain the government's capacity to justify its deterrence and detention policies. While the notion of the 'alien' has important legal and constitutional meanings, its broader ideological connotations are of greater significance. The capacity of the state to alienate unauthorised migrants underpins its ability to criminalise and abuse them. Because the alien is constructed as a defining feature of nationalism, existing outside the realm of the legitimate citizen and any formal obligations owed by the nation state, being an alien usually represents a disturbing embodiment of difference, a threatening 'other', who needs to be controlled. For Western states, the construction of the 'other', through a combination of legal and ideological mechanisms, not only helps reinforce a particular conception of national identity but also provides lawful and institutional rationales for racism.

It is in this general context and the specific circumstances of the White Australia policy that the concept of the 'alien' was embedded in the Australian constitution. Its practical purpose in terms of immigration control was to enforce the exclusion of primarily Asian, non-white migrants. As has already been discussed, this was one of the hegemonic imperatives of early Australian nationalism that until the 1960s, shaped official perceptions of the legitimate migrant. The abandonment of the White Australia policy and the evolution of multiculturalism in the 1970s signaled the beginning of a period of contested hegemony in relation to migration and border policing policy and while the resettlement of a substantial community of Indo-Chinese refugees played a defining role in the demise of the White Australia policy, measures to prevent unauthorised boat arrivals laid the ground for contemporary border policing arrangements.

In legitimising their border policing practices, successive governments since the 1970s sought to reshape deeply rooted associations of threat with ethnic and cultural difference. To some extent, these associations were confronted, especially by the Fraser

State crime and the ideologies of exclusion

government, as obstacles to the consolidation of a non-discriminatory migration and refugee resettlement policy. However, the implementation of a border policing regime targeting unauthorised migrants from backgrounds historically excluded by the White Australia policy also allowed the ideological reference points of the past to be revived and reformulated. While officially deploring racism, the Howard government was especially proactive in this regard, promoting and implementing a political agenda that drew heavily on elements of 'race based nationalism' (Markus 2001: x). Contrary to the Fraser government's emphasis on multiculturalism as a source of social cohesion, Howard's government progressively undermined official multiculturalism on the basis that it represented a threat to social cohesion. Central to this process was the rejection of the so-called claims to special rights the Howard government attributed to advocates of multiculturalism in general and unauthorised migrants and 'queue jumpers' in particular.

While maintaining a formal adherence to multiculturalism, in so far as it signaled a willingness to allow migration from non white European sources, the Howard era gave rise to an alternate discourse of integration. At an official level, this was characterised in 2006 by the renaming of the Department for Immigration and Multicultural Affairs to the Department of Immigration and Citizenship. This reflected a policy emphasis on citizenship that required of migrants a commitment to 'Australian values', knowledge of which was to be formally tested. At the more informal level it formed part of a concerted attempt to promote the virtues of Australia's colonial heritage and its Western identity. In these contexts, unauthorised refugees were alienated by their illegal methods of transit and typically since the 1990s by their association with Islam. In short, while the exclusion of certain types of migrant was no longer legitimised by direct reference to the White Australia policy, the idea that those legally designated as aliens are 'not really like us' operated as a powerful and enduring ideological undercurrent to arguments that justified their exclusion.

The Howard government's policies on migration, refugees and citizenship had their ideological roots in the 'new conservatism' of the 1980s when Howard and others such as historian Geoffrey Blainey first advanced critiques of multiculturalism and Asian immigration. Blainey and Howard were marginalised within the conservative establishment at the time, although various networks promoting 'new conservative' ideas remained an important component of conservative intellectual and institutional life, especially in relation to the 'history wars' (MacIntyre and Clark 2003: 93–141; Markus 2001: 49–81). However, the practical impetus for the revival and mainstreaming of these ideas came from Pauline Hanson's challenge to the Coalition's hegemony over conservative politics.

Hanson was elected as an Independent member of the federal parliament in 1996 after being deselected as the Liberal Party candidate for the same seat. In April 1997, she formed One Nation, an unstable but high profile political formation that attracted assorted fragments from the fractious far-right fringe and a wider support base drawn by Hanson's racist populism. One Nation had an immediate and substantial electoral impact, most notably at the Queensland state election in June 1998, when it won 11 seats with 22.7 percent of the vote. This led to predictions that One Nation could hold the balance of power in the forthcoming federal election but when the election took place in October 1998, One Nation's vote fell to 14.5 percent in Queensland and was just under 9 percent nationally. Hanson failed in her bid to be re-elected but still received 36.8 percent of the vote and remained a high profile national figure. At the 2001 federal election, One Nation's vote fell further to 4.34 percent in the House of Representatives and 5.54 percent in the Senate. While this signaled the demise of One Nation as an immediate electoral force, its impact on the public discourse and government policy on migration was nevertheless significant.

From the outset, Hanson portrayed herself as an anti-establishment figure fighting to preserve Australia's 'cultural identity' and 'social harmony' from the 'threats' posed by 'minority interests'. In her maiden speech to the parliament in September 1996, she threw down a challenge to the newly elected Howard government, by drawing on some of the ideological materials of traditional, mainstream Australian nationalism. She denied being a

State crime and the ideologies of exclusion

racist but then proceeded to mount a sustained attack on multiculturalism and to invoke the threat of invasion from heavily populated Asian states:

> I and most Australians want our immigration policy radically reviewed and that of multiculturalism abolished. I believe we are in danger of being swamped by Asians...They have their own culture and religion, form ghettos and do not assimilate...A truly multicultural country can never be united....

> Time is running out. We have only 10 to 15 years to turn things round. Because of our resources and our position in the world we will not have a say because neighbouring countries such as Japan, with 125 million people, China, with 1.2 billion people, India with 846 million people, Indonesia with 178 million people, and Malaysia with 20 million people are well aware of our resources and our potential. Wake up Australia before it is too late (ON 1996).

The Howard government's response to Hanson was belated and ambivalent but the prime minister did move to claim the populism that had propelled Hanson into parliament as part of the wider conservative project. Two weeks after Hanson addressed the parliament, Howard told a gathering of Queensland Liberal Party members,

> It was no accident that we won [the election]....Our opponents more than any group of people I have seen ...had not only lost touch with the mainstream of the Australian community, they had quite literally stopped listening to the mainstream of the Australian community. The only people they had listened to were the flatterers and the fawners among those in the national Press Gallery who themselves had become a self-deluded political elite and the leaders of noisy minority groups....One of the great changes that have come over Australia in the last six months is that people do feel able to speak a little more freely and a little more openly about what they feel. In a sense the pall of censorship on certain issues has been lifted...I welcome the fact that people can now talk about certain things without living in fear of being branded as a bigot or a racist. There is an

important caveat...Freedom of speech carries with it a responsibility on all those who exercise that freedom to do so in a tolerant and moderate fashion (quoted, Ricklefs 1997: 52).

Howard's carefully measured comments seemed designed to distance the government from Hanson's more extreme formulations and followers, while simultaneously legitimising much of her message. While other government ministers were more forthright in their criticisms of One Nation (Ricklefs 1997: 52–55), a pattern was established of the government seeking to undercut One Nation electorally by combining personal criticisms of Hanson with the embrace of much of One Nation's political agenda. The ways in which this pattern unfolded became more apparent after the 1998 federal election. One Nation's 1998 election policy on 'immigration, population and social cohesion' (ON 1998), listed a number of principles, including:

> Freedom of speech should be extended to all discussions on immigration and multicultural policies and the cry of 'racism' should not be used to silence debate or to promote violence against those who wish to debate these issues...

> Australians, like other peoples of the world, have the right to maintain their unique identity and culture...

> Our migrant intake will be non-discriminatory on the condition that the numbers do not significantly alter the ethnic and cultural make up of the country...

> English is the official language of Australia and government policy will encourage widespread use of English within all communities and in all institutions of the land...

> Compassion must be extended to genuine refugees but temporary refuge need not extend to long-term permanent settlement...

> The Government institutionalised, publicly funded policy of Multiculturalism is not in the best interests of migrants, nor of Australia, and will be abolished...

State crime and the ideologies of exclusion

No person other than an Australian citizen, or a permanent resident of the Australian community, has a basic right to enter Australia...

Even though One Nation's electoral impact was starting to wane, such 'principles' set the terms and tone of mainstream political debate. The central element of Hanson's racism, the notion that social cohesion was at risk of being undermined by the nature of the migrant intake, was to become an increasingly unchallenged orthodoxy, while specific One Nation policies were simply appropriated by the government. The most important of these in relation to unauthorised arrivals was the introduction in 1999 of temporary protection visas for unauthorised arrivals subsequently granted refugee status. When first raised by One Nation, Immigration Minister Ruddock condemned the proposal 'as being highly unconscionable' (quoted, Mansouri and Leach: 2003: 103). However, Ruddock's back flip twelve months later not only embraced the principle underlying the One Nation policy but arguably went further by denying family reunion. This change of heart could hardly be attributed to a sudden change in the nature of temporary protection; it was clearly motivated by a desire to undercut One Nation's electoral support.

The introduction of temporary protection visas was just one of a number of measures, including the excision of Christmas Island from Australia's migration zone, which originated as One Nation proposals and ended up as government policy by 2001. Even when One Nation policies, such as its call for a 'zero net immigration program' (ON 1998), were dismissed by the government the surrounding rhetoric had an enduring effect. In particular, One Nation's persistent references to being 'swamped' by 'alien cultures' fitted into the developing fever over the arrival of unauthorised refugees in the late 1990s and the run-up to the 2001 election.

The nature of political debate during that period was very much reflected by the media, which in turn helped set the terms of public discourse and the frameworks of interpretation around themes that the government was keen to promote. In relation to asylum seekers, there was an almost unchallenged orthodoxy that unauthorised boat arrivals represented a serious threat to Australia's borders. The concept of the alien was a constant undercurrent within this orthodoxy. Pickering's analysis of articles on the subject of refugees in the *Sydney Morning Herald* and *Brisbane Courier Mail* during the period January 1997 to December 1999 demonstrates the extent to which by the late 1990s, the 'quality press' was prepared to encourage the categorisation of refugees as 'invading', 'racially different' and 'diseased' (Pickering 2001: 172). Such representations of refugees also intersected with 'a highly racialised framing of current events, around crime and terrorism, on a local and national level' (Poynting et al 2004: 14). 'Ethnic crime gangs', 'race rapes', 'invasions' of asylum seeking boat people, and the terrorist attacks in the United States and Bali were tied together by common perceptions that associated these incidents with people of 'Middle Eastern' ancestry, and 'formed the basis of a series of cycles of moral panic which have centred around those of Arabic-speaking background and especially, but not exclusively, those of Muslim faith' (Poynting et al 2004: 11).

One such cycle revolved around the *Tampa* events, when there was an intensely racist response to Middle Eastern refugees. In his analysis of the coverage in the *Sydney Morning Herald* and *Daily Telegraph,* Manning (2004: 36–37) concluded:

> Both newspapers' columns were filled for the next two months with an outpouring of fear about the refugee "onslaught". According to the *SMH,* the letters editor had never seen more letters to the Editor on any other issue…Commercial radio commentator and Herald columnist Mike Carlton wrote that he had received an overwhelming number of calls on the *Tampa* crisis that expressed a hatred of Islam…ABC radio commentator Richard Glover wrote in his column that his callers were saying that Muslims were "by nature inclined to be violent"… An *SMH* editorial referred to the "constant waves of illegal arrivals"…Letters spoke of refugees as "Muslim invaders"…"criminals and parasites"…"scum" and "demonic"… *SMH* columnist Paddy McGuinness suggested that refugees may indeed be terrorists…and that Islam seemed to encourage a "culture of violence".

State crime and the ideologies of exclusion

Similarly, Kelly (2002a: 29–30) noted an authoritative survey of opinion on talkback radio which revealed 'that in the first week of the crisis half the talkback radio callers stressed that the boat people were Muslim'. The expression of such sentiments was not limited to the airwaves. In a study commissioned by the Human Rights and Equal Opportunity Commission, Poynting and Noble (2004:17) highlighted the increasing levels of discrimination, racial vilification, threats of violence and actual violence experienced by Muslims in Australia since the late 1990s:

> The nature of these experiences of racism varied widely, from the most egregious forms of physical violence or threats of violence, to active discrimination in work places and other sites, to verbal abuse and general feelings of discomfort and being made to feel ill at ease, especially in public places. Incidents took place in shopping centres, on the street, when driving or on public transport, through the media, at work and in leisure places, in schools and in government institutions. The perpetrators of these various acts were typically identified by respondents as of English-speaking background, and more often male than female. Religion was cited as the most common reason for these acts, as perceived by the interviewees, while some of the abuse clearly indicated references to terrorism and other domestic events that have become ideologically linked to people of Islamic faith. One of the most disturbing findings of the study was the frequency of these incidents of racism – these were often everyday experiences and accepted as commonplace by the interviewees. The pervasive nature of these incidents suggest that for many citizens of Arab and Muslim background racism, abuse and violence form part of an everyday landscape of fear and civility.

While both the Prime Minister Howard and the Immigration Minister Ruddock made official calls for tolerance in the wake of September 11 and 'condemned scapegoating of Arab and Muslim Australians' (HREOC 2004b: 98), the whole tenor of the government's border protection and migration policies, not to mention its explicit linkages of refugees and terrorism helped sustain the actions they criticised. As Collins et al (2000) and Poynting et al

Border Crimes

(2004) detail, Islamophobia is a defining ingredient of contemporary Australian racism and was plainly evident in the 2005 'Cronulla riots' in Sydney (Poynting 2007). Moreover, the Australian experience of racism increasingly taking the form of Islamophobia is consistent with a developing post-Cold War discourse, shaped by writers such as Samuel Huntington (1998), in which cultural difference becomes the basis of identifying threats to the Western states, and Islam a defining opposite of Western identity. Muslims living in Australia are implicitly targeted within this discourse, with their religion being attributed a capacity to produce 'extremists' or 'terrorists' not shared by Christianity or other more 'tolerant' religions.

The linkages drawn between Islam and terrorism are central to the wider institutional problematisation of Islam as a religious and cultural force that is fundamentally non-Western, undemocratic and socially disruptive. In such circumstances, the onus is on Muslims to comply with different cultural norms, and co-option of 'Muslim community' leaders an integral element of the government's strategy. Accordingly, the federal government attempted to incorporate representative Muslim opinion through bodies such as the Muslim Community Reference Group (MCRG 2006) and to 'support Australian Muslims to participate effectively in the broader community through its National Action Plan to Build on Social Cohesion, Harmony and Security' (MCIMA 2006).

Such moves formed part of a wider government initiated focus on citizenship that interwove legal legitimacy with a willingness to embrace Western cultural and political norms in ways which inevitably reinforced the wider ideological demarcation between migrants from British or European backgrounds, and those who are not. The main practical expression of this was the introduction of a citizenship test and a values statement for people applying for permanent residence. 'The central principle behind such a test and statement', according to former Immigration Minister Kevin Andrews (2007), was to ensure that those people who wish to become an Australian citizen do so by way of demonstrating a level of understanding and commitment to Australia and our way of life'. 'This way of life', he continued, 'is influenced by a history that includes the Judeo Christian beliefs and traditions brought by

State crime and the ideologies of exclusion

British settlers. Also present were the values and institutions that form the basis of a free and open democratic society, particularly our British political heritage, and the spirit of the European enlightenment'.

The introduction of the citizenship test, and the renewed emphasis on English language skills as a requirement of residence, reinforced a clear institutional divide between those people who are born citizens, usually in Australia, and those who seek to acquire citizenship. For the latter, 'citizenship is a privilege, not a right' (AG 2006: 8). It is something that is bestowed by the state on the basis of compliance with formally established norms. It is the juridical opposite of the alien, regulated, carefully defined and conditional. It is the product of the nation state imposing its conceptions of legitimacy over and above claims to universal rights or transnational loyalties. It is a legal construct designed to reinforce particular forms of knowledge and interpretations of history; for example, the test, which purported to outline 'Australian values' (AG 2007), made no reference to multiculturalism or human rights but did ensure that prospective citizens were familiar with the Anzac legend, the race horse Phar Lap and the cricketing achievements of Donald Bradman.

The introduction of a citizenship test and other prescriptive integration mechanisms for migrants reaffirmed the high level of state control over human movement in and out of Australia, the state's role in the construction of the legitimate migrant, and its role in the conceptualisation of Australian identity. The origins of these proposals lay in the ideological rejection of migration from non-English speaking, non-Western regions as an enriching source of cultural diversity and social advance and an ahistorical world view that saw cultures and 'ways of life' as fixed, self-perpetuating, devoid of interaction and prone to mutual incompatibility. This narrow conception of identity that presents multiculturalism as a force for separatism and fragmentation has become an increasingly common feature of Western political discourse. In Australia, this has taken the form of attacks on multiculturalism as a threat to social cohesion, personal security and the preservation of 'Western values'. Unauthorised asylum seekers from states such as Afghanistan and

Iran were the embodiment of such threats. Although their physical exclusion was rendered almost total by the Pacific Solution and acted as a metaphor for the treatment of all unauthorised migrants, they continue to exist within the national imaginings promoted by the state as symbols of alien danger, as the anti-citizen whose deviance must be repelled, punished and controlled by measures that ensure their criminalisation and abuse.

Exclusion and state crime

By employing particular conceptions of national identity, sovereignty and citizenship to help justify the forced exclusion of unauthorised migrants, the Australian state has drawn on deeply-rooted nationalist sentiments that pit an ideal national type against an unwanted or threatening outsider. While it can be argued that this is a dynamic essential to all nationalist ideologies, the state's role in constructing the deviance of the outsider is particularly acute in the implementation of border controls. It is within the border policing complex that superficially benign, everyday, peaceful expressions of national solidarity are translated into systems of organised control. These operate along a continuum that links the administrative processes of passport and visa control; the policing imperatives of detention, forced removal and disruption; and the military's involvement in interdiction.

Despite the strong institutional consensus against unauthorised migration, opposition to the Australian state's actions has arisen at many points along this continuum. These challenges have ranged from the episodic to the sustained and have come from a variety of sources including a substantial and diverse grass-roots political campaign; individual critics within the government's own ranks; statutory bodies such as the Human Rights and Equal Opportunity Commission; and unauthorised migrants themselves. Such opposition facilitates the development of an alternative framework of state crime to critically analyse the government's actions. However, state crime cannot simply be defined by the existence of opposition to particular government policies. Patterns of organised abuse need to be identified and their justifications and neutralising explanations rejected on the basis of over-riding moral imperatives, social norms or claims to human rights. For Australia's border policing practices to be understood as criminally deviant, we need to distil the sources of tension between the state's claims to legitimate actions and the rights of unauthorised migrants to enter and move within Australia's national boundaries. Using this approach, this book has identified a series of focal points where the state's claims to legitimacy break down or operate in direct conflict with the legitimate aspirations of unauthorised migrants. These focal points are not mutually exclusive; rather they are the broad areas of contradiction and inquiry where the state's hegemony can be challenged and its cultures of forced exclusion delegitimised.

The alienation of unauthorised migrants

The construction of the unauthorised migrant as the outsider is perhaps the most powerful legitimising process underpinning the implementation of border controls. It rests at the centre of legal perceptions of the legitimate migrant and sustains wider and more complex cultural and ideological expressions of identity, difference and threat. However, while the general concept of the alien is entrenched within the institutional fabric of the nation state, specific perceptions of the alien shift according the wider political and strategic priorities of those running the state.

In Australia, the legal and constitutional essence of the alien at the time of federation meshed with and helped promulgate a very specific and legitimising sense of Australian national identity. However, this was not fixed. The program of mass migration instituted after the Second World War and the reorientation of the Australian economy towards Asia inevitably resulted in the abandonment of the White Australia policy ensuring that the regulation of migration operated within very different contexts of exclusion and inclusion. This was consistent with the broad pattern in Western states where combinations of colonial history; shifting trends in trade and commerce; large-scale often state-encouraged migration; and increased capacities to travel resulted in the consolidation of substantial communities of people who could be defined as ethnic minorities. As in Australia, from the 1970s, there were moves, often strongly contested, towards official forms of multiculturalism in states such as Canada, the United States, the United Kingdom and France. By the 1990s, the consolidation and expansion of the European Union within which certain rights to free movement were guaranteed opened up the prospect of transnational forms of identity for some Western citizens and residents, while simultaneously excluding many guest workers and asylum seekers with origins outside the core states of Western Europe.

From the perspective of the state what constitutes an alien is therefore partly a relative question. As the natal origins and demographic make-up of the national population become more complex, so too do the debates about identity, culture and acceptability. As migration targets and residence requirements change, often disrupting established migration patterns and cross border family and social networks, the inconsistencies in migration policy destabilise prevailing views of the legitimate migrant. What is consistent is the impact that alienation has on forced and unauthorised migrants. For refugees, displacement and the disruption of their social world is compounded by the absence of any claim to formal legitimacy. Their capacity to operate as social subjects within a national polity is lost and their ability to survive made dependent on necessarily illicit social and economic activity. For unauthorised migrants more generally, alienation superimposes over the legal limits to movement, a generalised lack of authenticity that helps popularise and legitimise their exclusion.

In such circumstances, there is permanent tension between the state and the prospective migrant but a more variable relationship between state institutions and their official citizenry. In formal constitutional terms, the alien and the nation are defining opposites but in sociological terms the relationship is more volatile and productive of a range of social responses to potential migrants, many of which will be in conflict with the particular migration control policies of the state especially once they become the focus of activist campaigns against government policy.

The criminalisation of unauthorised migrants

The state's capacity to criminalise unauthorised migrants is fundamental to its ability to legitimise their exclusion. As the High Court has emphasised, unauthorised migrants are not legally defined as criminals. They have not been convicted of a criminal offence and even when they are held in prisons or police cells, they are not formally subject to the criminal justice process. Instead, their detention is administrative, designed to facilitate civilian decision-making processes about their rights of entry and residence and their possible removal. However, their necessarily clandestine means of travel; their association with illicit people smuggling networks; their detention in prison-like institutions and their forced removal combine to transform popular perceptions of the unauthorised migrant into the deviant; if not criminal, illegal immigrant. Such perceptions are heavily mediated by the state's construction of specific types of migrant with different and competing claims to legitimacy. As with alienation, criminality does not automatically flow from the fact of being a migrant. Rather, it is the consequence of conscious decision-making processes by the state, normally in the context of wider migration policy. In absolute terms, nothing compels the state to exclude certain types of prospective migrant. Immigration controls can be relaxed or even abandoned, amnesties granted for illicit migrants and particular groups of refugees welcomed.

In practice, the construction of exclusion zones by Australia and other Western states normalises the criminalisation of unauthorised migrants from the developing world, but does so in quite a contradictory context. On one hand, in many parts of Europe and North America, there is a reliance on irregular migration to sustain key sectors of the economy. In this sense, while the front door is shut, the back door is left open (Marfleet 2006: 172–186). While this trend is not so pronounced in Australia, the impact of the criminalisation of illicit workers is to provide a vulnerable workforce, whose wages and conditions can be pushed below prevailing minimum standards. On the other hand, criminalisation operates counter to understandings and expectations of human rights. At a global level, the discourse on human rights gained considerable momentum during the latter part of the twentieth century. The popularisation of human rights ideals has been accompanied by the growth of formal institutions such as human rights commissions and the 'very rapid growth of transnational rights campaigns' (Marfleet 2006: 220). Non government organisations have been particularly important in the promotion of rights that are relevant to migrants. They 'have endorsed the centrality to migrant networks of the rights discourse, with its formal universalism, its critiques of the state and the state's excesses and its appeal to specific rights, notably the right to freedom of movement, the right to return and the right of asylum' (Marfleet 2006: 220).

They have increased the level of consciousness and expectation of many migrants, especially refugees, and affected the responses to unauthorised migration in receiving states. Consequently, unauthorised migrants facing exclusion and criminalisation highlight the disjuncture between the formal commitments of states and the impact of border restrictions. The ability of non-government and human rights organisations to document and campaign around this disjuncture provides the space for the alleged criminality of the migrant to be refocused onto the actions of the state. This is especially the case when exclusion and criminalisation gives rise to organised abuse.

The abuse of unauthorised migrants

The abuse of unauthorised migrants provides the most obvious framework for analysing state behaviour as sociologically criminal. Through policies such as mandatory detention, Australia's border policing regime has given rise to multiple breaches of widely adopted human rights instruments. These include the Refugee Convention; the International Covenant on Civil and Political Rights; the Convention against Torture; and the Convention on the Rights of the Child. However, international humanitarian law does not always capture the extent of the social harm generated by experiences of loss, displacement, forced movement, alienation and disempowerment. As the official responses to the various inquiries

State crime and the ideologies of exclusion

conducted by the Human Rights and Equal Opportunity Commission and others highlight, there has also been a profound reluctance on the part of successive governments to acknowledge the extent of these breaches, or to accept responsibility for them. Instead, techniques of denial and neutralisation have been deployed, typically by using arguments that emphasise the legality of mandatory detention or by presenting egregious and undeniable human rights breaches as exceptional. Establishing the systemic nature of these breaches and the patterns of accountability is therefore an important task and has been a major focus of this book.

Australia's systemic breaches of particular conventions have also established a precedent that can be used by other Western states to normalise the forced exclusion of forced and unauthorised migrants. The whole infrastructure of border protection, particularly the Pacific Solution, was designed to prevent and obstruct informal migration into Australia and to undermine the rights of refugees to determine the locations and circumstances in which they claim asylum. This had immediate implications for some refugees and continues to undermine the international framework for refugee protection developed since the Second World War. While this framework had its limitations and was primarily developed on terms that suited the West, it nevertheless established some expectation of universal rights for refugees, especially an entitlement to enter a state in order to claim protection. Such rights are now being challenged by Australia and other Western states pressing for refugees to be contained near their regions of origin from where they can be resettled or repatriated.

The dominant rationale for this approach is that large-scale illicit movement represents a threat to the national sovereignty of Western states, particularly their capacity to fully regulate movement across their borders. The theme of sovereignty runs through each of the focal points outlined above and is a primary source of legitimacy for the state's monopoly and exercise of force. Unchallenged it can provide a justification for almost any state actions, especially when invoked to support engagements in war or to defend the national entity from external or internal threats. However, the sovereign

Border Crimes

power of the nation state is exercised in a contradictory context. On one hand, to the extent that sovereignty provides the basis for imposing a national rule of law, treaties and international legal obligations need to be taken into account. This is the paradigm within which human rights critiques of the government have generally been formulated.[32] On the other hand, state sovereignty, particularly in relation to border controls, runs counter to the increasingly globalised nature of economic and social activity; meaning the restrictions on the freedom of movement stand in contrast to the demands for and trends towards the denationalisation and deregulation of trade and commerce.

The availability of unprecedented means of travel and communication; the growth of transnational migrant networks; the existence of substantial and diverse groups of migrants within the boundaries of most national states; and the increasing normality of international movement and resettlement for a significant portion of the world's population, suggest that the contradictions between the state's enforcement of border controls and the expectations of and pressures towards migration are likely to sharpen. In such circumstances, the potential deviance of the state rests not just in particular measures it may adopt to prevent migration (although the violent and abusive nature of many of these may demand critical analysis), or the arbitrary and seemingly capricious changes that might be made to visa requirements, but in the assertion that migration control is a legitimate activity in and of itself. For this reason, the deviance of the Australian state examined in this book should not be regarded as an aberration or the product of a policy gone wrong, but as the consequence of organised exclusionary practices authorized by the government and supported by an elaborate policing and judicial infrastructure.

Notes

[1] See *Minister for Immigration, Local Government and Ethnic Affairs v Msilinga* (1992) ALR 301.
[2] Section 54R *Migration Act* 1958.
[3] *Chu Kheng Lim and Others and the Minister for Immigration*, Local Government

and Ethnic Affairs and Another (1992) CLR 1.

[4] Judgment of Brennan, Deane and Dawson JJ at 29.

[5] Judgment of McHugh J at 70-76; and JSCM (1994:51-53).

[6] Judgment of McHugh J at 72.

[7] *Minister for Immigration and Multicultural and Indigenous Affairs v Al Masri* (2003) 197 ALR 241.

[8] Mr Al Masri was subsequently removed from Australia in September 2002 after arrangements had been made with the Palestinian Territories. On 1 August 2009, he was shot dead 'at close range by a militant gunman in front of the magistrates court in Khan Younis in the southern Gaza Strip' (PSC 2009).

[9] *Al Masri*, as cited at 241.

[10] *Al Masri*, as cited at 272.

[11] *Al Masri*, as cited at 273-277.

[12] Extensive evidence was before the Court on the damaging impact of detention on Mr. Al Masri.

[13] *Al-Kateb v Godwin* (2004) 208 ALR 124

[14] *Minister for Immigration and Multicultural and Indigenous Affairs v Al Khafaji* (2004) 208 ALR 201.

[15] *Al-Kateb* as cited, at 179.

[16] *Al-Kateb* as cited, at 180.

[17] *Al- Kateb* as cited, at 181.

[18] *Al- Kateb* as cited, at 190-191.

[19] *Al-Kateb* as cited, at 162.

[20] *Al-Kateb* as cited, at 158.

[21] *Behrooz v Secretary, Department of Immigration and Multicultural and Indigenous Affairs and Others* (2004) 208 ALR 271.

[22] Quoted in *Behrooz* as cited, at 273.

[23] *Behrooz* as cited, at 275.

[24] *Behrooz* as cited, at 277.

[25] *Re Woolley; Ex parte Applicants M276/2003 by their next friend GS* [2004] HCA 49 (7 October 2004).

[26] *Re Woolley* as cited, at par.422.

[27] *Re Woolley* as cited, at par.58.

[28] *Re Woolley* as cited, at par.61.

[29] *Re Woolley* as cited, at par.63.

[30] *Ruhani v Director of Police* [2005] HCA 42 (31 August 2005).

[31] *Ruhani v Director of Police* [No 2] [2005] HCA 43 (31 August 3005).

[32] For example, see HREOC (2004b: 89-91).

Epilogue: A new beginning?

Endgames

In the November 2007 federal election, the Australian Labor Party led by Kevin Rudd defeated John Howard's Coalition government. Border policing policy barely featured in the election campaign. For the Coalition, the treatment of asylum seekers had become a liability and episodes such as the 'Children Overboard' affair an indicator of the government's cynicism and illegitimacy. Within a parliamentary Labor Party committed to strict border controls, the prevailing wisdom was that while reforms should be implemented, these should be low key and not capable of being a vehicle for attacking Labor as weak on border protection.

Despite this uneasy consensus, the endgame of the Pacific Solution continued to unfold, albeit with relatively little publicity. On 12 September 2007, Immigration Minister Andrews announced that 72 of the Sri Lankan Tamil asylum seekers detained on Nauru since February 2007 had been granted refugee status (MIC 2007a). Being stranded on Nauru had already taken its toll on this group. In July, concerns had been raised about the possible deterioration of their mental health (PSC 2007) and on 1 September 2007, 50 of the group had commenced a hunger strike demanding that decisions be made on their claims. In an open letter to the immigration minister, they declared their disappointment 'that no decision has been taken about our plea for political asylum' and their frustration at being 'reduced to walking zombies' (ASRC 2007; Topsfield 2007b). The hunger strike was called off after six days but those who were granted refugee status were also told that they would not be resettled in Australia and that they would remain detained on Nauru while the Australian government explored other resettlement options (MIC 2007a). In effect, the refugees were told they would be detained in an indefinite state of limbo. This was brought to an end soon after the election, when the new government announced

Epilogue

that it would close the Nauru detention centre and shortly after agreed to resettle the 75 remaining Sri Lankan detainees in Australia (Evans 2008a).

On 2 October 2007, Immigration Minister Andrews announced that the proportion of African refugees included in Australia's annual resettlement quota of 13,000 would be cut to 30 percent. This was down from 50 percent in 2005–2006 and 70 percent in 2004–2005 (MIC 2007b). Resettled Sudanese refugees were the main target of these cuts, which were accompanied by a series of sensationalist media reports about Sudanese gangs (Attard 2007). According to the Victorian police commissioner, there was no African gang culture in the areas concerned or evidence that Sudanese youths were disproportionately engaged in offending behaviour (Attard 2007). This did not stop the minister condemning '...as not reflecting "the Australian way of life"' an incident in which a detective was allegedly assaulted[1] by a group that 'included Sudanese youths' (Holroyd 2007), even though such public order incidents can hardly be described as extraordinary. Indeed, as the assistant Victorian police commissioner pointed out, two similar incidents not involving Sudanese youths that occurred on the same night in other parts of Melbourne received no media coverage (Brown 2007).

Such conscious attempts by a government in its death throes to shape its restrictive integrationist agenda around anti-African and anti-Muslim racism reiterated the official problematisation of refugees as outsiders. And even though the minister's announcement coincided with the allocation of an additional $210 million in federal funds for resettlement services (MIC 2007b), the notion that refugees require careful management denied their right of agency, delegitimised their status and undermined their rights to free movement. The passing of the Howard government did not bring an end to this, but it did result in a shift in tone.

The new approach?

There were some notable changes to border policing during the first year of the Rudd government. In addition to closing down the

Nauru centre and resettling the remaining refugees, the government announced in May 2008 that it would abolish temporary protection visas and provide permanent visas to all people determined to be refugees, regardless of their mode of arrival (Evans 2008c). In July 2008, the government announced further changes to the detention system. Under the new framework, children (and where possible their families) would not be detained in an immigration detention centre and the length and conditions of detention 'would subject to regular review'. More significantly, detainees would be released following health, identity and security checks unless they are deemed to be 'a risk to the community'. The onus would be on the immigration department to justify ongoing detention (Evans 2008d) although one of the tests for the future will be how risk is determined, especially if unauthorised arrivals come from regions likely to generate adverse security assessments. Further amending legislation in 2009 codified the new framework and abolished the perverse practice of imposing a financial charge on detainees for the costs of their detention (although not for deportation).[2]

Claims that these reforms represent a new direction in government are somewhat overstated. Most of the changes were announced in 2008, when with little media attention only 161 people sought unauthorised entry by boat[3]. However, the new framework should be considered in the context of the renewed cycle of unauthorised boat arrivals generated largely by the conflicts and repression in Afghanistan and Sri Lanka. Between 17 January and 13 October 2009, 31 unauthorised boats arrived carrying a total of 1,770 people,[4] with little sign of the numbers abating in the immediate future. While the government has so far avoided the state sanctioned invasion phobias of 2001, and been dismissive of opposition suggestions that the new policy has attracted people smugglers, much of the language is redolent of the Howard era and key criminogenic elements of Australia's border policing infrastructure remain intact.

Externalisation

The Rudd government remains fully committed to the externalisation of border controls. The excision of key landfalls such

Epilogue

as Ashmore reef and Christmas Island remains, leaving those seeking unauthorised entry via such routes vulnerable to naval interception and removal. Through the Bali Process and other diplomatic mechanisms, the government has focused its energies on securing regional implementation of its forward border policing strategy. Indonesia, which is still not a signatory to the 1951 Refugee Convention, has been at the centre of these efforts. During October 2009, Prime Minister Rudd met personally with his Indonesian counterpart in a bid to secure further co-operation. The gist of the bi-lateral arrangements is that the Australian government is funding the operation and refurbishment of detention centres in Indonesia, either directly or through the International Organisation for Migration; providing logistical support to the Indonesian navy; and working with Indonesia's policing agencies to prevent and disrupt further boat departures (Maiden 2009; Fitzpatrick and Walters 2009).

Providing a bleak reminder of the *Tampa* events, an Australia bound fishing boat carrying 255 Tamil asylum seekers was intercepted on 13 October by the Indonesian Navy at the direct request of the Australian government. The boat was towed to the port of Merak in Western Java, where a number of the Tamils went on a 52 hour hunger strike demanding resettlement in Australia or another safe western country and thereafter refused to disembark (Thompson 2009; Murdoch 2009). In the same week, another 78 Tamil asylum seekers were picked up in Indonesia's search and rescue zone by an Australian Customs ship, the *Oceanic Viking*. When told they were being taken to Tanjung Pinang detention centre near Singapore, they also went on hunger strike demanding refuge in Australia and refused to leave the ship. At the time of writing,[5] there were indications that Indonesian officials would begin processing the asylum claims on board the *Oceanic Viking* but no sign that the refugees would willingly leave either boat.

While various members of the Australian government have hailed such interventions as examples of good co-operation (ABC News 2009b), the refugees face years of warehousing and uncertainty in dangerous and degrading conditions. Up to 3,000 people were believed to be in Indonesian detention centres in

October 2009 (Black 2009). As the 78 Tamils were being taken to Tanjung Pinang, Afghan refugees who had been detained there for over 7 months behind razor wire and barred windows, told journalists of being 'locked in during the day and suffering night-time beatings' (Kearney and Fitzpatrick 2009). An eyewitness account by documentary maker, Jessie Taylor,[6] of Indonesia's detention facilities described asylum seekers being 'treated like animals' and continued:

> At the Pontianak jail there was an escape of a few people in late July and the people left behind have been in lock down without permission to leave their cell since that day. There are children in there.
>
> In places like Mataram, Lombok, there are rats running around, very young babies and children in putrid houses....
>
> Some people reside in extremely cramped conditions. In Jakarta...there's a small office with two prison cells attached on the third floor of the immigration building. People can't lie down at the same time.
>
> In a prison in Pontianak...around 50 men and unaccompanied boys are locked up in a big cell just smaller than a tennis court, a concrete cell behind bars. It's very hot and steamy and when the men do their business it flows into a ditch behind the building and just sits there and the stench is unbelievable.
>
> The women and kids are kept in a three room house with no walls or windows or doors that you can lock, a shell of a house.
>
> At the time there was a strange bunch of illegal Thai fisherman [sic] who'd been caught and put in jail. They were not under lock and key and had full access to the women and children...One of the mother came up to me with tears in her eyes and said that very often she can't find her daughters and she's horrified at the prospect of them being s-xually [sic] assaulted (quoted, Black 2009).

The Rudd government resorted to the language of denial and blame shifting about the circumstances facing refugees in Indonesia. When questioned about the 255 refugees re-routed to Merak,

Epilogue

Deputy Prime Minister Julia Gillard responded bluntly that these were matters for the Indonesian government, repeating the line of numerous predecessors:

> Our message is very clear. We say to people who are engaged in people smuggling, they are engaged in a vile trade that seeks to profit off human misery, and anything we can do to stop people smugglers plying that vile trade, we will do (quoted, ABC News 2009a).

Gillard's language replicated the prime minister's response to the fatal explosion on board an unauthorised boat off Australia's north-west coast on 16 April 2009. Rather than concede that Australia's exclusion zone was a central driver of illicit movement, he declared:

> People smugglers are engaged in the world's most evil trade and they should all rot in jail, because they represent the absolute scum of the earth. We see this lowest form of life in what we saw on the high seas yesterday (quoted, Griffiths 2009).

The alternative to the strategy employed by the government, which would undercut both people smuggling and the institutional abuse of refugees would be to dedicate the resources devoted to policing people smuggling to processing refugees in Afghanistan, Sri Lanka and Indonesia with a view to re-settling them in Australia or another destination of their choice. Instead, we have the construction of the Indian Ocean or Indonesian Solution, backed up by the continued use of offshore processing at the Christmas Island detention centre.

Mandatory detention and offshore processing

The new Christmas Island detention centre was opened in December 2008 after the interception of seven unauthorised vessels carrying 164 people. This coincided with an aggressive campaign by states in the region, especially, Thailand, to physically remove and repel refugees from Burma and Sri Lanka (Percy 2009; UNHCR 2009). By October 2009, the centre was almost full with contingency plans in place to re-open a centre in Darwin.

The Rudd government's policy leaves unauthorised boat arrivals in a similar state of physical and legal limbo to the Pacific Solution. All asylum seekers who arrive at excised offshore places are detained on Christmas Island as a matter of policy. Isolating detainees on Christmas Island is not fundamentally different to isolating them on Nauru. Because of the continued excision of Christmas Island, asylum seekers are denied access to the refugee determination processes available on the Australian mainland and are allowed only very limited access to Australian courts. Whether they are granted a protection visa rests entirely in the discretion of the immigration minister.

In October 2009, the Australian Human Rights Commission (AHRC 2009) condemned the inherently discriminatory and abusive dynamics of this policy. In a report based on inspections conducted in July 2009, the commission made 22 recommendations including: the repeal of the excision provisions; access to the full refugee determination system; the cessation of detention on Christmas Island or failing that, an end to mandatory detention of all unauthorised boat arrivals on the island; rights to prompt review by a court of detention decisions; an end to the detention of children in any of the three secure facilities on the island; urgent amendments s to the detention laws to ensure full compliance with the UN Convention on the Rights of the Child; the appointment of an independent guardian for unaccompanied children; the removal of all caged walkways, perspex barriers and electrified fencing from the new detention centre; and an extensive list of improvements to the detention regime (AHRC 2009: 4–9).

Resuming hostilities

Such an extensive critique during the first sustained period of unauthorised arrivals suggests that the first year of the Rudd government is better viewed as a lull in hostilities rather than a period of substantial reform, and that the concerns raised by this book are live and ongoing issues.

The recent history of border policing in Australia has not been an aberration but the product of deeply rooted state practice and

Epilogue

ideology. The Pacific Solution was not inevitable – governments have choices about the decisions they make – but it could be legitimised by drawing on ideas from the political mainstream. No doubt, the fears associated with Australian nationalism and racism will again be mobilised but there is no reason for this to be accepted as hegemonic.

A proper account of the substantial opposition to Australia's border policing policies that developed during period of the Howard government has yet to be written and has not been attempted here. However, it is significant that in October 2009, Paul Howes, the president of the Australian Workers Union and vice-president of the Australian Council of Trade Unions condemned the policy of returning refugees to Indonesia and argued for their right to be processed in Australia (Kirk 2009).[7] The scale and diversity of the opposition to the Howard government's policies,[8] while often unacknowledged, demonstrates the capacity for widely-accepted assumptions about border protection and the legitimacy of abusive state practice to be challenged.

The key argument of this book is that many of these practices should be understood as criminal and that the absence of any formal legal mechanism for identifying and targeting state crime should not deter criminologists, or anyone else, from using this concept to analyse and challenge organised human rights abuses committed in our name. Governments are not in habit of acknowledging collective responsibility, let alone criminality. But it is possible for criminology to accommodate the concept of deviance from below; that is a deviance that is defined within civil society and the wider international polity, rather than by the determinations of particular states or enforcement agencies. A deviance that is understood by reference to the experiences of Amal Basry, with whom this book started, rather than out of a fear of un-named people, on un-named boats, employing 'criminal' gangs, to 'threaten' Australia's border controls and 'ways of life'.

Notes

[1] The officer's injuries amounted to 'a chipped tooth and a sore leg' (Holroyd 2007).
[2] See Migration Amendment (Immigration Detention Reform) Bill 2009 and *Migration Amendment (Abolishing Detention Debt) Act* 2009.
[3] Statistics provided by Customs and Border Protection media and published in The Australian, 16 October 2009.
[4] As above
[5] 26 October 2009
[6] See http://www.vimeo.com/6328019
[7] See also ACTU (2009).
[8] For some insights into some of the opposition, see O'Neill (2008).

References

11 Million (2009) *The Arrest and Detention of Children Subject to Immigration Control*, Children's Commissioner for England, London.

AAP (Australian Associated Press) (1990) 'More refugees headed this way' *The Australian*, 4 June.

AAP (2005) 'Detention company fined over breaches', *The Age*, 17 October.

AAP (2006a) 'Payout a "landmark"', *The Age*, 3 March.

AAP (2006b) 'Government unveils "prison hulk" patrol boat', *The Age*, 10 December.

AAP (2007a) 'Andrews won't intervene for sick refugee', *Sydney Morning Herald*, 12 June.

AAP (2007b) 'Hanson calls for halt to Muslim immigration', *Sydney Morning Herald*, 16 August.

AAP (2007c) 'Nile wants Muslim pause', *Sydney Morning Herald*, 11 March.

Aarons, M (2001) *War Criminals Welcome: Australia, a Sanctuary for Fugitive War Criminals Since 1945*, Black Inc., Melbourne.

ABA (Australian Broadcasting Authority) (2003) *Investigation Report*, File 2002/1296, Investigation Number 1203, http://SIEV X.com/articles/psdp/ABAInvestigationIntoSundayProgram.pdf, accessed 2 July 2007.

ABC (Australian Broadcasting Corporation) (2009) 'Asylum Seekers', *Unleashed Voices,* 28 January, http://www.abc.net.au/unleashed/stories/s2474952.htm, accessed 29 January 2009.

ABC News (2006) 'Police to consider Villawood abuse report', 23 June, http://www.abc.net.au/news/stories/2006/06/23/1669786.htm, accessed 8 August 2007.

ABC News (2009a) 'Asylum seekers' fate up to Indonesia: Gillard', 16 October, http://www.abc.net.au/news/stories/2009/10/15/2715184.htm, accessed 16 October 2009.

ABC News (2009b) 'Indonesia agrees to take asylum seekers', 21 October, http://www.abc.net.au/news/stories/2009/10/20/2719513.htm, accessed 21 October 2009.

ABC Online (2004a) 'Vanstone Critical of Human Rights Commission report', 13 May, http://www.abc.net.au/pm/content/2004/s1107800.htm, accessed 14 May 2004.

ABC Online (2004b) 'Australian aid to help ease Nauru crisis', 20 October, http://www.abc.nt.au/news/newsitms/200410/s1224147.htm, accessed 21 October 2004.

ABC Online (2006a) 'Australian treatment of Nauru detainee shameless, lawyer says', 4 December, http://www.abc.net.au/newsitem/200612/s1803435.htm, accessed 4 December 2006.

ABC Online (2006b) 'Sexual abuse widespread in detention centres, doctor says', 13 June, http://www.abc.net.au/news/newsitems/200606/s1661330.htm, accessed 13 June 2006.

ABS (Australian Bureau of Statistics) (1974) *Official Year Book of Australia*, Number 60, Author, Canberra.

ABS (1978) *Official Year Book of Australia,* Number 64, Author, Canberra.

ACTU (Australian Council of Trade Unions) (2009) 'Union statement in support of the humane treatment of asylum seekers', *Media Release,* 26 October.

Adepoju, A (2005) 'Review of Research and Data on Human Trafficking in Sub-Saharan Africa' in F. Laczko and E.Gozdziak (eds) *Data and research on human trafficking: A global survey*, IOM, Geneva.

AFP (Australian Federal Police, 2002 'Sunday Program continues with People Smuggling Allegations', *Media Release*, 29 August.

AFP (2005) *2004–2005 Annual Report*, Author, Canberra.

AG (Australian Government) (2006) *Australian Citizenship: Much more than a ceremony*, Author, Canberra.

References

AG (2007) *Becoming an Australian Citizen*, Draft, Author, Canberra.

Agamben, G (1998) *Homo Sacer: Sovereign Power and Bare Life*, trans. Daniel Heller-Roazen, Stanford University Press, Stanford.

Agamben, G (2000) *Means Without End: Notes on Politics*, trans.Vincenzo Binetti and Cesare Casarino, University of Minnesota Press, Minneapolis.

A-GD (Attorney-General's Department) (1994) *Report of the Investigations of War Criminals in Australia*, AGPS, Canberra.

A-GD (2002) 'Response to Lateline program and Curtin Detention Centre Video', *Media Release,* Justice Minister, 23 April, Author, Canberra.

A-GD (2004) *Australian Government's Action Plan to Eradicate Trafficking in Persons*, Author, Canberra.

Age (*The Age*) (1888) 'News of the Day', 28 April.

Age (1907) 'Editorial', 28 December.

AHRC (Asian Human Rights Commission) (2001) 'Australia: The denial of the right to asylum and inhumane treatment', *Urgent Appeal*, Number 17, 29 May, http://www.ahrchk.net/au/mainfile.php/2001/105/, accessed 21 August 2001.

AHRC (Australian Human Rights Commission) (2008) *2008 Immigration Detention Report*, http://www.humanrights.gov.au/human_rights/immigration/idc2008.html, accessed 2 February 2009.

AHRC (2009) *Immigration detention and offshore processing in Christmas Island*, Author, Sydney.

AI (Amnesty International) (1996a) *The Refugee Crisis in the Great Lakes Region,* AI Index: AFR 02/01/96, Author, London.

AI (1996b) *Zaire – Hidden from Scrutiny: human rights abuses in Eastern Zaire*, AI Index: AFR 62/29/96, Author, London.

AI (2005a) 'Refugee rights are being eroded in central Africa', *Amnesty Wire*, February, http://web.amnesty.org/wire/February2005/refugee, accessed 14 March 2005.

AI (2005b) *Amnesty International Appeal to the European Union Regarding Expulsions from Italy to Libya*, 28 June, B472, Amnesty International EU Office, Belgium.

AI (2006) *Families Divided: The Impact of Temporary Protection Visas*, Author, Sydney.

Akers, R (2000) *Criminological Theories: Introduction, Evaluation and Application*, Roxbury Publishing, Los Angeles.

ALP (Australian Labor Party) (2007) *National Platform and Constitution*, 44th National Conference, Author, Canberra.

Amor, M and Austin, J (eds) (2003) *From Nothing to Zero: Letters from Refugees in Australia's Detention Centres*, Lonely Planet Publications, Melbourne.

AMSA (Australian Maritime Safety Authority) (2001) 'Timeline for *Tampa* Incident', *Submission to Senate Select Committee Inquiry into a Certain Maritime Incident,* Author, Canberra.

ANAO (Australian National Audit Office) (2002) Management Framework for Preventing Unlawful Entry into Australian Territory, *Audit Report,* No.57, 2001–02, Author, Canberra.

ANAO (2004) 'Management of the Detention Centre Contracts – Part A', *Audit Report*, No.54, 2003–4, Author, Canberra

Anderson, B (2000) *Imagined Communities: Reflections on the Origin and Spread of Nationalism*, Revised edition, Verso, London.

Andreas, P (2000) *Border Games: Policing the US-Mexico Divide*, Cornell University Press, New York.

Andreas, P and Nadelmann, E (2006) *Policing the Globe: Criminalization and Crime Control in International Relations*, Oxford University Press, New York.

Andreas, P and Snyder, T (2000) *The Wall Around the West*, Rowman and Littlefield, New York.

Andrews MP, K (2007) 'Citizenship – committing to a way of life', *Address to the Sydney Institute*, 31 July.

APC (Australian Press Council) (2002) 'Access to refugees', *Australian Press Council News*, Volume 14, Number 1.

Arendt, H (1976) *The Origins of Totalitarianism*, Harvest, Harcourt Inc., New York.

References

ASRC (Asylum Seeker Resource Centre) (2006) *Submission to Senate Legal and Constitutional References Committee Inquiry into the Administration and Operation of the Migration Act 1958*, Author, Melbourne.

ASRC (2007) 'Open letter to the Minister for Immigration and Citizenship', http://www.asrc.org.au/uploads/File/Nauru%20Asylum%20Seekers.doc., accessed 19 September 2007.

Athwal, H (2004) *Death Trap: The human cost of the war on asylum*, Institute of Race Relations, London.

Attard, M (2007) 'Ganging Up', *Media Watch*, ABC Television, 8 October, http://www.abc.net.au/mediawatch/transcripts/s2054150.htm, accessed 10 October 2007.

Bailey, R (2007) 'Power, resistance and bare life in Australian Immigration detention', *Paper presented at 'Disciplines and Punishments': Interdisciplinary Approaches to Crime and Justice*, Criminal Justice and Research Network Conference, University of New South Wales, Sydney, 9–10 July 2007.

Bakewell, O (2002) 'Refugee Aid and Protection in Rural Africa: Working in Parallel or Cross Purposes?' *Refugee Survey Quarterly*, Volume 21, Numbers 1 and 2.

Bales, K (2004) *Disposable People: New Slavery in the Global Economy*, Revised Edition, University of California Press, Berkeley.

Banham, C (2004) 'Detained children freed in policy flip', *Sydney Morning Herald*, 6 July.

Barak, G (ed) (1991) *Crimes by the Capitalist State: An Introduction to State Criminality*, State University of New York Press, New York.

Barker, G (2007) 'The public service', in C. Hamilton and S.Maddison (eds) *Silencing Dissent: How the Australian government is controlling public opinion and stifling debate*, Allen and Unwin, Sydney.

Barnes, D (2002) *A Life Devoid of Meaning: Living on a Temporary Protection Visa in Western Sydney*, Centre for Refugee Research, University of New South Wales.

Bass, G (2000) *Stay the Hand of Vengeance: the politics of war crimes tribunals*, Princeton University Press, New Jersey.

Bayart, J-F, Ellis, S and Hibou, B (1999) *The Criminalization of the State in Africa,* James Currey, Oxford.

Beare, M (1997) 'Illegal Migration: Personal Tragedies, Social Problems, or National Security Threats?' *Transnational Organised Crime,* Volume 3, Number 4.

Bem, K, Field, N, Maclellan, N, Meyer, S and Morris, T (2007) *A price too high: the cost of Australia's approach to asylum seekers,* A Just Australia and Oxfam Australia, Sydney and Melbourne.

Bender, L (2007) 'Compelled to act', in S. Mares and L. Newman (eds) *Acting from the Heart: Australian advocates for asylum seekers tell their stories,* Finch Publishing, Sydney.

Biddulph, S (2007) 'Memorial is also hope for humanity', *Sydney Morning Herald,* 30 August.

Black, R (1998) 'Putting Refugees in Camps', *Forced Migration Review,* Number 2.

Black, R (2001) 'Environmental refugees: myth or reality', *New Issues in Refugee Research,* Working Paper, Number 34, UNHCR, Geneva.

Black, S (2007a) 'Christmas Island – building our own private Guantanamo', *Crikey,* 28 March, http://www.crikey.com.au/Politics/20070328–Christmas-Island-the-full-plans.html, accessed 5 June 2007.

Black, S (2007b) 'Going, going, gone: Baxter chattels on the block', *Crikey,* 8 May, http://www.crikey.com.au/Politics/20070508–Grand-sale-Baxter, accessed 10 May 2007.

Black, S (2009) 'A tour of Indonesia's detention centres' *Crikey,* 23 October, http://www.crikey.com.au/2009/10/23/bali-it-aint-a-tour--of-indonesias-detention-centres.html, accessed 26 October 2009.

Blainey, G. (1984) *All for Australia,* Methuen Hayes, Sydney.

Blainey, G (1991) *Eye on Australia: speeches and essays of Geoffrey Blainey,* Schwartz Books, Melbourne.

Blakeney, M (1984) *Australia and the Jewish Refugees* 1933–1948, Croom Helm, Sydney.

Boggs, C (1976) *Gramsci's Marxism,* Pluto Press, London.

Brennan, F (2003) *Tampering with Asylum: A Universal Humanitarian Problem,* University of Queensland Press, St.Lucia.

References

Britain, I (1969) 'Victoria, the Chinese and the federal idea', *ANU Historical Journal*, Number 6.

Brown, M (2007) 'Sudanese community unfairly singled out over street violence', *ABC News,* 11 October, http://www.abc.com.au/news/stories/2007/10/11/2056606.htm , accessed 11 October 2007.

Budapest Group (1999) *The Relationship Between Organised Crime and Trafficking in Aliens,* International Centre for Migration Policy Development, Vienna.

Burgmann, V (1978) 'Capital and Labour' in A.Curthoys and A.Markus (eds) *Who Are Our Enemies?: Racism and the Australian Working Class*, Hale and Ironmonger and Australian Society for the Study of Labour History, Sydney and Canberra.

Burke, A (2001) *In Fear of Security: Australia's Invasion Anxiety*, Pluto Press Australia, Sydney.

Burke, E (1961) *Reflections on the Revolution in France*, Doubleday, New York.

Caldwell, A (2006) 'SIEV X memorial plans thwarted: organisers', *AM*, ABC Radio National, 14 October, http://SIEV X.com/articles/5thAnniversary/20061014AlisonCaldwell.html, accessed 1 June 2007.

Callinicos, A (2000) *Equality,* Polity Press, Cambridge.

Calwell, A (1945) *How Many Australians Tomorrow?* Reed and Harris, Melbourne.

Carey, C (2007) 'Woomera: victims of the war zone', *Sydney Morning Herald,* 25 February.

Carnegie Commission (1997) *Carnegie Commission on Preventing Deadly Conflict,* Carnegie Corporation of New York, Washington D.C.

Carrington, K and Hearn, J (2003) 'Trafficking and the Sex Industry: From Impunity to Protection', *Current Issues Brief*, Number 28, 2002–2003, Parliamentary Library, Canberra.

Cass, M (1978) 'Stop this unjust queue jumping', *The Australian*, 29 June.

Castles, S (2001) 'Environmental Change and Forced Migration', *Text of Lecture*, 6 December, Preparing for Peace Initiative, www.preparingforpeace.org/castles_environmntal_change_and_forced_migration, accessed 24 August 2005.

Castles, S (2003) 'Towards a Sociology of Forced Migration and Social Transformation' *Sociology,* Volume 37, Number 1.

CEC (2005a) *Communication from the Commission to the Council and the European Parliament on Regional Protection Programmes*, COM (2005) 388 final, 1 September, Brussels

CEC (2005b) *Communication from the Commission to the European parliament and the Council: Fighting trafficking in human beings – an integrated approach and proposals for an action plan*, COM (2005) 514 final, 18 October, Brussels.

CG *(Commonwealth Government) (2007) Government Response to Senate Committee Report: Legal and Constitutional References Committee*, March 2006, Author, Canberra.

Chambliss, W (1989) 'State-Organised Crime', *Criminology,* Volume 27, Number 2.

Chen, G (2005) 'Confinement and Dependency: The Decline of Refugee Rights in Tanzania', *World Refugee Survey 2005,* USCRI, Washington D.C.

CIVIPOL (2003) *Feasibility Study on the control of the European Union's maritime borders*, Final Report, 11490/1/03, 19 September, Council of the European Union, Brussels.

CO (Commonwealth Ombudsman) (2006a) *Report on Referred Immigration Cases: Mr T*, Report No. 04/2006, Author, Canberra.

CO (2006b) *Report Into Referred Immigration Cases: Mr G*, Report No. 06/2006, Author, Canberra.

CO (2006c) *Report Into Referred Immigration Cases: Mental Health and Incapacity*, Report No. 07/2006, Author, Canberra.

CO (2006d) *Report Into Referred Immigration Cases: Children in Detention*, Report No. 08/2006, Author, Canberra.

CO (2007a) *Report Into Referred Immigration Cases: Detention Process Issues,* Report No. 07/2007, Author, Canberra.

CO (2007b) *Report Into Referred Immigration Cases: Data Problems, Report No.* 08/2007, Author, Canberra.

CO (2007c) *Report Into Referred Immigration Cases: Notification Issues*, Report No. 09/2007, Author, Canberra.

References

CO (2007d) *Report Into Referred Immigration Cases: Other Legal Issues*, Report No. 10/2007, Author, Canberra.

CO (2007e) *Immigration reports tabled in Parliament by number*, Author, Canberra.

CoA (Commonwealth of Australia) (1946) 'Immigration-Government Policy', Statement by the Minister for Immigration', 22 November, *Parliamentary Papers*, Session 1946–1947–1948, Volume II, 1045, Commonwealth Government Printer, Canberra.

CoA (1947) 'Immigration-Government Policy', Ministerial Statement, 28 November, *Parliamentary Papers*, Session 1946–1947–1948, Volume II, 1061, Commonwealth Government Printer, Canberra.

Cockburn, M (1990) 'Evans has doubts over Cambodians', *Sydney Morning Herald*, 16 June.

Cohen, R and Deng, F (1998) *Masses in Flight: The Global Crisis of Internal Displacement*, Brookings Institution Press, Washington D.C.

Cohen, S (1993) 'Human Rights and Crimes of the State: the Culture of Denial', *Australian and New Zealand Journal of Criminology*, Volume 26, Number 97.

Cohen, S (2001) *States of Denial: Knowing about Atrocities and Suffering*, Polity Press, Cambridge.

Cohen, S (2002) *Folk Devils and Moral Panics*, Third Edition, Routledge, London.

Collins, J., Noble, G., Poynting, S., and Tabar, P. (2000) *Kebabs, Kids, Cops and Crime*, Pluto, Sydney.

Comrie, N (2005) *Inquiry into the Circumstances of the Vivian Alvarez Matter*, Commonwealth Ombudsman, Canberra.

Coombs, M (2005) 'Excising Australia: Are we really shrinking?', *Research Note*, Number 5, 2005–06, Parliamentary Library, Canberra.

Corlett, D (2005) *Following Them Home: The Fate of the Returned Asylum Seekers*, Black Inc., Melbourne.

CPD (Commonwealth Parliamentary Debates) (House of Representatives) (1977) '*Refugee Policies and Mechanisms*', Ministerial Statement, 24 May.

CPD (1983) *Ministerial Statement*, 18 May.

CPD (1988) *Ministerial Statement*, 8 December.
CPD (1992a) *Second reading speech*, 5 May.
CPD (1992b) *Second reading debate*, 11 November.
CPD (1994) *Second reading speech*, 8 November.
CPD (1999a) *Second reading speech*, 22 September.
CPD (1999b) *Second reading debate*, 21 October.
CPD (2001a) *Ministerial Statements*, 29 August.
CPD (2001b) *Second reading debate*, 29 August.
CPD (Senate) (2002), *Debates*, 10 December.
Crawford, J (1990) 'Australian Immigration Law and Refugees: the 1989 Amendments', *International Journal of Refugee Law*, Volume 2, Number 4.
Crawford, J (1998) Special Rapporteur, *First report on State responsibility*, International Law Commission, UN General Assembly, A/CN.4/490/Add.3
Crawford, J (2002) *The International Law Commission's Articles on State Responsibility: Introduction, Text and Commentaries*, Cambridge University Press, Cambridge.
Crisp, J (1999) *"Who has counted the refugees?" UNHCR and the politics of numbers*, Working Paper, Number 12, UNHCR, Geneva.
Crock, M (ed) (1993) *Protection or Punishment: The detention of asylum seekers in Australia*, The Federation Press, Melbourne.
Crock, M (1995) 'The Peril of the Boat People: Assessing Australia's Responses to the Phenomenon of Border Asylum-Seekers', in H. Selby (ed) *Tomorrow's Law*, The Federation Press, Sydney.
Crock, M (1998) *Immigration and Refugee Law in Australia*, The Federation Press, Sydney.
Crock, M and Saul, B (2002) *Future Seekers: Refugees and the Law*, The Federation Press and the Justice Foundation of New South Wales, Sydney.
Cubby, B (2006) 'Report on detention abuse due', *Sydney Morning Herald*, 12 June.
Dastyari, A, Saul, B and Crock, M (2006) *Future Seekers II: Refugees and Irregular Migration in Australia*, Federation Press, Sydney.

References

Dastyari, A (2007) 'Trading in refugees', *On Line Opinion,* 28 May, http://www.onlineopinion.com.au/view.asp?article=5896, accessed 29 May 2007.

Davis, M (2001) *Late Victorian Holocausts: El Niño Famines and the Making of the Third World*, Verso, London.

Davis, M (2004a) 'Planet of Slums', *New Left Review*, Volume 26, Number 2.

Davis, M (2004b) 'Poor, Black and Left Behind', *TomDispatch*, 24 September, http://www.tomdispatch.com/index.mhtml?pid=1849, accessed 31 October 2005.

Davis, M (2006) *Planet of Slums*, Verso, London.

De Waal, A (1997) *Famine Crimes: Politics and the Disaster Relief Industry in Africa,* The International African Institute, James Currey and Indiana University Press, Oxford and Bloomington.

Detter, I (2000) 2nd edition, *The Law of War*, Cambridge University Press, Cambridge.

DFAT (Department of Foreign Affairs and Trade) (1990) *Cambodia: An Australian Peace Proposal,* AGPS, Canberra.

DFAT (2006) *Agreement Between the Republic of Indonesia and Australia on the Framework for Security Cooperation*, http://www.dfat.gov.au/geo/indonesia/ind-aus-sec06.html, accessed 23 November 2006.

DIAC (Department of Immigration and Citizenship) (2007a) 'Immigration Detention', *Fact Sheet 82*, Author, Canberra.

DIAC (2007b) 'Palmer report – two years of progress', *Media release,* 1 July.

DIAC (2007c) 'Reintegration Package for Afghans', *Fact Sheet 80,* Author, Canberra.

DIAC (2007d) 'Reintegration package for Iranians', *Fact Sheet 80b,* Author, Canberra.

DIEA (Department of Immigration and Ethnic Affairs) (1976) *Review of Activities to 30 June 1976*, AGPS, Canberra.

DIEA (1977) *Review of Activities to 30 June 1977*, AGPS, Canberra.

DIEA (1979) *Review of Activities to 30 June 1979,* AGPS, Canberra.

DIEA (1980) *Review of Activities to 30 June 1980*, AGPS, Canberra.
DIEA (1981) *Review of Activities to 30 June 1981*, AGPS, Canberra.
DIEA (1982) *Review of Activities to 30 June 1982*, AGPS, Canberra.
DIEA (1983) *Annual Review*, AGPS, Canberra.
DIEA (1984) *Annual Review*, AGPS, Canberra.
DIEA (1985) *Annual Review*, AGPS, Canberra.
DIEA (1986) *Annual Review*, AGPS, Canberra.
DILGEA (Department of Immigration, Local Government and Ethnic Affairs) (1988) *Annual Review*, AGPS, Canberra.
DILGEA (1989) *Annual Review*, AGPS, Canberra.
DILGEA (1990) *Annual Review*, AGPS, Canberra.
DIMIA (Department of Multiculturalism, Immigration and Indigenous Affairs) (2004) 'Boat Arrival Details', *Fact Sheet 74a*, Author, Canberra.
DIMIA (2005a) *Annual Report 2004–2005*, Author, Canberra.
DIMIA (2005b) 'Secretary Deplores Incident', *Media Release*, DPS 025/2005, 10 August
DIMIA (2005c) *Managing the Border: Immigration Compliance*, Author, Canberra.
DIMIA (2006) *Key Facts in Addressing the Recommendations of the Palmer Report*, Author, Canberra.
Di Nicola, A (2007) 'Researching into human trafficking: issues and problems', in M. Lee (ed) *Human Trafficking*, Willan Publishing, Devon.
Dietrich, H (2005) 'The desert front – EU refugee camps in North Africa?' *Statewatch News Online*, March, http://statewatch.org/news/2005/mar/12eu-refugee-camps.htm, accessed 14 April 2005.
Dodd, M (2007) 'SAS to train with Indonesians', *The Australian*, 2 February.
Douzinas, C (2000) *The End of Human Rights: Critical legal thought at the end of the century*, Hart Publishing, Oxford.
Dow, M (1994) 'A Refugee Policy to Support Haiti's Killers', *New Politics*, Volume 5, Number 1 (new series).

References

Draper, H (1977) *Karl Marx's Theory of Revolution, Volume 1: State and Bureaucracy*, Monthly Review Press, New York.

Dudley, M (2003) 'Contradictory Australian national policies on self-harm and suicide: the case of asylum seekers in mandatory detention', *Australasian Psychiatry*, Volume 11 Supplement.

Duffield, M (2001) *Global Governance and the New Wars: The Merging of Development and Security*, Zed Books, London.

Engels, F (1973) 'The Origins of the Family, Private Property and the State', in Marx, K and Engels, F, *Selected Works*, Volume III, Lawrence and Wishart, London.

ERC (Edmund Rice Centre) (2004) *Deported to Danger: A Study of Australia's Treatment of 40 Rejected Asylum Seekers*, Australian Catholic University, Sydney.

ERC (2006) *Deported to Danger II: A Continuing Study of Australia's Treatment of Rejected Asylum Seekers*, Australian Catholic University, Sydney.

Europol (2004a) *Trafficking of Human Beings: A Europol Perspective*, Author, http://www.europol.eu.int/publications/SeriousCrimeOverviews/2004/OverviewTHB2004.pdf, accessed 10 October 2005.

Europol (2004b) *Annual Report 2004*, Author, http://www.europol.eu.int/publications/ar2004/annualreport2004.pdf, accessed 10 October 2005.

Evans, G and Grant, B (1991) *Australia's Foreign Relations in the World of the 1990s*, Melbourne University Press, Carlton.

Evans, R (1999) *Fighting Words: Writing About Race*, University of Queensland Press, St.Lucia.

Evans, R, Moore, C, Saunders, K and Jamison, B (1997) *1901 Our Future's Past: Documenting Australia's Federation*, Pan MacMillan Australia, Sydney.

Evans, Senator C (2008a) 'Sri Lankans granted humanitarian entry', *Media Release*, 11 January, Minister for Immigration and Citizenship.

Evans, Senator C (2008b) 'Cornelia Rau's settlement offer finalised', *Media Release*, 7 March, Minister for Immigration and Citizenship.

Evans, Senator C (2008c) 'Budget 2008–09 – Rudd Government scraps Temporary Protection visas', *Media Release,* 13 May, Minister for Immigration and Citizenship.

Evans, Senator C (2008d) 'New Directions in Detention – Restoring Integrity to Australia's Immigration System', *Speech delivered at Australian National University, Canberra,* 29 July, Minister for Immigration and Citizenship.

Everitt, J (2008) *The Bitter Shore,* MacMillan, Sydney.

Falk, R, Kolko, G and Lifton, R (eds) (1971) *Crimes of War: A legal, political-documentary, and psychological inquiry into the responsibility of leaders, citizens, and soldiers for criminal acts in wars,* Random House, New York.

Fekete, L (2003) *Canary Islands tragedy: did the RAF put border security before human safety?* Institute of Race Relations, London.

Feller, E, Türk, V and Nicholson, F (eds) (2003) *Refugee Protection in International Law: UNHCR's Global Consultations on International Protection,* Cambridge University Press, Cambridge.

Femia, J (1981) *Gramsci's Political Thought,* Clarendon, Oxford.

Ferro, M (2007) '*Communism, Nazism, colonialism, assessing the analogy'*, in M.Haynes and J.Wolfreys (eds) *History and Revolution: Refuting Revisionism,* Verso, London.

Findlay, M (2008) *Governing through Globalised Crime: Futures for international criminal justice,* Willan Publishing, Devon.

Fischer, G (1989) *Enemy Aliens: Internment and the home front experience in Australia 1914–1920,* University of Queensland Press, St.Lucia

Fitzgerald, S (chair) (1988) *Immigration: A Commitment to Australia,* The Report of the Committee to Advise on Australia's Immigration Policies, AGPS, Canberra.

Fitzpatrick, P (2001) 'Bare Sovereignty: *Homo Sacer* and the Insistence of Law', *Theory and Event,* Volume 5, Number 2.

Fitzpatrick, S (2006a) 'UN "concerns" over asylum policy', *The Australian,* 19 April.

Fitzpatrick, S (2006b) 'Papuan refugees were hand-picked', *The Australian,* 25 September.

Fitzpatrick, S and Walters, P (2009) 'Indonesia key to boat solution as aid millions to stop arrivals', *The Australian,* 17 October.

References

Flood, P (2001) *Report of the Inquiry into Immigration Detention Procedures*, DIMA, Canberra, http://spareroomsforrefugees.com/pages/flood.htm, accessed 1 May 2007.

Foster, L and Stockley, D (1988) *Australian Multiculturalism: A Documentary History and Critique*, Multilingual Matters 37, Multilingual Matters, Clevedon.

Fraser, M (1981) *Multiculturalism: Australia's unique achievement*, AGPS, Canberra.

Friedrichs, D (1995) 'State Crime or Governmental Crime: Making Sense of the Conceptual Confusion', in J. Ross (ed) *Controlling State Crime: An Introduction*, Garland Publishing, New York.

Friman, R and Andreas, P (1999) *The Illicit Global Economy and State Power,* Rowman and Littlefield, New York.

Frost, F (1997) 'Labor and Cambodia', in D.Lee and C.Waters (eds) *Evatt to Evans: The Labor Tradition in Australian Foreign Policy,* Allen and Unwin, Sydney.

Galbally, F (chair) (1978) *Migrant Services and Programs: report of the Review of Post-Arrival programs and Services for Migrants*, AGPS, Canberra.

Gellner, E (1998) *Nationalism*, Phoenix, London.

Gellner, E (2001) *Nations and Nationalism*, Blackwell Publishers, Oxford.

Germov, R and Motta, F (2003) *Refugee law in Australia,* Oxford University Press, Melbourne.

GIDPP (Global IDP Project) (2005a) *Internal Displacement: Global Overview of Trends and Developments in 2004*, Author/Norwegian Refugee Council, Geneva.

GIDPP (2005b) *Sri Lanka: political instability hampers IDP return*, Author/Norwegian Refugee Council, Geneva.

GIDPP (2005c) 'Sudan: thousands of IDPs forcibly relocated from Khartoum camp', *IDP News Alert*, 8 September, http://www.idpproject.org/weekly_news/2005/weekly_news_sep05_1.htm., accessed 10 October 2005.

Goodwin-Gill, G (1984) *The Refugee in International Law,* Oxford University Press, Oxford.

Gordon, M (2002) 'No turning back', *The Age*, 24 August.

Gordon, M (2005) *Freeing Ali: The Human Face of the Pacific Solution*, UNSW Press, Sydney.

Gordon, M (2006a) 'Asylum seeker No.43 has a new start', *The Age*, 14 August.

Gordon, M (2006b) 'Loneliest refugee finds a home', *The Age*, December 4.

Gordon, M (2007) 'Freedom for Nauru man', *The Age*, 1 February.

Graham, D (1990) 'Invasion in the north', *Sunday Age*, 3 June.

Graham, J (1984) '"A danger that no language could magnify": the *Newcastle Morning Herald* and the Chinese question', *Journal of the Royal Australian Historical Society*, Volume 69, Part 4.

Gramsci, A (1971) *Selections from the Prison Notebooks*, eds. Q.Hoare and G.Nowell-Smith, Lawrence and Wishart, London.

Gramsci, A (2000) *The Gramsci Reader: Selected Writings 1916–1935*, ed. D.Forgacs, New York University Press, New York.

Grant, B (1979) *The Boat People: An 'Age' Investigation*, Penguin Books, Ringwood.

Grassby, A (1973) *Australia's Decade of Decision*, AGPS, Canberra.

Green, P and Grewcock, M (2002) 'The War Against Illegal Immigration' *Current Issues in Criminal Justice*, Volume 14, No. 1.

Green, P and Ward, T (2000a) 'Legitimacy, Civil Society and State Crime', *Social Justice*, Volume 27, Number 1.

Green, P and Ward, T (2000b) 'State Crime, Human Rights and the Limits of Criminology', *Social Justice*, Volume 27, Number 4.

Green, P and Ward, T (2004) *State Crime: Governments, Violence and Corruption*, Pluto Press, London.

Gregory, P and Middleton, K (1994) 'Boat people fail to stop deport order', *The Age*, 18 November.

Grewcock, M (2003) 'Irregular Migration, Identity and the State – the Challenge for Criminology', *Current Issues in Criminal Justice*, Volume 15, Number 2.

Grewcock, M (2005) 'Slipping through the net? Some thoughts on the Cornelia Rau and Vivian Alvarez Inquiry', *Current Issues in Criminal Justice*, Volume 17, Number 2.

References

Grewcock, M (2007) 'Shooting the passenger: Australia's war on illicit migrants', in M. Lee (ed) *Human Trafficking*, Willan Publishing, Devon.

Grewcock, M (2008) 'State Crime: Some Conceptual Issues', in T. Anthony and C.Cunneen (eds) *The Critical Criminology Companion*, Hawkins Press, Sydney.

Grewcock, M (2009) 'Multiple punishments: the detention and removal of convicted non-citizens', *Paper presented to Australia and New Zealand Critical Criminology Conference,* Monash University, Melbourne, 8–9 July, http://papers.ssrn.com/sol3/papers.cfm?abstract_id=1489733#.

Griffiths, E (2002) 'Government to reduce detainee numbers at Woomera', *Lateline,* ABC Television, 11 April, http://www.abc.net.au/lateline/s529574.htm, accessed, 6 March 2007.

Griffiths, E (2009) 'People smugglers should rot in hell: Rudd', *PM*, ABC Radio National, 17 April, http://www.abc.net.au/pm/content/2008/s2546098.htm, accessed 20 April 2009.

Griffiths, P (2006) *The Making of White Australia: Ruling class agendas, 1876–1888,* PhD Thesis, The Australian National University, Canberra.

Grimm, A (1999) 'Border Protection Legislation Amendment Bill 1999', *Bills Digest*, Number 70 1999–2000, Parliamentary Library, Canberra.

Groves, M (2004) 'Immigration Detention vs Imprisonment: Differences explored', *Alternative Law Journal,* Volume 29, No. 5.

Hall, R (1998) *Black Armband Days: Truth from the dark side of Australia's past*, Vintage, Sydney.

Hall, S (1984) 'The State in Question', in G.McLennan, D.Held and S.Hall (eds) *The Idea of the Modern State,* Open University Press, Milton Keynes.

Haller, J (1975) *Outcasts from Evolution: Scientific attitudes of racial inferiority, 1859–1900*, McGraw Hill, New York.

Hamburger, K (2005) Findings *and Recommendations from the Report of Investigation on behalf of the Department of Immigration and Multicultural and Indigenous Affairs Concerning Allegations of Inappropriate Treatment of Five Detainees during Transfer from Maribyrnong Immigration Detention Centre to Baxter Immigration Detention Facility*, Knowledge Consulting, DIMIA, Canberra.

Hamilton (1993a) 'Three years hard', Part 1, *Eureka Street,* Volume 3, Number 1.

Hamilton (1993b) 'Three years hard', Part 2, *Eureka Street,* Volume 3, Number 2.

Hancock, N (2001) 'Border Protection Bill 2001', *Bills Digest No.41 2001–02,* Parliamentary Library, Canberra.

Hannaford, I (1996) *Race: the History of an Idea in the West*, Woodrow Wilson Press, Washington D.C.

Hanson, P (1997) *The Truth: On Asian Immigration, the Aboriginal Question, the Gun Debate and the Future of Australia*, St.George Publications, Parkholme, SA.

Hanson, P (2007) 'Multiculturalism and Immigration', *Pauline's Political Messages,* http://www.paulinehanson.com.au/messages-06.08.php, accessed 6 September 2007.

Harding, R (1996) *Private Prisons and Public Accountability*, Open University Press, Milton Keynes.

Harding, R (2001) 'Standards and Accountability in the Administration of Prisons and Immigration Detention Centres: A Description of the Role of the Western Australian Inspector of Custodial Services and a Proposal for Bringing Equity and Decency to the Operation of Australia's Immigration Detention Centres', *A Speech to the International Correction and Prisons Association Conference,* 30 October, Perth.

Harrell-Bond, B (1986) *Imposing Aid: Emergency Assistance to Refugees*, Oxford University Press, Oxford.

Harrell-Bond, B (2002) 'Can humanitarian work with refugees be humane?' *Human Rights Quarterly*, Volume 24, pp.51–85.

Hart, C (2006) 'Government to bury Alvarez payout details', *The Australian,* 1 December.

Hart, C (2007) 'Returning asylum seekers 'scandalous'', *The Australian*, 27 September.

References

Hathaway, J (1993) 'Labelling the "Boat People": The Failure of the Human Rights Mandate of the Comprehensive Plan of Action for Indo-Chinese refugees', *Human Rights Quarterly*, Volume 15, 686.

Hayes, B (2003) *Cover Up! Proposed Regulation on European Border Guard hides unaccountable, operational bodies*, Statewatch, London.

Hayes, B (2004) *Killing me softly? "Improving access to durable solutions": doublespeak and the dismantling of refugee protection in the EU*, Statewatch, London.

Hayter, T (2000) *Open Borders: The case against immigration controls*, Pluto Press, London.

Head, M (2005) 'Detention Without Trial: Is there no limit?', *Alternative Law Journal*, Volume 30, Number 2.

Hedman, E-L (2005a) 'A State of Emergency, A Strategy of War: Internal Displacement, Forced Relocation, and Involuntary return in Aceh', in E-L Hedman (ed) *Aceh Under Martial Law: Conflict, Violence and Displacement*, Working Paper Number 24, Refugee Studies Centre, University of Oxford.

Hedman, E-L (2005b) 'The politics of the tsunami response', *Forced Migration Review*, July Special Issue, Refugee Studies Centre, University of Oxford.

Heinrichs, P (1999) 'Holding back the tide', *Sunday Age*, 21 November.

Henderson, R, Harcourt, F and Harper, R (1971) *People in Poverty: A Melbourne Survey*, Cheshire, Institute of Applied Economic and Social Research, University of Melbourne.

Hill, K (1994) 'Firm action sought on boat people', *The Age*, 29 December.

Hill, K (1995) 'Boat people surge feared', *The Age*, 6 January.

Hinch, D (2001) Interview with Peter Reith MP, Radio 3AK, 13 September 2001, http://www.defence.gov.au/minister/2001/1309013.doc, accessed 6 February 2007.

Hirst, P and Thompson, G (1999) *Globalisation in Question: The International Economy and the Possibilities of Governance*, Second Edition, Polity, Cambridge.

Holborn, L (1956) *The International Refugee Organization*, Oxford University Press, London.

Holroyd, J (2007) 'Attack on officer is un-Australian: Andrews', *The Age*, 11 October.

Hooker, J (2005) 'The Baxter detention centre', *NewMatilda.com*, 23 February.

Hovy, B (2002) 'Statistics on Forced Migration', *Migration Information Source*, http://www.migrationinformation.org/Feature/display.cfm?ID=49, accessed 28 October 2005.

Howard PM, J (2001) *Speech to Liberal Party federal election campaign launch*, http://www.australianpolitics.com/news/2001/01-10-28.shtml., accessed 4 November 2004.

HRCOA (Human Rights Council of Australia), Children Out of Detention, Brotherhood of St.Laurence, Rights and Accountability in Development, and International Committee of Jurists (2005) *Submission to the Australian National Contact Point – Global Solutions Limited: Supplementary evidence on operations of GSL*, Brotherhood of St.Laurence, Melbourne.

HREOC (Human Rights and Equal Opportunity Commission) (1997) *Bringing them home: Report of the National Inquiry into the Separation of Aboriginal and Torres Strait Islander Children from Their Families*, Author, Sydney.

HREOC (1998) *Those Who've Come Across the Seas: Detention of Unauthorised Arrivals*, Author, Sydney.

HREOC (2002) *Report of an inquiry into a complaint by Mr. Mohammed Badraie on behalf of his son Shayan regarding acts or practices of the Commonwealth of Australia (the Department of Immigration, Multicultural and Indigenous Affairs)*, Report Number 25, Author, Sydney.

HREOC (2004a) *A last resort? National Inquiry into Children in Immigration Detention*, Author, Sydney.

HREOC (2004b) *Ismaε - Listen: national consultations on eliminating prejudice against Arab and Muslim Australians*, Author, Sydney.

HREOC (2006) *Breach of Ms CD's human rights at the Curtin Immigration Reception and Processing Centre*, Report Number 36, Sydney.

References

HREOC (2007) *Summary of Observations following the Inspection of mainland Immigration Detention Facilities*, Author, Sydney.

Hughes, H. (2004), 'From Riches to Rags What Are Nauru's Options and How Can Australia Help?' *Issues Analysis*, Number 50, Centre for Independent Studies, Sydney.

Hugo, G (2001) 'From compassion to compliance? Trends in refugee and humanitarian migration in Australia', *GeoJournal*, Number 55.

HRW (Human Rights Watch) (1999) *Backgrounder: The Indonesian Army and Civilian Militias in East Timor April 1999*, Author, New York.

HRW (2002) 'Afghanistan Unsafe for Refugee Returns: UN Refugee Agency Sending "Misleading" Message', *Press Release,* 23 July, New York.

HRW (2003a) *An Unjust 'Vision' for Europe's Refugees: Commentary on the UK's 'New Visions' Proposal for the Establishment of Refugee Processing Centres Abroad*, Author, New York.

HRW (2003b) *Human Rights Watch Commentary on Australia's Temporary Protection Visas for Refugees*, Author, New York.

HRW (2005a) *Time to Take Stock: The U.S. Cluster Munition Inventory and the FY 2006 Department of Defense Budget*, HRW Briefing Paper, Author, New York.

HRW (2005b) 'Overview of human rights issues in the European Union', *World Report 2005,* Author, New York.

HRW (2005c) *Getting Away with Torture? Command responsibility for the US Abuse of Detainees*, Author, New York.

Huntington, S (1998) *The Clash of Civilizations and the Remaking of the World Order*, Simon and Schuster, London.

Hutton, M (2006a) *'No Happy Ending: Vale Amal Basry'*, http://sievx.com/archives/2006/20060319.shtml, accessed 17 September 2007.

Hutton, M (2006b) *'On the Fifth Anniversary – Release the Names'*, http://sievx.com/, 19 October, accessed 12 February 2007.

IDMC (Internal Displacement Monitoring Centre) (2009a) *Global IDP estimates (1990–2008)*, http://www.internal-displacement.org, accessed 22 October 2009.

IDMC (2009b) *Internal Displacement: Global Overview of Trends and Developments in 2008,* http://www.internal-displacement.org, accessed 22 October 2009.

IOM (International Organisation for Migration) (2000) *Trafficking in Migrants Quarterly Bulletin,* Number 21.

IOM (2005a) '5+5 Dialogue on Migration in the Western Mediterranean', *Dialogue 5+5 Newsletter,* June, http://www.iom.int/en/know/dialogue5–5/index.shtml, accessed 10 October 2005.

IOM (2005b) 'IOM and Libya Sign Agreement', *IOM Press Briefing Notes,* 9 August, http://www.iom.int/en/news/PBN090805.shtml., accessed 10 October 2005.

IRR (Institute of Race Relations) (2006) *Driven to Desperate Measures,* Author, London.

Jacobsen, K (2000) 'A Framework for Exploring the Political and Security Context of Refugee Populated Areas', *Refugee Survey Quarterly,* Volume 19, Number 1.

Jacobsen, K (2001) *The forgotten solution: local integration for refugees in developing countries,* Working Paper, Number 45, UNHCR, Geneva.

Jakubowicz, A, Morrissey, M and Palser, J (1984) *Ethnicity, Class and Social Policy in Australia,* SWRC Reports and Proceedings Number 46, Social Welfare Research Centre, University of New South Wales.

James, CLR (1980) *The Black Jacobins,* Revised edition, Allison and Busby, London.

Jefferson, T (1939) *Thomas Jefferson on Democracy,* ed. S.Padover, The New American Library, New York.

Jones, T (2002) 'Experts respond to video', *Lateline,* ABC Television, 22 April, http://www.abc.net.au/lateline/s537864.htm, accessed 6 March 2007.

Jørgenson, N (2003) *The Responsibility of States for International Crimes,* Oxford University Press, Oxford.

JSCM (Joint Standing Committee on Migration) (1994) *Asylum, Border Control and Detention,* AGPS, Canberra.

References

JSCM (2008) *Immigration detention in Australia: A new beginning*, Commonwealth of Australia, Canberra.

JSCMR (Joint Standing Committee on Migration Regulations) (1992) *Australia's Refugee and Humanitarian System: Achieving a balance Between Refuge and Control*, AGPS, Canberra.

Jupp, J (1986) *Don't settle for less*, Report of the Committee of Review of Migrant and Multicultural Programs and Services, AGPS, Canberra.

Jupp, J (2003) *From White Australia to Woomera: The story of Australian immigration*, Cambridge University Press, Cambridge.

Jureidini, J (2005) *Submission to Senate Legal and Constitutional References Committee Inquiry into the Administration and Operation of the Migration Act 1958*, Submission 31, http://www.aph.gov.au/Senate/committee/legcon_ctte/migratio n/submissions/sub31.pdf, accessed 17 March 2006.

Jureidini, J (2007) 'It is not courage', in S. Mares and L. Newman (eds) *Acting from the Heart: Australian advocates for asylum seekers tell their stories*, Finch Publishing, Sydney.

Kagan, M (2002) *Assessment of Refugee Status Determination Procedure at UNHCR's Cairo Office, 2001–2002*, Forced Migration and Refugee Studies Working Paper, Number 1, The American University in Cairo, Cairo.

Kalantzis, M (2003) 'Immigration, multiculturalism and racism' in S. Ryan and T. Bramston (eds) *The Hawke Government: A Critical Retrospective*, Pluto Press Australia, Melbourne.

Kaldor, M (2002) *New and Old Wars: Organised Violence in a Global Era*, Polity, Oxford.

Kälin, W (2005) *Protection of Internally Displaced Persons in Situations of Natural Disaster: A Working Visit to Asia by the Representative of the United Nations Secretary General on Human Rights of Internally Displaced Persons*, UNOHCHR, Geneva.

Kauzlarich, D and Kramer, R (1998) *Crimes of the American Nuclear State at Home and Abroad*, Northeastern University Press, Boston.

Kearney, S and Fitzpatrick, S (2009) '"Life of brutality' in crowded Indonesian lock-up', *The Australian*, 24 October.

Kelly, L (2002) *Journeys of Jeopardy: A Review of Research on Trafficking in Women and Children in Europe*, IOM Migration Research Series, Number 11, IOM, Geneva.

Kelly, P (1992) *The End of Certainty: The story of the 1980s*, Allen and Unwin, Sydney.

Kelly, P (2002a) 'The Race Issue in Australia's 2001 Election: A Creation of Politicians or the Press?', *Working Paper #2002-8,* The Joan Shorenstein Center on the Press, Politics and Public Policy, Harvard University, Massachusetts.

Kenny, M, Silove, D and Steel, Z (2004) 'Legal and ethical implications of medically enforced feeding of detained asylum seekers on hunger strike', *Medical Journal of Australia*, Volume 180, pp. 237–40.

Kerr, J (2005) 'Free at last, but a prisoner still of his tortured mind', *Sydney Morning Herald,* 21 June.

Kevin, T (2004) *A Certain Maritime Incident: the sinking of the SIEV X*, Scribe Publications, Melbourne.

Kibreab, G (1990) 'Host Governments and Refugee Perspectives on Settlement and Repatriation in Africa', *Paper for the Conference on 'Development Strategies on Forced Migration in the Third World'*, Institute of Social Studies, the Hague, Refugees Studies Programme Documentation Centre, University of Oxford.

Kingston, M (1993) 'Politics and Public Opinion', in M.Crock (ed) *Protection or Punishment? The detention of asylum seekers in Australia,* The Federation Press, Melbourne.

Kirk, A (2006) 'UN asks Australia to change asylum policy', *AM,* ABC Radio National, 4 May, http://www.abc.net.au/am/content/2006/s1630432.htm, accessed 16 June 2006.

Kirk, A (2009) 'Open doors to asylum seekers: union boss', *ABC News,* 19 October, http://www.abc.net.au/news/stories/2009/10/19/2718331.htm, accessed 21 October 2009.

Kleemans, E (2003) 'The Social Organisation of Human Trafficking', in D.Siegel, H. van de Bunt and D. Zaitch (eds)

References

Global Organised Crime: Trends and Developments, Kluwer Academic Publishers, Dordrecht.

Koser, K (2001) 'The Smuggling of Asylum Seekers into Western Europe: Contradictions, Conundrums and Dilemmas', in D. Kyle and R. Koslowski (eds) *Global Human Smuggling: Comparative Perspectives,* The John Hopkins University Press, London.

Koslowski, R (2001) 'Economic Globalization, Human Smuggling and Global Governance', in D. Kyle and R. Koslowski, R (eds) *Global Human Smuggling: Comparative Perspectives,* The John Hopkins University Press, London.

Kunz, E. (1988) *Displaced Persons: Calwell's new Australians,* Pergamon Press, Sydney.

Kushner, T and Knox, K (2001) *Refugees in an Age of Genocide,* Frank Cass, London.

Kyle, D and Koslowski, R (eds) (2001) *Global Human Smuggling: Comparative Perspectives,* The John Hopkins University Press, London.

Lack, J and Templeton, J (1995) *Bold Experiment: A Documentary History of Australian Immigration since 1945,* Oxford University Press, Melbourne.

Laczko, F and Collett, E (2005) *Assessing the Tsunami's Effects on Migration,* Migration Information Source, Migration Policy Institute, Washington, www.migrationinformation.org/Feature/print.cfm?ID=299, accessed 17 June 2005.

Laczko, F and Gozdziak, E (eds) (2005) *Data and research on human trafficking: A global survey,* International Organization for Migration, Geneva.

Langfield, M (1999) *More People Imperative: Immigration to Australia, 1901–39,* National Archives of Australia, Canberra.

Lavelle, K and Feagin, J (2006) 'Hurricane Katrina: The Race and Class Debate', *Monthly Review,* Volume 58, Number 3.

Lawrence, C (2003) 'Port Hedland Detention Centre: Carmen's eye witness report', *Sydney Morning Herald,* 2 September.

LCHR (Lawyers Committee for Human Rights - now Human Rights First) (1989) *Inhumane Deterrence: the Treatment of Vietnamese Boat People in Hong Kong,* Author: New York.

Leach, M and Mansouri, F (2004) *Lives in Limbo: Voices of refugees under temporary protection,* UNSW Press, Sydney.

Lee, M (2005) 'Human trade and the criminalization of irregular migration', *International Journal of the Sociology of Law,* Number 33.

Lee, M (ed) (2007) *Human Trafficking,* Willan Publishing, Devon.

Lever-Tracy, C and Quinlan, M (1988) *A Divided Working Class,* Routledge and Keegan Paul, London.

Lischer, S (2005) *Dangerous Sanctuaries: Refugee Camps, Civil War and Dilemmas of Humanitarian Aid,* Cornell University Press, New York.

Lockwood, D (1968) *The Front Door: Darwin 1869–1969,* Rigby Limited, Adelaide.

Loescher, G (2001) *The UNHCR and World Politics,* Oxford University Press, Oxford Scholarship Online, www.oxfordscholarship.com/oso/public/content/politicalscience/0199246912/toc.html, accessed 3 March 2005.

Losurdo, D (2004) 'Towards a Critique of the Category of Totalitarianism', *Historical Materialism,* Volume 12, Number 2.

Loughna, S (2005) 'What is Forced Migration?', *Forced Migration Online,* http://www.forcedmigration.org/whatisfm.htm., accessed 1 February 2006.

Love, D (2001) *Straw polls, paper money,* Viking, Ringwood.

Lowth, A (1999) 'New centre planned for illegal immigrants', *PM,* ABC Radio, 9 November, http://www.abc.net.au/pm/stories/s63745.htm, accessed 4 December 2006.

Lygo, I. (2004) *News Overboard: The Tabloid Media, Race Politics and Islam,* Southerly Change Media, Geelong.

MacDonald, J (1999) 'Refugee crisis warning', *The Age,* 18 November.

MacIntyre, S and Clark A (2003) *The History Wars,* Melbourne University Press, Carlton.

Maiden, S (2009) 'Sri Lankans face "Indonesia Solution" in centres funded by Australia', *The Australian,* 23 October.

References

Maley, P (2008) 'John Howard's detention centre to open', *The Australian,* 19 December.

Maley, W (2001) 'Security, People-Smuggling, and Australia's New Afghan Refugees', *Australian Journal of International Affairs,* Volume 55, Number 3.

Maley, W (2005) 'Detention: Australian Government's policy has been built on a myth', *Australian Policy Online,* 15 June, http://www.apo.org.au/webboard/results.chtml?filename_num=12125, accessed 6 March 2007.

Maley, W (2006) *Rescuing Afghanistan,* UNSW Press, Sydney.

Manderson, D (1993) *From Mr.Sin to Mr.Big,* Oxford University Press, Melbourne.

Manning, P (2004) *Dog Whistle Politics and Journalism: reporting Arabic and Muslim people in Sydney newspapers,* Australian Centre for Independent Journalism, University of Technology, Sydney.

Mansouri, F and Leach, M (2003) 'Temporary Protection of Refugees: Australian Policy and International Comparisons', *Critical Perspectives on Refugee Policy in Australia: The Challenges of Globalisation Symposium on Refugee Rights,* Institute for Citizenship and Globalisation, Deakin University, Melbourne.

Maogoto, J (2004) *War Crimes and Realpolitik: International justice from World War 1 to the 21st century,* Lynne Rienner Publishers, Colorado.

Mares, P (2001) *Borderline: Australia's treatment of refugees and asylum seekers,* UNSW Press, Sydney.

Marfleet, P (2006) *Refugees in a Global Era,* Palgrave MacMillan, Basingstoke.

Markus, A (1979) *Fear and hatred: Purifying Australia and California 1850–1901,* Hale and Ironmonger, Sydney.

Markus, A. (2001) *Race: John Howard and the remaking of Australia,* Allen and Unwin, Sydney.

Marr, D and Wilkinson, M (2003) *Dark Victory,* Allen and Unwin, Sydney.

Marston, G (2003) *Temporary Protection Permanent Uncertainty: The experiences of refugees living on temporary protection visas,* Centre for Applied Research, Royal Melbourne Institute of Technology University.

Marx, K (1963) *Karl Marx: Early Writings*, ed.and trans T.B.Bottomore, C.A.Watts, London.

Mathew, P (1994) 'Sovereignty and the Right to Seek Asylum: The case of the Cambodian Asylum-Seekers in Australia', *Australian Yearbook of International Law,* Volume 15, Number 37.

McAllister, I (1993) 'Immigration, bi-partisanship and public opinion', in J.Jupp and M. Kabala (eds) *The Politics of Australian Immigration,* Australian Government Publishing Service, Canberra.

McBride, M (1999) *The evolution of US immigration and refugee policy: public opinion, domestic politics and UNHCR, New Issues in Refugee Research,* Working Paper, Number 3, UNHCR, Geneva.

MCIMA (Ministerial Council on Immigration and Multicultural Affairs) (2006) *A National Action Plan to Build on Social Cohesion, harmony and Security,* Author, Canberra.

McKay, D and C (2002) *The Worst of Woomera,* Authors, Sydney.

McKiernan, J (1993) 'The Political Imperative: Defend, Deter, Detain', in M.Crock (ed) *Protection or Punishment? The detention of asylum seekers in Australia,* The Federation Press, Melbourne.

McLennan, G (1984) 'Capitalist state or democratic polity? Recent developments in Marxist and pluralist theory', in G.McLennan, D.Held and S. Hall (eds) *The Idea of the Modern State,* Open University Press, Milton Keynes.

McMaster, D (2002) *Asylum Seekers: Australia's Response to Refugees,* Melbourne University Press, Melbourne.

McMaster, D (2006) 'Temporary Protection Visas: Obstructing Refugee Livelihoods', *Refugee Quarterly Survey,* Volume 25, Number 2.

MCRG (Muslim Community Reference Group) (2006) *Building on Social Cohesion, Harmony and Security: An action plan by the Muslim Community Reference Group,* Author, Sydney.

Melvern, L (2000) *A People Betrayed: The Role of the West in Rwanda's Genocide,* Zed Books, London.

Merton, R (1938) 'Social Structure and Anomie', *American Sociological Review,* Volume 3, Number 5.

Merton, R (1968) *Social Theory and Social Structure,* Free Press, New York.

References

MHA (Minister for Home Affairs) (2009) 'Improved Support for Trafficking Victims', *Media Release*, 22 October.

Middleton, K (1994) 'China "no" to boat people – Bolkus demands end to "racket"', *The Age*, 29 December.

MIC (Minister for Immigration and Citizenship) (MIC) (2007a) 'Status of Sri Lankan Asylum Seekers', *Media Release*, 12 September.

MIC (2007b) 'Refugee and Humanitarian Intake 2007–2008', *Media Release*, 4 October.

MIC (2007c) 'Interview with Neil Mitchell, Radio 3AW', *Media Release and Transcript*, 2 October.

MILGEA (Minister for Immigration, Local Government and Ethnic Affairs) (1989a) *News Release*, 8 December.

MILGEA (1989b) *News Release*, 18 December.

MILGEA (1990a) *Media Release*, 27 June.

MILGEA (1990b) *Media Release*, 10 July.

Miliband, R (1976) *The State in Capitalist Society*, Quartet Books, London.

Millar, C (2004) *'Combating Trafficking in Persons through the Bali Process', Speech to International Symposium on People Trafficking, Human Society and Development*, Australian National University, 1 September, personal copy of transcript.

MIMA (Minister for Immigration and Multicultural Affairs) (1999a) *Media Release*, MPS 143/99, 13 October.

MIMA (1999b) *Media Release*, MPS 164/99, 18 November.

MIMA (2001) *Media Release*, MPS 131/2001, 6 September.

MIMA (2005) *Media Release*, VPS, 059/2005, 17 May.

MIMA (2006) *Media Release*, MPS 48/2006, 13 April.

Molenaar, B and Neufeld, R (2003) 'The Use of Privatized Detention Centers for Asylum Seekers in Australia and the UK', in A.Coyle, A.Campbell and R.Neufeld (eds) *Capitalist Punishment: Prison Privatization and Human Rights*, Zed Books and Human Rights Internet, London.

Moore, C (1985) *Kanaka: A History of Melanesian Mackay*, Institute of Papua New Guinea Studies and University of Papua New Guinea Press, Port Moresby.

Morrison, J and Crosland, B (2001) *The Trafficking and Smuggling of Refugees: the End Game in European Policy?*, New Issues in Refugee Reform, Working Paper, Number 39, UNHCR, Geneva.

Morton, T (2004) 'The Detention Industry', *Background Briefing*, ABC Radio, 20 June, http://www.abc.net.au/rn/talks/bbing/stories/s1137813.htm, accessed 25 June 2007.

Moyle, P (2000) *Profiting from Punishment, Private Prisons in Australia: Reform or Regression*, Pluto Press, Sydney.

MRI (Migrant Rights International) (2003) 'Background on US Border Militarization: failed Immigration Enforcement Strategy Is Causing More Migrant Deaths', *MRI Press Statement*, July, http://migrantwatch.org/mri/background_doc_to_press_statement.htm, accessed 16 April 2005.

Murdoch, L (1990) 'Cambodians paying up to $5,000 for escape to Australia', *The Age*, 24 April.

Murdoch, L (2009) 'Hunger strike ends: "too many died"', *Sydney Morning Herald*, 18 October.

Myers, N (2005) '*Environmental Refugees: An Emergent Security Issue*', Paper presented at 13th Economic Forum, Prague, 23–27 May 2005, EF.NGO/4/05, http://www.osce.org/documents/eea/2005/05/14488_en.pdf, accessed 24 August 2005.

NAA (National Archives of Australia) (A1, 1908/1320) '*Report of Inspector Lewis*, 30 December 1907.

NAA (A1, 1908/13342) '*Memoranda on rewards from the Secretary of the Department of External Affairs*' October 1908.

NAA (A1, 1912/19251) '*Customs and Excise Memoranda on the fumigation of boats arriving from China*', November 1912.

NAA (2004) *A Doubtful Character: Wolf Klaphake*, http://uncommonlives.naa.gov.au/contents.asp?sID=3, accessed 22 November 2004.

References

Nagata, Y (1996) *Unwanted Aliens: Japanese Internment in Australia*, University of Queensland Press, St.Lucia.

Neumann, K (2004) *Refuge Australia: Australia's Humanitarian Record*, UNSW Press, Sydney.

Nevins, J (2002) *Operation Gatekeeper: The Rise of the "Illegal Alien" and the Making of the U.S. - Mexico Boundary*, Routledge, London.

Newland, K (1995) 'Impact of U.S. Refugee Policies on U.S. Foreign Policy: A Case of the Tail Wagging the Dog?' in M.Teitelbaum and M.Weiner (eds) *Threatened Peoples, Threatened Borders: World Migration and US Policy*, The American Assembly, New York.

Newman, E (2003) 'Refugees, international security, and human vulnerability: Introduction and Survey', in E. Newman and J. van Selm (eds) (2003) *Refugees and Forced Displacement: International Security, Human Vulnerability and the State*, United Nations University Press, New York.

Newman, E and van Selm, J (eds) (2003) *Refugees and Forced Displacement: International Security, Human Vulnerability and the State*, United Nations University Press, New York.

Nicholls, G (2007) *Deported: A History of Forced Departures from Australia*, UNSW Press, Sydney.

NPC (National Population Council) (1991) *The National Population Council's Refugee Review*, Australian Government Publishing Service, Canberra.

NSWLA (New South Wales Legislative Assembly) (1888) 'Minutes of Proceedings of the Conference on Chinese Question', *Votes and Proceedings, 1887–1888*, Volume 2.

O'Brien, N and Walker, J (1994) 'Boat people fail to halt air charter deportations', *The Australian*, 18 November.

O'Connor, C (2005 unpublished) *Submission by Cornelia Rau Regarding her Unlawful Detention in Immigration Detention*, Legal Services Commission, South Australia. Personal copy obtained from Counsel.

OMA (Office of Multicultural Affairs) (1989) *An Agenda for Multicultural Australia*, Author, Canberra.

O'Neill, M (2002) 'Video reveals the extent of Curtin protests', *Lateline,* ABC Television, 22 April, http://www.abc.net.au/lateline/stories/s537853.htm, accessed 12 October 2004.

O'Neill, M (2005) 'Immigration official gives insight into department', *Lateline,* ABC Television, 13 June, http://www.abc.net.au/lateline/content/2005/s1391140.htm, accessed 15 June 2005.

O'Neill, M (2008) *Blind Conscience,* UNSW Press, Sydney.

ON (One Nation) (1996) *'Pauline Hanson's Maiden Speech',* House of Representatives, 10 September, http://nswonenation.com.au/parliamentaryspeeches/paulinhansonsspeech.htm, accessed 28 August 2007.

ON (1998) *Immigration, Population and Social Cohesion Policy,* http://www.australianpolitics.com/cgi-bin/MasterPFP.cgi?doc=self, accessed, 11 December, 2006.

Ortiz, O (2006) 'The Battle for New Orleans' in J. Childs (ed) *Hurricane Katrina: Response and Responsibilities,* New Pacific Press, Santa Cruz.

Oxfam (2005) *Foreign Territory: The Internationalisation of EU Asylum Policy*, Author, Oxford.

Paine, T (1961) *The Rights of Man,* Doubleday, New York.

Palfreeman, A (1967) *The Administration of the White Australia policy*, Melbourne University Press, Melbourne.

Palmer, M (2005) *Report of the Inquiry into the Circumstances of the Immigration Detention of Cornelia Rau,* DIMIA, Canberra.

Parish, G (2000) 'Allegations spread to WA refugee detention centre', *7.30 Report*, ABC Television , 8 December, http://www.abc.net.au/7.30/stories/s221765.htm, accessed 23 August 2005.

Parkin, A and Hardcastle, L (1990) 'Immigration Policy', in C.Jennett and R. Stewart (eds) *Hawke and Australian Public Policy: Consensus and Restructuring,* MacMillan, Melbourne.

Passas, N (1990) 'Anomie and Corporate Deviance', *Contemporary Crises,* Volume 14, Number 3.

References

Peake, R (1989) '15,000 Chinese may be allowed to stay', *The Age*, 8 June.

Peake, R (2007) 'Asylum-seekers lost at sea but not forgotten', *Canberra Times*, 30 August.

Penovic, T (2004) 'The Separation of Powers': *Lim* and the "voluntary" immigration detention of children', *Alternative Law Journal*, Volume 29, Number 5.

Percy, K (2009) 'Thailand accused of mistreating Burmese asylum seekers', *PM*, ABC Radio National, 28 January, http://www.abc.net.au/pm/content/2008/s2476668.htm, accessed 29 January 2009.

Phillips, J (2004) 'People Trafficking: Australia's Response', *Research Note*, Number 20, 2004–2005, Parliamentary Library, Canberra.

Phillips, J (2007) 'Muslim Australians', *Parliamentary Library E-Brief*, 6 March, Parliamentary Library, Canberra.

Phillips, J and Lorimer, C (2005) 'Children in Detention', *Parliamentary Library E-Brief*, 13 October, updated 23 November, Parliamentary Library, Canberra.

Pickering, S (2001) 'Common Sense and Original Deviancy: News Discourses and Asylum Seekers in Australia', *International Journal of Refugee Studies*, Volume 14, Number 2.

Pickering, S (2005) *Refugees and State Crime,* The Federation Press, Sydney.

Pickering, S, Gard, M and Richardson, R (2003) *"We're working with people here": The impact of the TPV regime on refugee settlement service provision in NSW*, Charles Sturt University and Monash University.

Pickering, S and Weber, L (eds) (2006) *Borders, Mobility and Technologies of Control*, Springer, The Netherlands.

PICUM (Platform for International Cooperation on Undocumented Migrants) (2005a) 'Death at the Border' *PICUM Newsletter,* October, http://www.picum.org/, accessed 2 December 2005.

PICUM (2005b) 'Death at the Border' *PICUM Newsletter,* November, http://www.picum.org/, accessed 2 December 2005.

Piper, N (2005) 'A Problem by a Different Name? A Review of Research on Trafficking in South-East Asia and Oceania', in

F.Laczko and E. Gozdziak (eds) *Data and research on human trafficking: A global survey*, IOM, Geneva.

PL (Parliamentary Library) (2001) 'Migration Legislation Amendment (Immigration Detainees) Bill 2001, *Bills Digest No.131 2000–2001*, Author, Canberra.

PL (2002) 'Migration Legislation Amendment (Immigration Detainees) Bill (No.2) 2001, *Bills Digest No. 14 2001–2002*, Author, Canberra.

PMA (Prime Minister of Australia) (1999) '$124 million boost for the fight against illegal immigration', *Media Release*, 27 June.

PMA (2001a) 'MV Tampa – Unauthorised Arrivals', *Media Release*, 1 September.

PMA (2001b) *Prime Minister's Press Conference*, Parliament House, Canberra, 4 October 2001, http://www.pm.gov.au/news/interviews/2001/interview1269.htm, accessed 6 February 2007.

PMA (2001c) 'Agreement with Papua New Guinea to Process Unauthorised Arrivals', *Media Release*, 10 October.

Poynting, S and Noble, G (2004) *Living with Racism: The experience and reporting by Arab and Muslim Australians of discrimination, abuse and violence since 11 September 2001*, Report to the Human Rights and Equal Opportunity Commission, Centre for Cultural Research, University of Western Sydney, Sydney.

Poynting, S, Noble, G, Tabar, P and Collins, J (2004) *Bin Laden in the Suburbs: Criminalising the Arab Other*, Sydney Institute of Criminology and Federation Press, Sydney.

Poynting, S (2007) 'Thugs' and 'grubs' at Cronulla: From media beat-ups to beating up migrants', in S. Poynting S. Morgan, G (eds) *Outrageous*, ACYS Publishing, University of Tasmania, Hobart.

Poynting, S and Morgan, G (eds) (2007) *Outrageous*, ACYS Publishing, University of Tasmania, Hobart.

PPOEW (Prisons and Probation Ombudsman for England and Wales) (2004) *Investigation into Allegations of Racism, Abuse and Violence at Yarl's Wood Removal Centre*, Border and Immigration Agency, Home Office, London.

References

PPRI (Prison Privatisation Report International) (2001) 'Australia: ACM contract under scrutiny', *Prison Privatisation Report*, Number 39, Prison Reform Trust, London.

Prem Kumar, R and Grundy Warr, C (2004) 'The Irregular Migrant as Homo Sacer: Migration and Detention in Australia, Malaysia and Thailand', *International Migration*, Volume 42, Number 1.

Price, C (1981) 'Immigration Policies and Refugees in Australia', *International Migration Review*, Volume 15, Number 1.

PSC (Project SafeCom) (2007) 'Nauru Sri Lankans show first signs of mental health deterioration', *Media Release*, 5 July.

PSC (2009) 'Vale, Akram Al Masri', 2 August, http://www.safecom.org.au/vale-al-masri.htm, accessed, 2 October 2009.

Putt, J (2007) *Human trafficking to Australia: a research challenge*, Australian Institute of Criminology, Canberra.

Ramly, A (2005) 'Modes of displacement during martial law', in E-L Hedman (ed) *Aceh Under Martial Law: Conflict, Violence and Displacement*, Working Paper Number 24, Refugee Studies Centre, University of Oxford.

RANZCP (Royal Australian and New Zealand College of Psychiatrists) (2005) *Submission to Senate Legal and Constitutional References Committee Inquiry into the Administration and Operation of the Migration Act, 1958*, Author, http://www.ranzcp.org/pdffiles/submissions/Migration%20Act.pdf, accessed 17 March 2006.

RCOA (Refugee Council of Australia) (1999) *Statement on "Illegal" Boat Arrivals*, 15 November, Author, Sydney.

RCOA (2003) *Position Paper on the Use of Temporary protection Visas for Refugees*, Author, Sydney.

Reuters (2005) 'US says migrant deaths at record on Mexico border', *Reuters AlertNet*, 3 October, http://www.alertnet.org/thenews/newsdesk/N03594921.htm, accessed 4 October 2005.

Reynolds, H (2005) *Nowhere People: How international race thinking shaped Australia's identity*, Viking, Penguin Books, Camberwell.

Reynolds, P (2000) 'One Nation's Electoral Support in Queensland', in M.Leach, G.Stokes and I. Ward (eds) *The Rise and Fall of One Nation,* University of Queensland Press, St.Lucia.

Rheeney, A (2006) 'PNG: Somare Says No To Australia over Asylum Seekers', *Pacific Magazine,* 19 June.

Ricklefs, M (1997) 'The Asian immigration controversies of 1984–85, 1988–89 and 1996–97: A historical review', in G.Gray and C.Winter (eds) *The Resurgence of Racism: Howard, Hanson and the Race Debate,* Monash Publications in History, Clayton.

Robertson, G (2006) *Crimes Against Humanity: The struggle for global justice,* Third edition, Penguin, Camberwell.

Robinson, N (2005) 'Employment of detainees "slave labour"', *The Australian,* 6 December.

Robinson, W Courtland (1998) *Terms of Refuge: The Indo-Chinese Exodus and the International Response,* Zed Books, London.

Robinson, W Courtland (2004) 'The Comprehensive Plan of Action for Indo-Chinese Refugees, 1989–1997: Sharing the Burden and Passing the Buck', *Journal of Refugee Studies,* Volume 17, Number 3.

Rolls, E (1992) *Sojourners: The epic story of China's centuries-old relationship with Australia,* University of Queensland Press, St.Lucia.

Ross, J (ed) (1995) *Controlling State Crime: An Introduction,* Garland Publishing, New York and London.

Ross, J (ed) (2000) *Varieties of State Crime and its Control,* Criminal Justice Press, New York.

Ross, J, Barak, G, Ferell, J, Kauzlarich, D, Hamm, M, Friedrichs, D, Matthews, R, Pickering, S, Presdee, M, Kraska, P and Kappeler, V (1999) 'The State of State Crime Research', *Humanity and Society,* Volume 23, Part 3.

Rothe, D and Friedrichs, D (2006) 'The State of the Criminology of Crimes of the State', *Social Justice,* Volume 33, Number 1.

Roxtröm, E and Gibney, M (2003) 'The Legal and Ethical Obligations of UNHCR: The case of temporary protection in Western Europe', in N.Steiner, M. Gibney and G. Loescher, G (eds) *Problems of Protection: The UNHCR, Refugees and Human Rights,* Routledge, London.

References

Ruggiero, V (1997) 'Trafficking in Human Beings: Slaves in Contemporary Europe', *International Journal of Sociology of Law'*, Number 25.

Rumley, D, Forbes, V and Griffen, C (eds) (2006) *Australia's Arc of Instability: The Political and Cultural Dynamics of Regional Security*, Springer, Dordrecht.

Rummel, R J (1994) *Death by Government*, Transaction Publishers, New Brunswick, New Jersey.

Salna, K (2009) 'Security at detention centres over the top: inquiry', *The Australian,* 18 August.

Salomon, K (1991) *Refugees in the Cold War: Toward a New International Refugee Regime in the Early Postwar Era,* Lund University Press, Lund.

Salt J and Hogarth J (2000) *Migrant Trafficking and Human Smuggling in Europe: A Review of Evidence*, IOM/UN, Geneva.

Sara, S (1999a) 'Government struggles to stop flow of illegals', *PM*, ABC Radio National, 15 November, http://www.abc.net.au/pm/stories/s66365.htm, accessed 4 December 2006.

Sara, S (1999b) 'Opposition toes the Government line on immigration', *AM,* ABC Radio National, 22 November, http://www.abc.net.au/am/stories/s67640.htm, accessed 30 November 2006.

Saunders, K (2000) 'A Difficult Reconciliation: Civil Liberties and Internment Policy in Australia during World War Two', in K. Saunders and R. Daniels (eds) (2000) *Alien Justice: Wartime Internment in Australia and North America*, University of Queensland Press, St.Lucia.

Savona, E (1997) *Organised Criminality in Europe: A Descriptive Analysis,* Transcrime Working Papers, Number 16, University of Trento.

Savona, E (1998) *Recent Trends of Organised Crime in Europe: Actors, Activities and the Policies Against Them*, Transcrime Working Papers, Number 19, University of Trento.

Schwartz, P and Randall, D (2003) *An Abrupt Climate Change Scenario and its Implications for United States National Security*, Global Business Network/US Department of Defense, www.environmentaldefense.org/

documents/3566_AbruptClimateChange.pdf, accessed 24 August 2005.

Schwendinger, H and Schwendinger, J (1975) 'Defenders of order or guardians of human rights?' in I.Taylor, P.Walton and J.Young (eds) *Critical Criminology,* Routledge and Kegan Paul, London.

Schwendinger, H, Schwendinger, J and Lynch, M (2002) 'Critical Criminology in the United States: the Berkeley School and theoretical trajectories' in K.Carrington and R. Hogg (eds) (2002) *Critical Criminology: Issues, debates, challenges*, Willan Publishing, Devon.

Segrave, M, Milivojevic, S and Pickering, S (2009) *Sex Trafficking: International context and response,* Willan Publishing, Devon.

Sellin, T (1938) *Culture, Conflict and Crime*, Social Science Research Council, New York.

Serco (2009) 'Serco signs AU$370m contract with Australian Government to transform immigration centres, *Press Release,* 29 June.

Sexton, M (2003) 'Asylum seeker suicides while on temporary protection visa', *7.30 Report,* 27 May, ABC Television, http://www.abc.net.au/7.30/content/2003/s8655888.htm., accessed 10 October 2004.

Shanahan, D and Fitzpatrick, S (2006) 'Papuan refugees face closer scrutiny', *The Australian,* 4 October.

Sharkansky, I (1995) 'A State Action May Be Nasty But Is Not Likely To Be A Crime', in J. Ross (ed) *Controlling State Crime: An Introduction*, Garland Publishing, New York.

Silove, D and Steel, Z (1998) *The Mental Health and Well-Being of Onshore Asylum Seekers in Australia,* Psychiatric Research and Teaching Unit, University of New South Wales, Sydney.

Silove, D, Steel, Z and Watters, C (2000) 'Policies of deterrence and the mental health of asylum seekers in Western countries', *JAMA,* Number 284.

SIPRI (Stockholm International Peace Research Institute)(2005) *Recent Trends in Military Expenditure,* http://www.sipri.org/contents/milap/milex/mex_trends.html., accessed 1 March 2006.

References

Skehan, C (2007) 'Canberra silent on Nauru aid', *Sydney Morning Herald,* 18 July.

SLCAC (Senate Legal and Constitutional Affairs Committee) (2000) *A Sanctuary Under Review: An Examination of Australia's Refugee and Humanitarian Determination Processes*, Senate Printing Unit, Canberra.

SLCRC (Senate Legal and Constitutional References Committee) (2006) *Administration and Operation of the Migration Act 1958,* Senate Printing Unit, Canberra.

Sluga, G (1988) *Bonegilla: 'A Place of No Hope'*, Melbourne University History Monograph Series, The History Department, The University of Melbourne.

SMH (*Sydney Morning Herald*) (1888a) 'Editorial', 4 May.

SMH (1888b) 'The Chinese Question', 5 May.

SMH (1888c) 'The Chinese Question, 14 May.

SMH (1888d) 'The Chinese Question', 16 May.

SMH (1888e) 'Among the Chinese on the Tsinan', 19 May.

SMH (1888f) 'Editorial', 26 June.

Smith, M (2004) 'Warehousing Refugees: A Denial of Rights, a Waste of Humanity', *World Refugee Survey 2004*, USCRI, Washington D.C.

SSCCMI (Senate Select Committee on a Certain Maritime Incident) (2002) *Report of Senate Select Committee on a Certain Maritime Incident*, Senate Printing Unit, Canberra.

SSCFAD (Senate Standing Committee on Foreign Affairs and Defence) (1976) *Australia and the Refugee Problem: the plight and circumstances of Vietnamese and other refugees*, AGPS, Canberra.

SSCFAD (1982) *Indo-Chinese Refugee Resettlement – Australia's Involvement,* AGPS, Canberra.

Stani, N (2000) 'How the Media Treats National Diversity', *Media Report,* ABC Radio National, 27 January, http://www.abc.net.au/rn/mediareport/stories/2000/97348.htm, accessed 27 November 2006.

Statewatch (2003) 'UK asylum plan for "safe havens": full text of proposal and reactions', *Statewatch News Online,* April, http://.statewatch.org/news/2003/apr/10safe.htm, accessed 12 February 2004.

Statewatch (2005a) 'G5 Meeting in Evian, 4–5 July, Operational Conclusions', *Statewatch News Online*, July, http://.statewatch.org/news/2005/jul/03eu-g5–meeting.htm, accessed 21 July 2005.

Statewatch (2005b) 'Spain/Morocco: Migrants shot dead at border fence, Spain deploys army', *Statewatch News Online*, October, http://www.statewatch.org/news/2005/oct/01spain-morocco.htm., accessed 4 November 2005.

Steel, Z (2002) *Summary evidence regarding the psychological damage caused by long term detention*, MAPW Australia, http://www.mapw.org.au/refugees/02–07–03steel-psych.html., accessed 12 July 2007.

Steel, Z, Momartin, S, Bateman, C, Hafshegani, A, Silove, D, Everson, N, Roy, K, Dudley, M, Newman, L, Blick, B and Mares, S (2004) 'Psychiatrc status of asylum seekers families held for a protracted period in a remote detention centre in Australia', *Australia and New Zealand Journal of Public Health*, Volume 28.

Steel, Z, Silove, D, Brooks, R, Momartin, S, Alzuhairi, B and Susljik, I (2006) 'Impact of immigration detention and temporary protection on the mental health of refugees', *British Journal of Psychiatry*, Volume 188.

Stern, N (2006) *Review on the Economics of Climate Change*, pre-publication edition, HM Treasury, London.

Stevens, C (2002) *Tin Mosques and Ghantowns: A History of Afghan Camel Drivers in Australia*, Paul Fitzsimons, Alice Springs.

Suhrke, A (2003) 'Human security and the protection of refugees', in E.Newman and J. van Selm (eds) *Refugees and Forced Displacement: International Security, Human Vulnerability and the State*, United Nations University Press, New York.

Sultan, A and O'Sullivan, K (2001) 'Psychological disturbances in asylum seekers held in long term detention: a participant-observer account', *Medical Journal of Australia*, Volume 175, Number 4.

Sutherland, E (1949) *White Collar Crime*, Holt, Rhinehart and Winston, New York.

References

Sykes, G and Matza, D (1970) 'Techniques of Delinquency', in M.Wolfgang, L. Savitz and N. Johnston, N (eds) *The Sociology of Crime and Delinquency,* John Wiley and Sons, New York.

Taft-Morales, E (2005) *Haiti: Developments and US Policy Since 1991 and Current Congressional Concerns,* Report for Congress, Congressional Research Service, The Library of Congress, Washington D.C.

Tappan, P (1947) *Juvenile Delinquency,* McGraw-Hill Book Co., New York.

Tavan, G (2005) *The Long, Slow Death of White Australia,* Scribe Publications, Melbourne.

Taylor, P (2007) 'Christmas Island centre in limbo', *The Weekend Australian*, 6 March.

Taylor, S (2000) 'Protection or Prevention? A Close Look at the Temporary Safe Haven Visa Class', *UNSW Law Journal*, Volume 23, Number 3.

Thompson, G (2009) 'Asylum seekers declare hunger strike', *ABC News,* 15 October, http://www.abc.net.au/news/stories/2009/10/15/2715558.htm, accessed 16 October 2009.

TCJ (*Town and Country Journal*) (1888) 'The Absorbing Chinese Question – Incidents on the Steamships Tsinan and Afghan, while lying at the wharves in Sydney with Chinese immigrants on board', 9 June.

The Liberal Party (1988) *Future Directions*, Author, Canberra.

The Liberal and National Country Parties (1975) *Immigration and Ethnic Affairs Policy*, Liberal Party Federal Secretariat, Canberra.

Thompson, R (1980) *Australian Imperialism in the Pacific: The expansionist era 1820-1920*, Melbourne University Press, Carlton.

Tibaijuka, A (2005) *Report of the Fact-Finding Mission to Zimbabwe to assess the Scope and Impact of Operation Murambatsvina by the UN Special Envoy on Human Settlements Issues in Zimbabwe*, UN-Habitat, Nairobi.

Topsfield, J (2005a) 'Pacific Solution 'a success' as Nauru camp empties', *The Age,* 15 October.

Topsfield, J (2005b) 'Vanstone plays down self-harm', *The Age,* 20 September.

Topsfield, J (2007a) 'Refugees: Now for the US Solution', *The Age*, 19 April.

Topsfield, J (2007b) 'Nauru detainees 'walking zombies'', *The Age*, 4 September.

Towell, N (2007) 'Boat victims remembered SIEV X memorial approved', *Canberra Times*, 22 July.

Tran, My-Van (1981) *The Long Journey – Australia's Boat People*, CSAAR Research paper, No.15, Centre for the Study of Australian-Asian Relations, Griffith University, Brisbane.

Traverso, E (2007) 'Nazism and Communism. Re-readings of the twentieth century by Ernst Nolte, Francois Furet and Stephanie Courtois', in M.Haynes and J.Wolfreys (eds) *History and Revolution: Refuting Revisionism*, Verso, London.

Troeller, G (2003) 'Refugees and human displacement in contemporary international relations: Reconciling state and individual sovereignty', in Newman, E and van Selm, J (eds) *Refugees and Forced Displacement: International Security, Human Vulnerability and the State*, United Nations University Press, New York.

Trucco, L (2005) 'Lampedusa – a test case for the subcontracting of EU border controls', *Essays for civil liberties and democracy in Europe*, Number 13, European Civil Liberties Network, http://www.ecln.org., accessed 13 May 2006.

Tuitt, P (1996) *False Images: Law's Construction of the Refugee*, Pluto Press, London.

Turton, D (2003) *Conceptualising Forced Migration*, RSC Working Paper, Number 12, Refugee Studies Centre, University of Oxford.

UN (United Nations) (2004) *World Economic and Social Survey 2004: International Migration*, Author, New York.

UN (2005) *World Economic Situation and Prospects 2005*, Author, New York.

UNDP (United Nations Development Program) (UNDP) (1999) *Human Development Report 1999: Globalisation with a Human Face*, Oxford University Press, Oxford.

References

UNDP (2001) *Human Development Report 2001: Making New Technologies Work for Human Development*, Author, Oxford University Press, Oxford.

UNDP (2002) *Human Development Report 2002: Deepening democracy in a fragmented world*, Oxford University Press, Oxford.

UNGA (United Nations General Assembly) (2000) *'United Nations Millennium Declaration'*, A/RES/55/2, http://www.un.org/millennium/declaration/ares552e.pdf, accessed 10 October 2006.

UNGA (2005) *In larger freedom: towards, development, security and human rights for all*, A/59/2005, http://www.un.org/largerfreedom, accessed 10 October 2006.

UN-Habitat (United Nations Human Settlements Program) (2003) *The Challenge of the Slums: Global Report on Human Settlements 2003*, Earthscan Publications, London.

UNHCR (1996) *Lessons learned from the Rwanda and Burundi Emergencies*, Author, Geneva

UNHCR (1999) *Handbook for Emergencies*, Second Edition, Author, Geneva.

UNHCR (2000) *The State of the World's Refugees: Fifty Years of Humanitarian Action*, Oxford University Press, Oxford.

UNHCR (2002) *Human Rights and Immigration Detention in Australia*, http://smh.com.au/articles/2002/07/31/1027926913916.html, accessed 28 March 2006.

UNHCR (2003) *Summary of UNHCR proposals to complement national asylum systems through new multilateral approaches*, Author, Geneva.

UNHCR (2004) 'Europe's Next Challenge', *Refugees,* Volume 2, Number 135.

UNHCR (2005a) *Refugees,* Volume 2, Number 139.

UNHCR (2005b) 'Refugee Security At A Glance', *Refugees,* Volume 2, Number 139.

UNHCR (2007a) *2006 Global Trends*, Division of Operational Services Field Information and Coordination Support Section, UNHCR, Geneva.

UNHCR (2007b) *Statistics on Displaced Iraqis around the World: Global Overview September 2007*, http://www.unhcr.org/cgi-bin/texis/vtx/home/opendoc.pdf?tbl=SUBSITES&id=470387fc2, accessed 6 February 2009.

UNHCR (2009) 2008 *Global Trends: Refugees, Asylum –seekers, returnees, Internally Displaced and Stateless Persons*, http://www.unhcr.org/4a375c426.pdf, accessed 27 October 2009.

UNITED (2004) *List of 5017 documented refugee deaths through Fortress Europe*, 16 June, Author, Amsterdam.

UNITED (2005) *The Deadly Consequences of Fortress Europe*, Information Leaflet Number 24, http://united.non=profit.nl/pages/info24.htm, accessed 2 July 2006.

USCRI (United States Committee for Refugees and Immigrants) (2005) *World Refugee Survey*, Author, Washington D.C.

USDS (2005a) *Trafficking in Persons Report 2005*, Author, Washington D.C.http://www.state.gov/g/tip/rls/tiprpt/2005/, accessed 17 March 2006.

USDS (2005b) *Presidential Determination with Respect to Foreign Governments' Efforts Regarding Trafficking in Persons*, Presidential Determination No. 2005–37, http://www.state.gov/g/tip/rls/prsl/2005/53777.htm, accessed 17 March 2006.

Van Damme, W (1995) 'Do refugees belong in camps? Experiences from Goma and Guinea', *The Lancet*, Volume 346, Number 8971.

Van der Borght, S and Philips, M (1995) 'Do refugees belong in camps?' *The Lancet*, Volume 346, Number 8979.

Verdirame, G (1999) 'Human Rights and Refugees: the Case of Kenya', *Journal of Refugee Studies*, Volume 12, Number 1.

Verdirame, G and Harrell-Bond, B (2005) *Rights in Exile: Janus-Faced Humanitarianism*, Berghahn Books, Oxford.

Vincent, M (1999) 'Government calls new wave of boat people a border assault', *PM*, ABC Radio National, 2 November, http://www.abc.net.au/pm/stories/s63745.htm, accessed 4 December 2006.

Viviani, N (1984) *The Long Journey: Vietnamese Migration and Settlement in Australia*, Melbourne University Press, Carlton.

References

Viviani, N. (1996) *The Indo-Chinese in Australia 1975–1995,* Oxford University Press, Melbourne.

Webb, J and Enstice, A (1998) *Aliens and Savages: Fiction, Politics and Prejudice in Australia,* Harper Collins, Sydney.

Webber, F (2006) *Border wars and asylum crimes,* Statewatch, London.

Weber, D (2001) 'Refugee group attacks state of detention centres', *PM,* ABC Radio, 30 January, http://www.abc.net.au/pm/stories/s239407.htm, accessed 5 March 2007.

Weber, L (2002) 'The Detention of Asylum Seekers: 20 Reasons Why Criminologists Should Care', *Current Issues in Criminal Justice,* Volume 14, Number 1, Institute of Criminology, Sydney.

Weber, L (2003) 'Decisions to detain asylum seekers – routine, duty or individual choice?' in L.Gelsthorpe and D. Padfield (eds) *Exercising Discretion: Decision-making in the criminal justice system and beyond,* Willan Publishing, Devon.

Weber, L and Bowling B (2002) 'The policing of immigration in the new world disorder' in P.Scraton (ed) *Beyond September 11: An anthology of dissent,* Pluto Press, London.

Weber, L and Gelsthorpe, L (2000) *Deciding to detain: How decisions to detain asylum seekers are made at ports of entry,* Institute of Criminology, University of Cambridge.

Weber, L and Landman, T (2002) *Deciding to detain: The organisational context for decisions to detain asylum seekers at UK ports,* Human Rights Centre, University of Essex, Colchester.

Weber, M (1977) edited by H.Gerth and C. Wright Mills, *From Max Weber: Essays in Sociology,* Routledge and Kegan Paul, London.

Welch, M and Turner, F (2004) *'Tracking the Expansion of Private Prisons Around the World',* Paper presented at Prisons and Penal Policy: International Perspectives, City University, London, 23–25 June.

Welch, M and Turner, F (2007) "Private Corrections, Financial Infrastructure, and Transportation: The New Geo-Economy of Shipping Prisoners" *Social Justice,* Volume 34, Number 2–3, In press. Original manuscript provided by authors, July 2007.

Weller, P (2002) *Don't Tell the Prime Minister*, Scribe Publications, Melbourne.

White, R (1981) *Inventing Australia: Image and Identity, 1788–1980*, Allen and Unwin, Sydney.

Whitmont, D (2001) 'The Inside Story', *Four Corners*, ABC Television, 13 August.

Whitten, M (2005) 'Baxter Detention Centre', http://www.ajustaustralia.com/resource.php?act=attache&id=83, accessed 7 May 2007.

Willard, M (1967) *The history of the White Australia policy to 1920*, Melbourne University Press, Carlton.

Willey, K (1978) 'Australia's population' in A. Curthoys and A. Markus (eds) *Who Are Our Enemies?: Racism and the Australian Working Class*, Hale and Ironmonger and Australian Society for the Study of Labour History, Sydney and Canberra.

Williams, P and Vlassis, D (2005) *Combating Transnational Crime: Concepts, Activities and Responses,* Digital Print, Frank Cass, London.

Yarwood, A.T (1964) *Asian Migration to Australia: The Background to Exclusion 1896-1923*, Melbourne University Press, Parkville.

York, B (2003) *Australia and Refugees, 1901–2002: An Annotated Chronology Based on Official Sources*, Social Policy Group, Parliamentary Library, Canberra.

Zable, A (2003) 'Perilous Journeys', *Eureka Street,* April.

Zolberg, A, Suhrke, A and Aguayo, S (1989) *Escape from Violence: Conflict and the Refugee Crisis in the Developing World*, Oxford University Press, Oxford.

Index

1967 Protocol, *38, 72, 92, 96, 119*
2001 federal election, *247, 248, 262*
2007 federal election, *278*
2001 terrorist attacks, *245*
Absorbed Person Visa, *239*
Abu Ghraib, *14*
abuse in refugee camps, *6, 112, 130, 271*
Aceh, *48, 189*
Afghan crisis, *80, 81, 82, 83, 84, 85, 87, 88, 97, 115, 152, 177, 178, 191*
Afghanistan, *2, 44, 56, 153, 155, 165, 177, 178, 179, 180, 191, 223, 270, 280, 283*
    interim government, *177, 179*
Africa, *42, 43, 46, 53, 71, 73, 121*
    Addis Ababa, *46*
    Dakar, *46*
    Lagos, *46, 47*
Agamben, Giorgio, *50, 51, 71*
    'zone of exception', *50*
Agenda for Multicultural Australia, *111*
agricultural patterns
    changes, *46*
Ah Toy v Musgrove, *115*
aid, *43, 48, 51, 52, 53, 55, 56, 68, 101, 161, 170, 171, 193*
    agencies, *53*
    dependency, *54*
Akram, Abbas, *1, 2*
Al Kateb case, *254, 256*
Al Kateb, Ahmed, *254, 255, 256*
Al Khafaji case, *254, 256, 277*
Al Khafaji, Abbas Mohammad Hasan, *254*
Al Masri case, *253, 254, 277*
Al Masri, Akram, *253, 277*
    shooting death, *277*

Albania, *61*
Albany, *84*
alcohol prohibition, *63*
alienation, *9, 10, 18, 36, 70, 76, 79, 146, 153, 271, 272, 273, 274*
Al-Kateb v Godwin, *277*
Alliance of Health Professionals for Asylum Seekers, *239*
Alvarez Solon Inquiry, *185, 210, 211, 212, 213, 214, 215, 216, 217*
Alvarez Solon, Vivian, *185, 186, 208, 210, 212, 213, 214, 215, 216, 217, 239*
    unauthorised file note, *213*
Ambassador for People Smuggling Issues, *187*
American Declaration of Independence, *25*
Amnesty International, *155*
Andrews. Kevin, *268*
Anglo-Celtic identity, Australia, *90*
Angola, *56*
Annan, Kofi. *See* United Nations: Secretary General
anomie, *23, 37*
anti Muslim media commentary, *267*
anti-Chinese legislation, *80, 82, 83*
anti-Chinese rallies and violence, *85*
anti-Chinese sentiment, *85*
anti-discrimination, *29*
Anti-Slavery International, *66*
anti-terrorism, *37*
Anzac, *269*
'Arab Other', *243*
Arendt, Hannah, *27, 28, 37, 43, 71, 252*
Ashmore Island, *169, 192, 281*

Border Crimes

Asia, *9, 20, 42, 43, 46, 57, 60, 71, 77, 78, 87, 93, 94, 99, 130, 155, 185, 187, 190, 271*

Asia Pacific region, *9, 20, 68, 78, 90, 94, 130, 185, 187, 189, 190*

Association of Private Correctional and Treatment Organizations, *202*

asylum applications
　driving factors, *132*

asylum seeker boat arrivals, *9, 11, 88, 94, 96, 98, 100, 103, 119, 122, 126, 128, 129, 130, 131, 132, 136, 139, 142, 153, 154, 155, 162, 165, 170, 191, 229, 249, 260, 280, 284*
　construction as threat, *266*

asylum seekers, *2, 4, 5, 17, 34, 40, 41, 55, 62, 68, 70, 105, 119, 122, 124, 126, 129, 130, 131, 135, 136, 140, 150, 152, 159, 162, 164, 165, 166, 173, 174, 176, 177, 180, 182, 183, 184, 185, 244, 247, 249, 266, 270, 272, 278, 281, 284*
　Cambodian, *250*
　effects of detention, *223*
　treatment in Indonesia, *282*
　West Papuan, *170*

Attorney General's Department, *134, 143*

Ausaid, *171*

Australasian Correctional Management (ACM), *174, 202, 207, 229, 234, 235*

Australasian Correctional Services, *202*

Australasian Federal Convention, 1898, *78*

Australia and Indonesia
　bilateral arrangements, *281*

Australian armed forces, *5*

Australian Council of Churches, *143, 144*

Australian Council of Trade Unions, *285*

Australian Customs Service, *163*

Australian Defence Force (ADF), *162, 163, 164, 167, 172*

Australian Federal Police, *4, 63, 163, 171, 181, 182, 183, 187, 188, 189, 194, 195, 210, 244*
　joint undercover operations with INP, *182*

Australian Human Rights Commission
　condemnation of offshore processing policy 2009, *284*

Australian identity, *8, 9, 109, 269*

Australian Institute of Criminology, *144*

Australian Labor party, *5, 6, 11, 90, 95, 106, 108, 109, 110, 116, 117, 121, 128, 130, 138, 158, 159, 167, 168, 192, 199, 205, 237, 245, 246, 278*
　historic commitment to border protection, *245*
　Rudd government, *190*
　support for government's migration policy, *158*

Australian Liberal party, *95, 108, 112, 116, 118, 262, 263*

Australian Liberal Party/National Party coalition, *6, 95, 106, 108, 111, 112, 118, 151, 159, 245, 246, 250, 262, 278*

Australian Liberal Party/National Party coalition government, *248*

Australian National Audit Office, *156, 201, 202, 205*

Australian nationalism, *10, 76, 77, 78, 106, 113, 242, 260, 263, 285*
　cultural homogeneity, *242*

Australian navy, *2, 60*

Australian Protective Services, *143, 172, 234*

Australian public service, *247*

Index

Australian Public Service Code of Conduct, *217*
Australian Security Intelligence Organisation (ASIO), *162*, *163*, *190*
Australian sovereignty, *9*, *120*, *154*, *242*
Australian state's response to acts of resistance, *237*
Australian type, *87*
Australian values, *105*, *261*, *269*
Australian way of life, *279*
Baathist, *165*
Badraie, Shayan, *197*, *228*, *229*, *240*, *258*
    compensation, *229*
    diagnosis of PTSD, *228*
    HREOC investigation, *229*
    medical record, *229*
    symptoms of trauma, *228*
    transfer into foster care, *229*
    Westmead hospital, *229*
Bali, *187*, *195*, *281*
    terrorist attacks, *188*, *266*
Bali Process, *187*, *195*, *281*
Barrie, Admiral Chris, *247*, *248*
Bartlett Andrew, Senator, *1*
Barton, Edmund, *78*
Basry, Amal, *1*, *2*, *3*, *6*, *11*, *158*, *285*
Baxter Immigration Detention Facility, *198*, *199*, *200*, *204*, *205*, *207*, *208*, *209*, *210*, *214*, *217*, *220*, *221*, *223*, *231*, *240*, *259*
    conditions, *221*
    culture of abuse and voyeurism, *239*
    protests, *233*
Baxterwatch website, *210*
Beazley, Kim, *167*, *193*
Behrooz case, *256*, *277*
Behrooz, Mahran, *256*, *257*
bi-partisanship, *245*, *246*

Blainey, Geoffrey, *108*, *109*, *112*, *118*, *262*
Blair Government, UK, *5*, *73*
blanket detention policy, *146*
boat arrivals. *'boat people'*
'boat people', *60*, *76*, *98*, *100*, *110*, *117*, *124*, *126*, *127*, *128*, *129*, *145*, *149*, *150*, *266*, *267*
Bolkus, Nick, *128*
Bolshevism, *37*
Bonegilla Reception Centre, *91*
border control policy, *88*
border controls, *8*, *9*, *12*, *21*, *39*, *58*, *59*, *64*, *66*, *67*, *68*, *69*, *70*, *95*, *133*, *136*, *138*, *270*, *271*, *276*, *278*, *285*
    externalisation, *57*, *58*, *167*, *280*
    punitive, *8*, *151*
border policing, *2*, *7*, *9*, *10*, *11*, *12*, *13*, *35*, *36*, *39*, *51*, *57*, *58*, *59*, *68*, *70*, *76*, *77*, *80*, *83*, *88*, *94*, *115*, *162*, *171*, *174*, *180*, *185*, *201*, *216*, *222*, *242*, *243*, *244*, *245*, *246*, *250*, *259*, *260*, *261*, *270*, *271*, *274*, *279*, *281*, *284*, *285*
    criminogenic elements, *280*
border policing policy, *242*, *243*, *246*
border policing strategies, *51*, *58*
border protection, *3*, *6*, *9*, *10*, *50*, *57*, *58*, *70*, *88*, *152*, *154*, *163*, *165*, *180*, *185*, *190*, *201*, *216*, *244*, *245*, *249*, *253*, *258*, *275*, *278*
Border Protection Legislation Amendment Bill, 1999, *155*, *156*, *191*
border protection policy, *268*
Brisbane Courier Mail, *117*, *266*
Brisbane Women's Correctional Centre, *209*
Britain, *5*, *33*, *91*, *202*
    Home Office, *5*, *239*
    media, *5*

335

British migrants
   free and assisted passage, *91*
British National Party, *5*
Broome, Western Australia, *101, 126, 129*
Budapest Group, *65*
Burke, Edmund, *25, 26, 114*
Burma, *67, 283*
Burns Philp, *81*
Burnside, Julian QC, *178*
Burumbeet, *81*
Bush, George W, *67, 166*
Calwell Scheme, *91*
Calwell, Arthur, *91, 92, 116*
Cambodia, *67, 94, 122, 124, 126, 127, 131, 218, 252*
   peace agreement 1991, *125*
Campsfield House detention centre (UK), *202*
   disturbances, *204*
   disturbances High Court judgement, *207*
Cape York, *170, 173*
Carnegie Commission, *44*
Cartier Island, *169*
Central America, *44*
Chamarette, Senator Christabel, *144*
Changsa, *115*
chattel slavery. *See* slavery
'Children Overboard',*60, 148, 163,165, 166, 167, 247, 278*
Children's Commissioner for England, *206*
China, *16, 33, 45, 47, 55, 87, 101, 102, 114, 116, 119, 124, 128, 129, 132, 187, 263*
Chinese population in Australia, *87*
Chinese refugee 'crisis' 1994, *128*
Chinese Restriction Bill, *115*
cholera, *52*

Chomsky, Noam, *20*
Christmas Island, *2, 6, 160, 164, 169, 173, 197, 198, 201, 203, 204, 229, 230, 247, 249, 259, 265, 281, 283, 284*
   security, *200*
Circular Quay, *83*
citizenship, *50, 76, 105, 216, 243, 255, 261, 262, 268, 269, 270*
citizenship test, *269*
   rationale, *268*
civil society, *7, 17, 19, 23, 24, 26, 27, 29, 51, 77, 238, 243, 285*
civil war, *21, 43, 45*
Coastal Surveillance Task Force, *155, 156*
Coastwatch, *156, 163*
Cocos (Keeling) Islands, *169*
Cohen, Stan, *16, 23, 30, 36, 85*
Cold War, *5, 15, 20, 28, 32, 34, 43, 44, 45, 58, 92, 93, 101, 103, 113, 117*
College of Immigration, Border Security and Compliance, *249*
colonial secretary, *81, 89*
colonialism, *77*
   British, *78*
colonisation, *77, 87*
Coming Man', *86*
commercial-in-confidence, *206*
Commonwealth, *71, 78, 79, 91, 116, 146, 178, 184, 205, 207, 211, 215, 217, 239, 240*
Commonwealth Ombudsman, *210, 211, 213, 214, 215, 216, 248*
   reports, *215*
'Commonwealth Ombudsman systemic issues' reports, *210*
community activists, *232*
community detention, *230*
compensation, *208, 229, 239, 258*

Index

compliance, *67, 68, 133, 136, 187, 211, 225, 249, 269, 284*
compulsory registration, *89*
Comrie, Neil, *210*
concentration camp, *51*
concentration camp survivors, *116*
Congo, Democratic Republic of, *44, 56*
conscription, *28*
contract slavery. See slavery
Convention Against Torture, *143, 191*
Convention on the Rights of the Child, *143, 207, 219, 225, 253, 274, 284*
Convention Plus, *62*
corruption, *23, 64, 126, 189*
Country party, *116, 118*
crimes against humanity, *14, 15, 16*
Criminal Code Amendment (Slavery and Sexual Servitude) Act 1999, *186*
Criminal Code Amendment (Trafficking in Persons Offences) Act 2005, *186*
criminality, *8, 13, 16, 28, 148, 154, 191, 217, 224, 242, 273, 285*
criminology, *12, 13, 14, 16, 20, 23, 28, 37, 285*
    critical criminology, *14, 36*
    managerial, *35*
Croatia, *61*
Cronulla riots, 2005, *268*
Cuba, *67*
cultural difference, *76, 105, 203, 243, 261*
    basis of identifying threats, *268*
culture of containment, *10, 208, 217*
culture of control, *140, 165*
Curtin detention centre, *198, 206, 226, 231, 232, 233, 235, 238*
    allegations of attempted rape and sexual abuse, *239*

disturbances, *233*
    protests, *233*
cyber crime, *189*
Czarist Empire, *43*
Darwin, *97*
    East Arm quarantine station, *100*
    unathorised boat arrival April 1976, *97*
Darwin unathorised boat arrival April 1976, *149*
Deakin, Alfred, *78*
debt bondage. See slavery
declared country, *169*
decolonisation, *43*
Defence Department, *163*
defence department secretary, *248*
Defence Signals Directorate (DSD), *162*
defend, deter and detain', *159*
Democratic People's Republic of Korea, *67*
denationalisation, *50, 276*
Department of Customs, *89*
Department of Defence Public Affairs, *164*
Department of External Affairs, *79, 89, 114, 116*
Department of Foreign Affairs and Trade, *122, 134, 163, 189, 213*
Department of Immigration and Citizenship. See immigration department
Department of Immigration, Multiculturalism and Indigenous Affairs. See immigration department
Department of the Prime Minister and Cabinet, *156, 163*
Department of Trade and Customs, *79*
Derby detention centre, *198*
deserters, *89*

Border Crimes

designated person, *137, 251*
detainees, *9, 18, 142, 144, 147, 148, 178, 179, 190, 196, 197, 198, 199, 200, 203, 204, 205, 214, 217, 218, 219, 220, 222, 223, 224, 230, 231, 232, 233, 234, 235, 236, 239, 241, 248, 254, 280*
    abuse by detention centre staff, *231*
    acts of resistance, *232, 237*
    as commodities, *203*
    charged with offences after protests, *236*
    children, *2, 3, 6, 22, 46, 47, 66, 77, 78, 90, 95, 102, 117, 126, 143, 145, 148, 152, 165, 167, 183, 188, 192, 206, 207, 210, 221, 222, 224, 225, 226, 227, 229, 230, 234, 235, 238, 240, 244, 258, 280, 282, 284*
    children, exposure to self-harm, *228*
    children, symptoms of trauma, *227*
    children, witness abuse of parents, *228*
    children, witness self-harm by adults, *228*
    chronic depressive symptoms, *223*
    criminalisation, *237*
    duties of care towards, *207*
    effects of detention, *196*
    families with children, *230*
    forced labour in detention centres, *205*
    impact of detention, *198, 201*
    institutionalised child abuse, *225*
    international obligations regarding treatment, *207*
    isolation, *231*
    lip-stitching, *224, 227, 232, 233*
    non consensual medical treatment, *236*
    oral testimony, *227*
    organisation of protests, *232*
    participant-observer study, *223*
    psychosis, *223*
    repercussions from protests, *234*
    self-harm, *6, 162, 197, 222, 223, 224, 226, 227, 228, 234*
    strip searching, *236*
    suicidal behaviour rates, *223*
    unaccompanied children, *225*
Detective Inspector Gabriel, *89*
detention
    impact on detainees, *9*
detention camp, *6, 8, 42, 49, 50, 51, 52, 53, 54, 55, 56, 57, 59, 60, 71, 72, 91, 92, 95, 98, 99, 116, 122, 124, 125, 129, 140, 143, 146, 171, 178, 182, 200, 226, 232*
    definition, *52*
detention camps
    health risks, *52*
detention centre, *1, 5, 6, 52, 124, 137, 138, 141, 143, 169, 172, 173, 179, 197, 198, 201, 202, 204, 205, 206, 207, 218, 219, 225, 226, 228, 230, 231, 232, 235, 236, 237, 280, 281, 283, 284*
    Indonesia, *281*
    isolation units, *199, 220*
    monopoly of power over detainees, *231*
    privatisation, *201, 202, 205, 206, 207*
    protests by detainees, *142, 148*
    screening of visitors, *236*
    staff, *238*
    staff, *231*
    use of chemical restraints, *236*
    visiting procedures, *200*
detention regime
    abusive nature of regime, *230*
detention system
    changes under Rudd government, *280*
deterrence, *8, 11, 129, 139, 140, 148, 153, 157, 162, 169, 197, 258, 260*

Index

dictation test for immigrants, *79*
DIMIA
  Department of Immigration Multiculturalism and Indigenous Affairs (DIMIA). *See* immigration department
Dob-in Line, *249*
domestic law, *12, 14, 17*
Donald Bradman, *269*
Dover
  England, Chinese refugee deaths, *68*
Downer, Alexander, *185, 195*
drug smuggling, *54*
Dudley. Michael, *223*
East Timor, *170, 188, 189, 191*
economic migrants, *5, 62, 124, 129*
Edmund Rice Centre (ERC), *177, 178, 179, 180, 194*
Egypt, *61, 185, 195, 253*
entry permit
  abolition, *136, 137*
ethnic conflict, *45*
Ethnic crime gangs, *266*
Europe, *5, 21, 24, 28, 29, 32, 33, 34, 50, 57, 60, 71, 74, 91, 92, 101, 105, 116, 149, 153, 272, 273*
European Commission, *61, 66, 74*
European Court of Human Rights, *253*
European Union, *57, 59, 60, 61, 62, 64, 68, 71, 74, 272*
Evans, Senator Chris, *78, 85, 122, 150, 201, 279, 280*
Evian Conference, 1938, *90*
Ex Parte Lo Pak, *115*
excision, *169, 193, 265, 280, 284*
exclusion policy, *8, 12, 20, 35, 36, 39, 47, 49, 50, 51, 57, 58, 62, 63, 69, 75, 77, 79, 80, 88, 94, 104, 106, 112, 113, 129, 139, 140, 152, 172, 184,* *186, 190, 196, 238, 242, 244, 252, 255, 260, 261, 262, 270, 271, 272, 273, 274, 275, 283*
exclusion zone, *8, 20, 57, 63, 69, 188, 190, 232, 273*
exploitation, *47, 65, 69*
externalisation, *9, 57, 58, 59, 167*
family reunion, *2, 110, 121, 155, 157, 158, 265*
Farmer, Bill, *237*
far-right, *5, 118, 159, 262*
fascism, *50*
fascist, *5, 19*
Federal Court, *128, 137, 162, 166, 204, 207, 220, 250, 253*
federal election, 1998, *264*
feudalism, *22, 24, 26*
Fiji, *170*
Fitzgerald inquiry, *109, 110, 131, 141*
forced labour, *65, 205*
forced migration, *7, 11, 20, 22, 31, 33, 36, 39, 41, 42, 44, 45, 48, 49, 52, 55, 68, 69, 70, 71, 94, 103, 120, 122, 131, 157, 181, 252*
  driving factors, *7, 39, 40, 44, 48, 256*
  state responses, *57*
forced removal
  methods of restraint, *175*
foreign policy implications, *172*
forum shopping, *129, 154, 157*
France
  strikes, *28, 272*
Fraser government, *261*
Fraser, Malcolm, *103, 107, 117*
fraud, *65, 249*
Free the Slaves, *66*
free trade, *29*
French Declaration of the Rights of Man and of the Citizen, *25*

French Polynesia, *170*
French revolution, *25*
fumigation, *82, 83, 89, 116*
Future Directions, 112
G4S. *See* Global Soultions Limited (GSL)
Galbally inquiry, *107, 141*
Gaza Strip, *253, 277*
genocide, *13, 15, 16, 28, 43, 44, 45*
Genocide Convention, *28*
GIDPP, *48, 72*
Gillard, Julia, *283*
Gleeson, Chief Justice, *257*
Global North, *42, 71*
Global Solutions Limited (GSL), *202, 203, 204, 205, 206, 221, 231*
  management practices, *204*
Global South, *42, 71*
globalisation, *10, 58, 62, 69*
Glover, Richard, *266*
Goldie v Commonwealth, 239
Gramsci, Antonio, *23, 24, 26, 30*
Grassby, Al, *106*
Green, Penny, *7, 13, 16, 17, 19, 23, 24, 29, 35, 36, 37, 48*
Group 4 Falck, *202, 204, 239*
Guantanamo Bay, *60, 201, 259*
Gummow, Justice, *256*
gun running, *54*
Guthrie, 82, 84
Haiti, *25, 60, 72*
Hall, Richard, *77*
Halton, Jane, *247*
Hand, Gerry, *127, 138, 139, 150, 250*
Hanson, Pauline, *77, 262, 263, 264, 265*
Hawke Labor government, *5, 109, 120, 122, 127, 150*
Hawke, Robert, *127*

Hazara, *235*
hegemony, *23, 24, 29, 75, 85, 107, 112, 242, 260, 262, 271*
High Court, *137, 207, 239, 250, 251, 252, 253, 254, 256, 257, 259, 260, 273*
  willingness to license powers of detention, *258*
history wars, *262*
HMAS *Adelaide'*, *247*
Hoang, *97*
Holocaust, *4, 28*
Home and Territories Department, *79*
homo sacer, 50
Hong Kong, *84, 89, 93, 100, 115, 124, 125, 143*
Howard government, *152, 223, 242, 261*
  defeat, *279*
  ideological base for policies, *262*
  media strategy, *164*
  response to detention centre protests, *235*
  response to One Nation, *263*
Howard government reforms following Palmer Report, *249*
Howard, John, *3, 4, 5, 10, 58, 72, 101, 105, 111, 112, 130, 138, 159, 166, 167, 193, 197, 245, 247, 248, 261, 262, 263, 264, 267, 278, 280, 285*
Howes, Paul, *285*
human rights, *5, 6, 7, 9, 10, 13, 14, 15, 16, 17, 18, 20, 22, 23, 24, 26, 27, 28, 29, 30, 31, 32, 35, 36, 37, 39, 42, 44, 46, 47, 49, 50, 51, 53, 54, 56, 57, 58, 59, 63, 67, 68, 70, 75, 79, 92, 96, 101, 104, 106, 112, 117, 120, 124, 125, 130, 138, 143, 147, 149, 155, 159, 172, 176, 185, 186, 189, 203, 207, 232, 243, 249, 269, 271, 273, 274, 276*

Index

abuses, *7, 16, 28, 50, 60, 61, 66, 69, 75, 285*
breaches, *238*
discourse, *7, 24, 36*
obligations, *143, 146, 219*
Human Rights and Equal Opportunity Commission, *118, 143, 144, 145, 176, 199, 202, 207, 218, 219, 220, 225, 226, 227, 228, 229, 230, 233, 234, 235, 236, 239, 240, 267, 270, 275, 277*
    report on children in detention, *115, 149, 225, 226, 240*
human rights discourse, *27*
human rights violations, *17, 69*
human trafficking, *8, 46, 47, 54, 57, 58, 59, 62, 63, 64, 65, 66, 67, 68, 69, 70, 88, 89, 185, 186, 187, 188, 189, 249*
    anti-trafficking measures, *64*
    children, *46*
    definition, *65*
    sex, *187*
humanitarian protection visas, *135*
Hungarian Olympics team, 1956
    defection to Australia, *93*
hunger strike, *142, 148, 161, 179, 197, 227, 232, 233, 235, 278, 281*
Hurricane Katrina, *48*
Hutton, M, *3, 11, 195*
ideologies of exclusion, *242*
illegal fishing, *189*
illegal logging, *54*
illicit workers
    criminalisation, *273*
Immigration (Restriction) Act, 1901, 79, 80, 89
immigration compliance, *222, 249*
immigration department, *101, 107, 131, 134, 136, 139, 140, 143, 149, 151, 163, 172, 173, 175, 185, 186, 190, 191, 195, 199, 204, 206, 208, 209, 213, 214, 215, 217, 220, 229, 232, 238, 239, 240, 244, 245, 246, 277, 280*
    'mistakes', *208*
    contract with private detention centre operators, *66, 202, 203, 204, 205, 206, 207, 214*
    culture of compliance, *208*
    internal culture, *211, 214*
    renaming, *261*
Immigration Restriction Act, 116
Immigration Review Tribunal, *134*
income
    ratio between rich and poor, *45*
Independent and Multicultural Broadcasting Corporation, *107*
India, *16, 33, 43, 45, 263*
Indian Ocean, *2, 283*
Indian subcontinent, *2, 33*
indigenous people, *21*
Indigenous people. Australia, *77, 113*
Indo-China, *43, 55, 121, 122*
Indonesia, *2, 99, 100, 129, 143, 155, 160, 162, 170, 173, 181, 184, 187, 217, 263, 281, 282, 283, 285*
    Aceh, *48*
    detention facilities, *282*
Indonesian National Police (INP), *182*
Indonesian Navy, *281*
Indonesian Solution, *283*
Indonesian Transnational Crime Coordination Centre, *188*
industrialisation, *46*
Inquiry into Immigration Detention Procedures, *202*
Intergovernmental Committee for European Migration (ICEM), *92, 93, 117*
Inter-governmental Committee for European Migration (ICEM), *92*
internal conflicts, *45*

Border Crimes

Internal Displacement Monitoring Centre, *41*
internally displaced persons (IDP), *40, 41, 44, 54, 55*
International Coffee Agreement, *45*
International Covenant on Civil and Political Rights, *117, 143, 191, 207, 219, 236, 251, 253, 274*
International Criminal Court, *16, 37*
international law, *14, 15, 16, 17, 20, 36, 158, 224*
International Monetary Fund, *29*
international obligations, *145*
International Organisation for Migration (IOM), *30, 61, 64, 170, 172, 177, 178, 179, 187, 281*
International Refugee Organisation (IRO), *33, 38, 91, 92*
international tribunals, *15*
Internment
    people of Japanese descent, *114*
Iran, *1, 2, 42, 61, 153, 165, 233, 270*
Iraq, *2, 4, 5, 42, 44, 56, 153, 155, 165, 191, 223, 254*
Islam, *165, 243, 261, 266, 268*
    link with terrorism, *268*
    problematisation, *268*
Islamophobia, *268*
Israel, *16, 33, 43, 253*
Italy, *23, 60, 147*
Jakarta, *2, 282*
    terrorist attacks, *188*
Japan
    Atomic bombing by Allies, *28*
Jefferson, Thomas, *25*
Jews, *43, 92*
Joint Senate Committee on Migration, *136, 137, 141, 143, 144, 145, 151, 277*

Joint Standing Committee on Migration, *130, 139, 141, 142, 144, 201*
Joint Standing Committee on Migration Regulations, *123, 130, 132, 133, 136, 141, 142, 144, 149, 151*
Judeo Christian beliefs, *269*
judiciary, *10, 18, 80, 244, 245, 250, 259*
Jureidini Dr, *221, 222, 240*
Kashmir, *43*
Keelty, Mick Australian Federal Police Commissioner, *181, 182*
Kevin, Tony, *11*
Khmer Rouge, *126*
Khogali, Abdul, *174*
Kinoon, William, *84*
Kirby, Justice, *256, 258*
Kiribati, *170, 187*
KM *Palapa 1*, *152, 159*
Kopassus, *189*
Korean peninsula, *33*
Kurdish, *5*
Latin America, *33, 71, 101, 121, 149*
Lawrence, Carmen, *199*
legal action by asylum seekers, *250*
Legal Services Commission SA, *239*
legitimacy, *23*
legitimate migrant, *57*
Leong, Virginia and Nancy, *237*
liberal democracy, *19, 25, 253*
Libya, *60*
Lim case, *151, 251, 252, 257, 259, 276*
lip sewing, *148*
Lombok, *182, 282*
Lombrum Naval Patrol Base, *171*
Malaysia, *1, 2, 98, 99, 102, 124, 129, 143, 155, 263*

Index

Management Unit, *220*, *See* detention centre:isolation units
Mandaean, *2*
mandatory detention, *5, 6, 8, 9, 10, 17, 18, 103, 110, 120, 126, 131, 136, 137, 138, 139, 140, 141, 142, 146, 147, 149, 151, 153, 159, 169, 196, 198, 201, 216, 219, 220, 224, 229, 238, 242, 243, 245, 246, 250, 254, 258, 274, 275, 283, 284*
Manus Island, *171, 173, 240*
Maribyrnong detention centre, *198, 204*
Maroko, *47*
martial law, *48*
Marx, Karl, *26, 27*
Marxism, *23, 26*
McGuinness, Paddy, *267*
McHugh, Justice, *251, 252, 258, 259*
McKiernan, Jim
    Senator, *138, 139, 140*
Médécins Sans Frontieres, *52*
media, *82, 86, 97, 102, 117, 123, 126, 153, 154, 162, 165, 231, 265, 267*
    reporting on Sudanese refugees, *279*
media strategy
    government, *164*
Melbourne Punch, *86*
Menmuir, *82*
mentally ill persons
    vulnerability, *215*
Merton, Robert, *23, 37*
Mexico, *57, 72*
'Middle Eastern' people, *266*
Migration Act, *119, 131, 136, 141, 151, 169, 178, 194, 198, 208, 209, 215, 216, 222, 230, 239, 240, 249, 250, 254, 255, 259, 276*
migration agents
    illicit, *63, 190*
Migration Amendment Act, 1992, *137, 151*
Migration Amendment Bill 1992, *151, 250*
Migration legislation, *244*
Migration Legislation Amendment Act 1989, *131, 155, 193*
migration legislation reforms
    penalites for protest and escape, *236*
Migration Reform Act, 1992, *136, 137, 151*
migration research, *40*
Migration Zone, *177, 193*
militarisation, *45, 54, 57, 63, 73*
military emergency, *48*
money laundering, *64, 189*
Moore, Claire, Senator, *1*
Moore-Wilton, Max, *156, 247*
moral panic, *85, 87, 266*
morality, *17, 24, 167*
Mr G wrongful detention case study, *208, 210, 215, 239*
Mr T wrongful detention case study, *208, 210, 215*
multiculturalism, *8, 28, 57, 75, 76, 96, 103, 104, 105, 106, 107, 109, 110, 111, 112, 113, 242, 243, 260, 261, 262, 263, 269, 272*
    ideological attacks, *270*
    presentation as a force for fragmentation, *269*
Muslim, *105, 165, 196, 266, 267, 268, 279*
Muslim Community Reference Group, *268*
Mussolini, *23*
MV Tampa, *5, 80, 97, 101, 152, 156, 159, 160, 161, 162, 164, 165, 167, 168, 169, 170, 172, 173, 178, 185, 189, 190, 216, 266, 281*

Border Crimes

Nairobi, *46, 47*
nation state, *25, 27, 32, 35, 36, 76, 255, 260, 269, 271, 275*
National Action Plan to Build on Social Cohesion, Harmony and Security, *268*
National Archives of Australia, *115*
national identity, *24, 76, 77, 88, 260, 270, 271*
National Population Council
    refugee review, *116*
national security, *18, 57, 63, 70, 71, 75, 79, 88, 91, 115, 117, 141, 146, 147, 152, 155, 160, 164, 190, 244, 246*
National Security Act 1939- 1940, *146*
National Security Council, *63*
nationalism, *35, 75, 76, 77, 88, 108, 260*
    race based, *261*
NATO, *44*
Nauru, *2, 5, 6, 61, 162, 169, 170, 171, 172, 173, 177, 178, 179, 180, 189, 192, 193, 229, 230, 232, 240, 244, 249, 259, 278, 284*
Nauru detention centre
    closure, *279, 280*
Nazi, *37, 51, 92, 118*
Nazi and SS officers migrate to Australia, *91*
Nazi Germany, *90*
Nazi war criminals
    recruitment to Australia, *92*
Nazis, *15*
negative depiction of Chinese immigrants, *86*
neoliberalism, *29, 45, 203*
Nettle, Kerry, Senator, *1*
new conservatism, *108, 262*
New South Wales Ethnic Affairs Commission, *128*

New South Wales Supreme Court
    Rau Settlement, *239*
New Zealand, *71, 172, 187, 189, 195*
Newman, Louise, *239*
NGOs, *29, 54, 134, 177*
Non Government Organisation, *66, 155, 173*
Non Government Organisations, *53, 57, 61*
non-citizen, *5, 9, 10, 18, 51, 110, 113, 120, 134, 137, 138, 143, 144, 147, 148, 155, 164, 191, 211, 215, 239, 248, 249, 254, 255*
    removal of legitimate agency, *257*
non-refoulement
    formal commitment to, *56, 93, 180*
Northern Ireland, *28*
NSW Legislative Assembly, *83, 115*
Nuremberg trials, *15*
Nuremberg Tribunal, *37*
Nuremburg tribunal, *15, 28*
Oceanic Viking, *281*
Office of Multicultural Affairs, *111*
Office of National Assessments, *156, 163*
Office of Strategic Crime Assessments, *163*
offshore detention, *4, 6, 10, 18, 57, 97, 120, 152, 169, 173, 176, 177, 283*
offshore processing, *60, 119, 141, 170, 173, 190*
offshore refugee and humanitarian program, *121*
One Nation, *77, 159, 262, 264, 265*
Operation Murambatsvina, *47*
Operation Relex, *162, 163, 164, 166, 172, 181, 189*
Operation Ulysses, *60*
opium, *86, 115*
organisational deviance, *17*

Index

organised crime, *37*, *54*, *65*, *66*, *139*, *148*
   Mafia, *65*
   snakehead gangs, *68*
   transnational, *57*, *62*, *63*, *64*, *182*, *188*, *196*
   Triads, *65*
otherness, *76*
Ottoman Empire, *43*
outsiders, *8*, *18*, *147*, *165*, *196*, *279*
Pacific Island labourers
   'blackbirding', *80*
Pacific Island Labourers Act, 1901, *79*, *80*
Pacific Rim, *57*
Pacific Solution, *2*, *4*, *6*, *8*, *9*, *11*, *60*, *63*, *95*, *103*, *120*, *130*, *152*, *156*, *158*, *162*, *164*, *167*, *169*, *173*, *174*, *176*, *177*, *179*, *180*, *189*, *190*, *196*, *216*, *225*, *230*, *232*, *242*, *244*, *245*, *259*, *270*, *275*, *278*, *284*, *285*
Paine, Thomas, *25*, *26*
Pakistan, *33*, *42*, *43*, *143*, *177*
Palau, *170*
Palestine, *33*, *43*
Palmer inquiry, *220*, *231*
Palmer Report, *197*, *199*, *205*, *209*, *210*, *211*, *214*, *216*, *217*, *220*, *231*, *248*, *249*
   findings, *215*
   nature of inquiry, *214*
   refusal to disclose evidence, *214*
Papua New Guinea, *5*, *169*, *170*, *171*, *172*, *173*, *188*, *244*
Parkes, Henry, *81*, *82*, *83*, *85*, *86*, *115*
parliamentary committee system, *245*
passport control, *76*
people smuggling, *2*, *3*, *4*, *6*, *8*, *9*, *22*, *46*, *57*, *58*, *59*, *62*, *63*, *64*, *65*, *68*, *69*, *70*, *74*, *88*, *89*, *99*, *117*, *132*, *139*, *148*, *154*, 155, 156, *159*, 160, *169*, *178*, 180, 181, 182, *184*, *185*, *187*, 188, 189, 190, 194, 195, *196*, *225*, 244, 247, 249, 259, 273, *280*, 283
   definition, *65*
People Smuggling Disruption Program, *184*
People Smuggling Task Force, *163*, *247*
People Smuggling Task Force (PST), *163*
permanent local integration, *51*
permanent protection visa, *2*, *190*
Petrov, Vladimir, 93
Phar Lap, *269*
Pontianak jail, *282*
Port Hedland detention centre, *129*, *141*, *142*, *198*, *199*, *219*, *233*, *235*
   Juliet block, *199*
   protests, *233*
   riots, *233*
post traumatic stress disorder, *226*, *228*
post-colonial, *45*
post-traumatic stress disorder, *228*
poverty, *13*, *45*, *106*
presumptive refoulement, *61*
Princess Alexandra Hospital, *209*
prison, *124*, *137*, *138*, *142*, *147*, *169*, *174*, *198*, *199*, *209*, *218*, *221*, *223*, *235*, *236*, *273*, *282*
   privatisation, *203*
prisoner of war, *147*
privatisation, *46*
processing centre, *171*
protection visa, *135*
protection visas, *129*, *158*, *189*
protective detention, *258*
   legal construct, *259*
Qasim, Peter, *217*

Border Crimes

quarantine, *81, 82, 83, 84, 97, 136, 232*
Quassey, Abu, *2, 185, 195*
Queensland Figaro, *86*
queue jumpers, *9, 117, 130, 140, 190, 261*
race rapes, *266*
racial discrimination, *15*
racism, *13, 76, 79, 86, 113, 159, 243, 260, 261, 264, 265, 268, 279, 285*
    experiences, *267*
racist abuse, *86*
Rau, Cornelia, *197, 208, 209, 210, 213, 214, 215, 220, 221, 222, 239, 240, 244, 249*
razor wire, *22, 198, 199, 227, 233, 282*
Re Woolley, *277*
Red One. *See* detention centre:isolation units
refugee
    rights, *158*
Refugee Council of Australia, *134*
refugee determination process
    control by state, *238*
refugee protection obligations, *58, 90, 170*
refugee quota
    African, *279*
Refugee Review Tribunal, *129, 134, 135, 191*
refugee status, *124*
refugee status review committee, *133, 134*
refugee villages, *52*
refugees, *1, 4, 5, 6, 7, 8, 9, 11, 17, 18, 20, 22, 26, 27, 29, 30, 31, 32, 33, 34, 35, 37, 38, 39, 40, 41, 42, 43, 45, 48, 49, 50, 51, 52, 53, 55, 56, 58, 59, 65, 68, 69, 70, 71, 72, 73, 76, 88, 89, 90, 92, 93, 94, 95, 96, 97, 98, 99, 100, 101, 102, 103, 104, 108, 110, 113,* *116, 117, 119, 120, 121, 122, 123, 124, 125, 126, 127, 128, 129, 130, 131, 132, 133, 134, 135, 136, 138, 139, 140, 141, 142, 145, 147, 148, 149, 150, 151, 152, 153, 154, 155, 157, 158, 159, 160, 161, 162, 164, 165, 166, 168, 169, 170, 171, 172, 173, 174, 176, 178, 179, 181, 189, 190, 191, 192, 196, 197, 208, 210, 218, 223, 225, 235, 237, 241, 245, 250, 252, 253, 254, 259, 261, 264, 265, 266, 272, 273, 274, 275, 278, 280, 281, 282, 283*
    'genuine', *197*
    abuse, *190*
    alienation, *148*
    alienation, *196*
    alienation, *238*
    alienation, *243*
    as victims, *53*
    bipartisan approach, *245*
    Burmese, *171*
    construction as a threat, *17, 57*
    construction as outsiders, *279*
    criminalisation, *9, 10, 11, 18, 36, 64, 69, 70, 75, 112, 129, 146, 147, 148, 153, 190, 191, 196, 238, 243, 270, 273*
    cycle of dependency, *53*
    dehumanisation, *164, 165*
    denial of access to determination process, *284*
    determination process, *190*
    development, *40*
    disaster, *40, 70, 135*
    environmental, *40, 41, 45, 48, 70, 71*
    Ethiopian, *121*
    European, *90, 119*
    formal rights, *7*
    host countries, *42*
    Indo-Chinese, *8, 76, 94, 95, 98, 100, 102, 103, 108, 120, 121, 125, 126, 129, 130, 136, 149, 245, 260*
    legal criteria, *5*

Index

legal definition, *30*
link with terrorism, *268*
media representation as threat, *266*
mid 1970's crises, *43*
post WWII intake by country, *33*
processing of applications, *61*
protest, *18*, *197*, *222*, *224*, *232*, *233*, *235*, *236*, *237*
punishment, *196*
refugee-like situations, *41*
removal techniques, *175*
representation as threat by media, *53*, *54*, *60*, *61*, *90*, *91*, *148*, *149*, *170*, *177*, *189*, *229*
resettled, *157*
Sri Lankan, *48*, *171*, *173*, *194*, *278*, *279*
status, *190*
stigmatisation, *124*, *147*
Sudanese, *174*, *279*
survivors of adversity, *53*
unauthorised arrival, *157*
universal rights, *275*
voluntary returnees, *177*
warehousing, *51*, *53*, *281*
West Papuan, *170*, *173*, *189*
World War II, *90*

Reith, Peter. Defence Minister, *165*, *193*, *247*, *248*

repatriation
    Afghanistan, *32*, *33*, *55*, *72*, *94*, *122*, *125*, *159*, *174*, *176*, *177*, *179*
    forced, *72*, *125*
    voluntary, *51*

reports into detention failures
    findings of recurring deficiencies, *211*

resettlement, *9*, *32*, *33*, *51*, *55*, *72*, *75*, *88*, *92*, *93*, *94*, *95*, *96*, *98*, *99*, *100*, *101*, *102*, *103*, *113*, *119*, *121*, *122*, *123*, *124*, *126*, *131*, *132*, *139*, *140*, *149*, *150*, *152*, *154*, *157*, *173*, *177*, *184*, *190*, *260*, *261*, *278*, *279*, *281*

resettlement agreement, *91*
resettlement processes, *197*
resettlement scheme, *91*
returned asylum seekers, *176*
Returned Servicemen's League, *116*
reward for conviction of prohibited immigrants, *89*
Robertson, Geoffrey, *15*, *16*, *20*, *28*, *37*
Roebourne prison, *142*
rogue states, *20*, *37*
Ross, Jeffrey, *13*
Royal Australian and New Zealand College of Psychiatrists, *223*
Royal Australian Navy (RAN), *162*, *184*
Royal Flying Doctor Service, *161*
Rudd government, *11*, *197*, *245*, *279*, *280*, *282*, *284*
    election, *11*, *12*
    maintenance of private detention centres, *205*
    policy on children in detention, *230*
Rudd, Kevin, *278*
Ruddock v Taylor, *239*
Ruddock, Phillip, *151*, *154*, *167*, *191*, *192*, *199*, *224*, *265*, *267*
Ruhani v Director of Police, *277*
Rwanda, *45*, *54*, *55*, *56*, *72*
    Burundi, *54*, *56*, *72*
    Goma refugee camp, *52*, *54*
    Hutu regime, *54*
'S' case, Baxter detention centre, *207*
safe haven visa, *157*
Saudi Arabia, *67*
Schwendinger, Herman and Julia, *13*, *14*, *16*, *28*, *37*
Seamen's Union, *85*

Border Crimes

Second World War, *30, 32, 43, 49, 90, 147, 271, 275*
security guards, *218*
self-harm by children in detention, *227*
self-harm by children in detention, *227*
Senate inquiries, *246*
Senate inquiry
  Migration Act, 246
Senate Joint Standing Committee on Migration Regulations, *130*
Senate Legal and Constitutional Affairs Committee, *175*
Senate Standing Committee on Foreign Affairs and Defence, *96*
separation of powers, *22, 243, 255*
September 11, 2001, *59, 152, 165, 166, 267*
Serco Group, *205, 206*
settler states, *21*
sex industry, *186*
sexual exploitation, *65*
sexual servitude, *186*
Sharkansky, Ira, *16*
SIEV X, *2, 3, 4, 11, 60, 73, 158, 166, 183, 184, 185, 192, 193, 195, 247*
Singapore, *89, 102, 124, 160, 281*
SIPRI, *44, 45*
slavery, *22, 25, 65, 66, 186, 218*
  contemporary forms, *46*
  sex, *213*
slums, *47*
Smith's Wharf, *83*
solitary confinement, *236*
Solomon Islands, *188*
Somalia, *5, 56, 61*
South Australian Department of Human Services, *227*

sovereignty, *7, 10, 19, 20, 26, 35, 36, 50, 55, 58, 124, 138, 140, 143, 146, 148, 189, 243, 244, 252, 270, 275*
Soviet Union, *29, 32, 62*
Special Air Services, *160, 161, 162, 164, 165, 192*
special response teams, *236*
Sri Lanka, *48, 56, 280, 283*
St Vincent de Paul charity, *97*
Stalinism, *37, 50*
Stalinist, *19, 37*
state
  as source of protection, *7*
state crime, *6, 7, 8, 10, 12, 13, 14, 15, 16, 17, 18, 19, 20, 21, 24, 27, 30, 32, 35, 36, 37, 39, 49, 52, 56, 58, 59, 61, 69, 70, 75, 91, 112, 113, 189, 191, 238, 242, 245, 270, 285*
state deviance, *7, 8, 24, 35, 39, 70, 217, 243*
state force, *129, 152, 231*
state repression, *47*
state violence, *21, 42*
stateless persons, *255*
statelessness, *18, 27, 37, 40, 41, 43, 252, 254, 255, 256*
stowaway organisation, *89*
stowaways
  Chinese, circa 1910, *90*
Straits Settlements, *89*
Suspected Illegal Entry Vessel (SIEV), *11, 162, 184*
suspected unauthorised non-citizens (SUNC), *165*
Sydney Morning Herald, 81, 83, 84, 85, 86, 115, 193, 266
Taliban, *165, 177, 178, 241*
talkback radio, *267*
Tamil, *48, 278, 281*
Tampa, 192, 193
'*Tampa* crisis', *159*

348

Index

censorship of images, *164*
Tanjung Pinang, *281, 282*
tear gas, *226, 234, 236*
techniques of neutralisation (Sykes and Matza), *197*
temporary entry permit, *133*
temporary protection regime, *158*
    effects, *158*
temporary protection visa, *1, 2, 34, 51, 157, 170, 173, 191, 229, 240, 265*
    abolition, *280*
    introduction, *265*
terrorism, *3, 57, 63, 148, 152, 165, 189, 201, 243, 266, 267, 268*
Thailand, *95, 126, 143, 155, 283*
The Age, *1, 3, 80, 116, 128, 131, 149, 150, 154*
The Bulletin, *86, 88*
the outsider
    as deviant, *270, 271*
the state
    accountability, *203*
    as source of criminality, *7*
    constitutional powers, *251*
    institutions, *242*
    maintenance of control over detainees, *238*
    monopoly of force, *12, 21*
    power to arbitrarily detain, *251*
    representation of asylum seekers, *270*
    responses to resistance, *230*
    theories of, *18, 19, 21*
Thiess Constructions, *202*
Tiananmen Square, *119, 132, 159*
Tokyo war crimes tribunal, *28*
Tonga, *170*
torture, *13, 14, 15, 20, 144, 145, 197*
totalitarianism, *19, 37*
totalitarianism theory, *37*
Trade Unions, *85*
transit camps, *57*

Tsinan, *81, 82, 83, 84, 86*
tsunami, *41, 48, 54*
Turkey, *5, 48, 61, 187*
Tuvalu, *170*
Ukraine, *61*
unauthorised migrants, *6, 7, 8, 9, 10, 11, 21, 27, 30, 35, 36, 39, 57, 58, 59, 60, 69, 70, 75, 88, 94, 104, 110, 112, 113, 130, 131, 135, 140, 146, 147, 153, 180, 189, 190, 191, 196, 197, 201, 204, 216, 221, 238, 243, 246, 248, 256, 259, 260, 261, 270, 271, 272, 273, 274, 275*
    abuse, *10, 18, 243, 274*
    alienation, *6*
    alleged criminality, *274*
    criminalisation, *6, 9, 10, 18, 273, 274*
    deaths, *59*
    organised abuse, *274*
    perception as a threat, *75*
    policing, *244*
    removal, *10*
    systematic abuse, *6*
UNGA, *45*
UNHCR Executive Committee Conclusions on detention, *143*
UNICEF, *66*
United Kingdom, *64, 69, 272*
    Dover 2000, *64*
United Nations, *29, 30, 32, 33, 34, 41, 42, 46, 47, 54, 71, 72, 96, 99, 105, 119, 122, 125, 155, 182, 186, 253, 284*
    Convention on Transnational Organised Crime, *156*
    Convention Relating to the Status of Refugees, 1951, *28, 31, 32, 34, 35, 40, 41, 53, 55, 56, 60, 61, 71, 72, 92, 96, 100, 101, 119, 121, 124, 134, 143, 153, 157, 158, 169, 170, 172, 181, 191, 251, 274, 281*
    Habitat, *46*

International Covenant on Civil Rights, *30*
International Covenant on Cultural Rights, *30*
International Covenant on Economic Rights, *30*
International Covenant on Political Rights, *30*
International Covenant on Social Rights, *30*
Organised Crime Convention, *64*
Relief and Rehabilitation Agency (UNRRA), *32*
Secretary General, *45*
Smuggling Protocol, *64*, *65*, *68*
Trafficking Protocol, *64*, *65*, *66*, *186*
Transnational Crime Convention, *64*
United Nations Charter, *28*
United Nations High Commissioner for Refugees, *30*, *33*, *34*, *40*, *41*, *42*, *43*, *44*, *51*, *52*, *53*, *54*, *55*, *56*, *61*, *62*, *71*, *72*, *73*, *95*, *99*, *100*, *101*, *102*, *117*, *122*, *124*, *125*, *129*, *134*, *149*, *159*, *172*, *173*, *177*, *178*, *179*, *187*, *189*, *190*, *283*
United States, *14*, *16*, *28*, *32*, *33*, *41*, *44*, *55*, *56*, *57*, *59*, *63*, *67*, *71*, *101*, *102*, *103*, *117*, *139*, *165*, *166*, *174*, *178*, *202*, *272*
    terrorist attacks, *266*
United States armed forces, *14*
United States Committee for Refugees and Immigrants (USCRI), *41*
United States Department of State Trafficking in Persons Report, *67*
Universal Declaration of Human Rights, *28*, *30*
Universal Declaration of Human Rights,, *31*
Universal Declaration on Human Rights, 1948, *117*

universal rights, *25*, *26*, *27*, *31*, *76*, *93*, *103*, *269*
unlawful detention cases, *216*, *217*
unlawful non-citizen, *138*, *169*, *255*
urbanisation, *46*
USCRI, *41*, *42*, *53*, *71*
values statement
    rationale, *268*
Vanstone, Amamda, *224*, *225*
Venezuela, *67*
Vietnam, *94*, *95*, *97*, *98*, *100*, *103*, *122*, *125*
    Saigon, *95*
Vietnam War, *28*, *95*, *103*
Vietnamese refugee intake, *55*, *95*, *97*, *98*, *100*, *101*, *102*, *103*, *122*, *124*, *125*, *126*, *128*, *129*, *149*
Vietnamese refugees
    Hong Kong, *125*
Villawood detention centre, *198*, *204*, *223*, *228*, *229*, *233*, *239*, *240*
    escapes, *233*
    protests, *233*
Villawood detention centre:, *239*
visa
    bridging, *144*, *145*, *186*, *217*
    criminal justice stay, *186*
    witness protection (trafficking), *186*
visa overstayers, *137*, *153*, *249*
visa queue, *42*
visas
    method of exclusion, *58*
voluntary repatriation, *72*, *100*, *177*
Wackenhut Corporation, *202*
Wacol Migrant Hostel, *97*
war, *9*, *14*, *15*, *16*, *20*, *21*, *33*, *44*, *48*, *52*, *54*, *57*, *58*, *62*, *63*, *67*, *69*, *71*, *73*, *77*, *90*, *114*, *117*, *146*, *152*, *163*, *180*, *244*, *275*
    as metaphor, *21*